Kamisama Kiss

Story & Art by
Julietta Suzuki

CHARACTERS

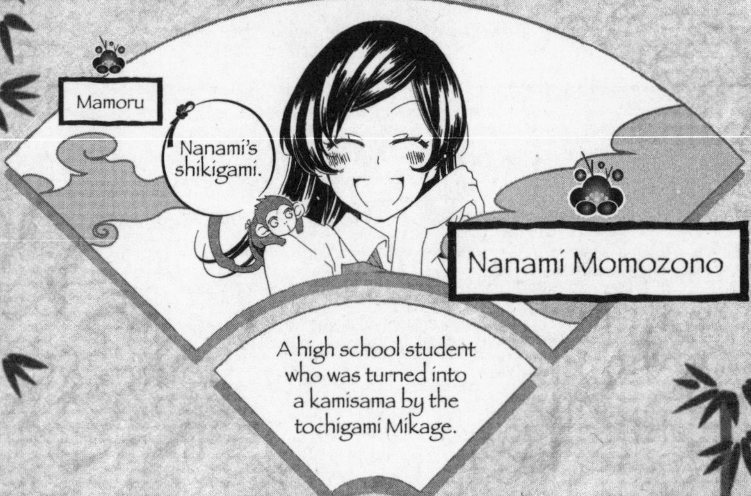
Mamoru
Nanami's shikigami.
Nanami Momozono
A high school student who was turned into a kamisama by the tochigami Mikage.

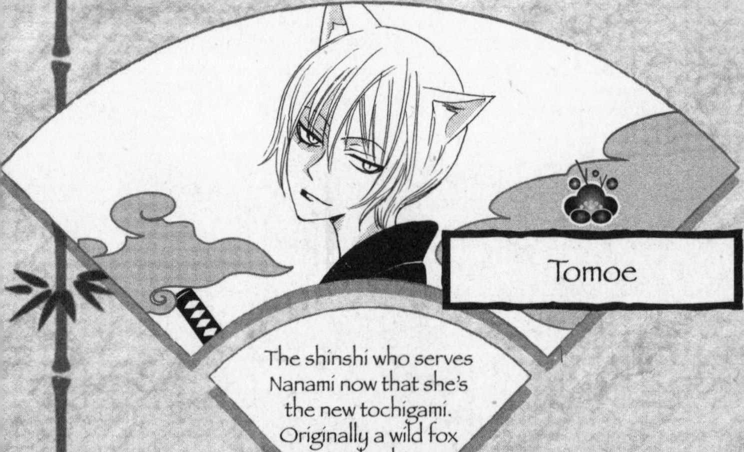
Tomoe
The shinshi who serves Nanami now that she's the new tochigami. Originally a wild fox ayakashi.

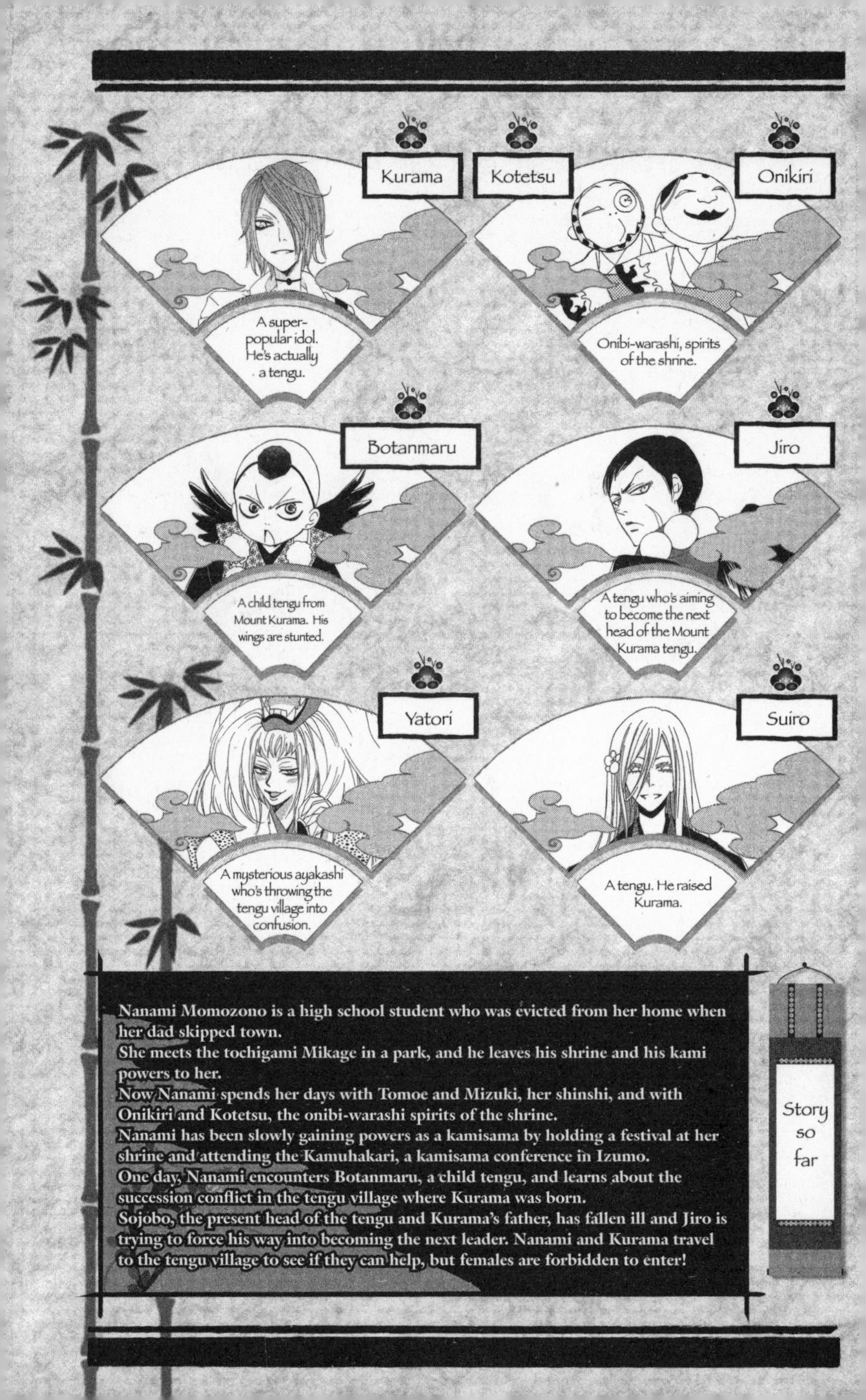
Kotetsu
Onikiri
Onibi-warashi, spirits of the shrine.
Kurama
A super-popular idol. He's actually a tengu.
Jiro
A tengu who's aiming to become the next head of the Mount Kurama tengu.
Botanmaru
A child tengu from Mount Kurama. His wings are stunted.
Suiro
A tengu. He raised Kurama.
Yatori
A mysterious ayakashi who's throwing the tengu village into confusion.

Story so far

Nanami Momozono is a high school student who was evicted from her home when her dad skipped town.
She meets the tochigami Mikage in a park, and he leaves his shrine and his kami powers to her.
Now Nanami spends her days with Tomoe and Mizuki, her shinshi, and with Onikiri and Kotetsu, the onibi-warashi spirits of the shrine.
Nanami has been slowly gaining powers as a kamisama by holding a festival at her shrine and attending the Kamuhakari, a kamisama conference in Izumo.
One day, Nanami encounters Botanmaru, a child tengu, and learns about the succession conflict in the tengu village where Kurama was born.
Sojobo, the present head of the tengu and Kurama's father, has fallen ill and Jiro is trying to force his way into becoming the next leader. Nanami and Kurama travel to the tengu village to see if they can help, but females are forbidden to enter!

Kamisama Kiss

Volume 10
CONTENTS

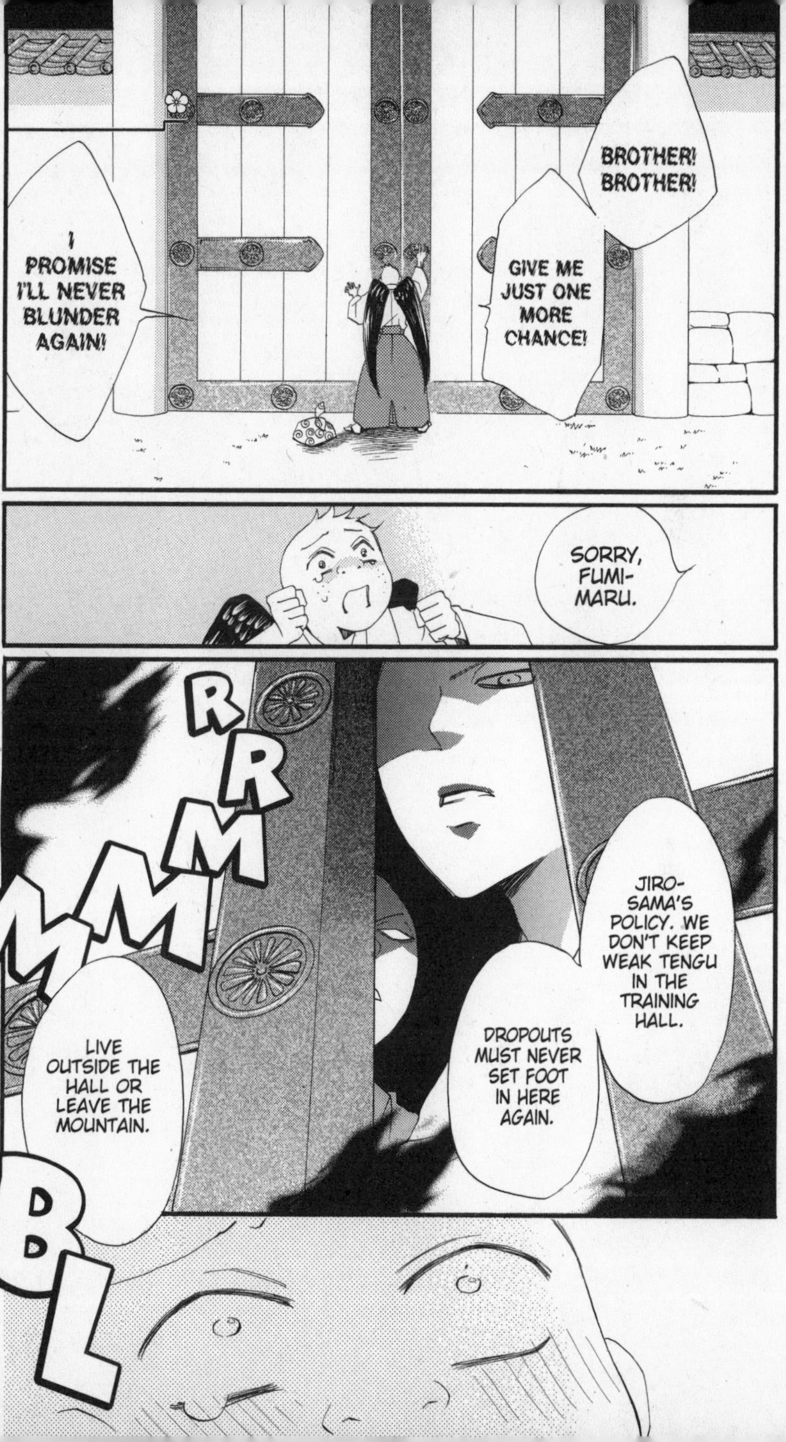
BROTHER! BROTHER!
GIVE ME JUST ONE MORE CHANCE!
I PROMISE I'LL NEVER BLUNDER AGAIN!
SORRY, FUMI-MARU.
RRMMM
JIRO-SAMA'S POLICY. WE DON'T KEEP WEAK TENGU IN THE TRAINING HALL.
DROPOUTS MUST NEVER SET FOOT IN HERE AGAIN.
LIVE OUTSIDE THE HALL OR LEAVE THE MOUNTAIN.
BL

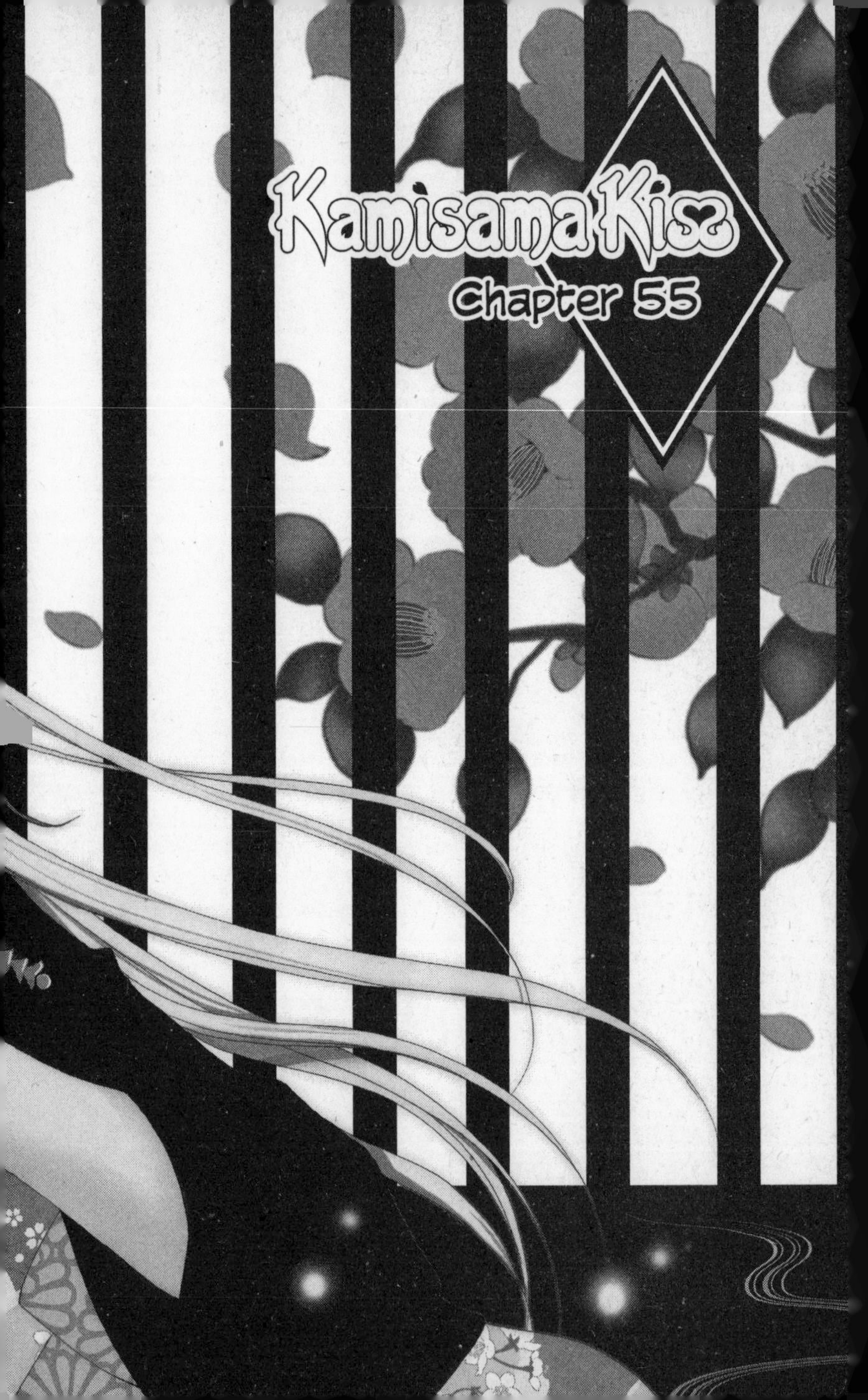

Kamisama Kiss
Chapter 55

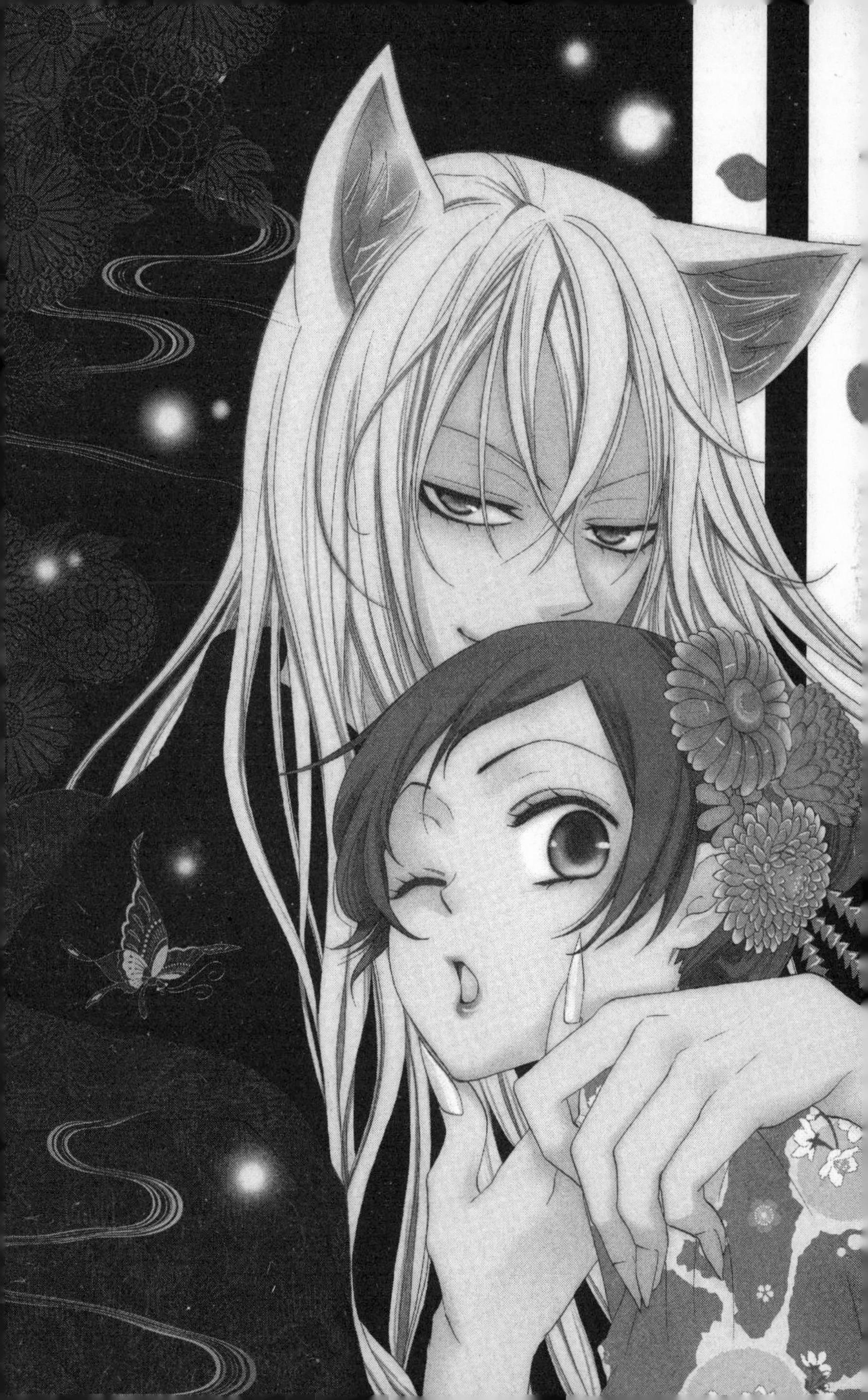

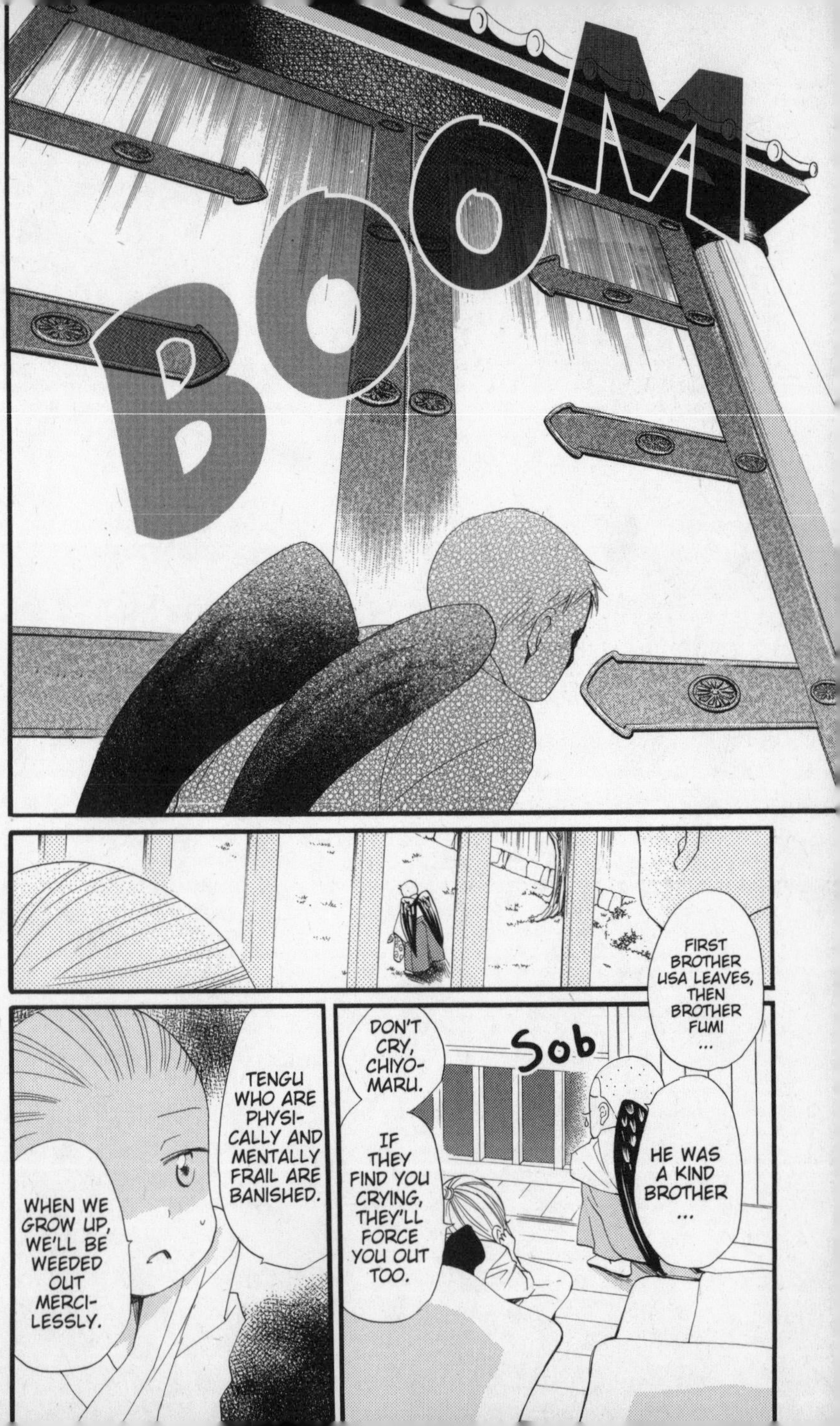
BOOM
FIRST BROTHER USA LEAVES, THEN BROTHER FUMI ...
HE WAS A KIND BROTHER ...
Sob
DON'T CRY, CHIYO-MARU.
IF THEY FIND YOU CRYING, THEY'LL FORCE YOU OUT TOO.
TENGU WHO ARE PHYSI-CALLY AND MENTALLY FRAIL ARE BANISHED.
WHEN WE GROW UP, WE'LL BE WEEDED OUT MERCI-LESSLY.

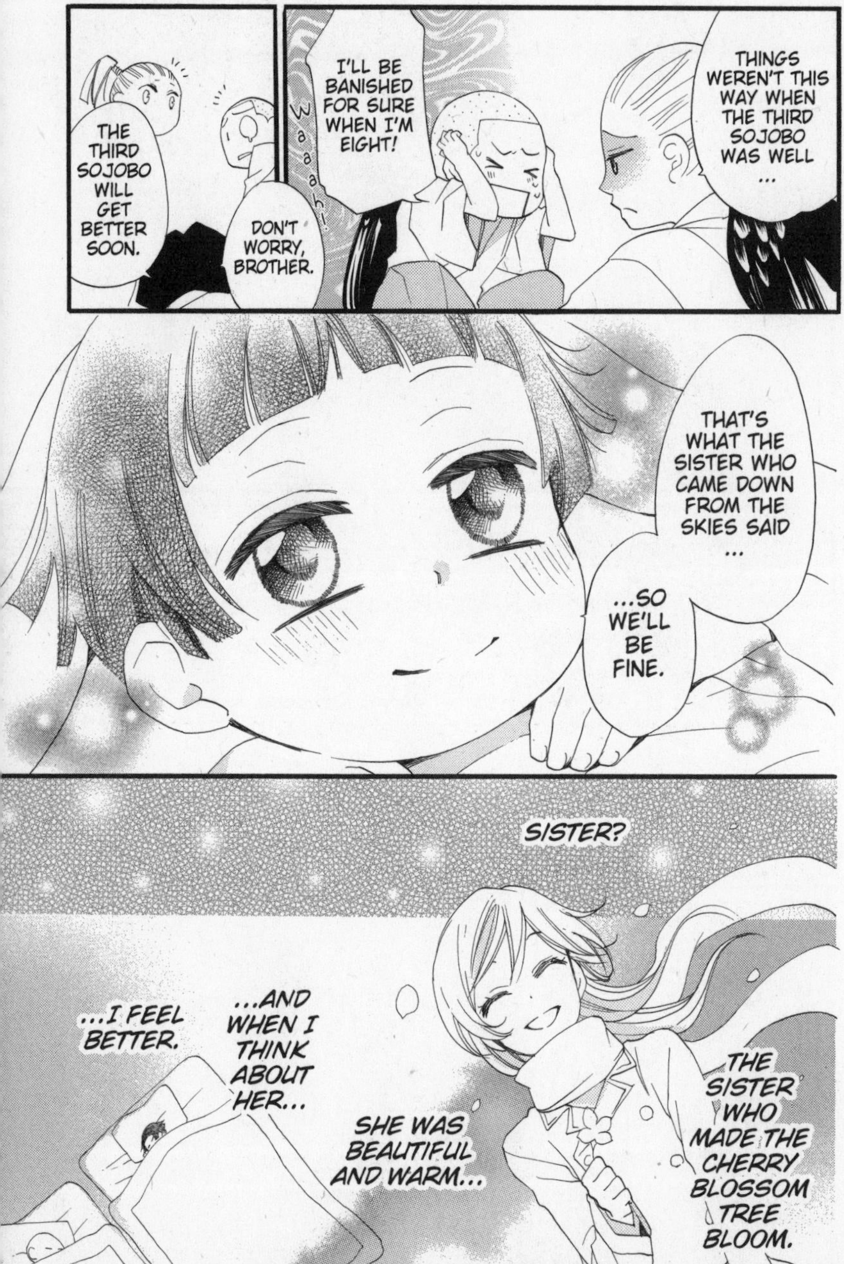
THINGS WEREN'T THIS WAY WHEN THE THIRD SOJOBO WAS WELL ...
I'LL BE BANISHED FOR SURE WHEN I'M EIGHT!
Waaah!
DON'T WORRY, BROTHER.
THE THIRD SOJOBO WILL GET BETTER SOON.
THAT'S WHAT THE SISTER WHO CAME DOWN FROM THE SKIES SAID ...
...SO WE'LL BE FINE.
SISTER?
THE SISTER WHO MADE THE CHERRY BLOSSOM TREE BLOOM.
SHE WAS BEAUTIFUL AND WARM...
...AND WHEN I THINK ABOUT HER...
...I FEEL BETTER.

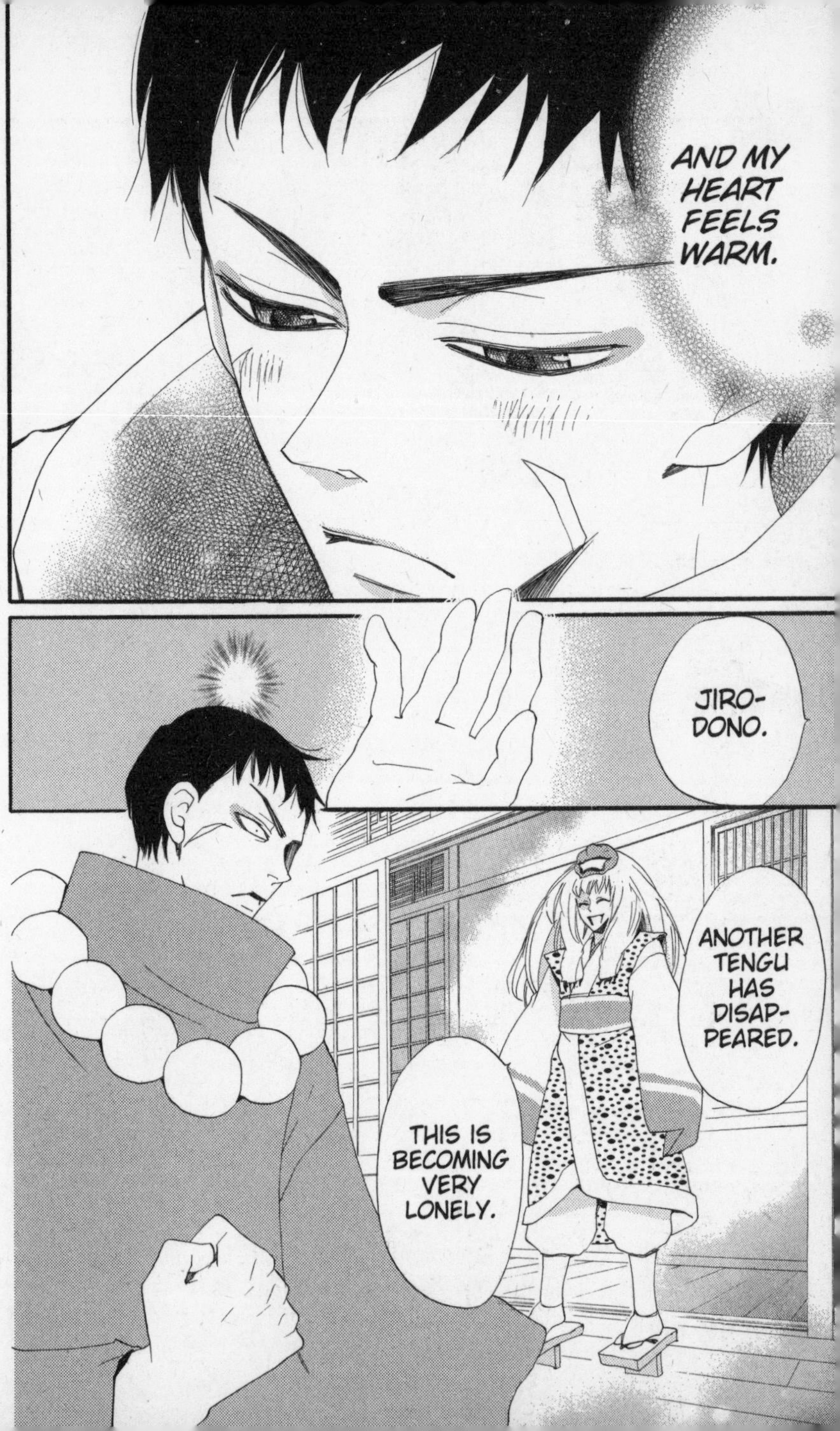
AND MY HEART FEELS WARM.
JIRO-DONO.
ANOTHER TENGU HAS DISAP-PEARED.
THIS IS BECOMING VERY LONELY.

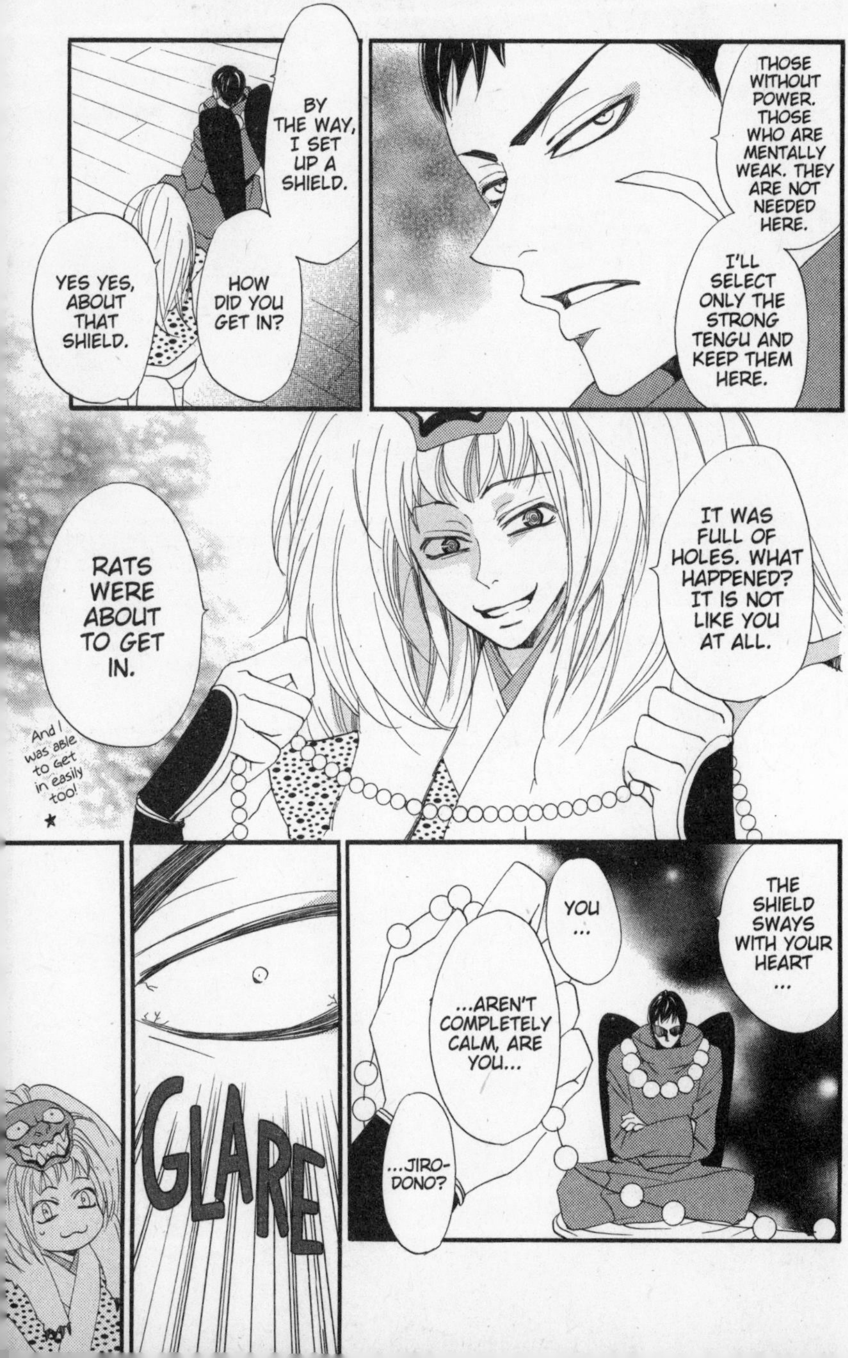
THOSE WITHOUT POWER. THOSE WHO ARE MENTALLY WEAK. THEY ARE NOT NEEDED HERE.
I'LL SELECT ONLY THE STRONG TENGU AND KEEP THEM HERE.
BY THE WAY, I SET UP A SHIELD.
HOW DID YOU GET IN?
YES YES, ABOUT THAT SHIELD.
IT WAS FULL OF HOLES. WHAT HAPPENED? IT IS NOT LIKE YOU AT ALL.
RATS WERE ABOUT TO GET IN.
And I was able to get in easily too! ★
THE SHIELD SWAYS WITH YOUR HEART ...
YOU ...
...AREN'T COMPLETELY CALM, ARE YOU...
...JIRO-DONO?
GLARE

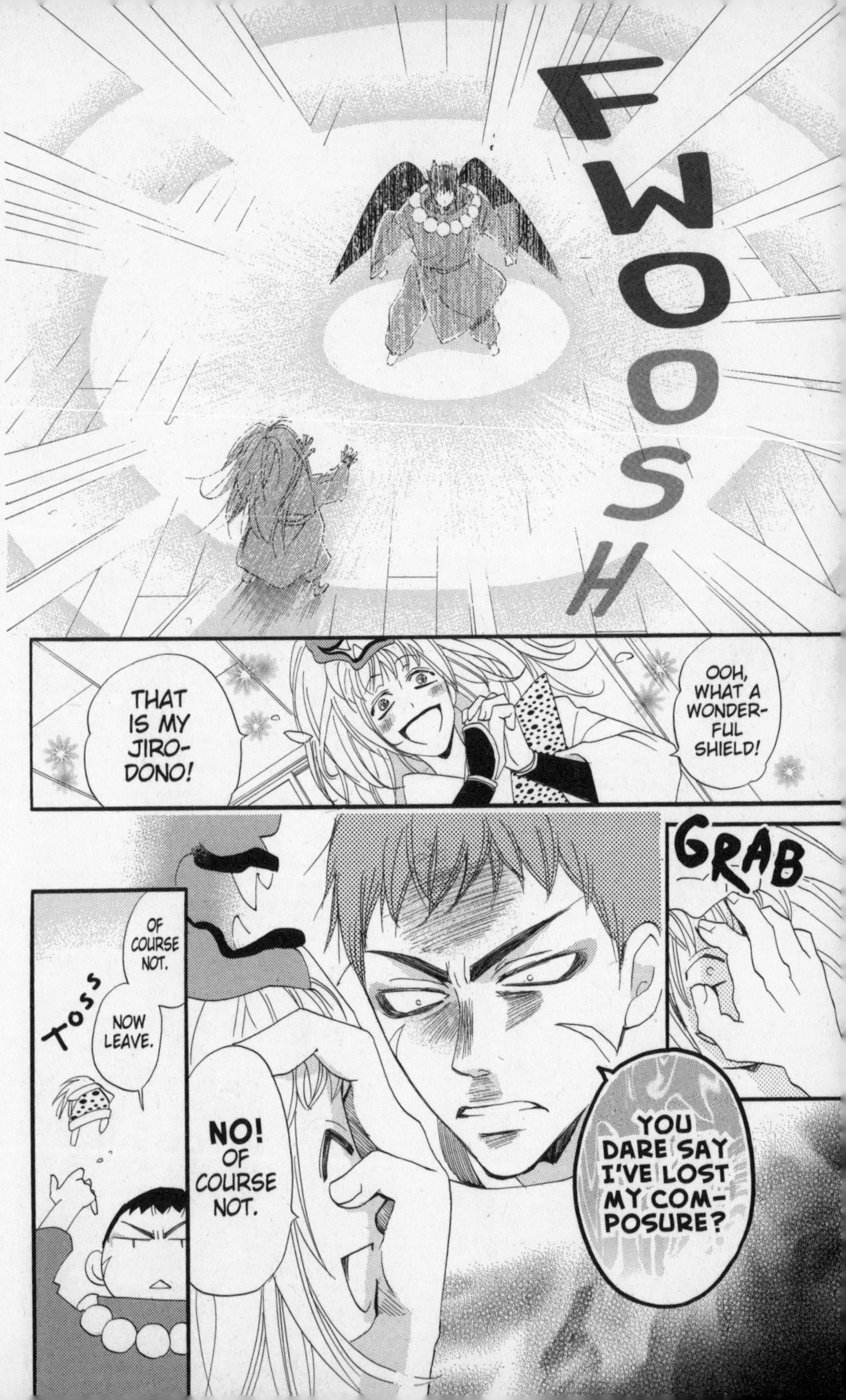
FWOOSH
OOH, WHAT A WONDERFUL SHIELD!
THAT IS MY JIRO-DONO!
GRAB
YOU DARE SAY I'VE LOST MY COMPOSURE?
NO! OF COURSE NOT.
OF COURSE NOT.
NOW LEAVE.
TOSS

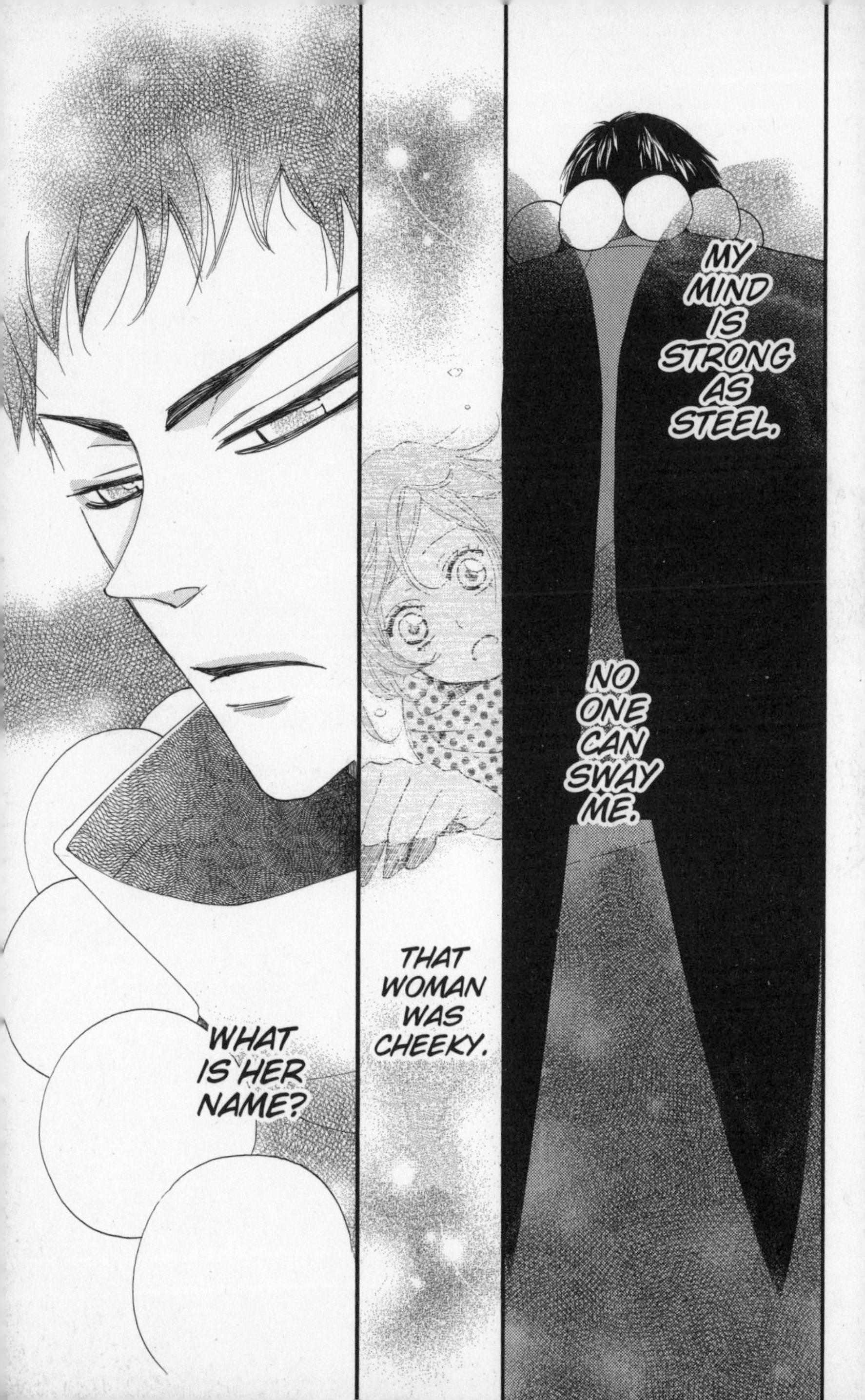
MY MIND IS STRONG AS STEEL.
NO ONE CAN SWAY ME.
THAT WOMAN WAS CHEEKY.
WHAT IS HER NAME?

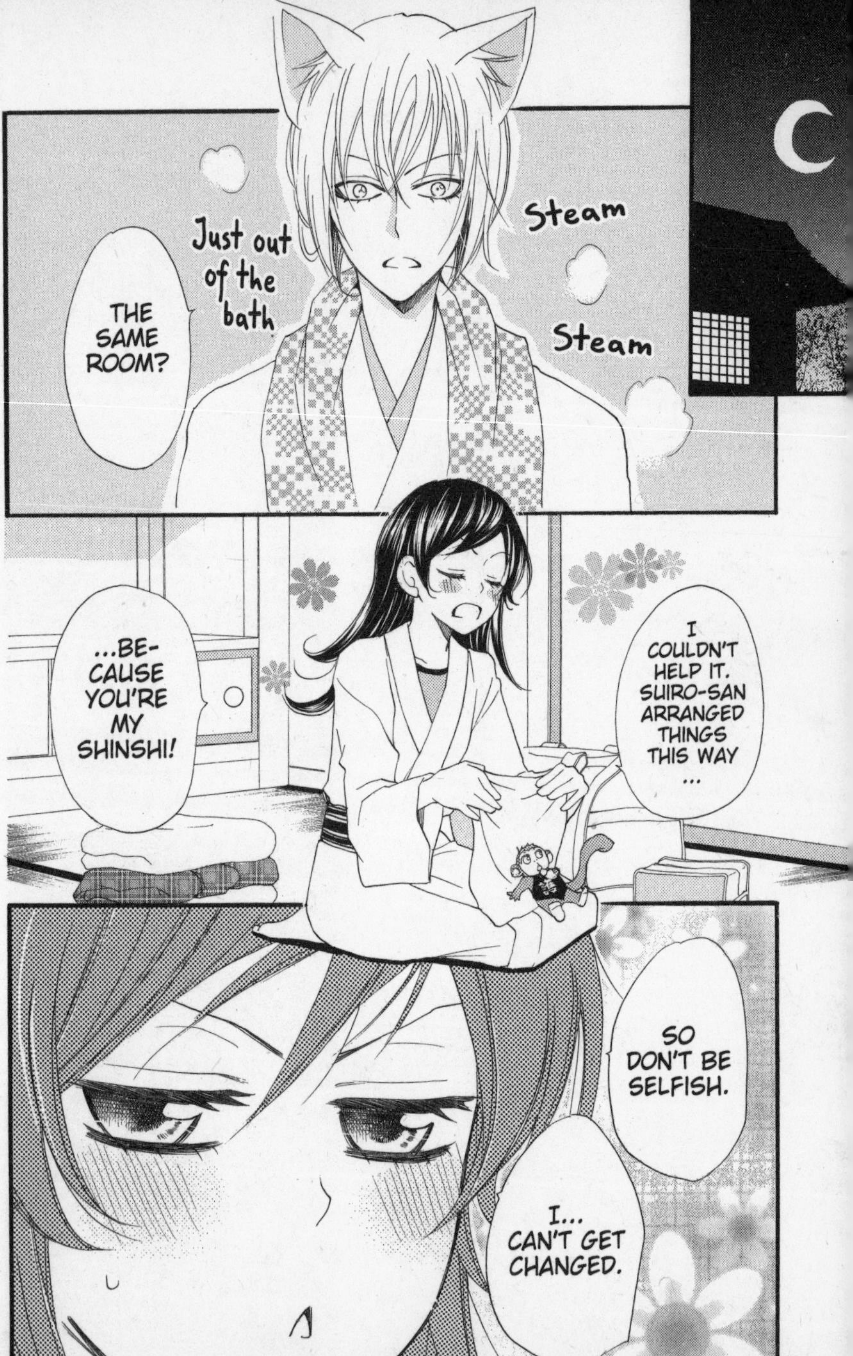
Steam
Steam
Just out of the bath
THE SAME ROOM?
I COULDN'T HELP IT. SUIRO-SAN ARRANGED THINGS THIS WAY ...
...BE-CAUSE YOU'RE MY SHINSHI!
SO DON'T BE SELFISH.
I... CAN'T GET CHANGED.

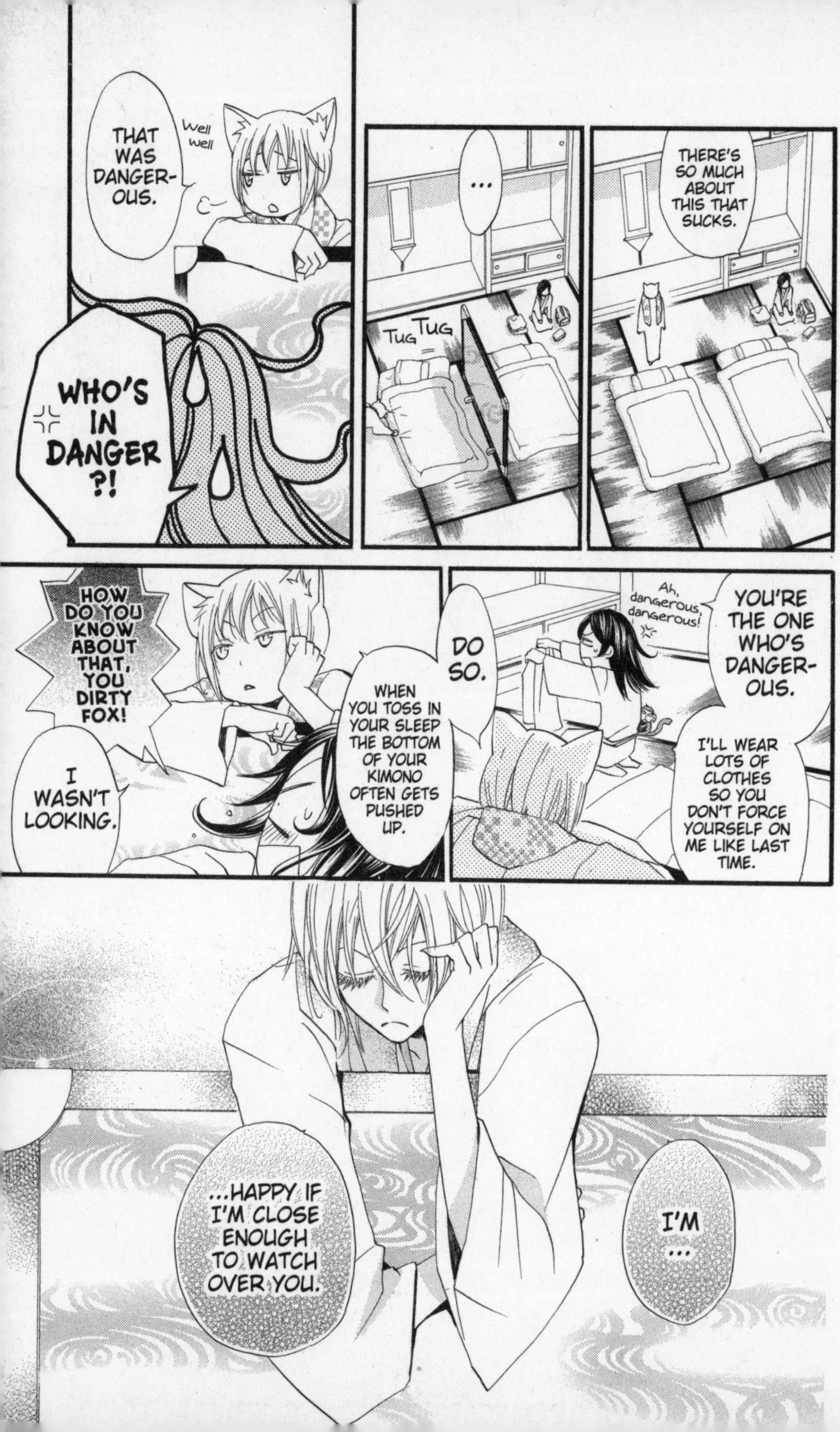
THERE'S SO MUCH ABOUT THIS THAT SUCKS.
...
TUG TUG
Well well
THAT WAS DANGER-OUS.
WHO'S IN DANGER?!
YOU'RE THE ONE WHO'S DANGER-OUS.
Ah, dangerous, dangerous!
I'LL WEAR LOTS OF CLOTHES SO YOU DON'T FORCE YOURSELF ON ME LIKE LAST TIME.
DO SO.
WHEN YOU TOSS IN YOUR SLEEP THE BOTTOM OF YOUR KIMONO OFTEN GETS PUSHED UP.
HOW DO YOU KNOW ABOUT THAT, YOU DIRTY FOX!
I WASN'T LOOKING.
I'M ...
...HAPPY IF I'M CLOSE ENOUGH TO WATCH OVER YOU.

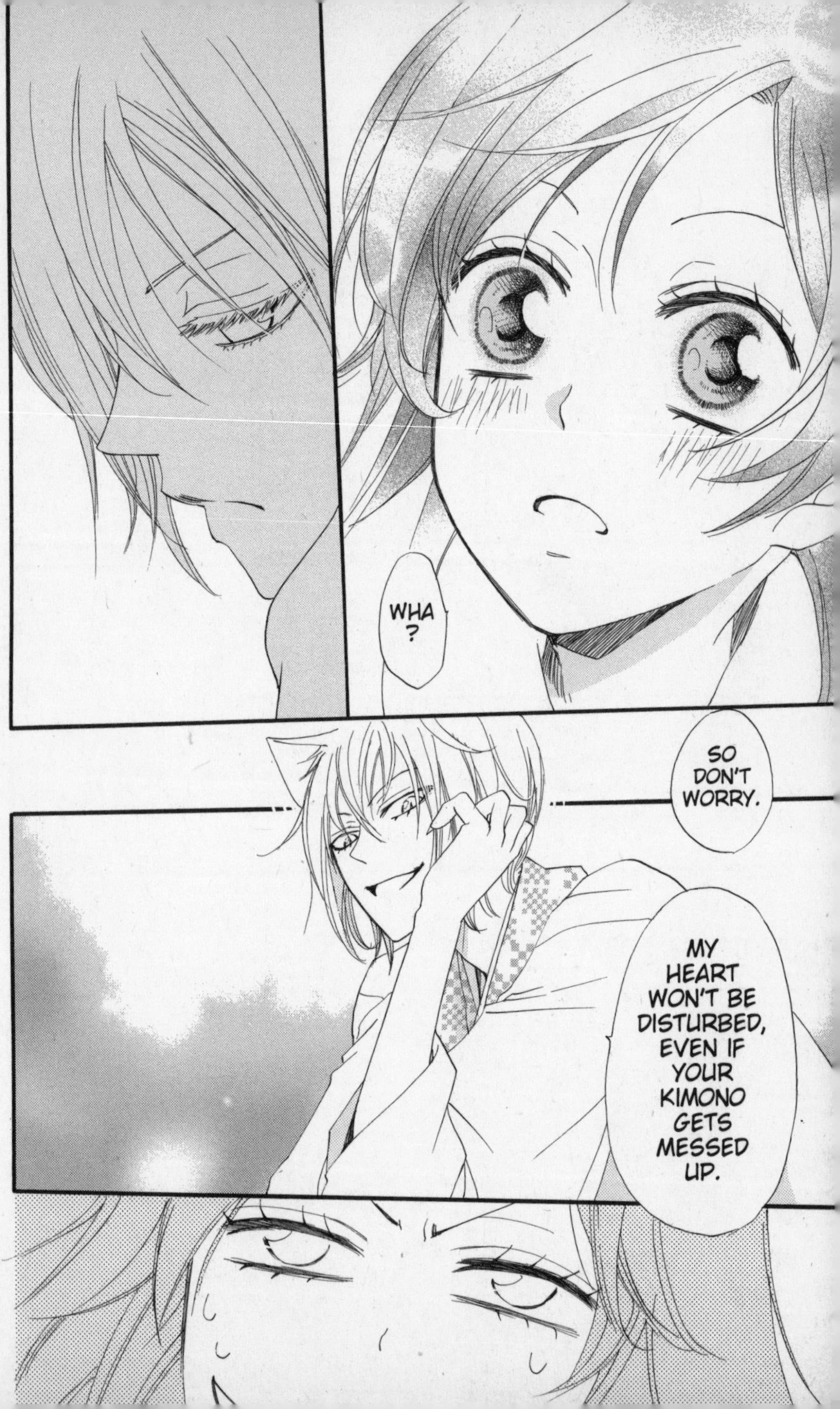
WHA?
SO DON'T WORRY.
MY HEART WON'T BE DISTURBED, EVEN IF YOUR KIMONO GETS MESSED UP.

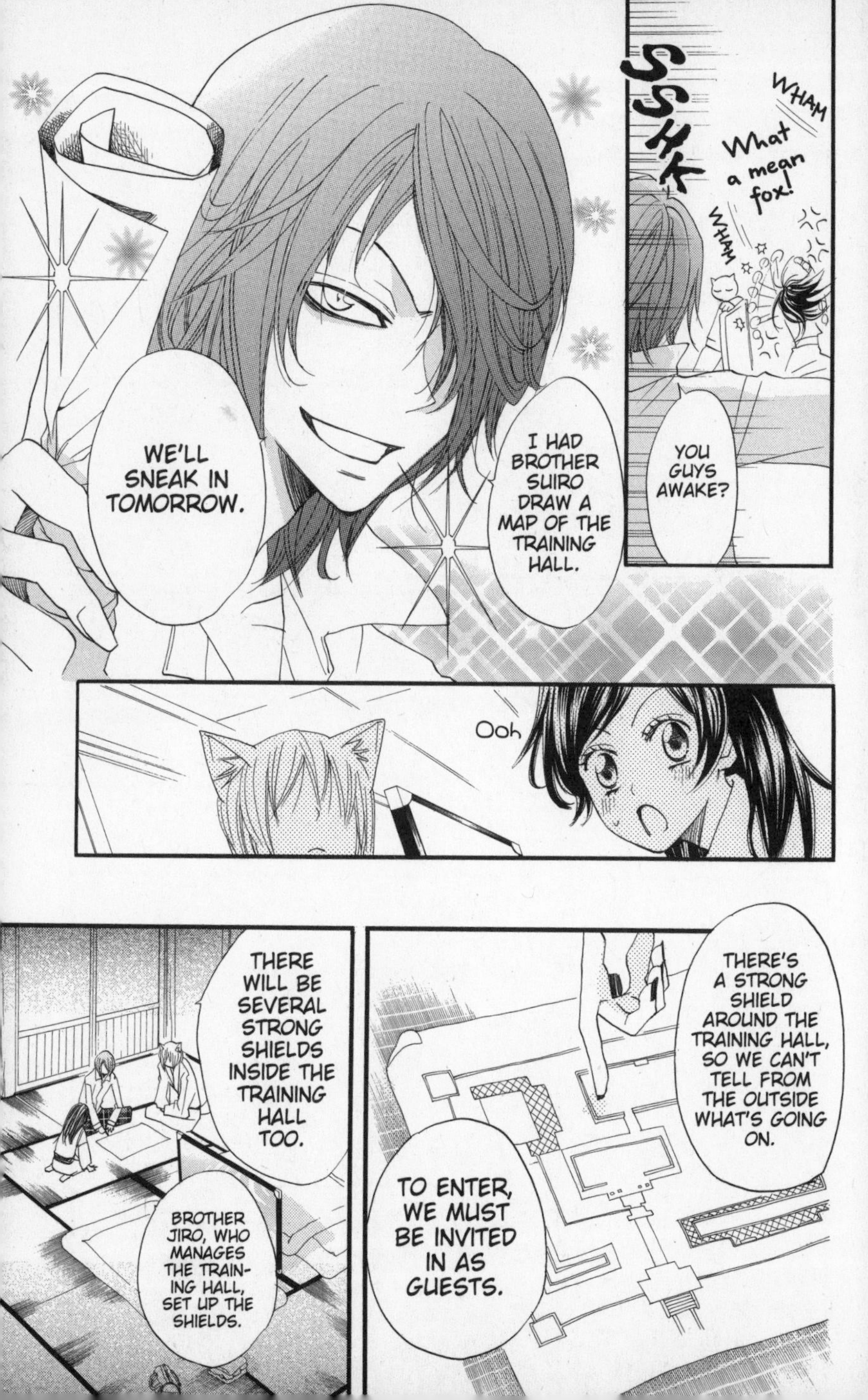
SSHK
WHAM
What a mean fox!
WHAM
YOU GUYS AWAKE?
I HAD BROTHER SUIRO DRAW A MAP OF THE TRAINING HALL.
WE'LL SNEAK IN TOMORROW.
Ooh
THERE'S A STRONG SHIELD AROUND THE TRAINING HALL, SO WE CAN'T TELL FROM THE OUTSIDE WHAT'S GOING ON.
TO ENTER, WE MUST BE INVITED IN AS GUESTS.
THERE WILL BE SEVERAL STRONG SHIELDS INSIDE THE TRAINING HALL TOO.
BROTHER JIRO, WHO MANAGES THE TRAIN-ING HALL, SET UP THE SHIELDS.

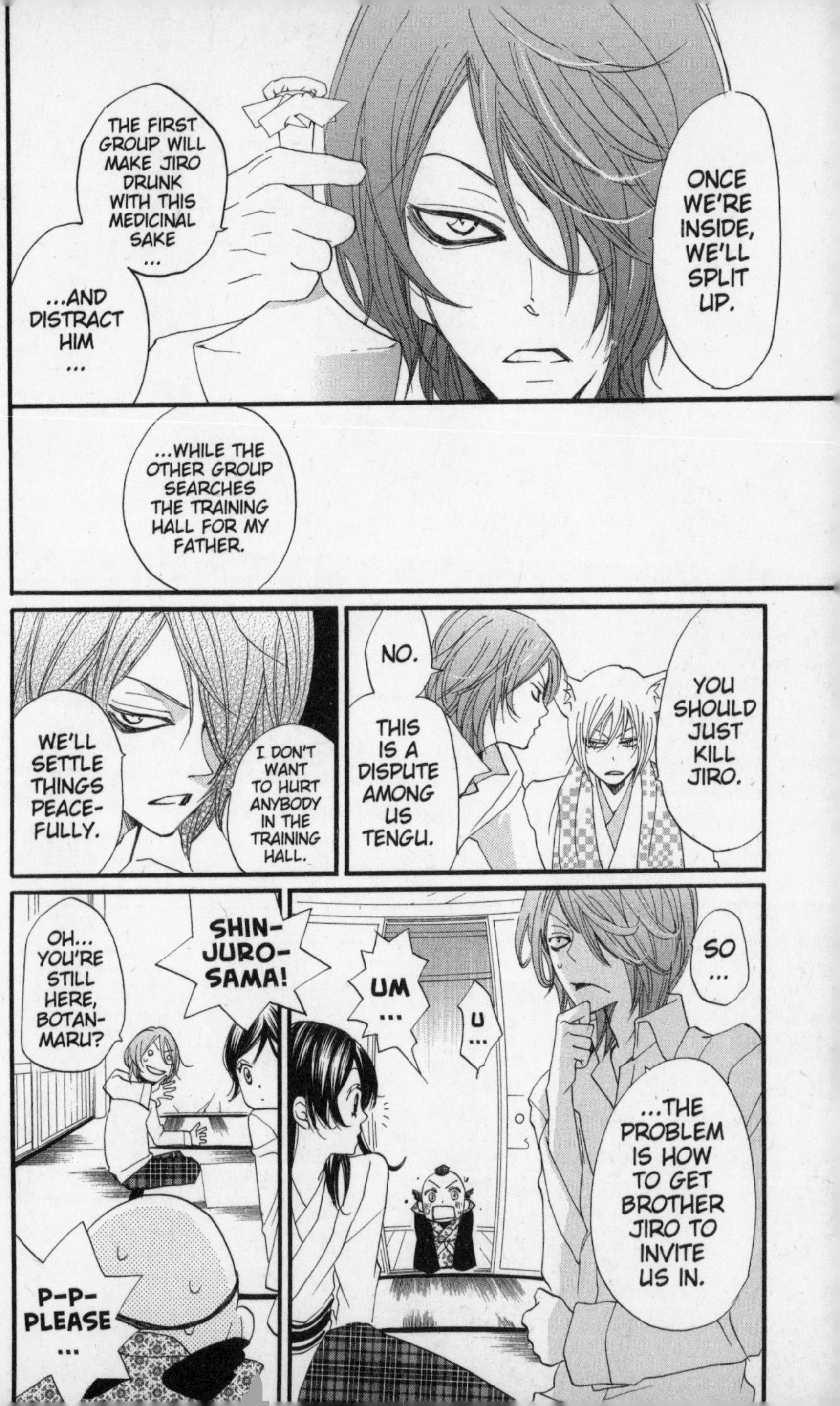
ONCE WE'RE INSIDE, WE'LL SPLIT UP.
THE FIRST GROUP WILL MAKE JIRO DRUNK WITH THIS MEDICINAL SAKE ...
...AND DISTRACT HIM ...
...WHILE THE OTHER GROUP SEARCHES THE TRAINING HALL FOR MY FATHER.
YOU SHOULD JUST KILL JIRO.
NO.
THIS IS A DISPUTE AMONG US TENGU.
I DON'T WANT TO HURT ANYBODY IN THE TRAINING HALL.
WE'LL SETTLE THINGS PEACE-FULLY.
SO ...
...THE PROBLEM IS HOW TO GET BROTHER JIRO TO INVITE US IN.
U ...
UM ...
SHIN-JURO-SAMA!
OH... YOU'RE STILL HERE, BOTAN-MARU?
P-P-PLEASE ...

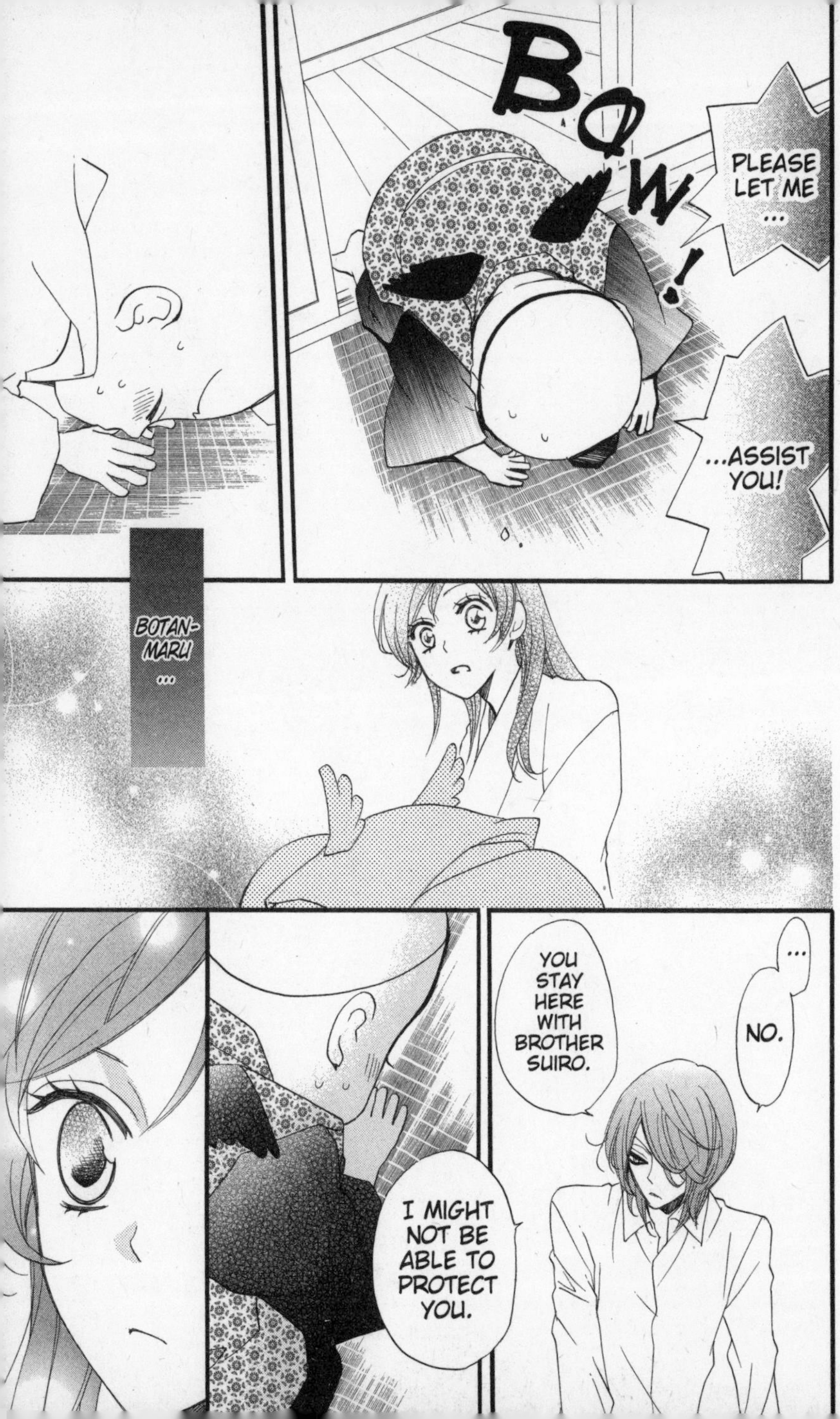
BOW!
PLEASE LET ME ...
...ASSIST YOU!
BOTAN-MARU ...
...
NO.
YOU STAY HERE WITH BROTHER SUIRO.
I MIGHT NOT BE ABLE TO PROTECT YOU.

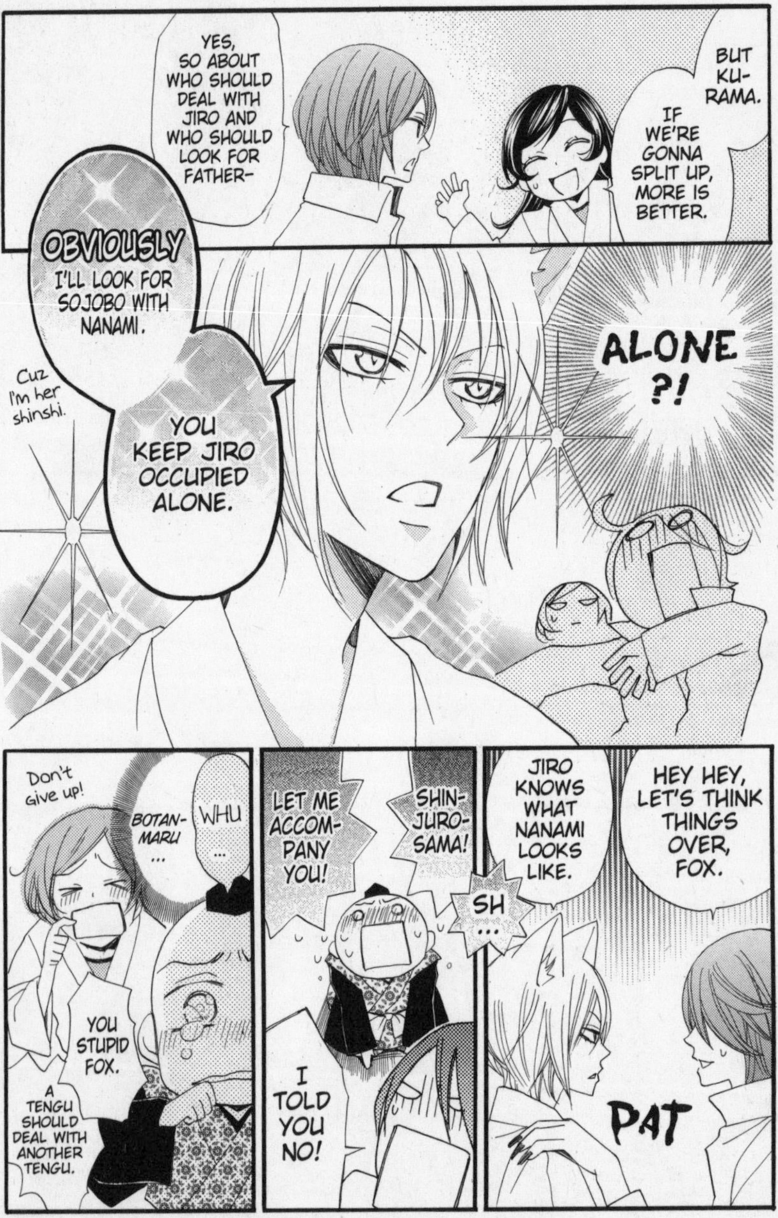
BUT KU-RAMA.
IF WE'RE GONNA SPLIT UP, MORE IS BETTER.
YES, SO ABOUT WHO SHOULD DEAL WITH JIRO AND WHO SHOULD LOOK FOR FATHER-
OBVIOUSLY I'LL LOOK FOR SOJOBO WITH NANAMI.
ALONE ?!
Cuz I'm her shinshi.
YOU KEEP JIRO OCCUPIED ALONE.
HEY HEY, LET'S THINK THINGS OVER, FOX.
JIRO KNOWS WHAT NANAMI LOOKS LIKE.
SH ...
PAT
SHIN-JURO-SAMA!
LET ME ACCOMPANY YOU!
I TOLD YOU NO!
WHU ...
BOTAN-MARU ...
Don't give up!
YOU STUPID FOX.
A TENGU SHOULD DEAL WITH ANOTHER TENGU.

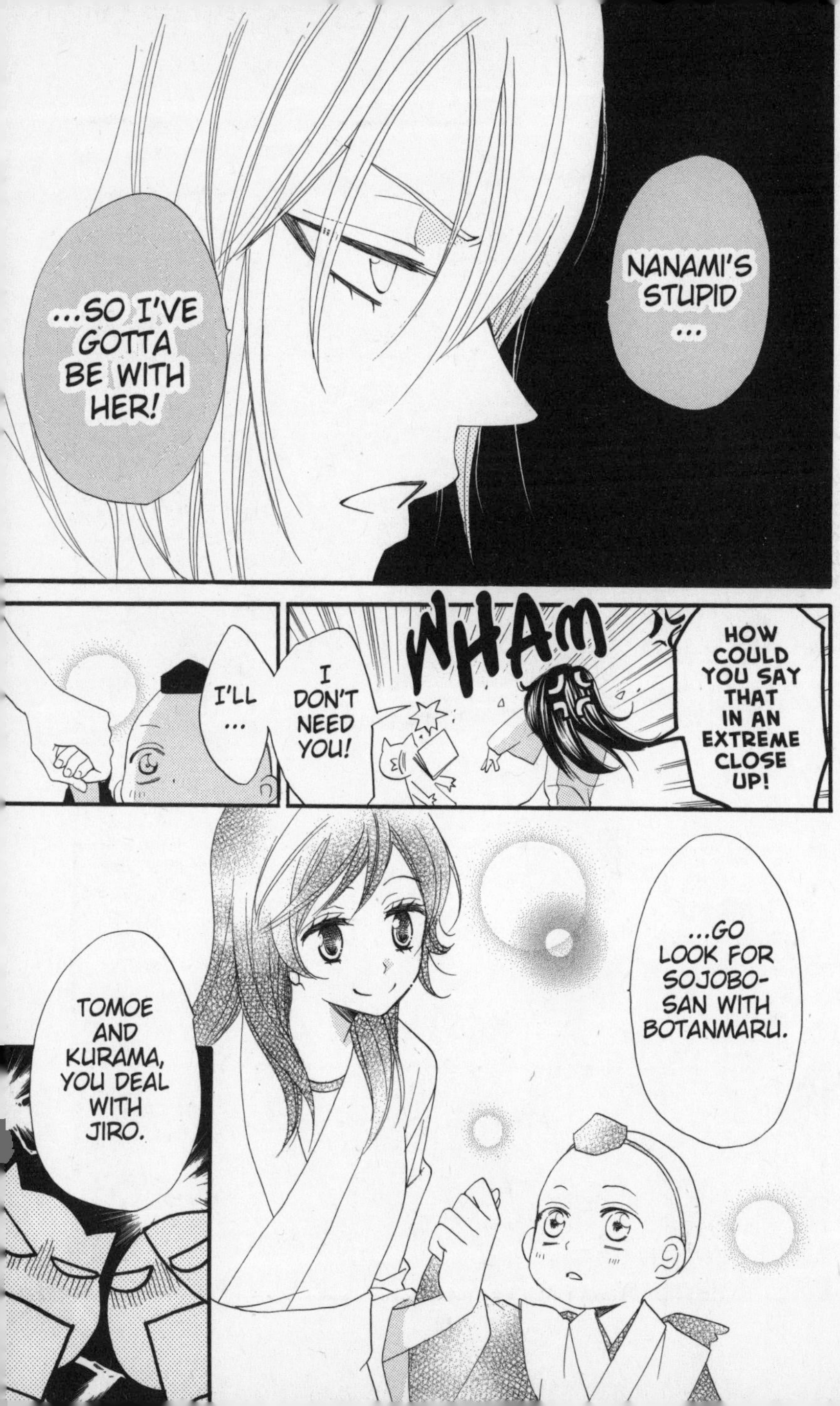
NANAMI'S STUPID ...
...SO I'VE GOTTA BE WITH HER!
HOW COULD YOU SAY THAT IN AN EXTREME CLOSE UP!
WHAM
I DON'T NEED YOU!
I'LL ...
...GO LOOK FOR SOJOBO-SAN WITH BOTANMARU.
TOMOE AND KURAMA, YOU DEAL WITH JIRO.

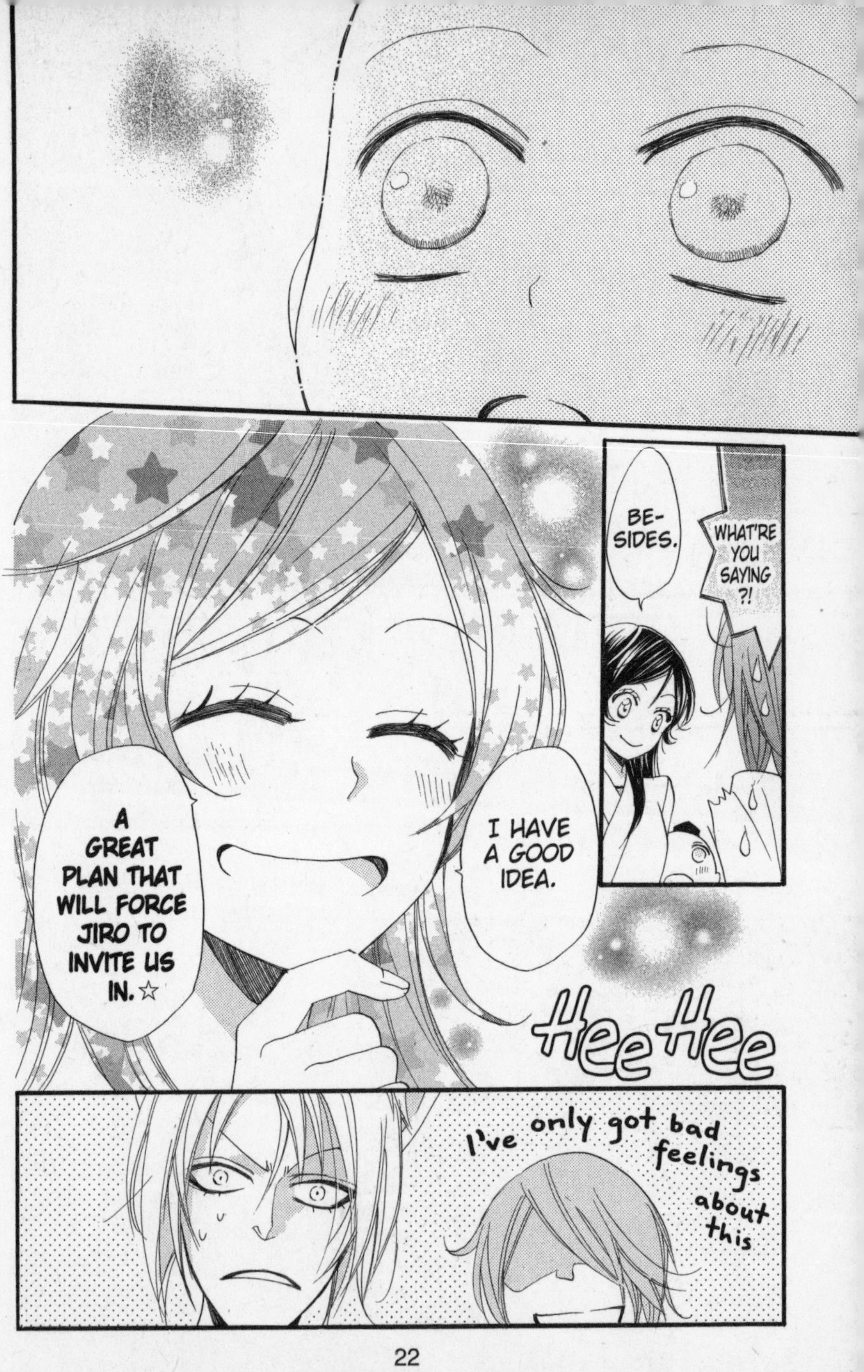
WHAT'RE YOU SAYING?!
BE-SIDES.
I HAVE A GOOD IDEA.
A GREAT PLAN THAT WILL FORCE JIRO TO INVITE US IN.☆
Hee Hee
I've only got bad feelings about this

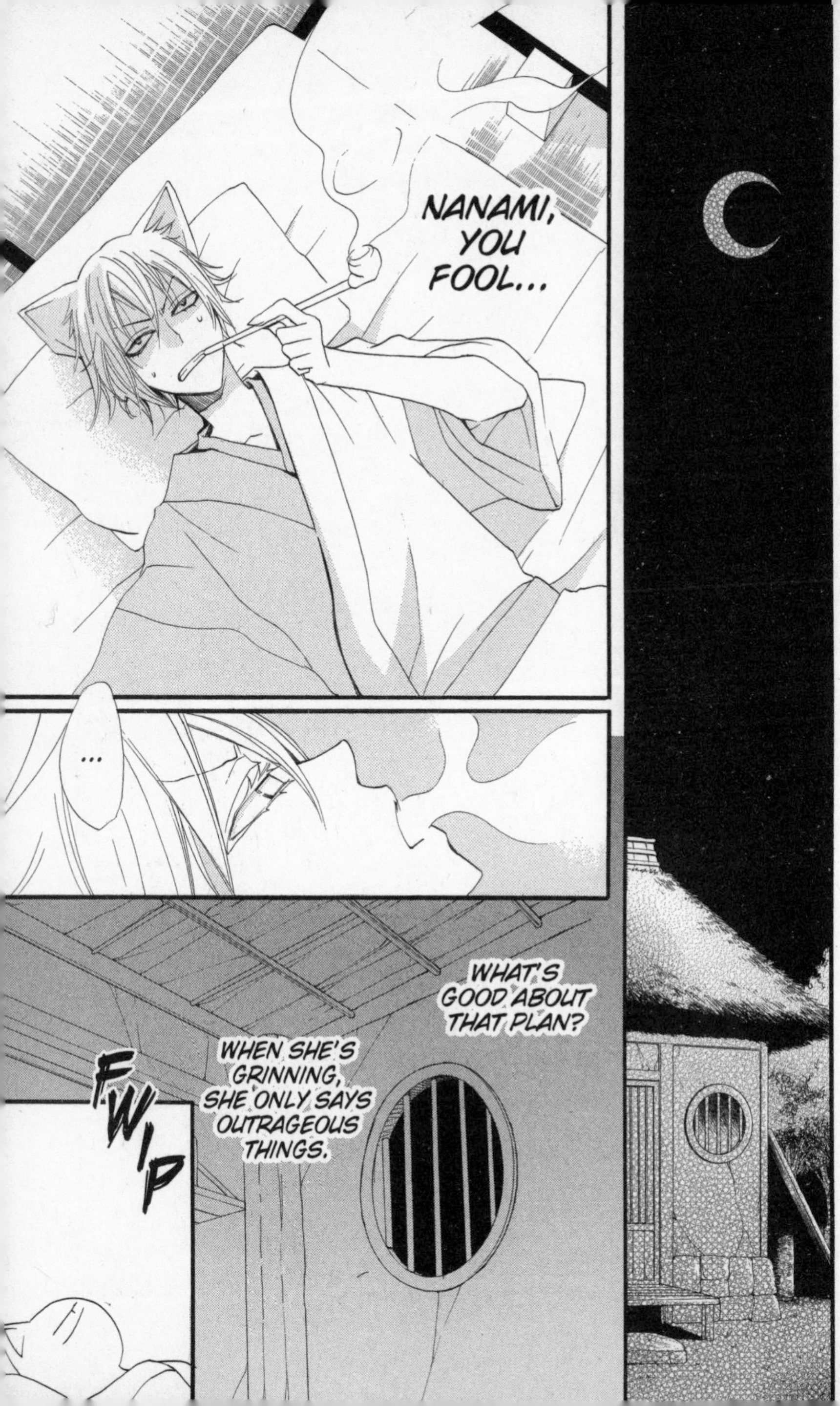
NANAMI, YOU FOOL...
...
WHAT'S GOOD ABOUT THAT PLAN?
WHEN SHE'S GRINNING, SHE ONLY SAYS OUTRAGEOUS THINGS.
FWIP

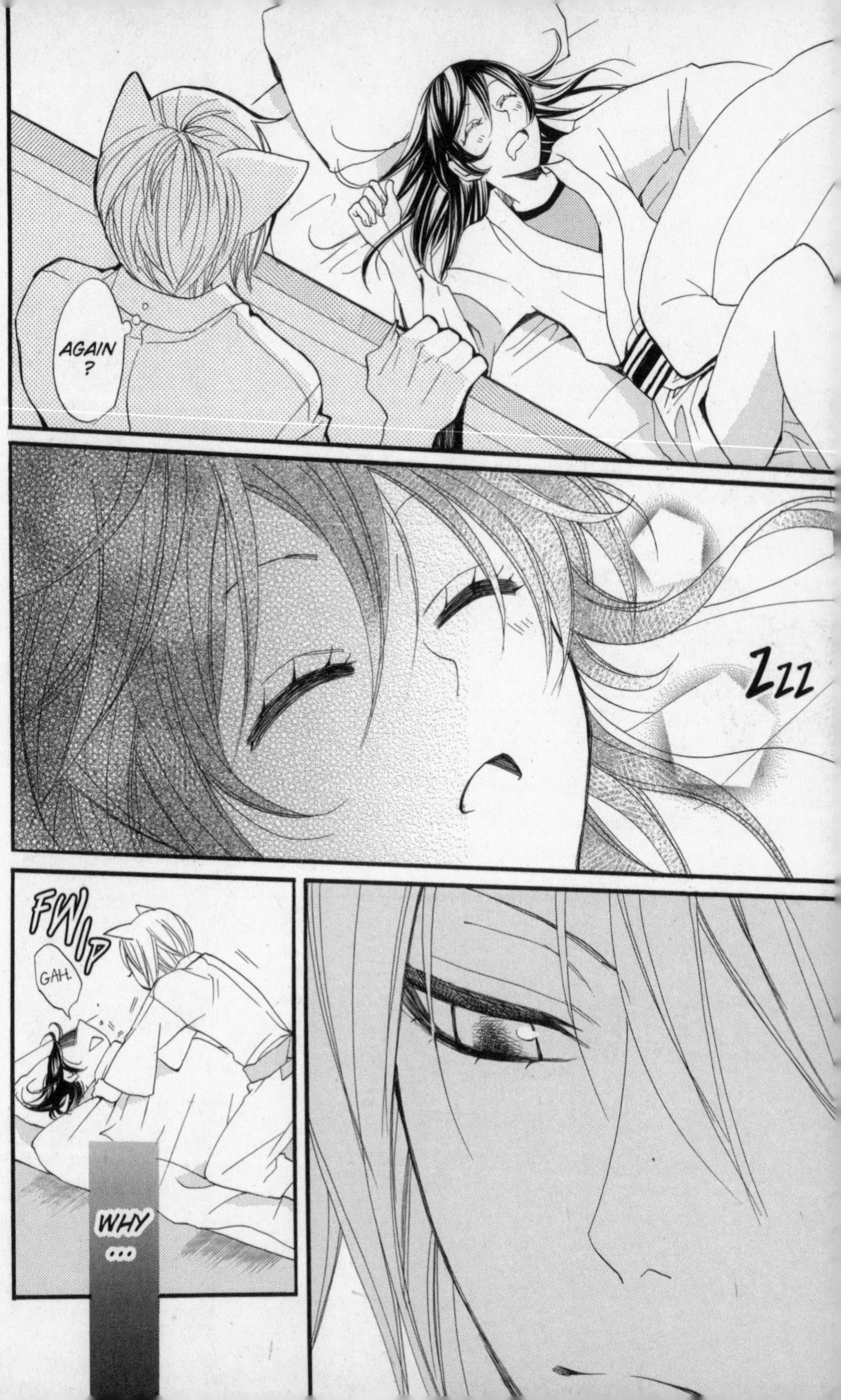
AGAIN ?
Zzz
WHY ...
FWIP
GAH.

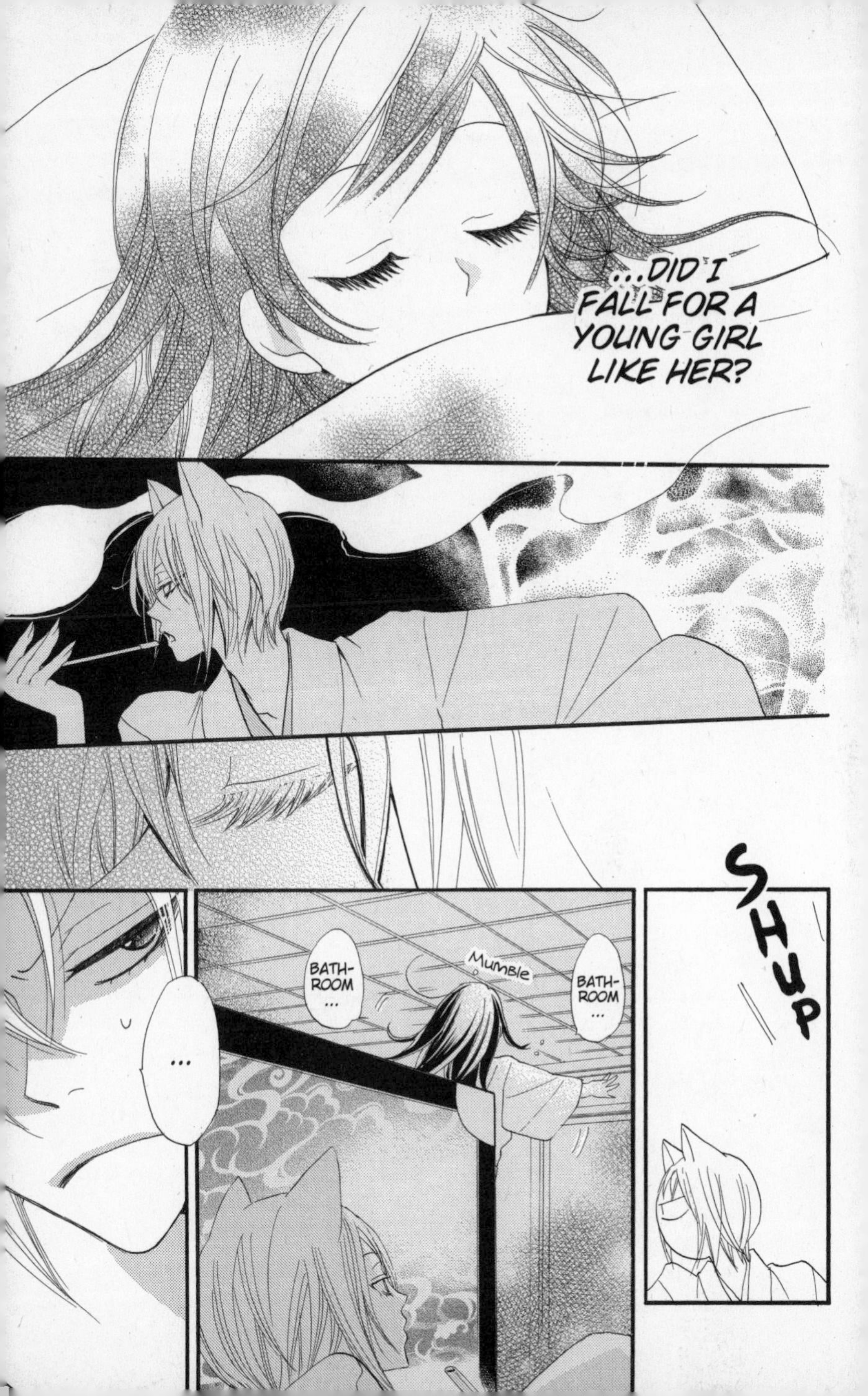
...DID I FALL FOR A YOUNG GIRL LIKE HER?
SHUP
BATH-ROOM ...
Mumble
BATH-ROOM ...
...

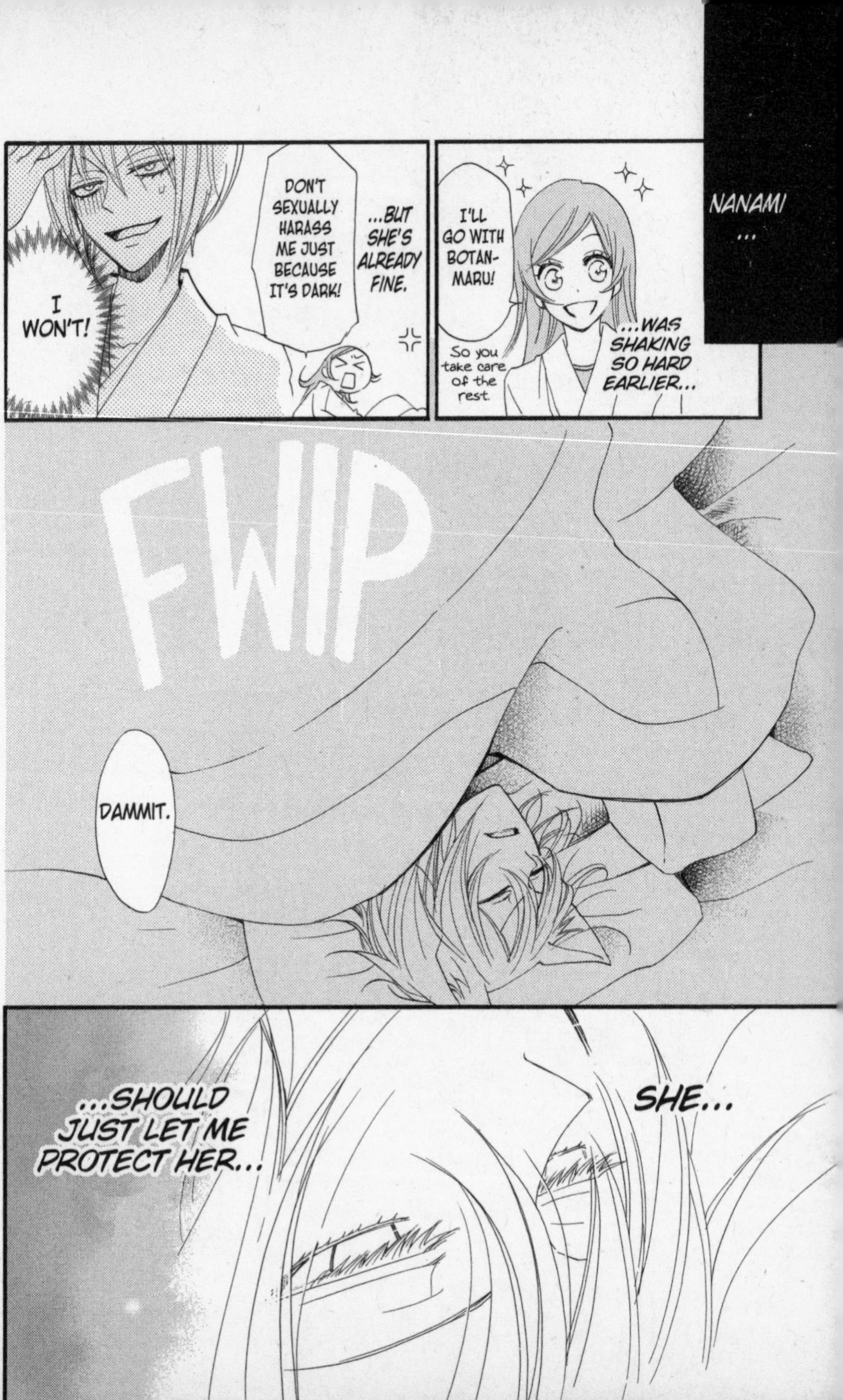
NANAMI ...
...WAS SHAKING SO HARD EARLIER...
I'LL GO WITH BOTAN-MARU!
So you take care of the rest.
...BUT SHE'S ALREADY FINE.
DON'T SEXUALLY HARASS ME JUST BECAUSE IT'S DARK!
I WON'T!
FWIP
DAMMIT.
SHE...
...SHOULD JUST LET ME PROTECT HER...

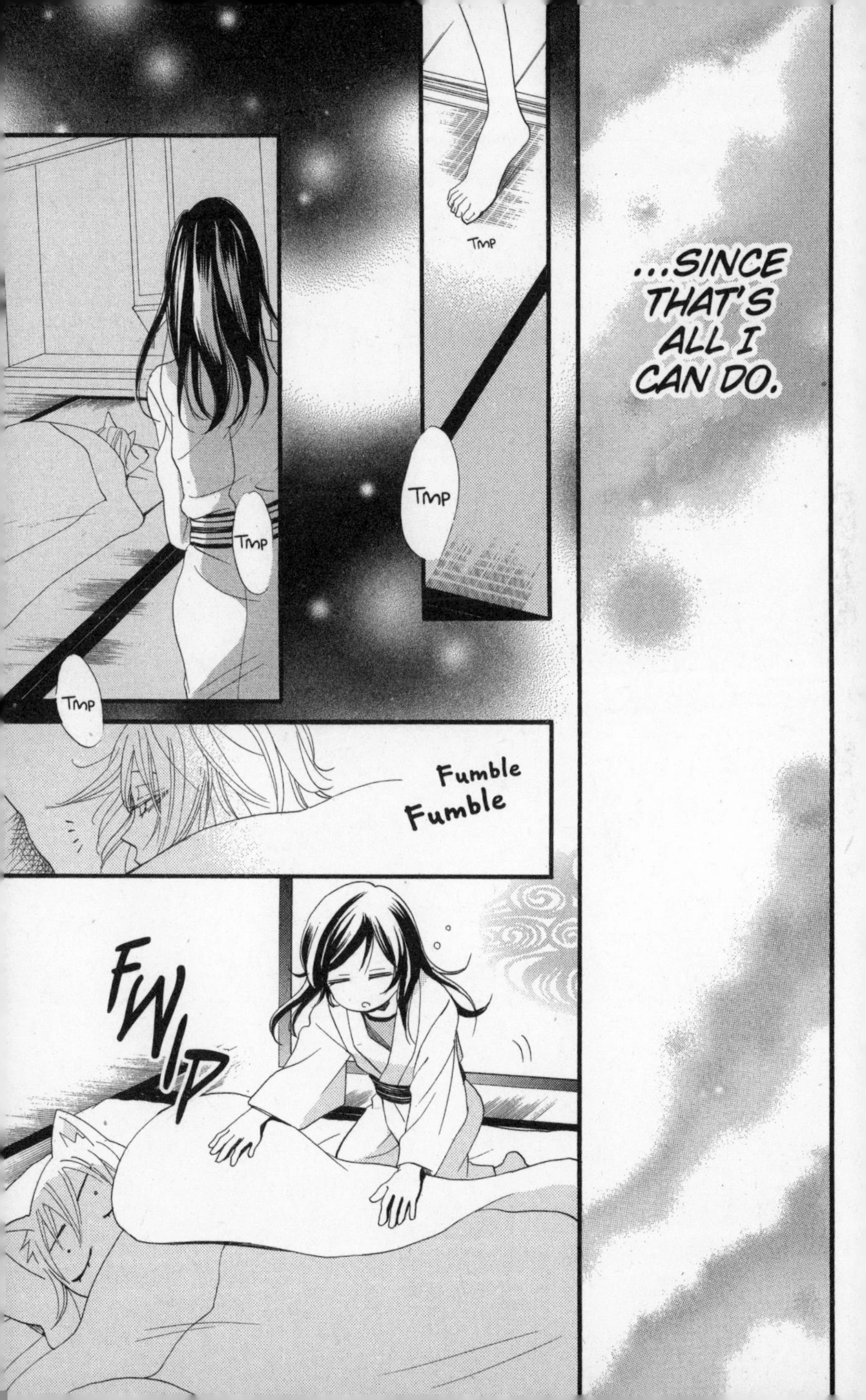
...SINCE THAT'S ALL I CAN DO.
TMP
Tmp
Tmp
Tmp
Fumble Fumble
FWIP

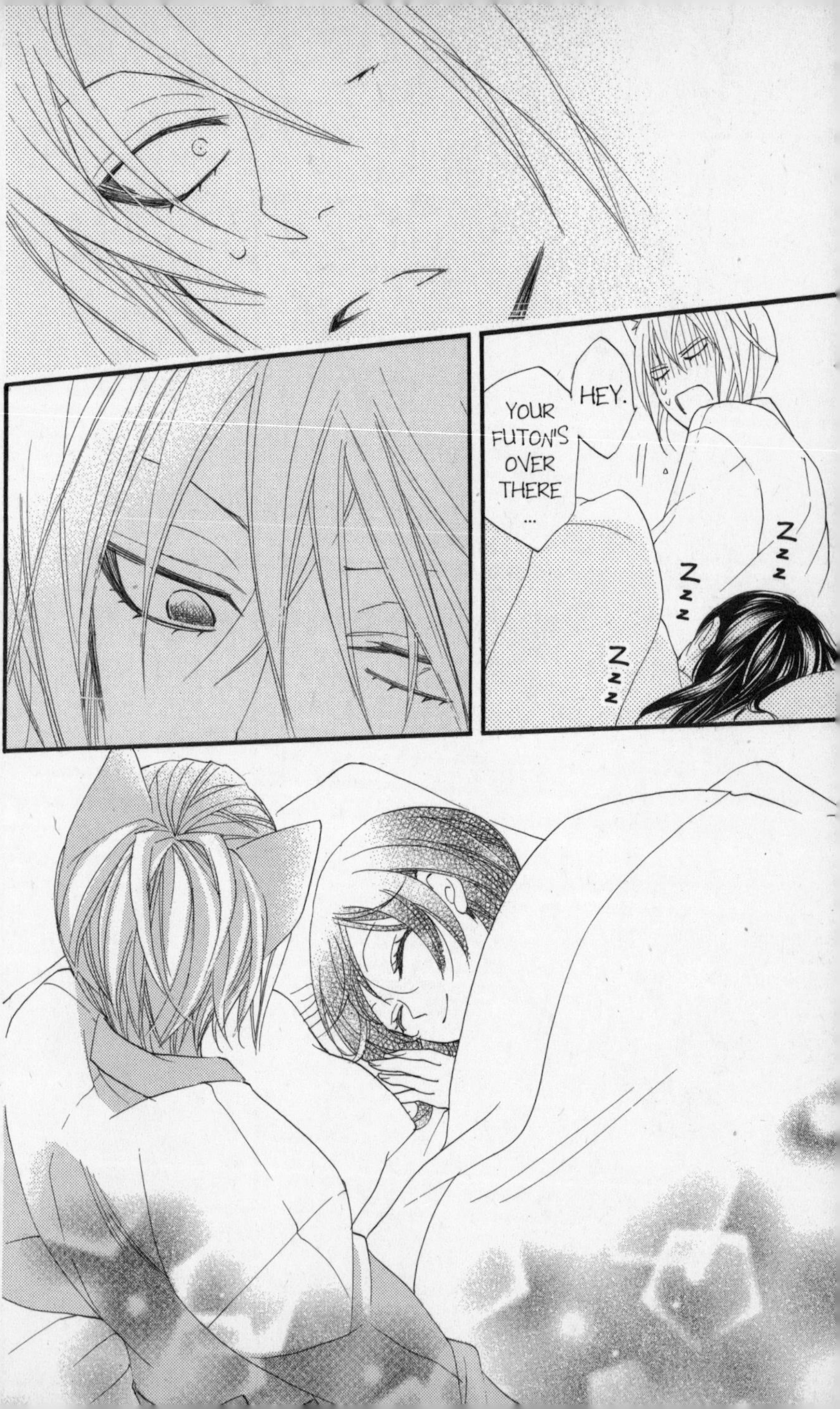
HEY.
YOUR FUTON'S OVER THERE ...
Z z z
Z z z
Z z z

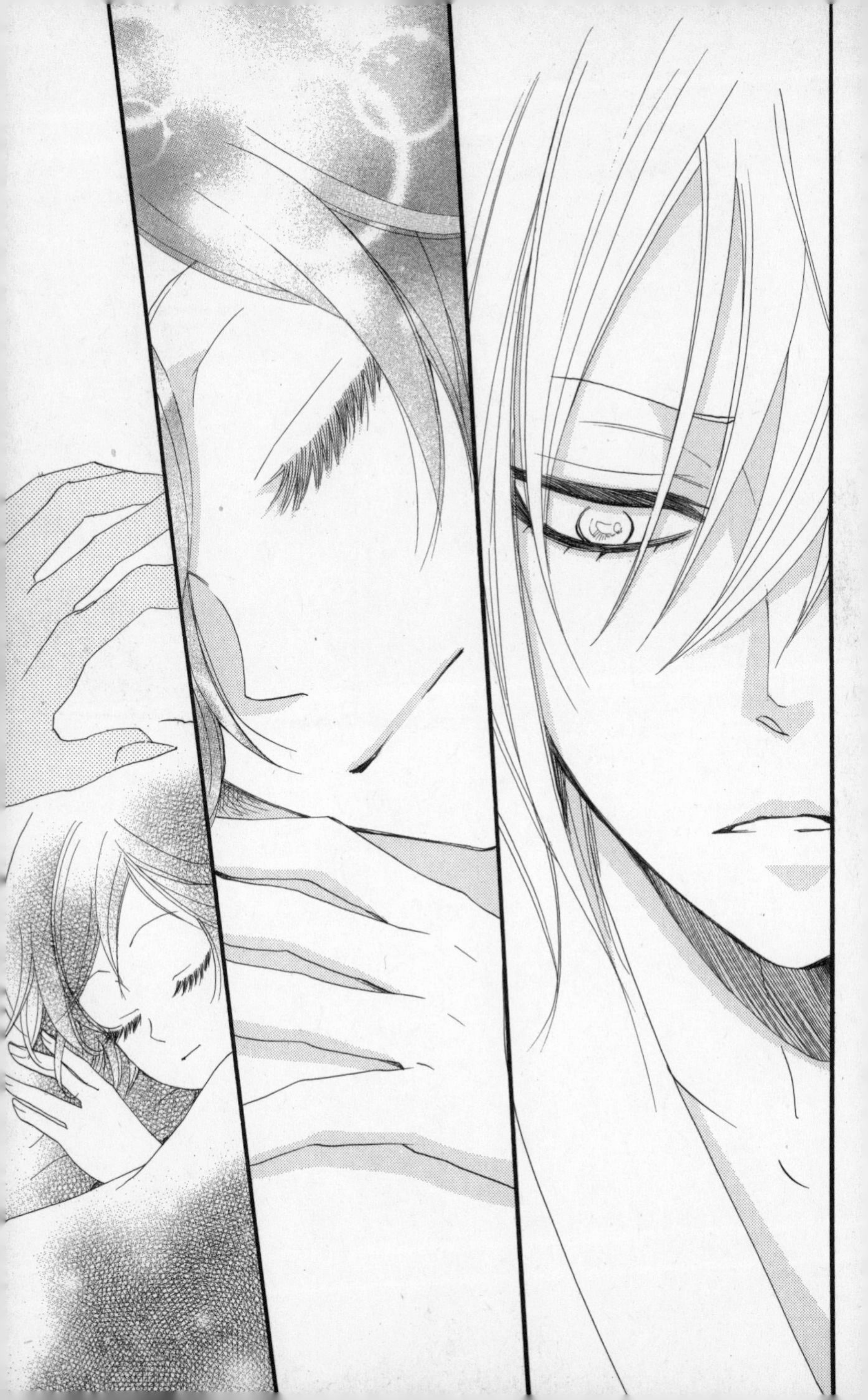

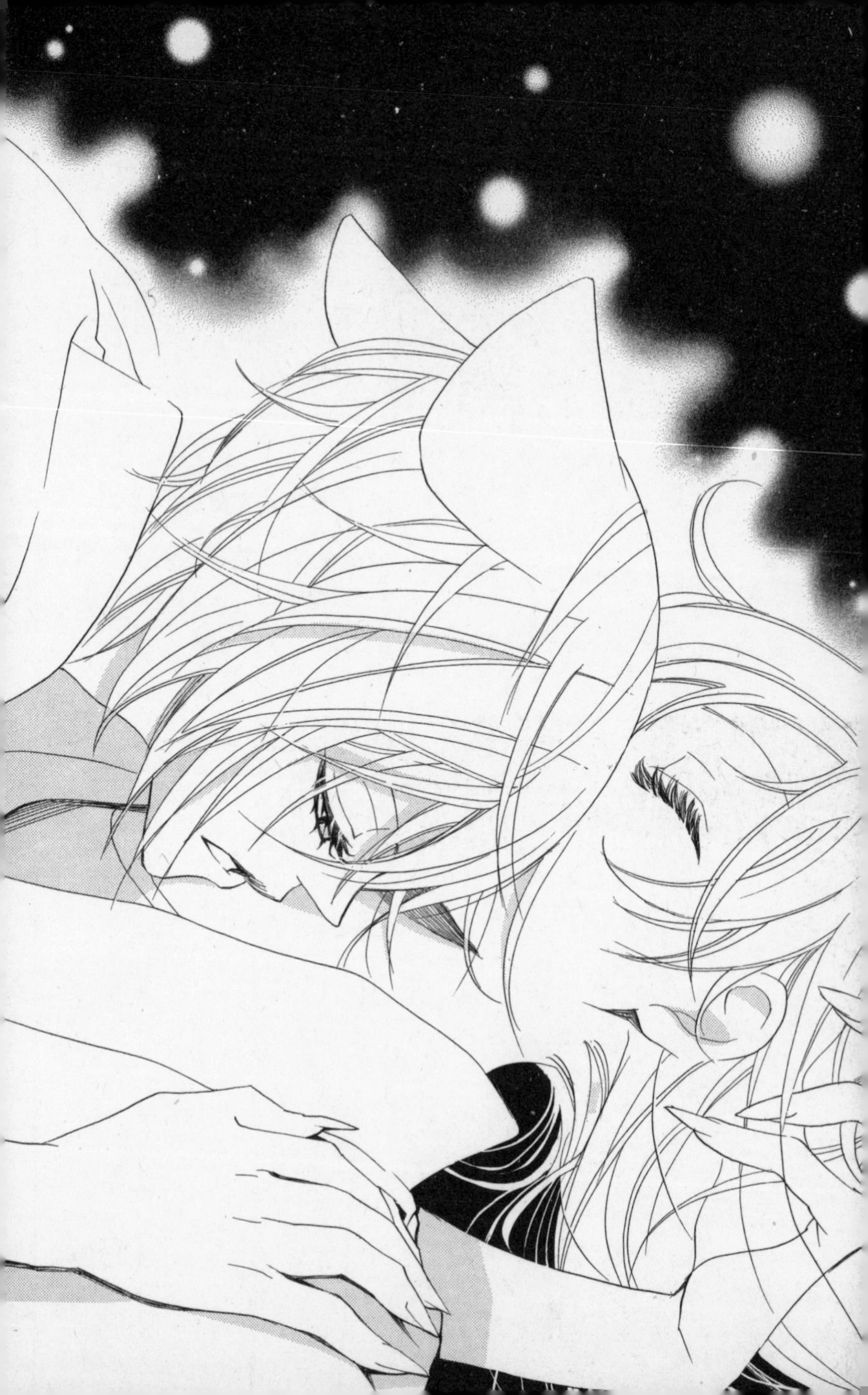

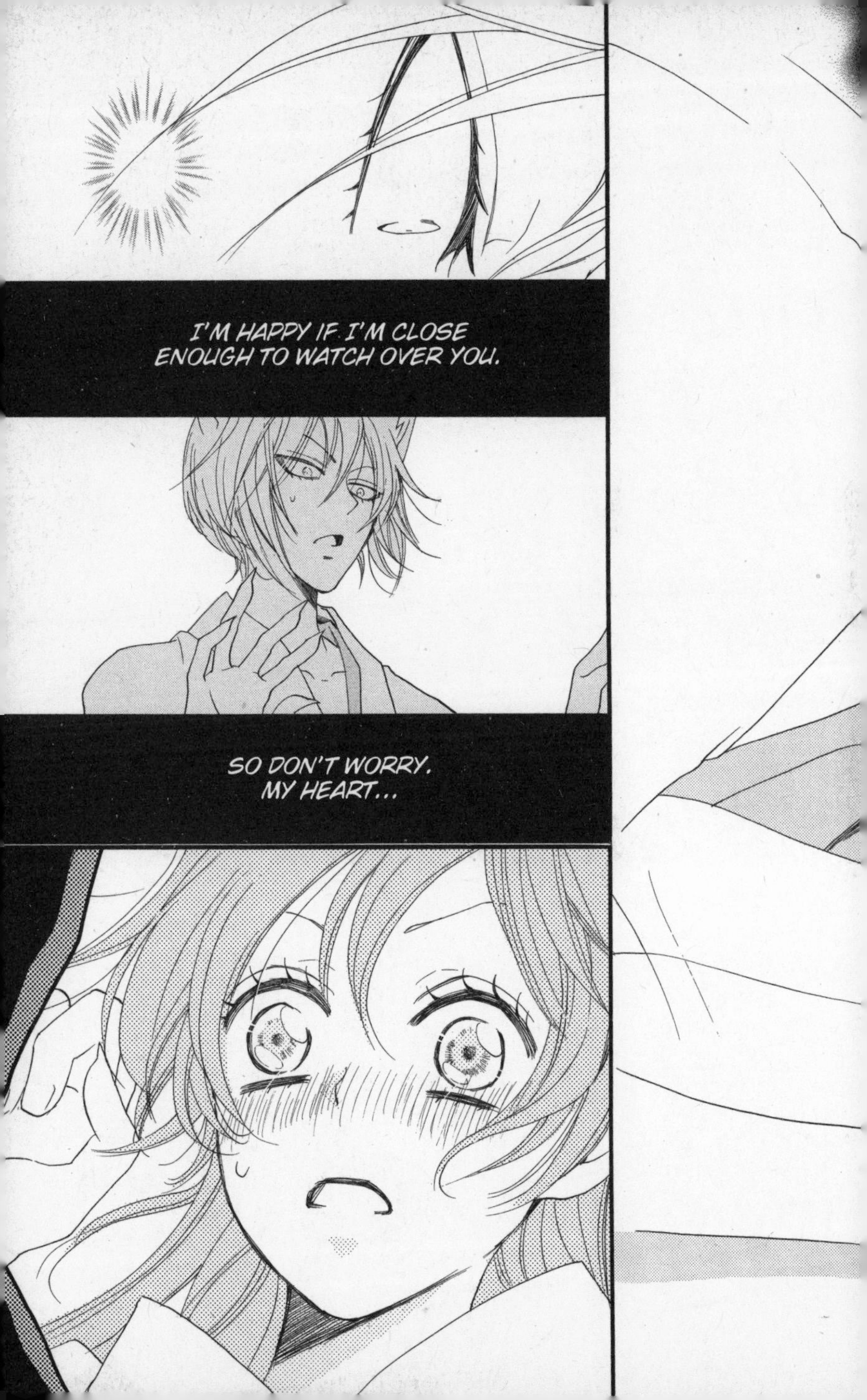
I'M HAPPY IF I'M CLOSE ENOUGH TO WATCH OVER YOU.
SO DON'T WORRY. MY HEART...

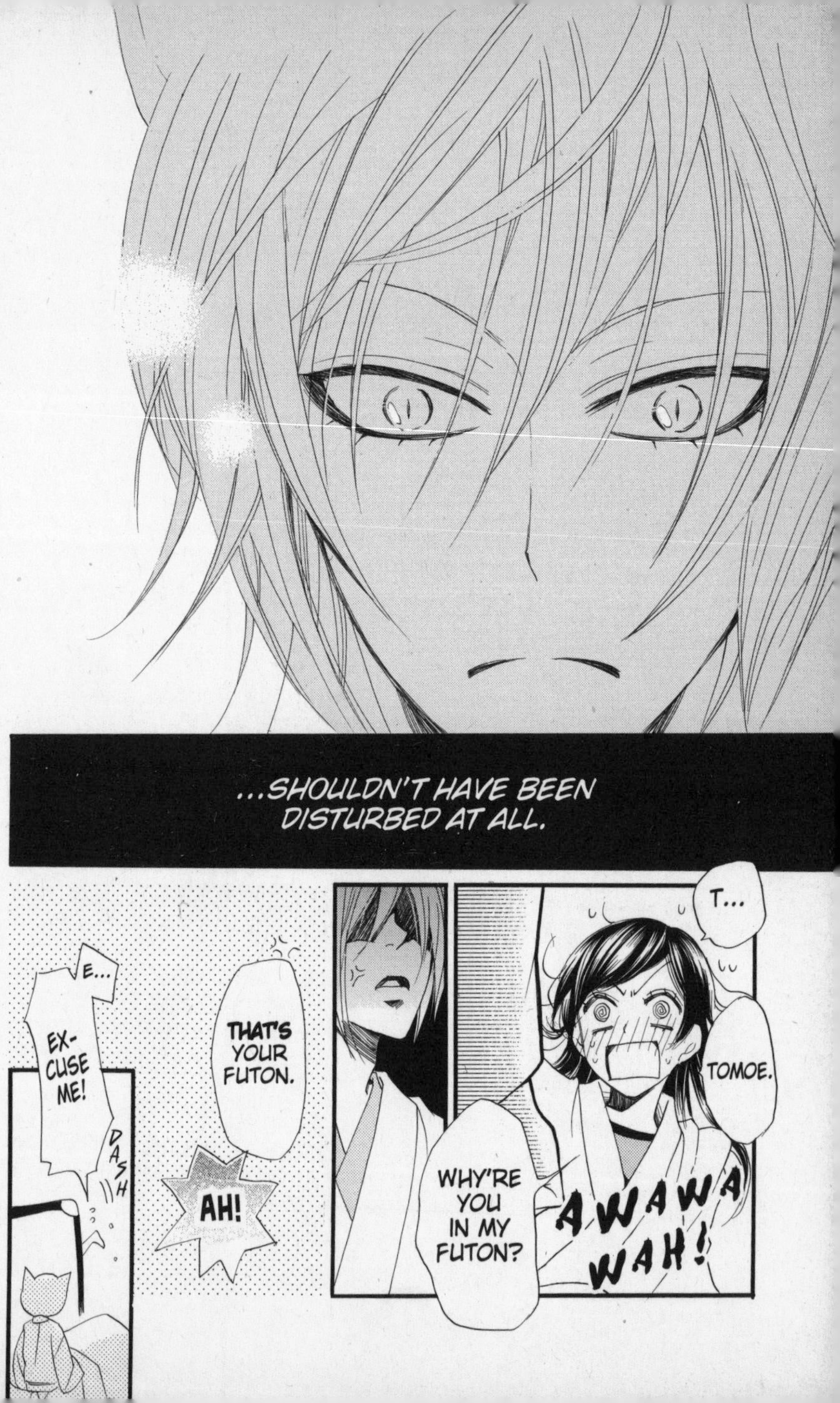
...SHOULDN'T HAVE BEEN DISTURBED AT ALL.
T...
TOMOE.
WHY'RE YOU IN MY FUTON?
AWAWA WAH!
THAT'S YOUR FUTON.
AH!
E...
EX-CUSE ME!
DASH

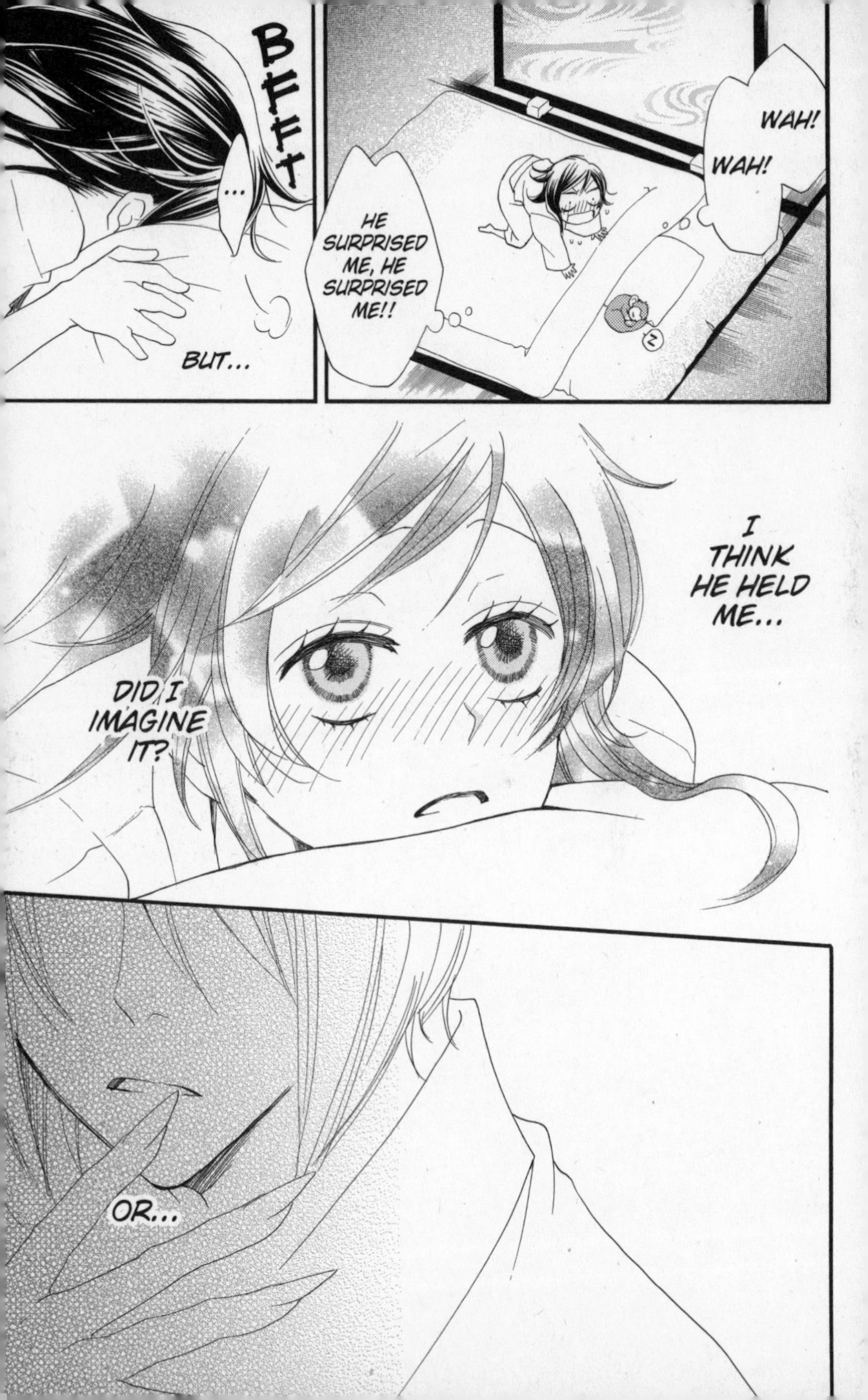
WAH!
WAH!
HE SURPRISED ME, HE SURPRISED ME!!
Z
BFFT
...
BUT...
I THINK HE HELD ME...
DID I IMAGINE IT?
OR...

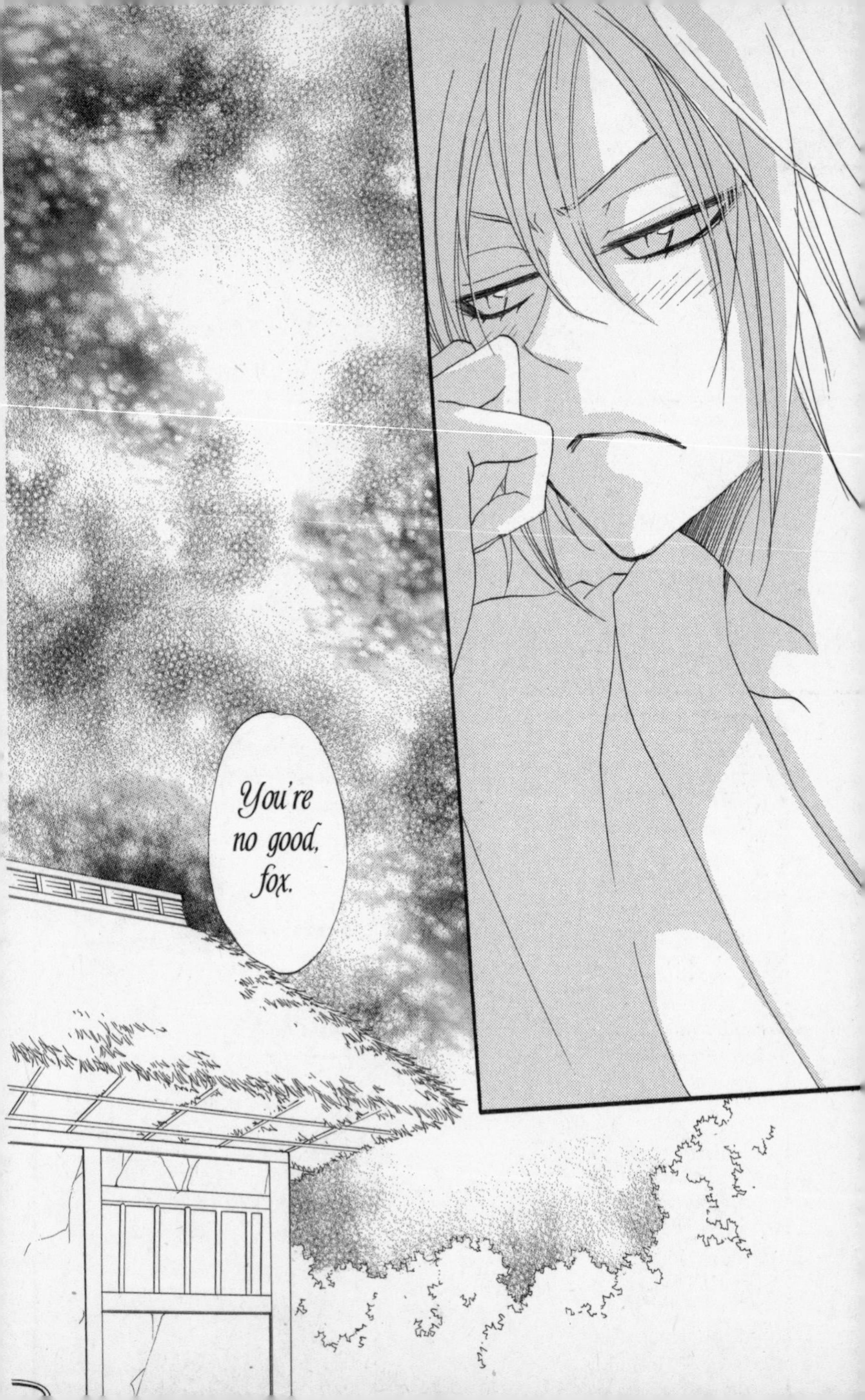
You're no good, fox.

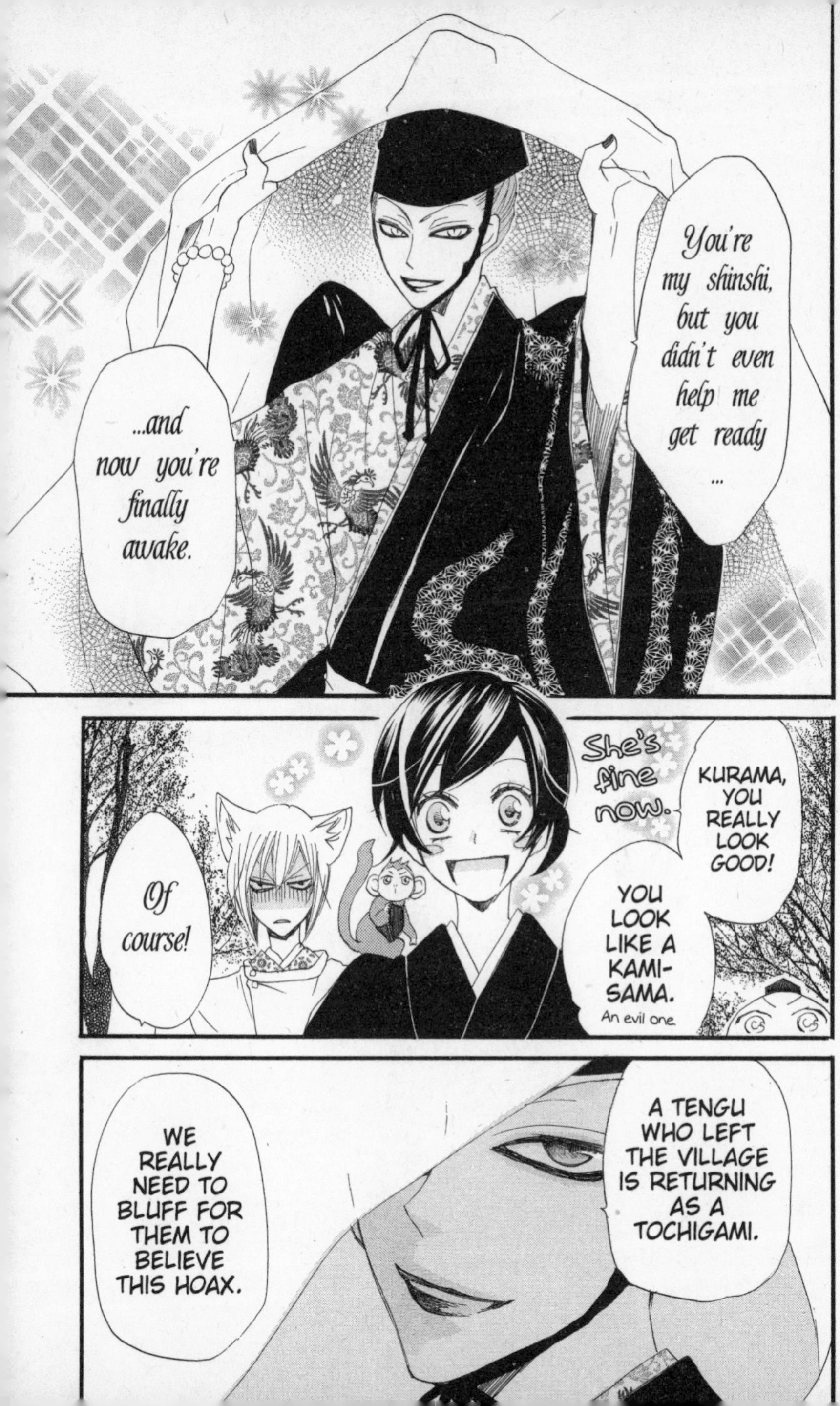
You're my shinshi, but you didn't even help me get ready ...
...and now you're finally awake.
KURAMA, YOU REALLY LOOK GOOD!
She's fine now.
YOU LOOK LIKE A KAMI-SAMA.
An evil one
Of course!
A TENGU WHO LEFT THE VILLAGE IS RETURNING AS A TOCHIGAMI.
WE REALLY NEED TO BLUFF FOR THEM TO BELIEVE THIS HOAX.

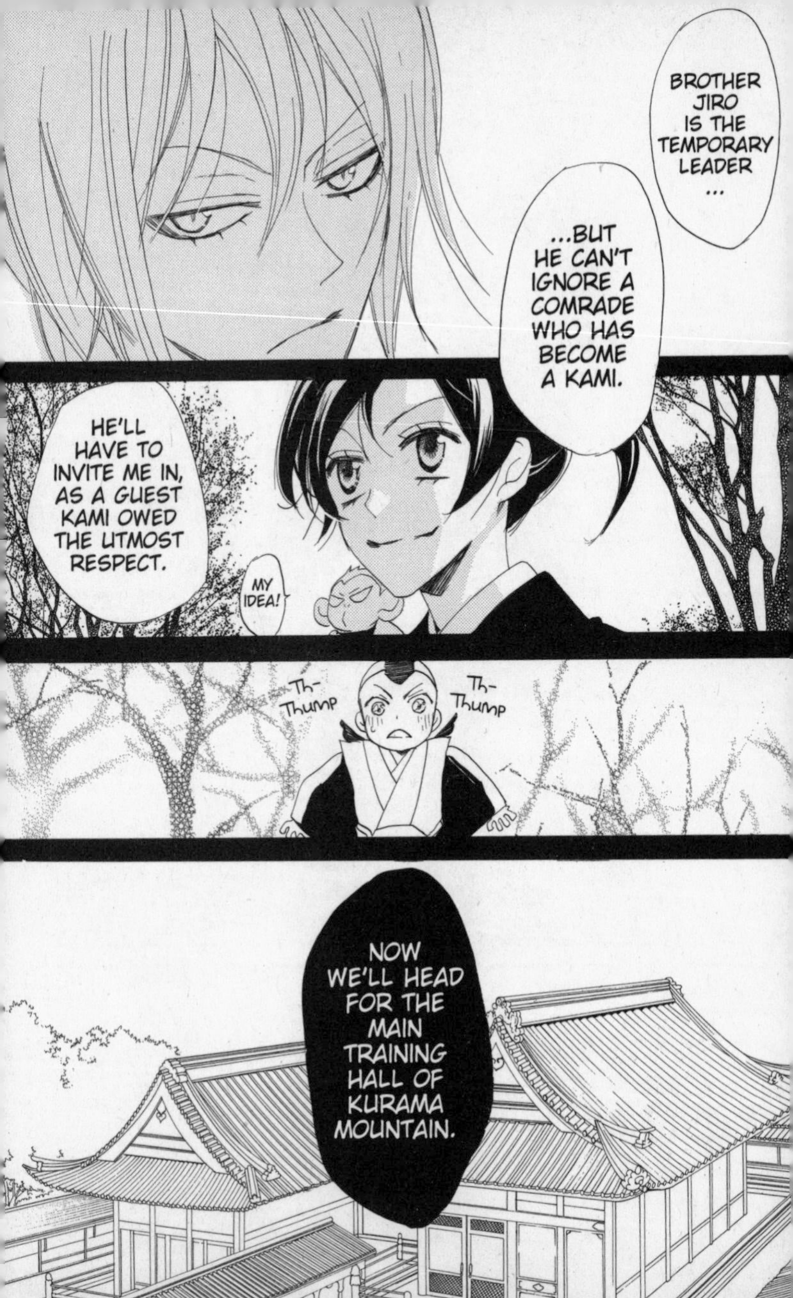
BROTHER JIRO IS THE TEMPORARY LEADER ...
...BUT HE CAN'T IGNORE A COMRADE WHO HAS BECOME A KAMI.
HE'LL HAVE TO INVITE ME IN, AS A GUEST KAMI OWED THE UTMOST RESPECT.
MY IDEA!
Th-Thump
Th-Thump
NOW WE'LL HEAD FOR THE MAIN TRAINING HALL OF KURAMA MOUNTAIN.

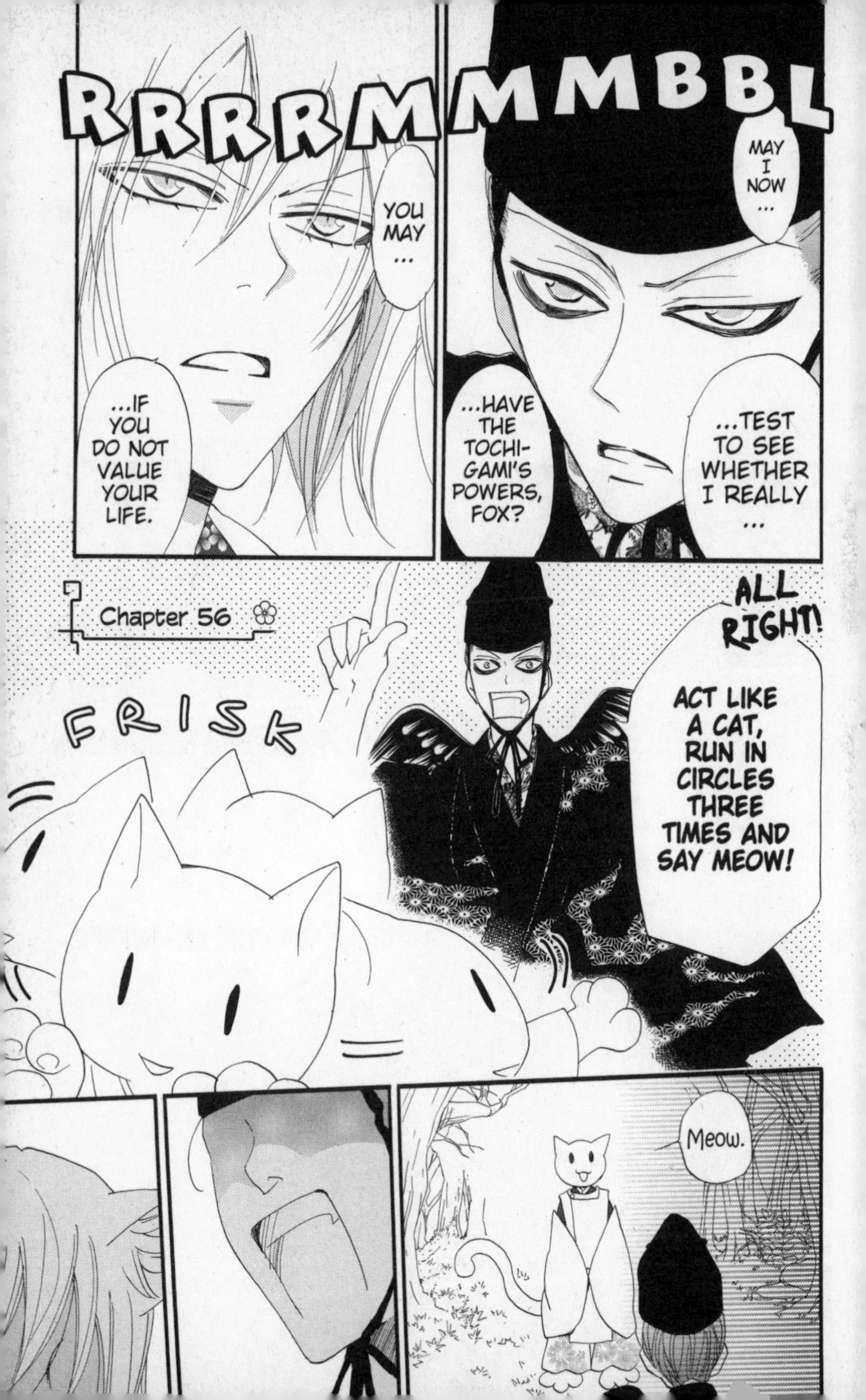
RRRRMMMMMBBL
MAY I NOW ...
...TEST TO SEE WHETHER I REALLY ...
...HAVE THE TOCHI-GAMI'S POWERS, FOX?
YOU MAY ...
...IF YOU DO NOT VALUE YOUR LIFE.
Chapter 56
ALL RIGHT!
ACT LIKE A CAT, RUN IN CIRCLES THREE TIMES AND SAY MEOW!
FRISK
Meow.

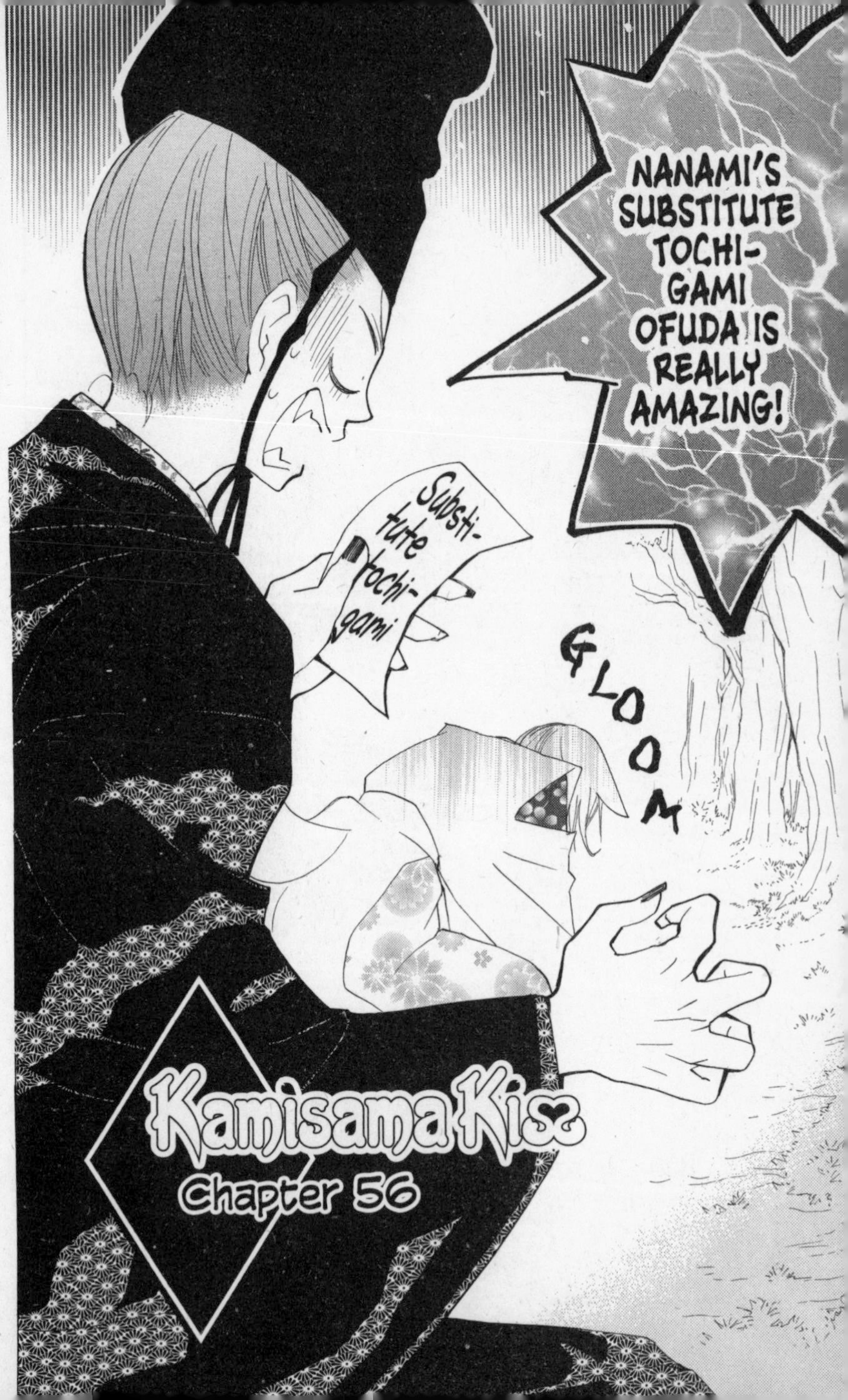
NANAMI'S SUBSTITUTE TOCHI-GAMI OFUDA IS REALLY AMAZING!
Substi-tute Tochi-gami
GLOOM
Kamisama Kiss
Chapter 56

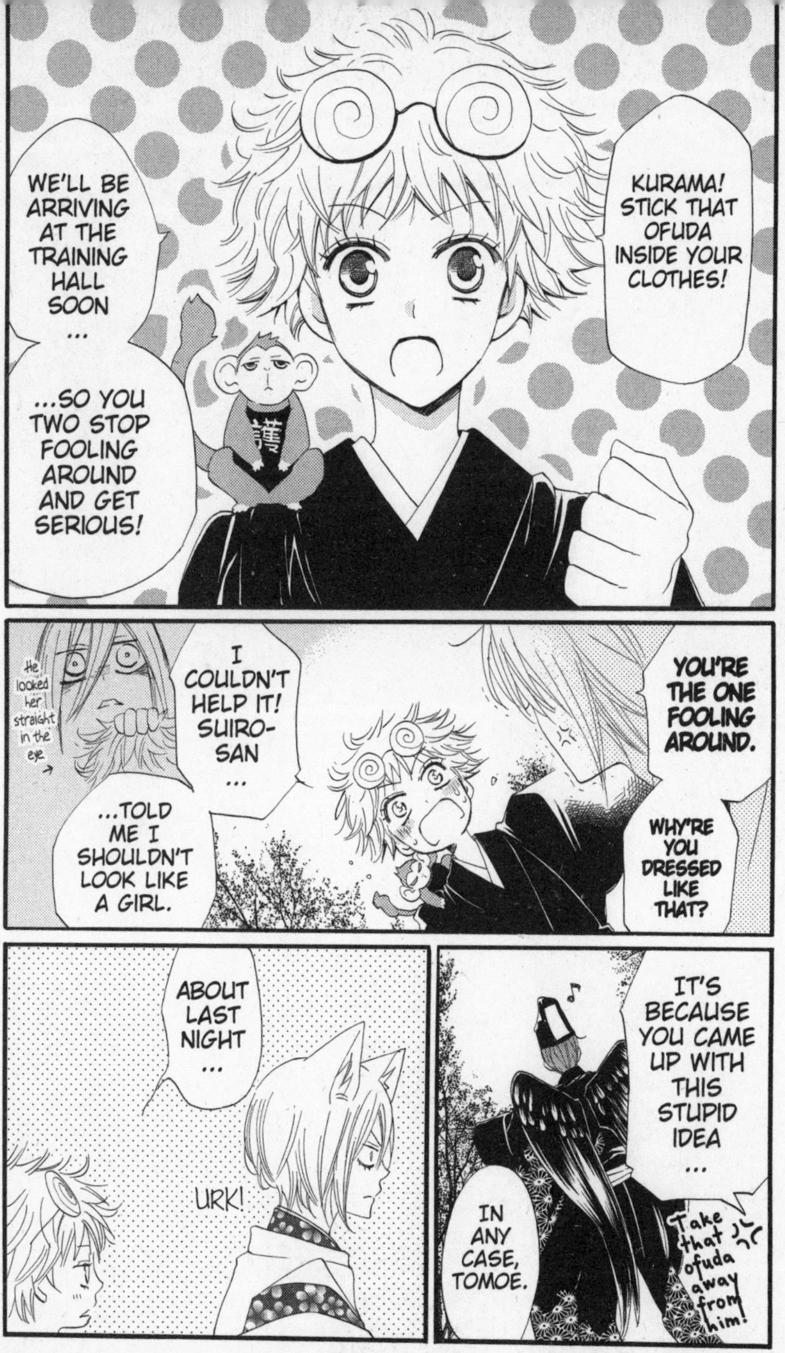
KURAMA! STICK THAT OFUDA INSIDE YOUR CLOTHES!
WE'LL BE ARRIVING AT THE TRAINING HALL SOON ...
...SO YOU TWO STOP FOOLING AROUND AND GET SERIOUS!
YOU'RE THE ONE FOOLING AROUND.
WHY'RE YOU DRESSED LIKE THAT?
I COULDN'T HELP IT! SUIRO-SAN ...
...TOLD ME I SHOULDN'T LOOK LIKE A GIRL.
He looked her straight in the eye
IT'S BECAUSE YOU CAME UP WITH THIS STUPID IDEA ...
Take that ofuda away from him!
IN ANY CASE, TOMOE.
ABOUT LAST NIGHT ...
URK!

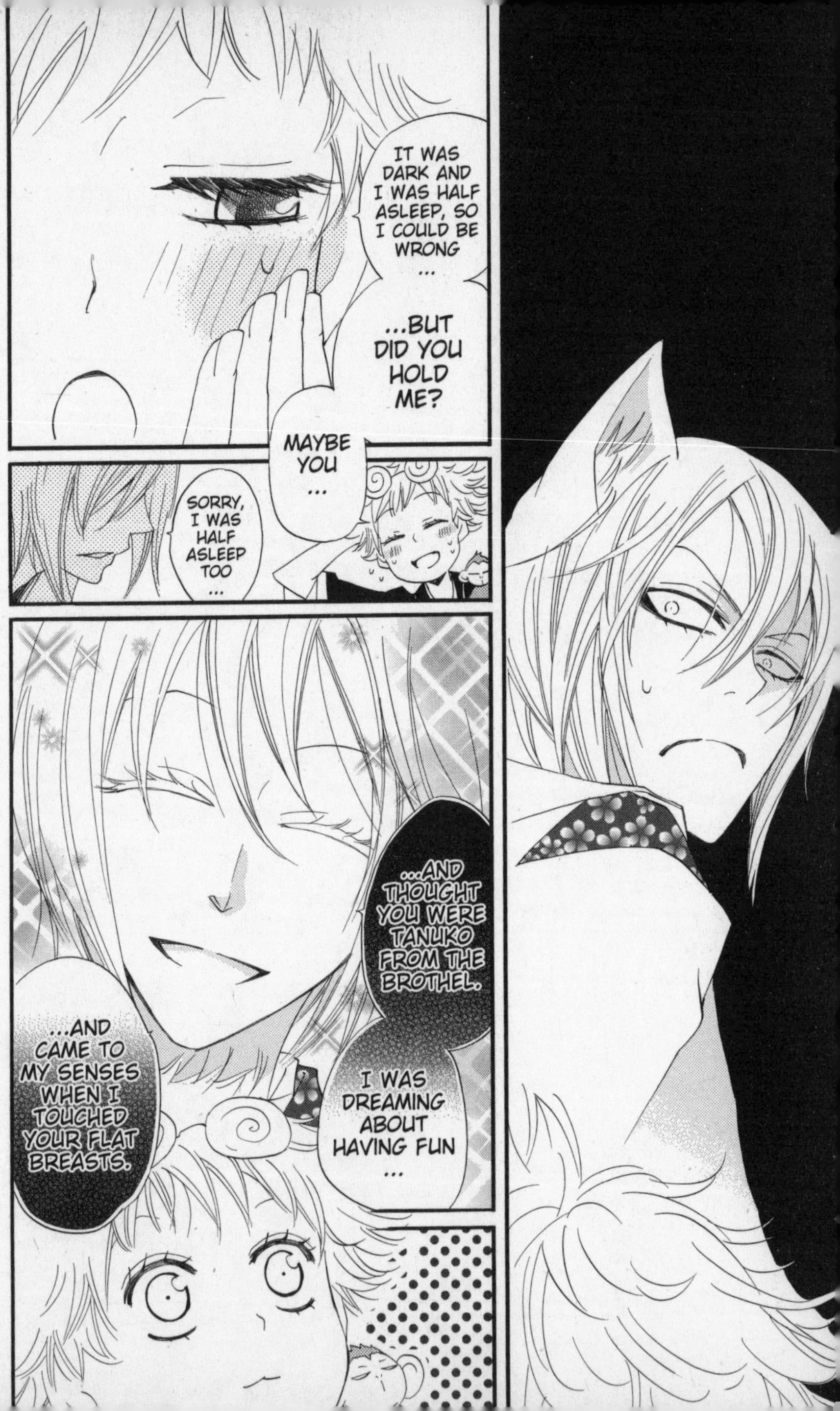
IT WAS DARK AND I WAS HALF ASLEEP, SO I COULD BE WRONG ...
...BUT DID YOU HOLD ME?
MAYBE YOU ...
SORRY, I WAS HALF ASLEEP TOO ...
I WAS DREAMING ABOUT HAVING FUN ...
...AND THOUGHT YOU WERE TANUKO FROM THE BROTHEL.
...AND CAME TO MY SENSES WHEN I TOUCHED YOUR FLAT BREASTS.

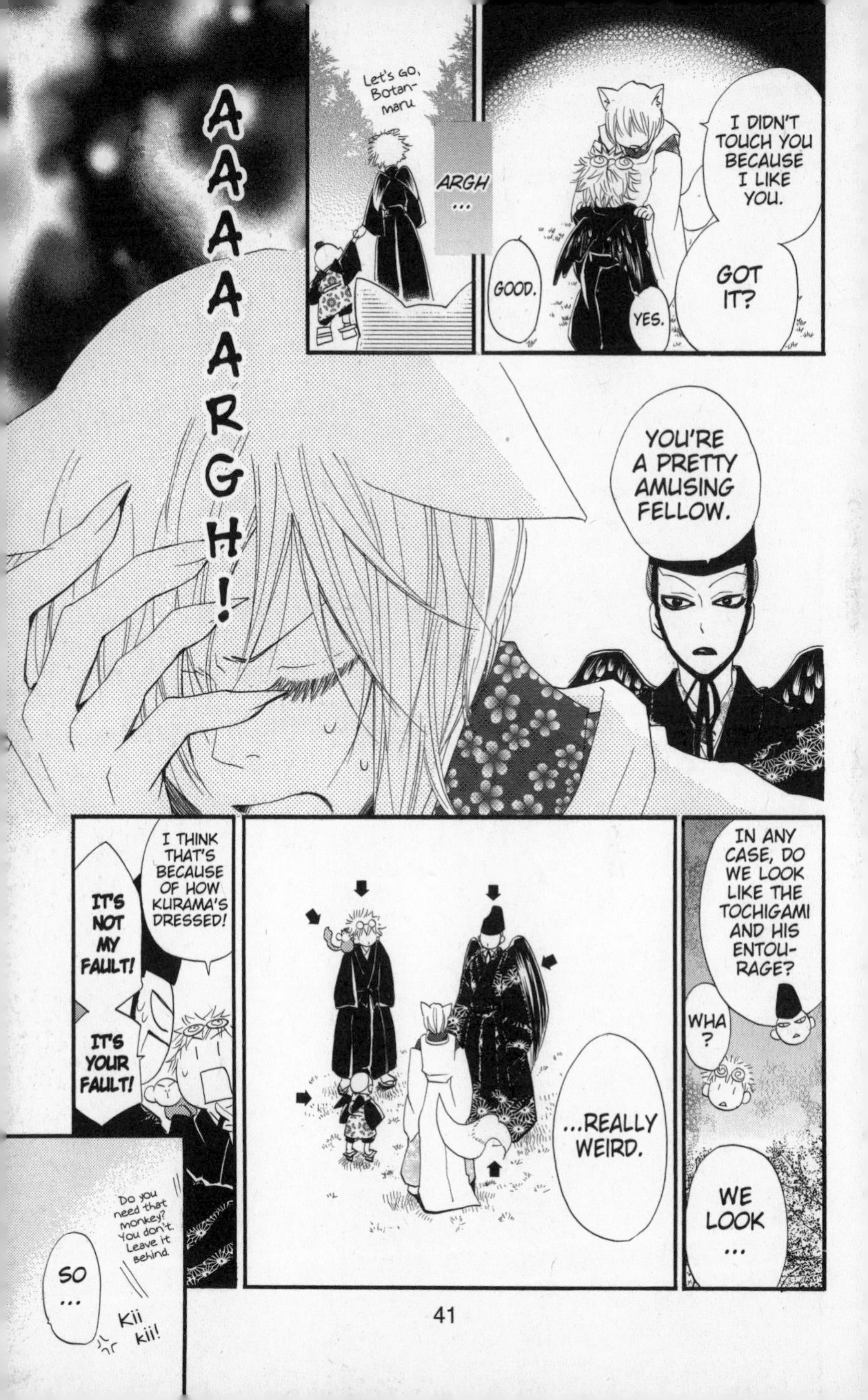
I DIDN'T TOUCH YOU BECAUSE I LIKE YOU.
GOT IT?
YES.
GOOD.
Let's go, Botan-maru
ARGH ...
YOU'RE A PRETTY AMUSING FELLOW.
AAAAAARGH!
IN ANY CASE, DO WE LOOK LIKE THE TOCHIGAMI AND HIS ENTOURAGE?
WHA?
WE LOOK ...
...REALLY WEIRD.
I THINK THAT'S BECAUSE OF HOW KURAMA'S DRESSED!
IT'S NOT MY FAULT!
IT'S YOUR FAULT!
Do you need that monkey? You don't. Leave it behind.
SO ...
Kii kii!

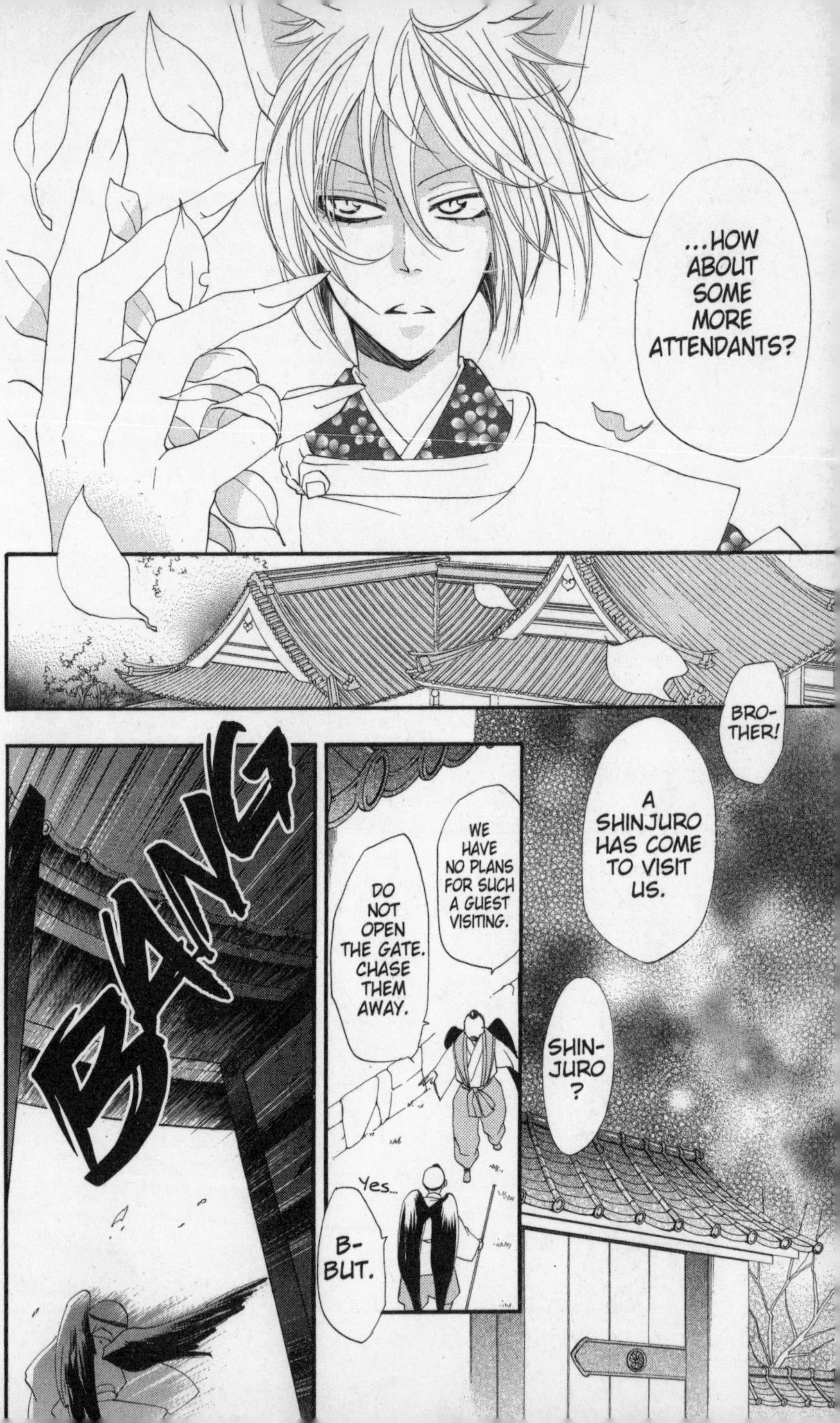
...HOW ABOUT SOME MORE ATTENDANTS?
BRO-THER!
A SHINJURO HAS COME TO VISIT US.
SHIN-JURO?
WE HAVE NO PLANS FOR SUCH A GUEST VISITING.
DO NOT OPEN THE GATE. CHASE THEM AWAY.
Yes...
B-BUT.
BANG

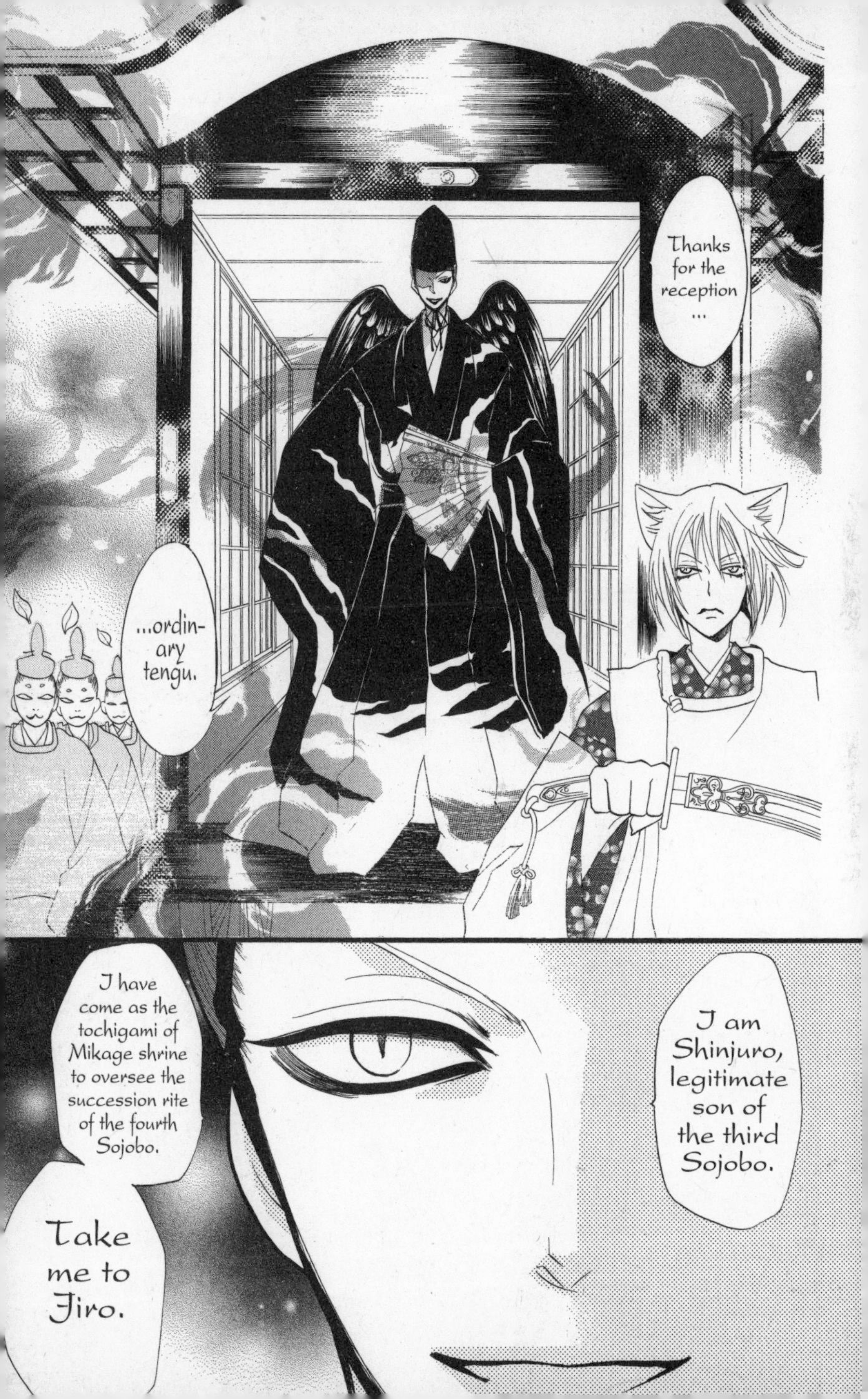
Thanks for the reception ...
...ordinary tengu.
I am Shinjuro, legitimate son of the third Sojobo.
I have come as the tochigami of Mikage shrine to oversee the succession rite of the fourth Sojobo.
Take me to Jiro.

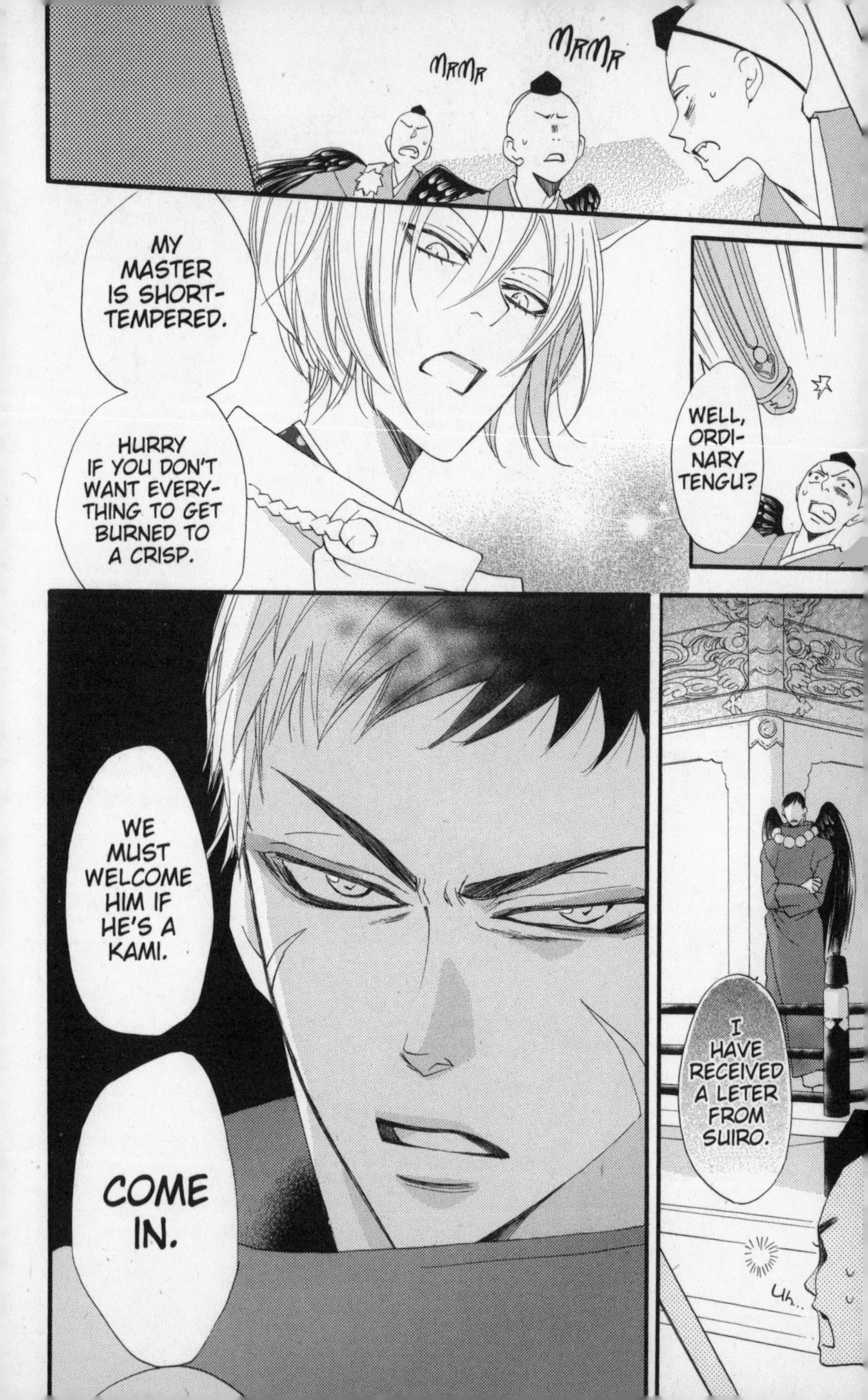
MRMR
MRMR
WELL, ORDINARY TENGU?
MY MASTER IS SHORT-TEMPERED.
HURRY IF YOU DON'T WANT EVERY-THING TO GET BURNED TO A CRISP.
I HAVE RECEIVED A LETER FROM SUIRO.
Uh..
WE MUST WELCOME HIM IF HE'S A KAMI.
COME IN.

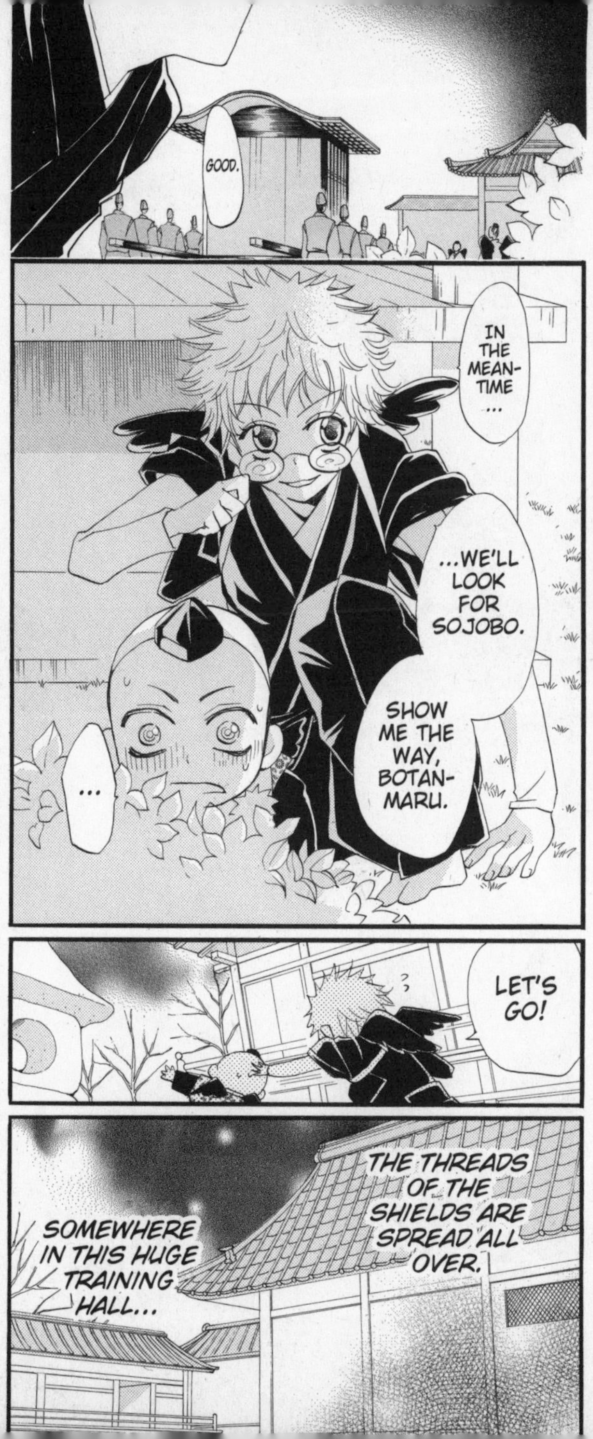
GOOD.
IN THE MEAN-TIME...
...WE'LL LOOK FOR SOJOBO.
SHOW ME THE WAY, BOTAN-MARU.
...
LET'S GO!
THE THREADS OF THE SHIELDS ARE SPREAD ALL OVER.
SOMEWHERE IN THIS HUGE TRAINING HALL...

1

Hello!

Thank you for picking up volume 10 of Kamisama Kiss!

When I started drawing Kamisama, my goal was ten volumes, so I'm very happy this volume is out. I'd like to thank the readers who have supported this series. Thank you so much! ✿

I hope you enjoy reading it! ☺

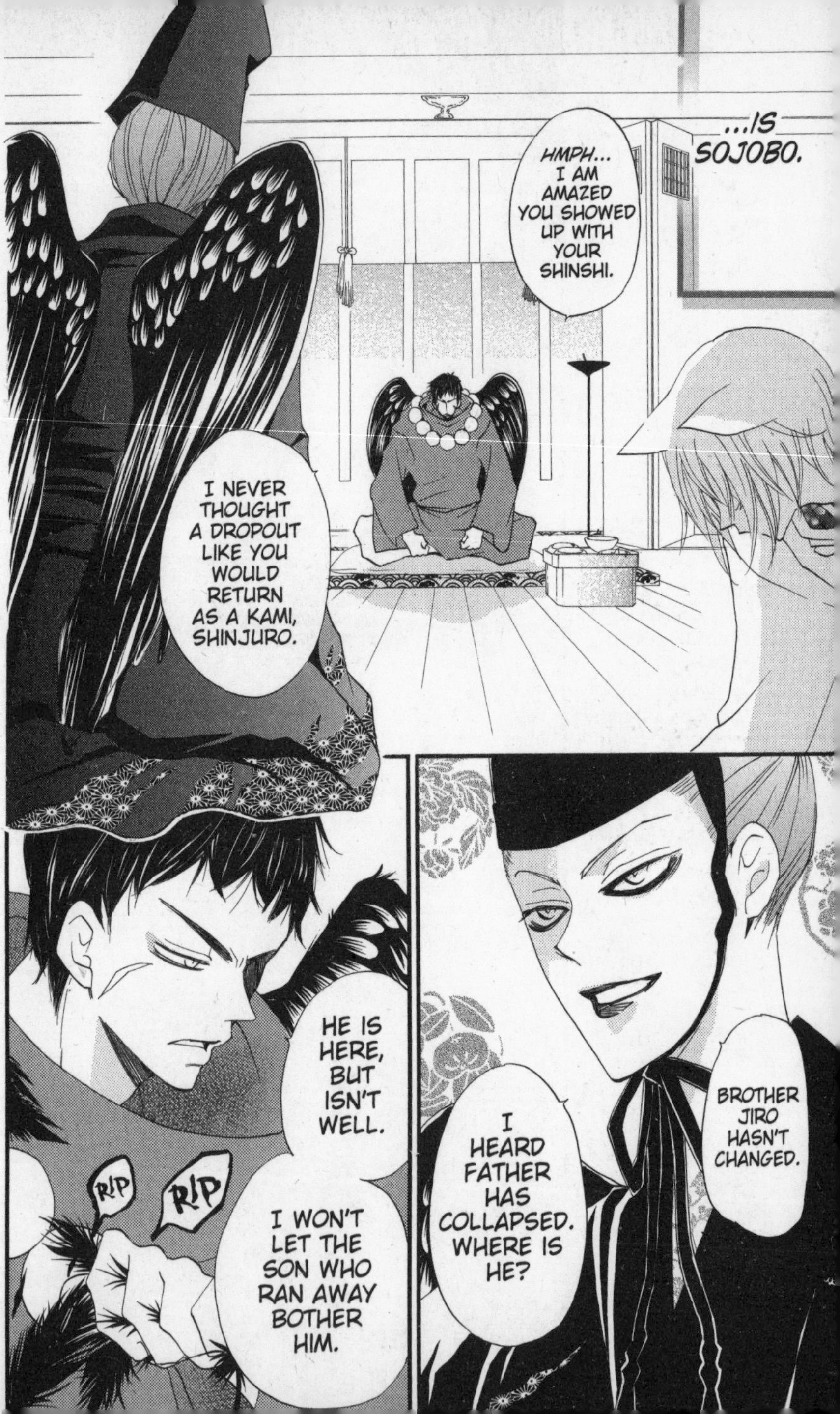
...IS SOJOBO.
HMPH... I AM AMAZED YOU SHOWED UP WITH YOUR SHINSHI.
I NEVER THOUGHT A DROPOUT LIKE YOU WOULD RETURN AS A KAMI, SHINJURO.
BROTHER JIRO HASN'T CHANGED.
I HEARD FATHER HAS COLLAPSED. WHERE IS HE?
HE IS HERE, BUT ISN'T WELL.
RIP
RIP
I WON'T LET THE SON WHO RAN AWAY BOTHER HIM.

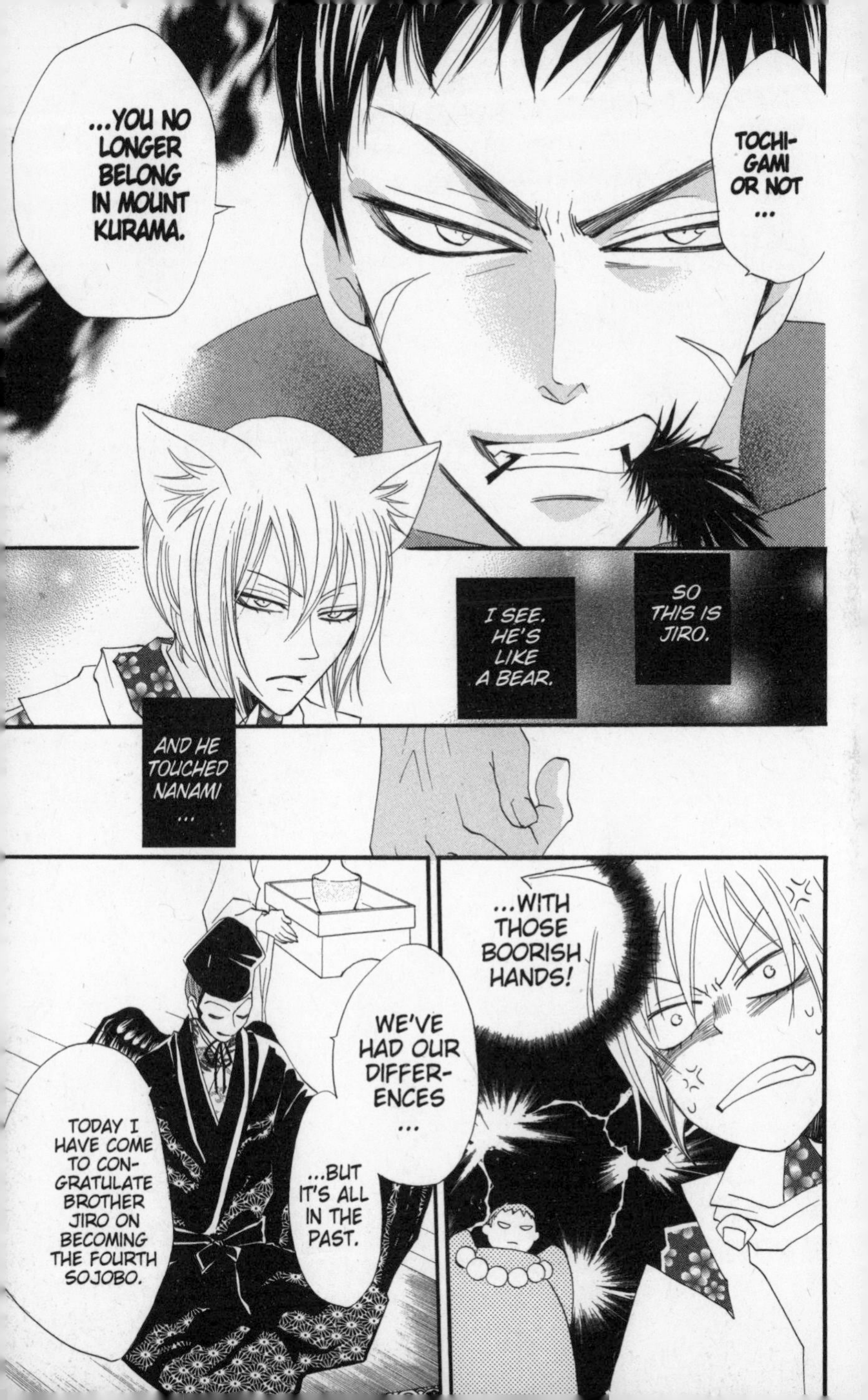
TOCHIGAMI OR NOT ...
...YOU NO LONGER BELONG IN MOUNT KURAMA.
SO THIS IS JIRO.
I SEE. HE'S LIKE A BEAR.
AND HE TOUCHED NANAMI ...
...WITH THOSE BOORISH HANDS!
WE'VE HAD OUR DIFFERENCES ...
...BUT IT'S ALL IN THE PAST.
TODAY I HAVE COME TO CONGRATULATE BROTHER JIRO ON BECOMING THE FOURTH SOJOBO.

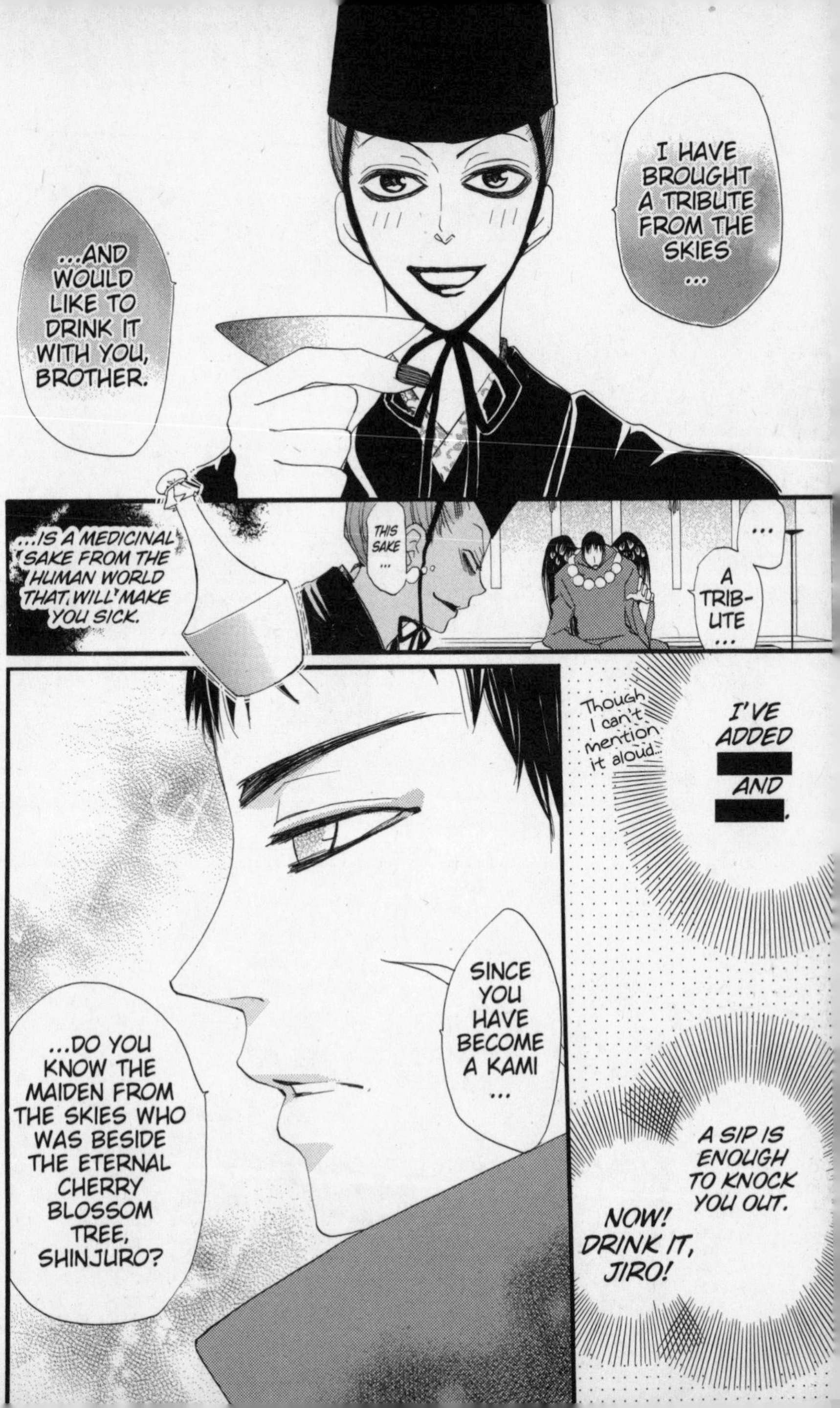
I HAVE BROUGHT A TRIBUTE FROM THE SKIES ...
...AND WOULD LIKE TO DRINK IT WITH YOU, BROTHER.
...
A TRIBUTE ...
THIS SAKE ...
...IS A MEDICINAL SAKE FROM THE HUMAN WORLD THAT WILL MAKE YOU SICK.
I'VE ADDED [redacted] AND [redacted].
Though I can't mention it aloud...
A SIP IS ENOUGH TO KNOCK YOU OUT.
NOW! DRINK IT, JIRO!
SINCE YOU HAVE BECOME A KAMI ...
...DO YOU KNOW THE MAIDEN FROM THE SKIES WHO WAS BESIDE THE ETERNAL CHERRY BLOSSOM TREE, SHINJURO?

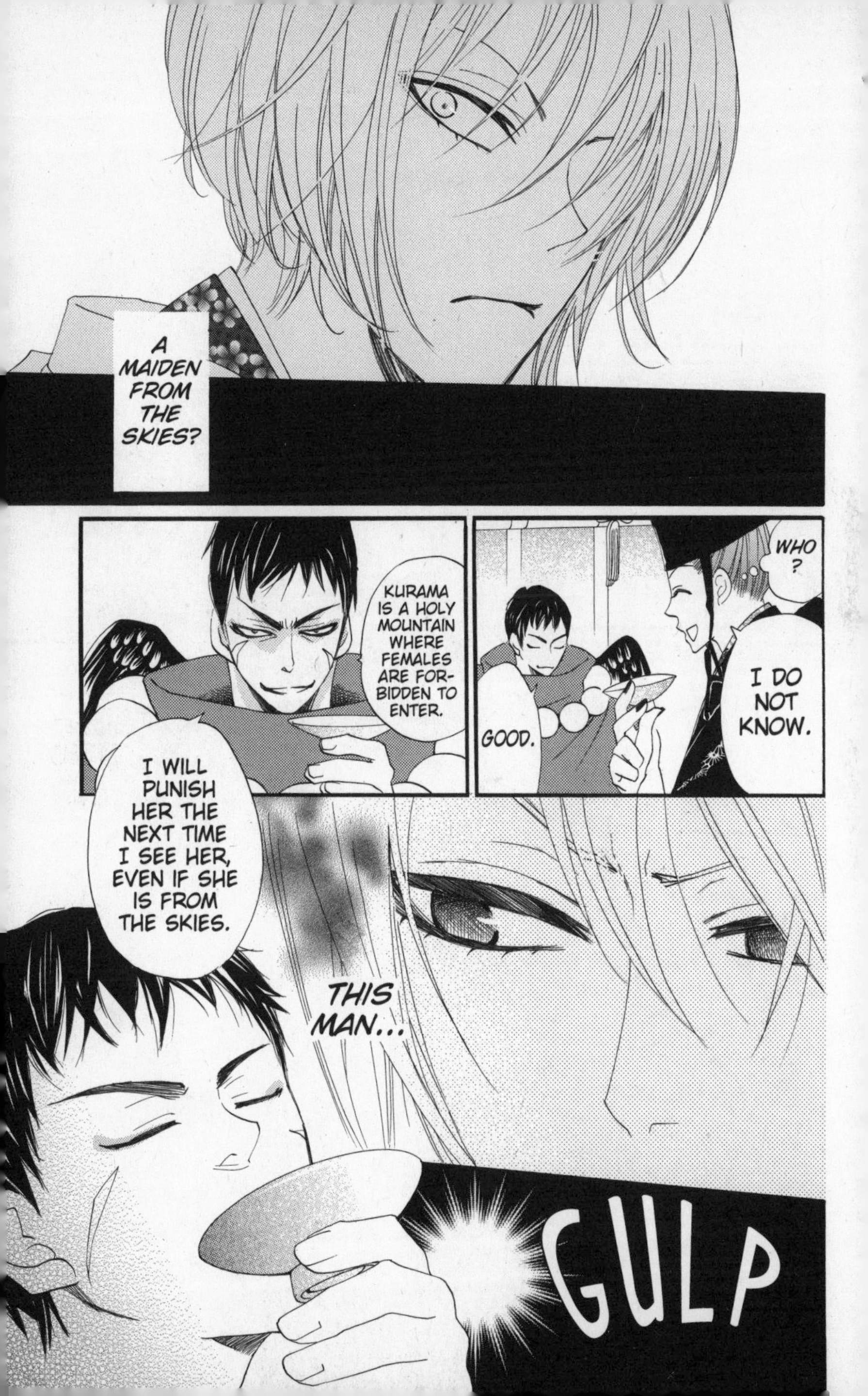
A MAIDEN FROM THE SKIES?
WHO?
I DO NOT KNOW.
GOOD.
KURAMA IS A HOLY MOUNTAIN WHERE FEMALES ARE FOR-BIDDEN TO ENTER.
I WILL PUNISH HER THE NEXT TIME I SEE HER, EVEN IF SHE IS FROM THE SKIES.
THIS MAN...
GULP

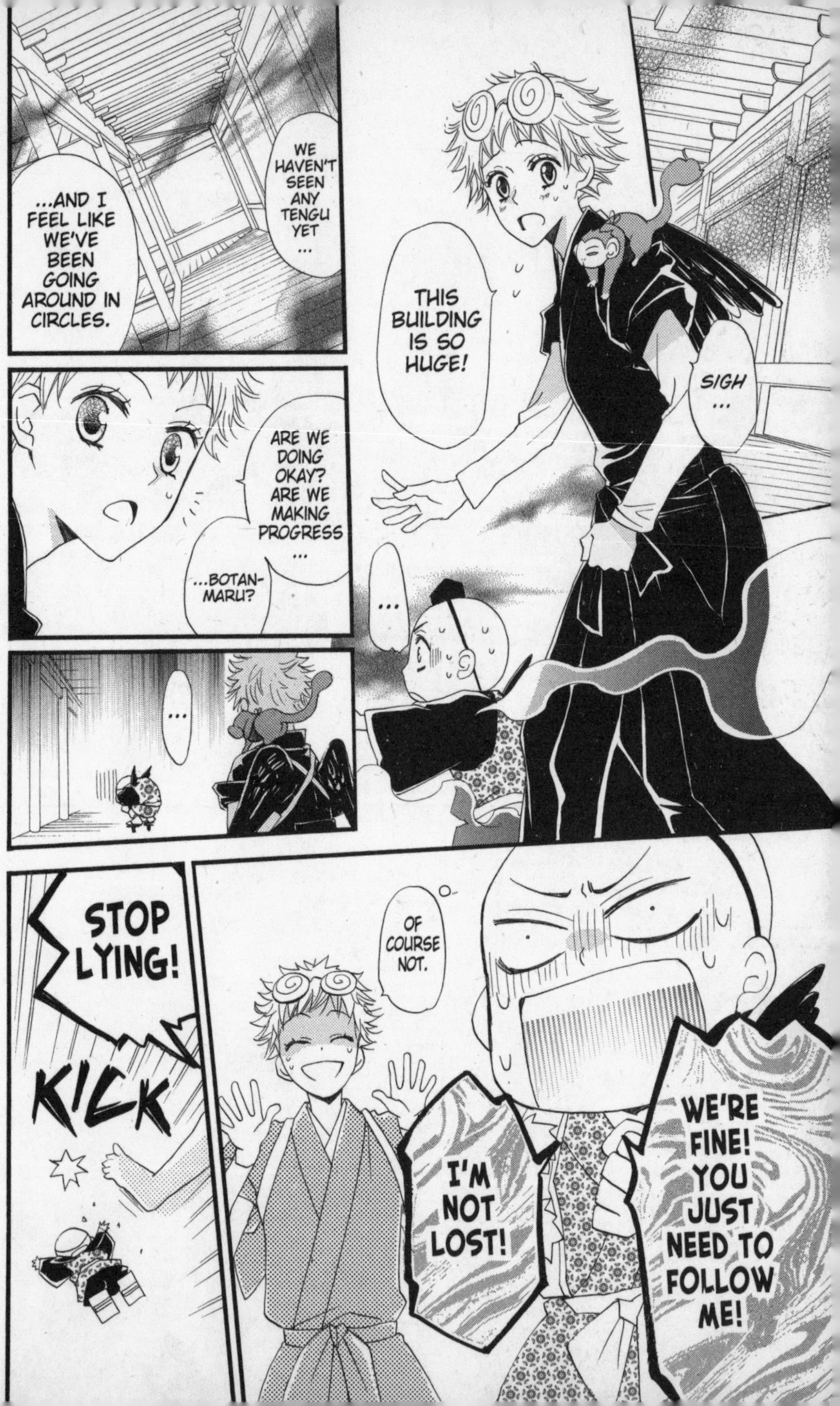
THIS BUILDING IS SO HUGE!
SIGH...
...
WE HAVEN'T SEEN ANY TENGU YET...
...AND I FEEL LIKE WE'VE BEEN GOING AROUND IN CIRCLES.
ARE WE DOING OKAY? ARE WE MAKING PROGRESS...
...BOTAN-MARU?
...
WE'RE FINE! YOU JUST NEED TO FOLLOW ME!
I'M NOT LOST!
OF COURSE NOT.
STOP LYING!
KICK

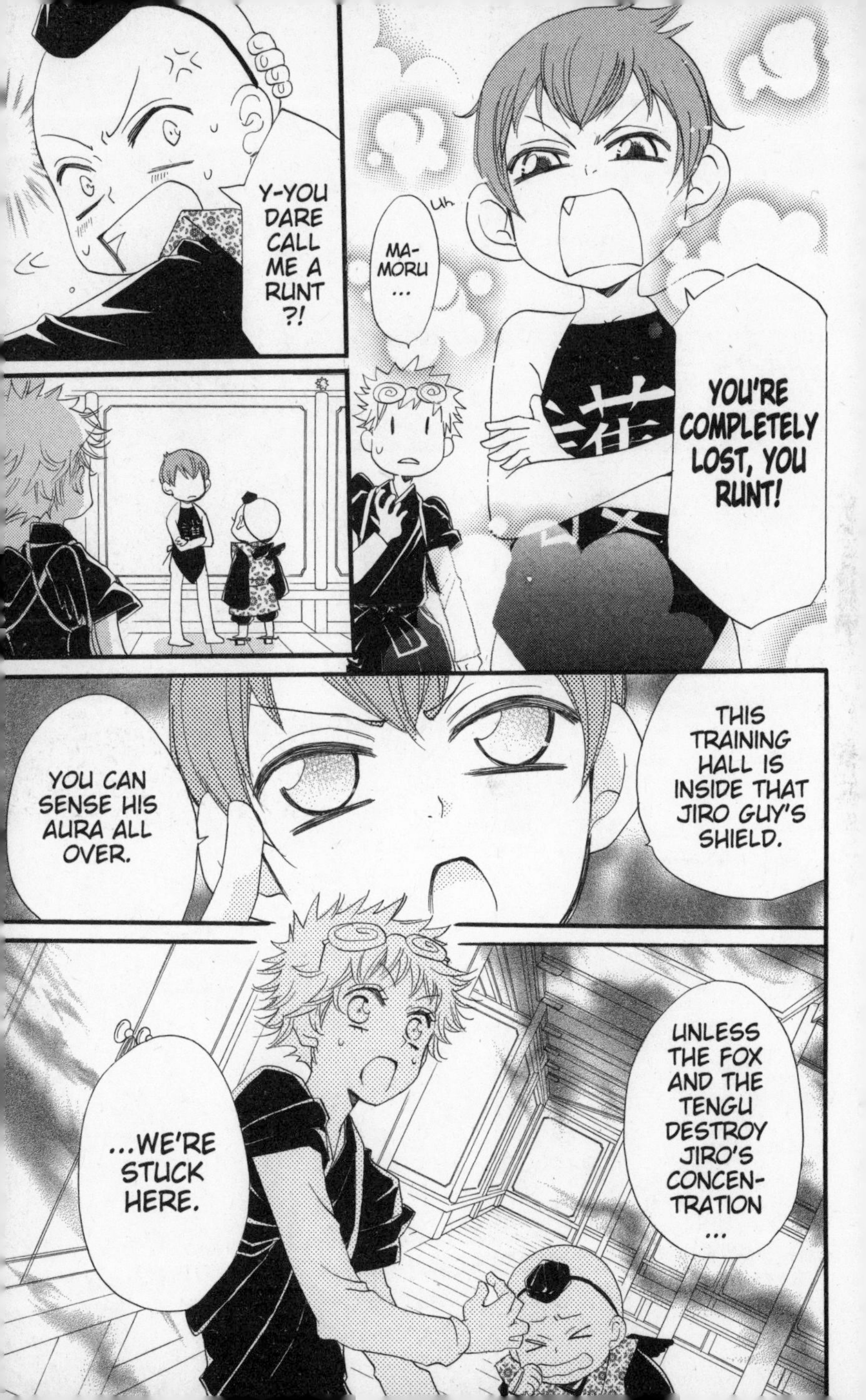
YOU'RE COMPLETELY LOST, YOU RUNT!
MA-MORU ...
Uh
Y-YOU DARE CALL ME A RUNT ?!
THIS TRAINING HALL IS INSIDE THAT JIRO GUY'S SHIELD.
YOU CAN SENSE HIS AURA ALL OVER.
UNLESS THE FOX AND THE TENGU DESTROY JIRO'S CONCEN-TRATION ...
...WE'RE STUCK HERE.

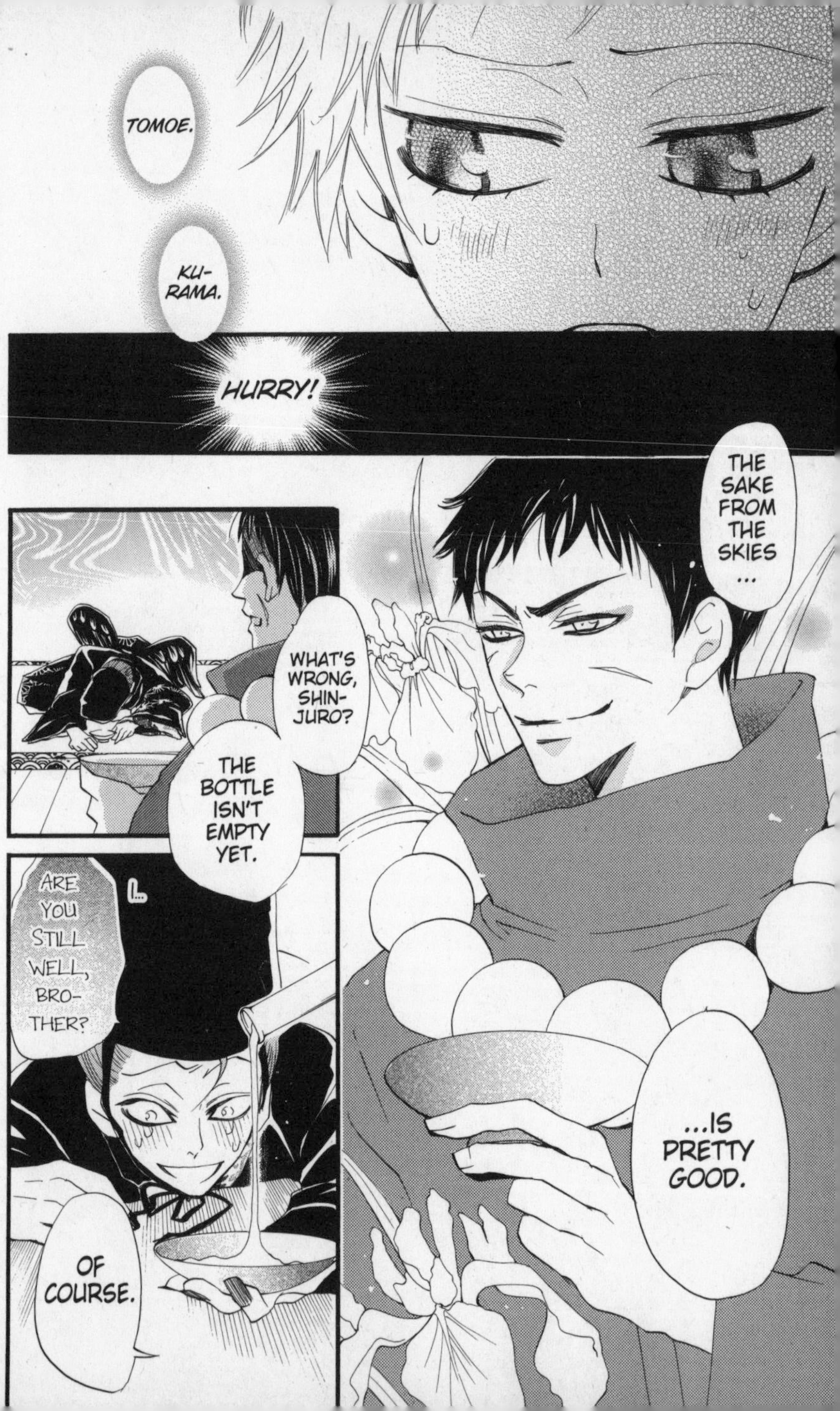
TOMOE.
KU-RAMA.
HURRY!
THE SAKE FROM THE SKIES...
...IS PRETTY GOOD.
WHAT'S WRONG, SHIN-JURO?
THE BOTTLE ISN'T EMPTY YET.
I...
ARE YOU STILL WELL, BRO-THER?
OF COURSE.

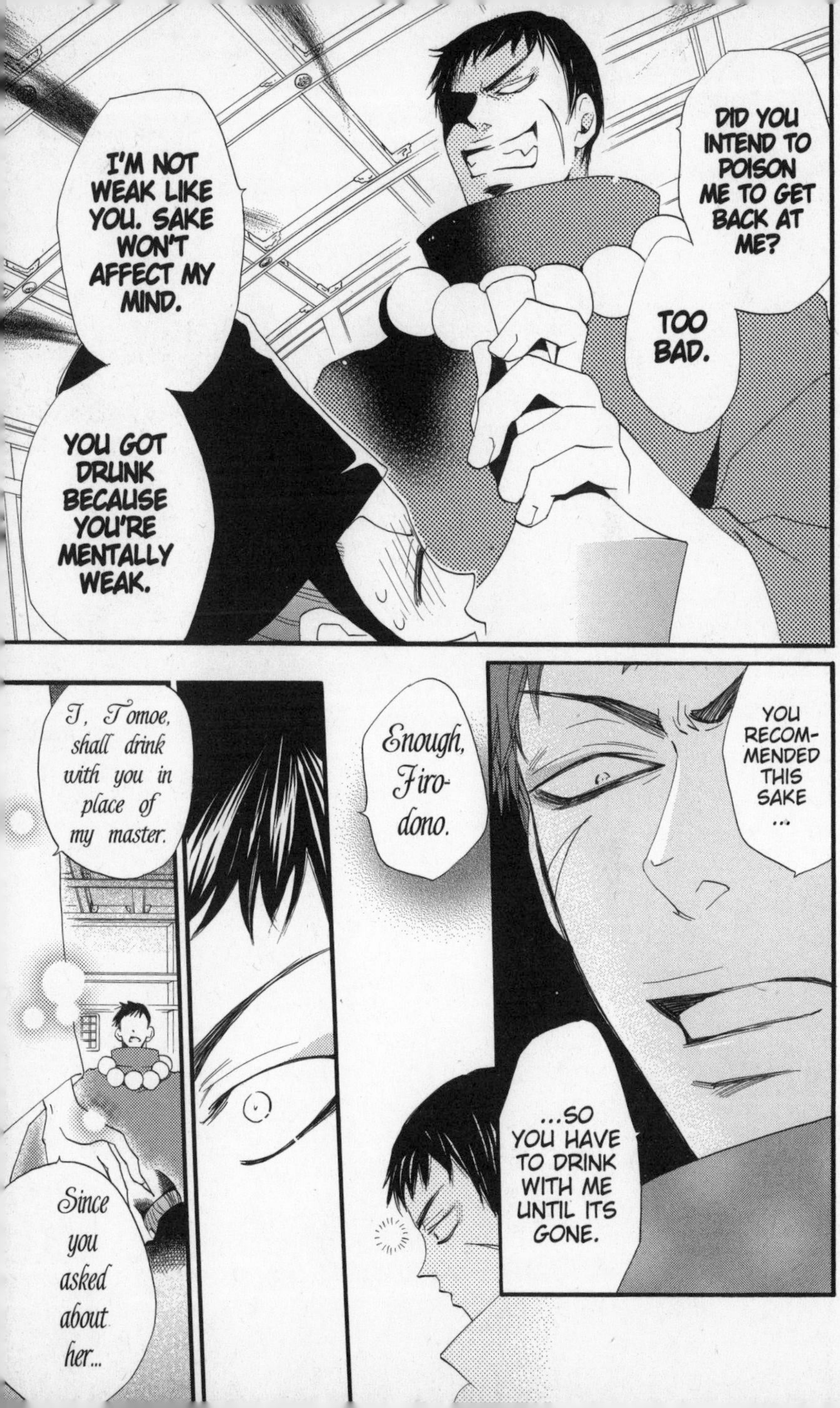
DID YOU INTEND TO POISON ME TO GET BACK AT ME?
TOO BAD.
I'M NOT WEAK LIKE YOU. SAKE WON'T AFFECT MY MIND.
YOU GOT DRUNK BECAUSE YOU'RE MENTALLY WEAK.
YOU RECOMMENDED THIS SAKE...
...SO YOU HAVE TO DRINK WITH ME UNTIL ITS GONE.
Enough, Jiro-dono.
I, Tomoe, shall drink with you in place of my master.
Since you asked about her...

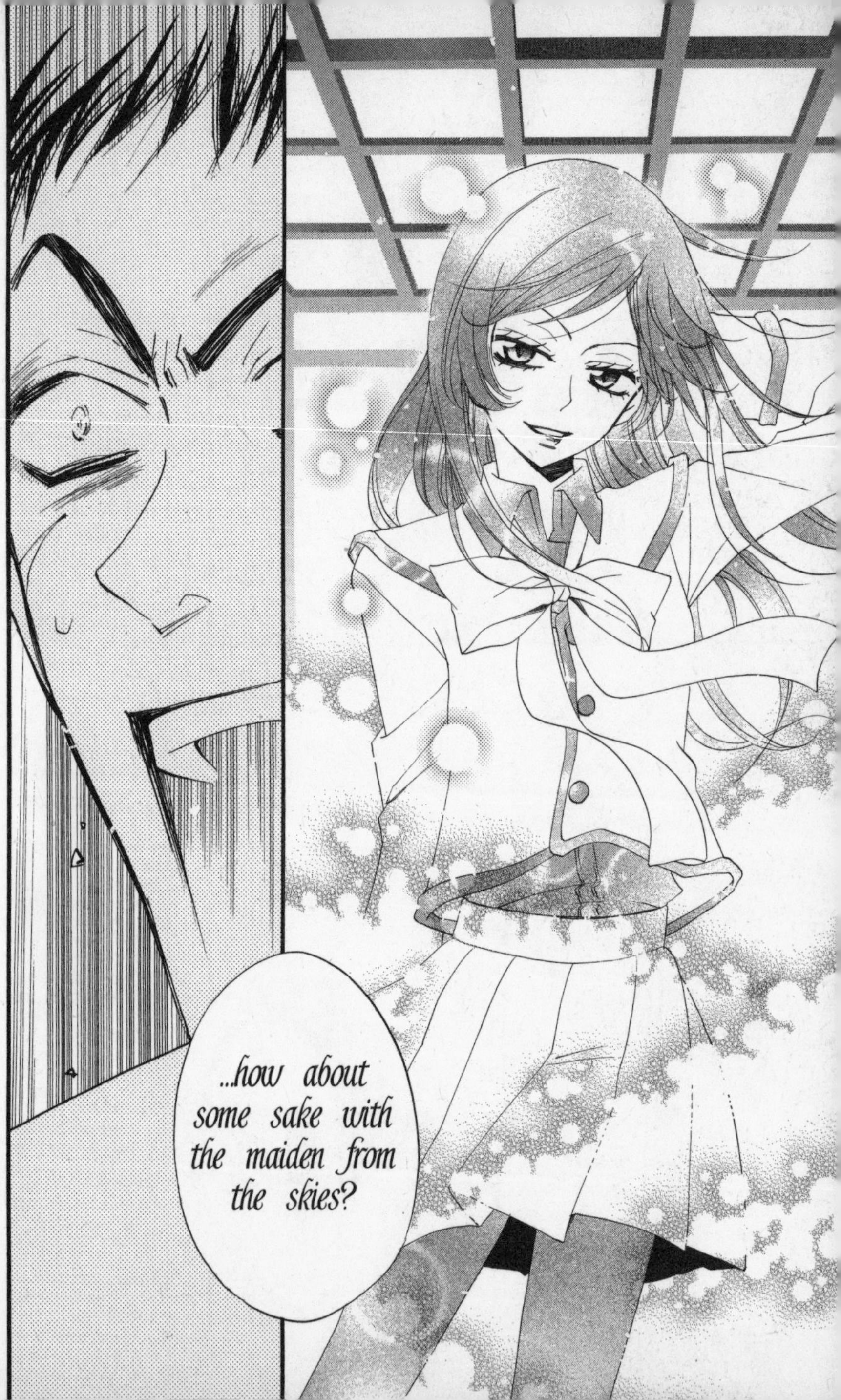
...how about some sake with the maiden from the skies?

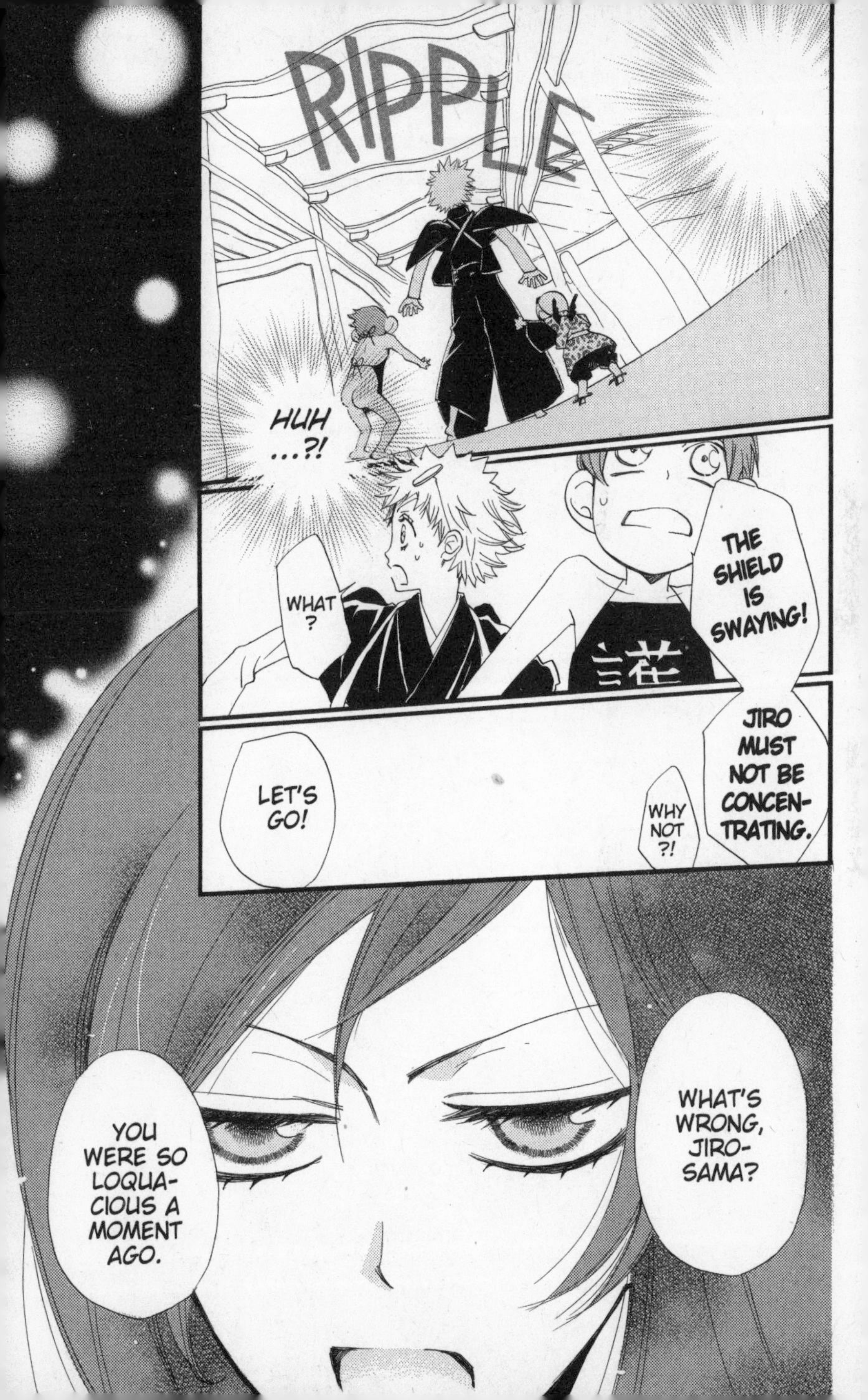
RIPPLE
HUH ...?!
THE SHIELD IS SWAYING!
WHAT?
JIRO MUST NOT BE CONCEN-TRATING.
WHY NOT?!
LET'S GO!
WHAT'S WRONG, JIRO-SAMA?
YOU WERE SO LOQUA-CIOUS A MOMENT AGO.

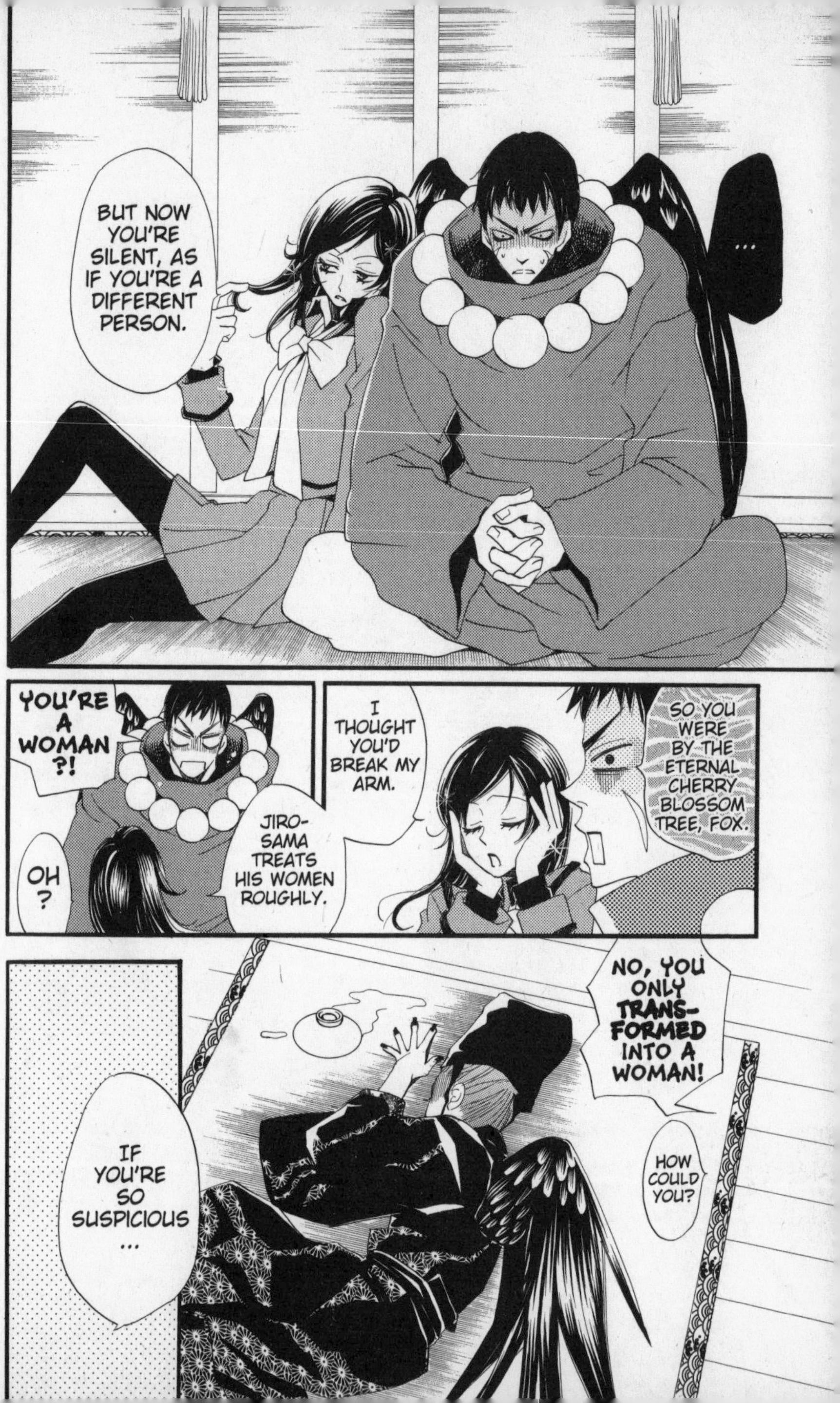
BUT NOW YOU'RE SILENT, AS IF YOU'RE A DIFFERENT PERSON.
...
SO YOU WERE BY THE ETERNAL CHERRY BLOSSOM TREE, FOX.
I THOUGHT YOU'D BREAK MY ARM.
JIRO-SAMA TREATS HIS WOMEN ROUGHLY.
YOU'RE A WOMAN ?!
OH ?
NO, YOU ONLY TRANS-FORMED INTO A WOMAN!
HOW COULD YOU?
IF YOU'RE SO SUSPICIOUS ...

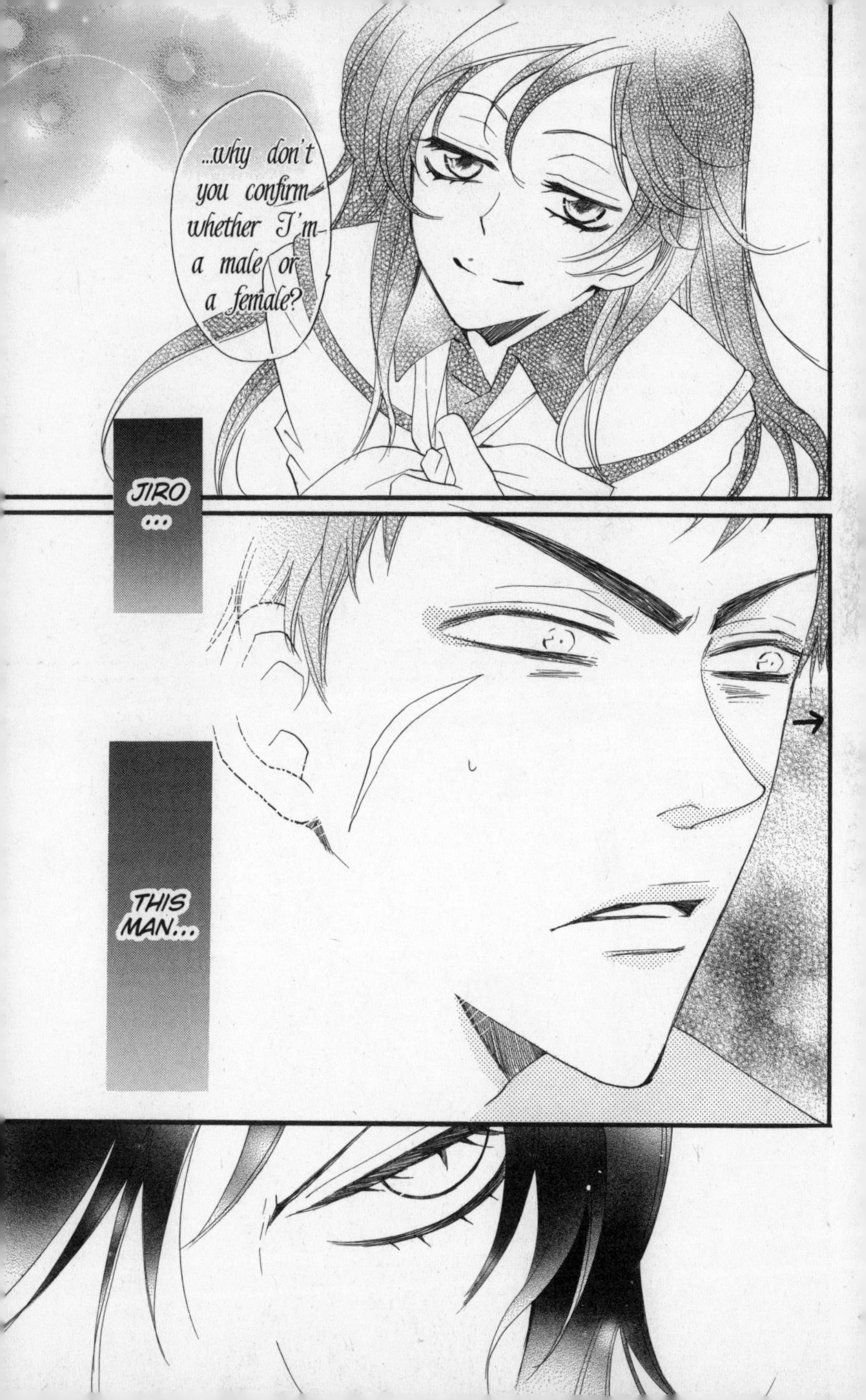
...why don't you confirm whether I'm a male or a female?
JIRO ...
THIS MAN...

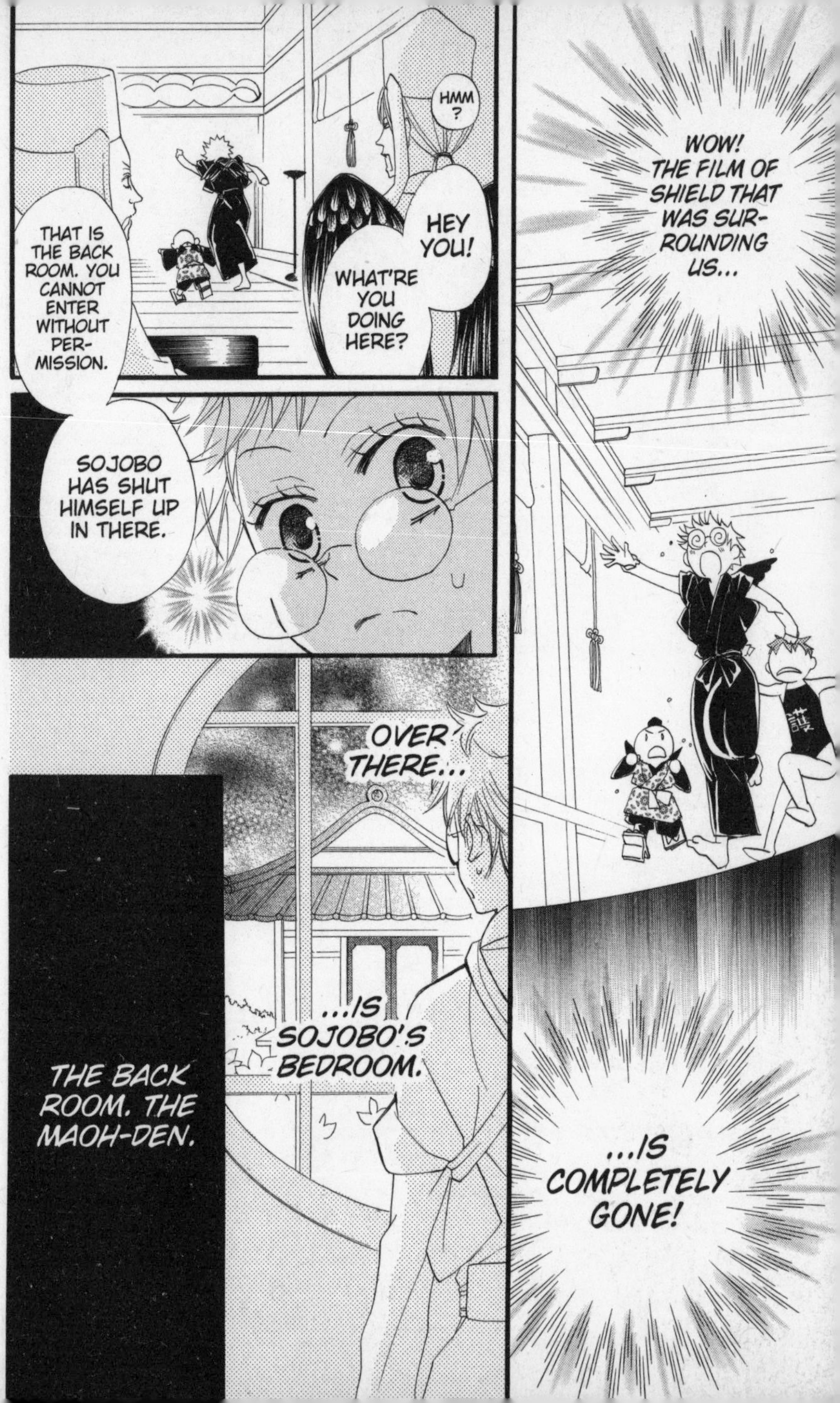
WOW! THE FILM OF SHIELD THAT WAS SUR-ROUNDING US...
...IS COMPLETELY GONE!
HMM?
HEY YOU!
WHAT'RE YOU DOING HERE?
THAT IS THE BACK ROOM. YOU CANNOT ENTER WITHOUT PER-MISSION.
SOJOBO HAS SHUT HIMSELF UP IN THERE.
OVER THERE...
...IS SOJOBO'S BEDROOM.
THE BACK ROOM. THE MAOH-DEN.

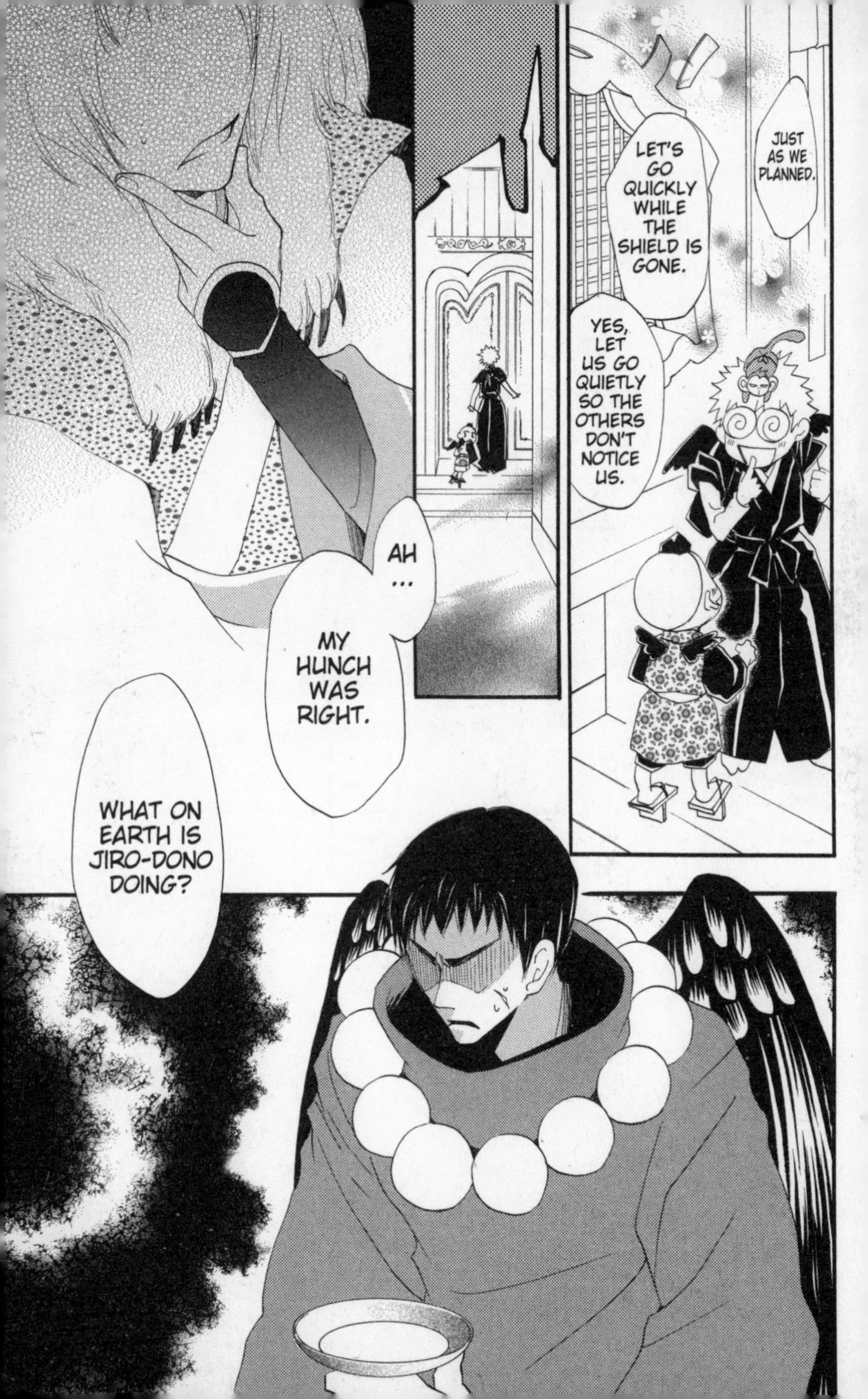
JUST AS WE PLANNED.
LET'S GO QUICKLY WHILE THE SHIELD IS GONE.
YES, LET US GO QUIETLY SO THE OTHERS DON'T NOTICE US.
AH ...
MY HUNCH WAS RIGHT.
WHAT ON EARTH IS JIRO-DONO DOING?

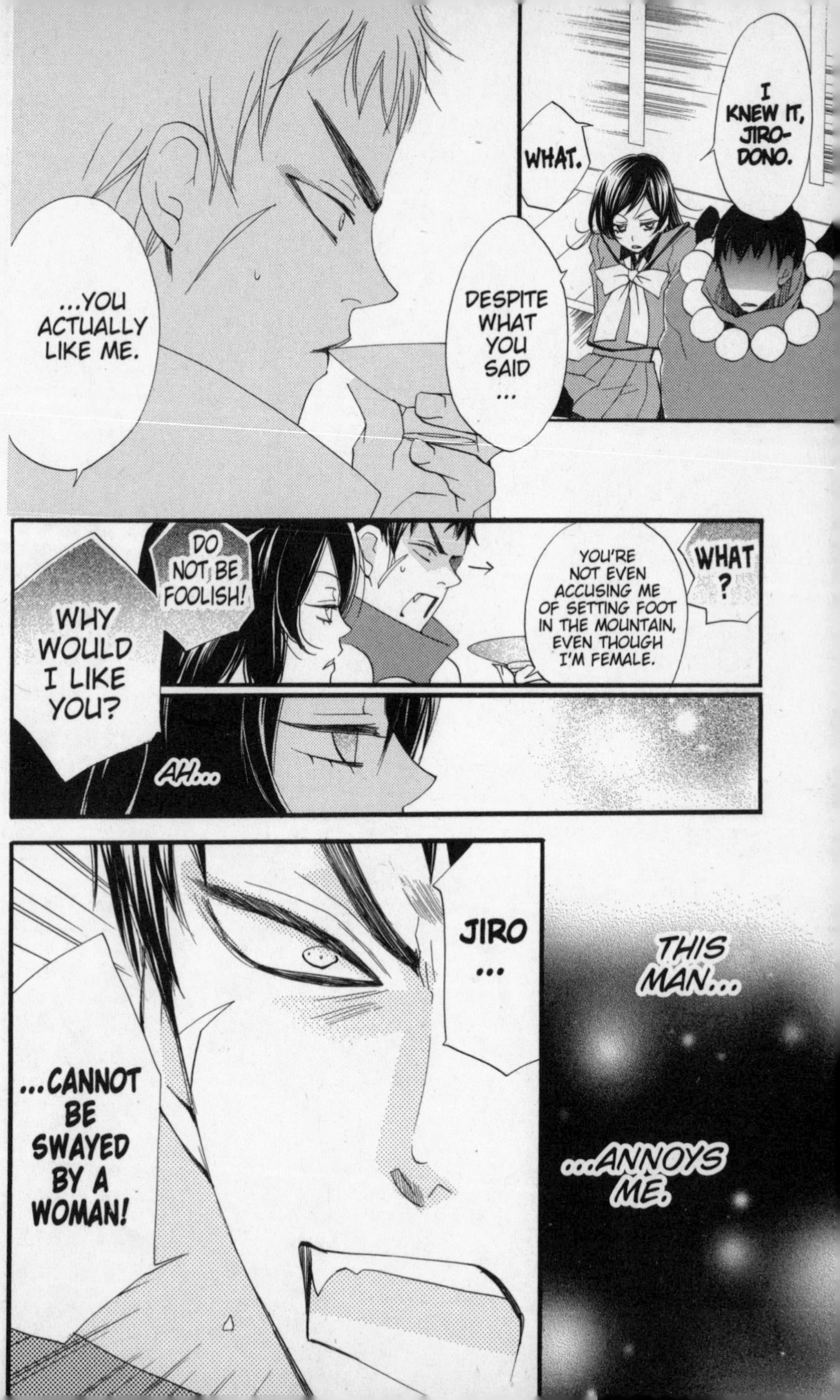
I KNEW IT, JIRO-DONO.
WHAT.
DESPITE WHAT YOU SAID...
...YOU ACTUALLY LIKE ME.
WHAT?
YOU'RE NOT EVEN ACCUSING ME OF SETTING FOOT IN THE MOUNTAIN, EVEN THOUGH I'M FEMALE.
DO NOT BE FOOLISH!
WHY WOULD I LIKE YOU?
AH...
JIRO...
THIS MAN...
...ANNOYS ME.
...CANNOT BE SWAYED BY A WOMAN!

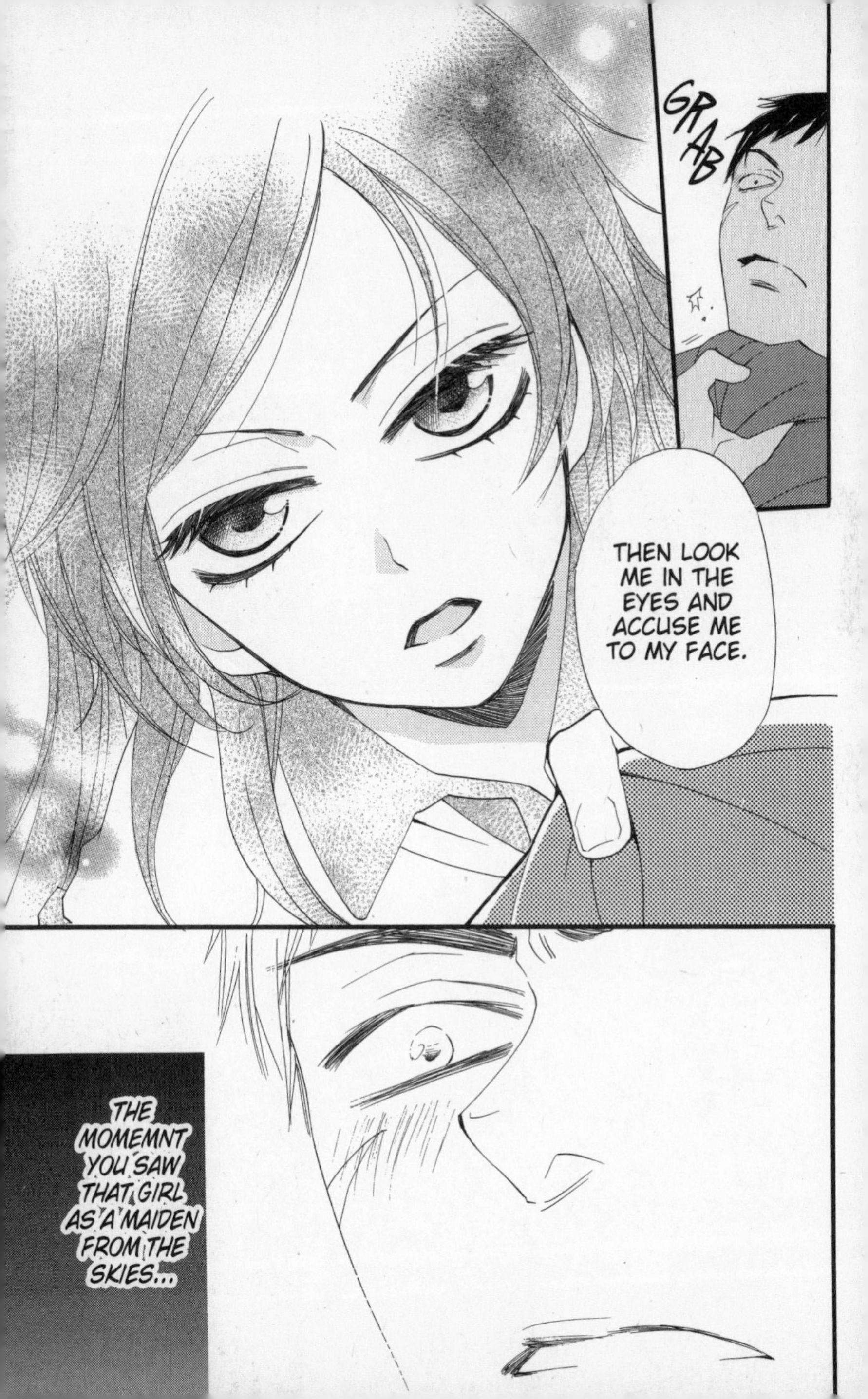
GRAB
THEN LOOK ME IN THE EYES AND ACCUSE ME TO MY FACE.
THE MOMEMNT YOU SAW THAT GIRL AS A MAIDEN FROM THE SKIES...

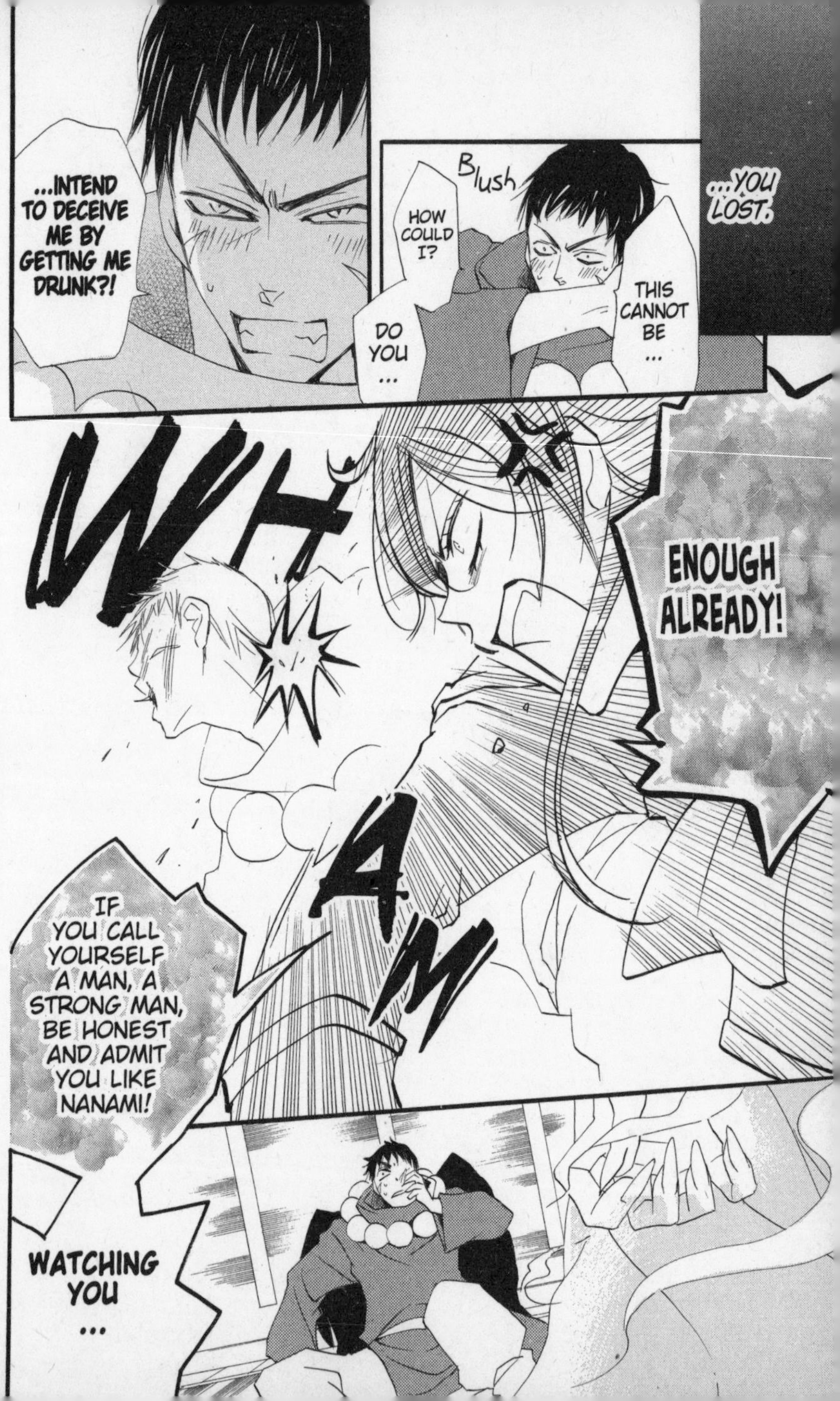
...YOU LOST.
Blush
THIS CANNOT BE ...
HOW COULD I?
DO YOU ...
...INTEND TO DECEIVE ME BY GETTING ME DRUNK?!
ENOUGH ALREADY!
WHAM
IF YOU CALL YOURSELF A MAN, A STRONG MAN, BE HONEST AND ADMIT YOU LIKE NANAMI!
WATCHING YOU ...

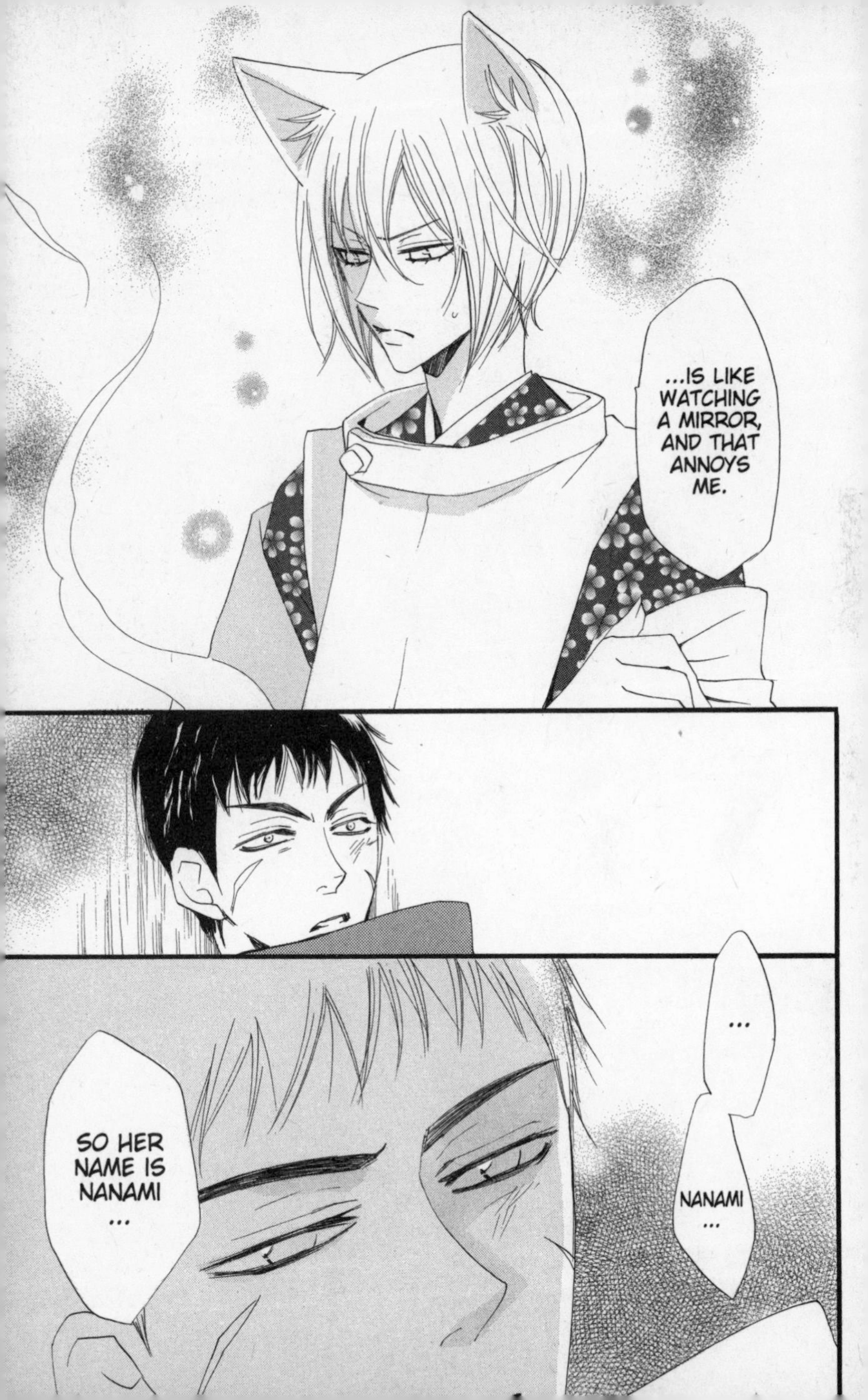
...IS LIKE WATCHING A MIRROR, AND THAT ANNOYS ME.
...
NANAMI ...
SO HER NAME IS NANAMI ...

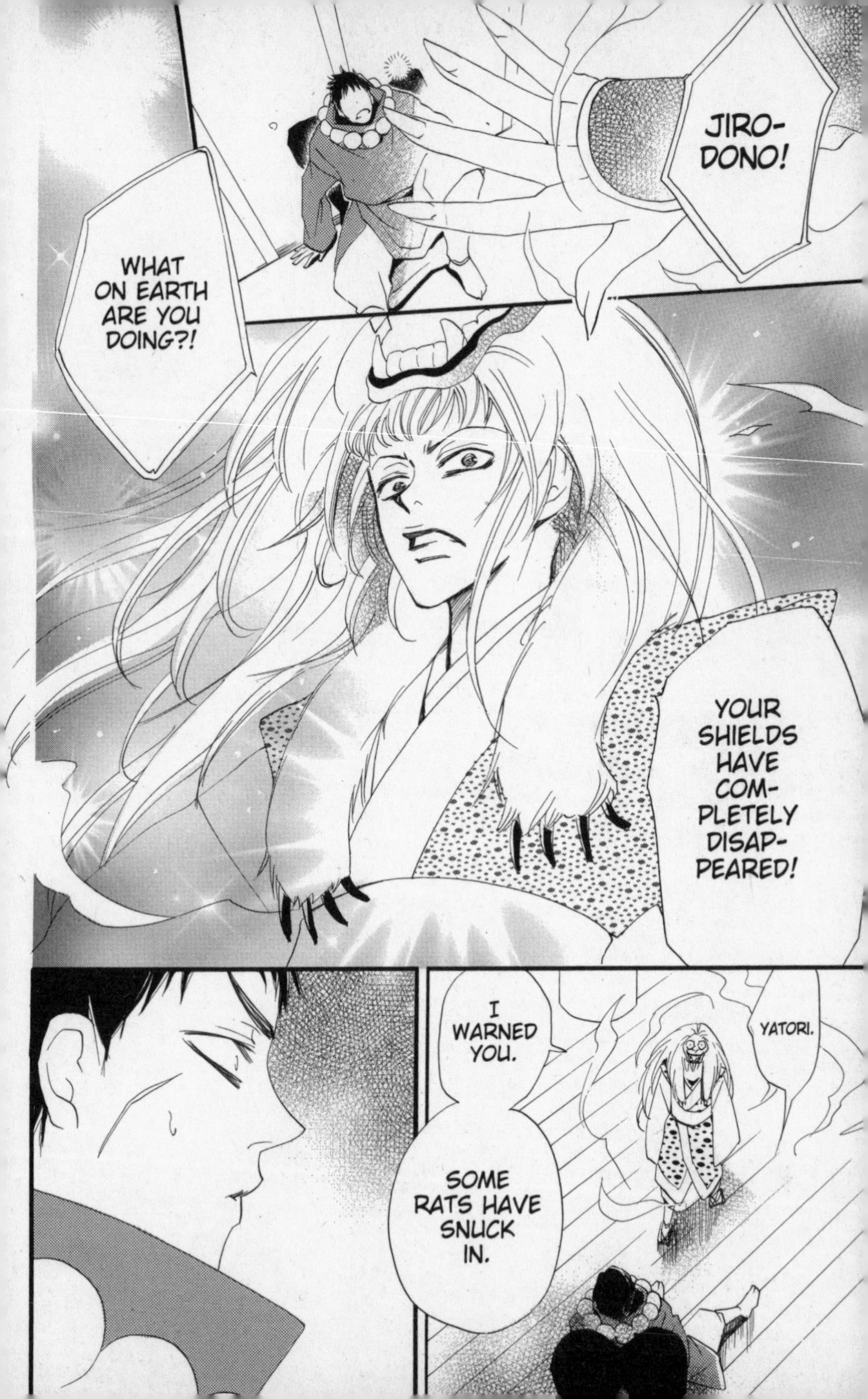
JIRO-DONO!
WHAT ON EARTH ARE YOU DOING?!
YOUR SHIELDS HAVE COMPLETELY DISAPPEARED!
YATORI.
I WARNED YOU.
SOME RATS HAVE SNUCK IN.

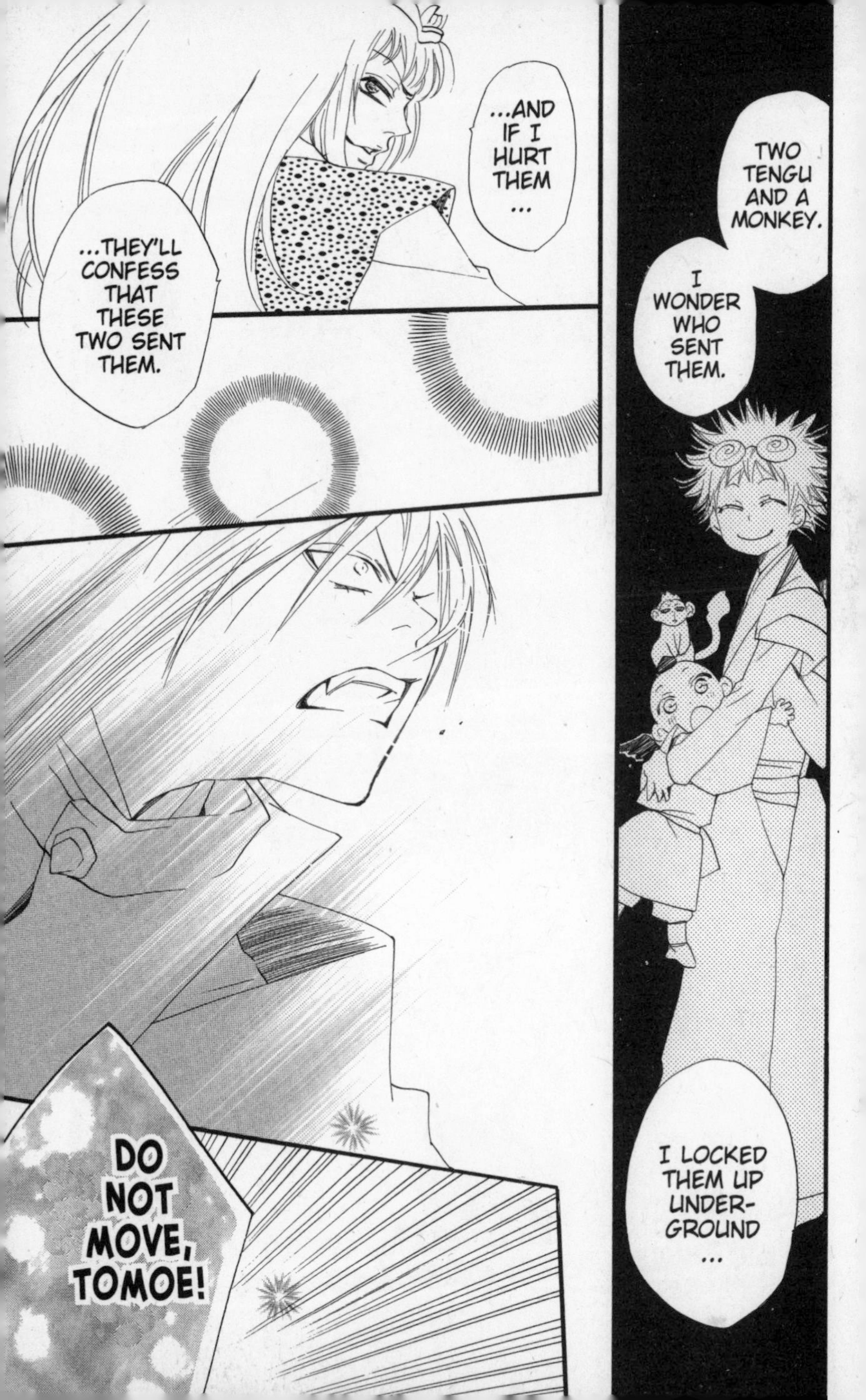
TWO TENGU AND A MONKEY.
I WONDER WHO SENT THEM.
I LOCKED THEM UP UNDER-GROUND ...
...AND IF I HURT THEM ...
...THEY'LL CONFESS THAT THESE TWO SENT THEM.
DO NOT MOVE, TOMOE!

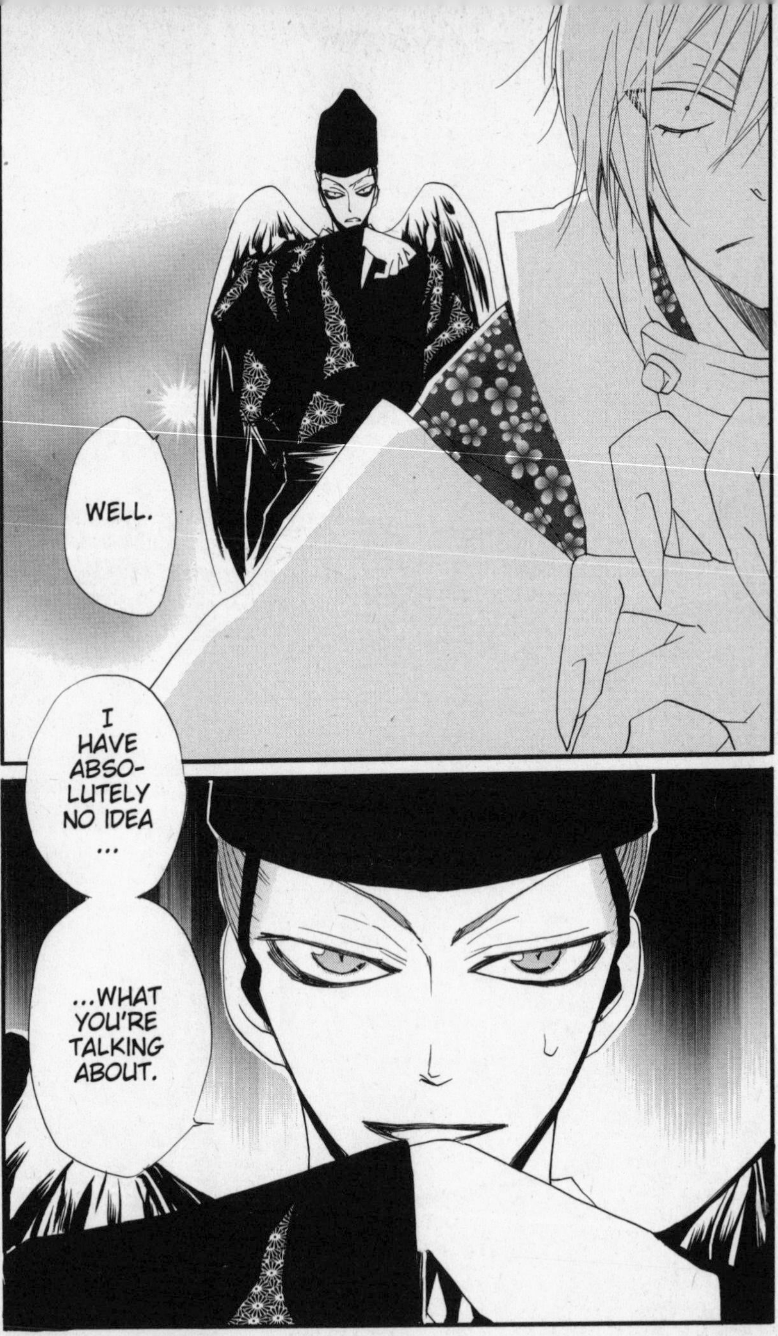
WELL.
I HAVE ABSO-LUTELY NO IDEA...
...WHAT YOU'RE TALKING ABOUT.

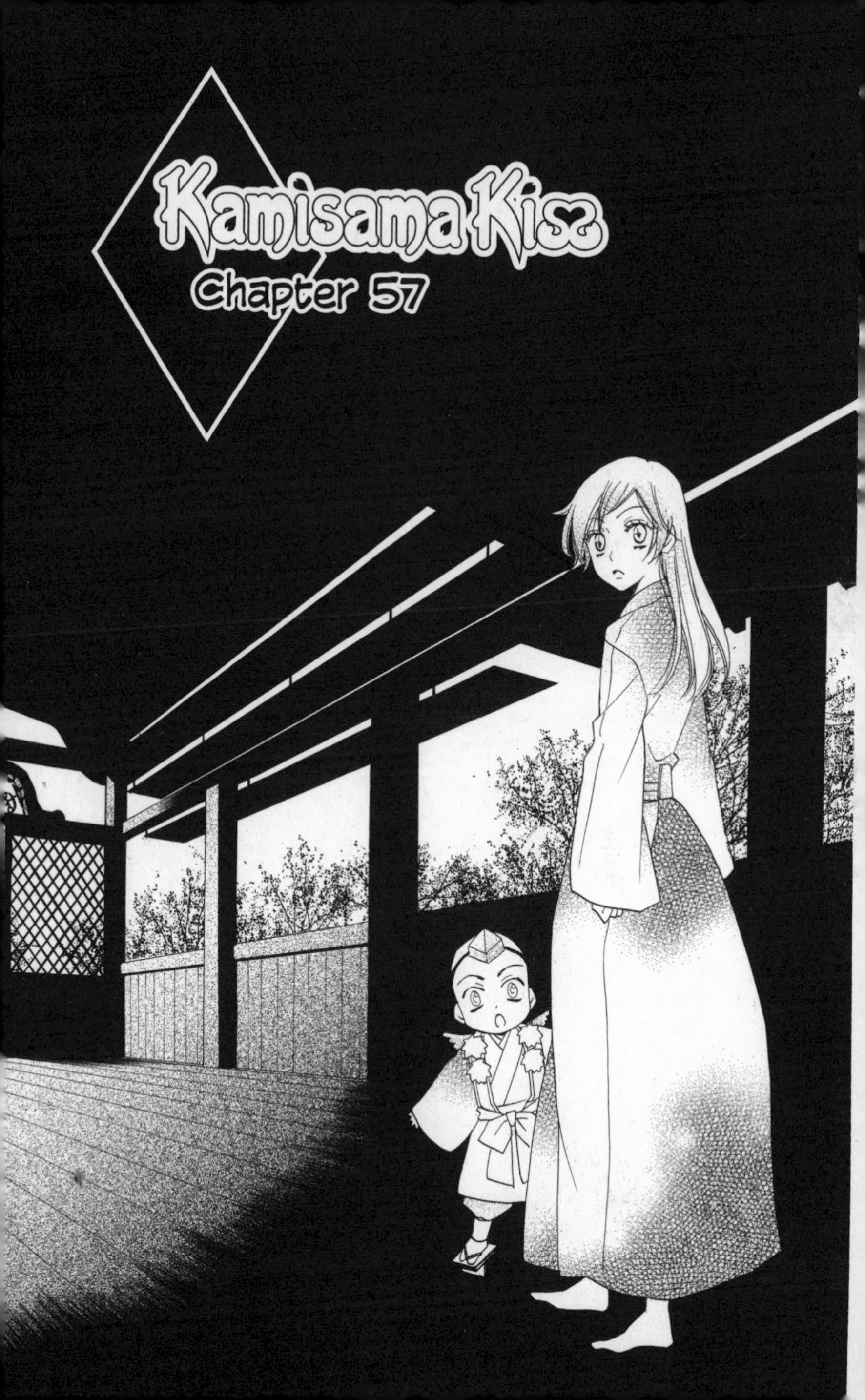
Kamisama Kiss
Chapter 57

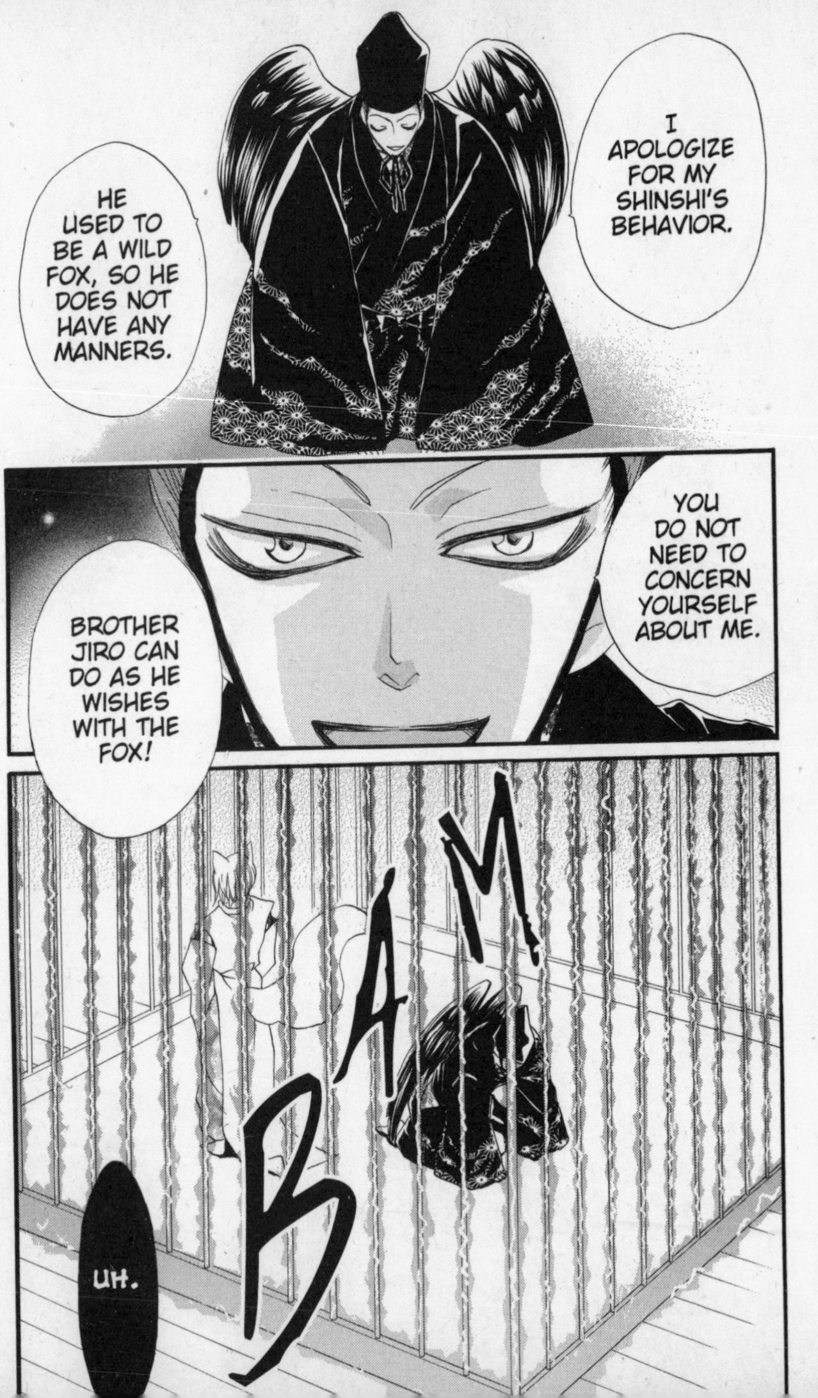
I APOLOGIZE FOR MY SHINSHI'S BEHAVIOR.
HE USED TO BE A WILD FOX, SO HE DOES NOT HAVE ANY MANNERS.
YOU DO NOT NEED TO CONCERN YOURSELF ABOUT ME.
BROTHER JIRO CAN DO AS HE WISHES WITH THE FOX!
BAM
UH.

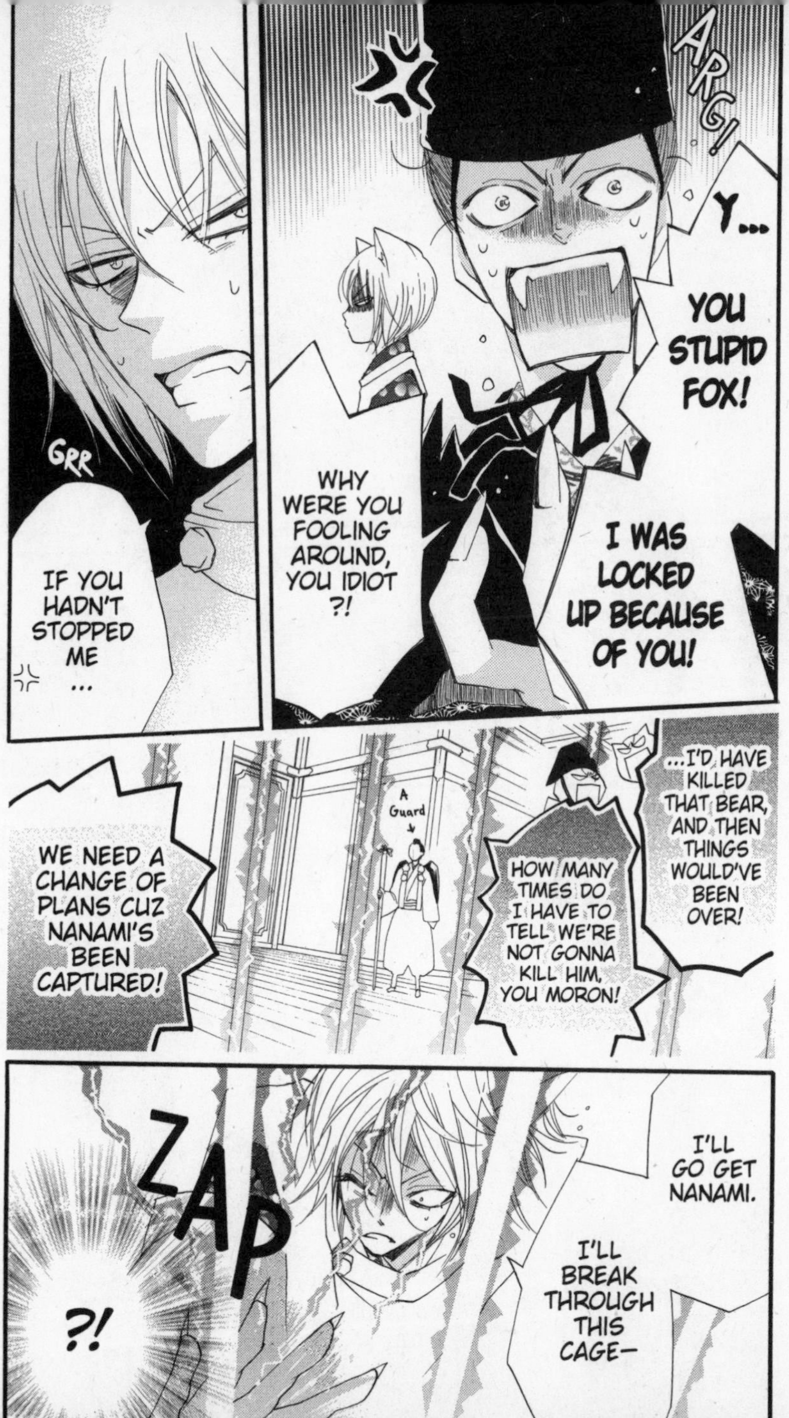
ARG!
Y...
YOU STUPID FOX!
I WAS LOCKED UP BECAUSE OF YOU!
WHY WERE YOU FOOLING AROUND, YOU IDIOT?!
GRR
IF YOU HADN'T STOPPED ME...
...I'D HAVE KILLED THAT BEAR, AND THEN THINGS WOULD'VE BEEN OVER!
HOW MANY TIMES DO I HAVE TO TELL WE'RE NOT GONNA KILL HIM, YOU MORON!
A Guard
WE NEED A CHANGE OF PLANS CUZ NANAMI'S BEEN CAPTURED!
I'LL GO GET NANAMI.
I'LL BREAK THROUGH THIS CAGE—
ZAP
?!

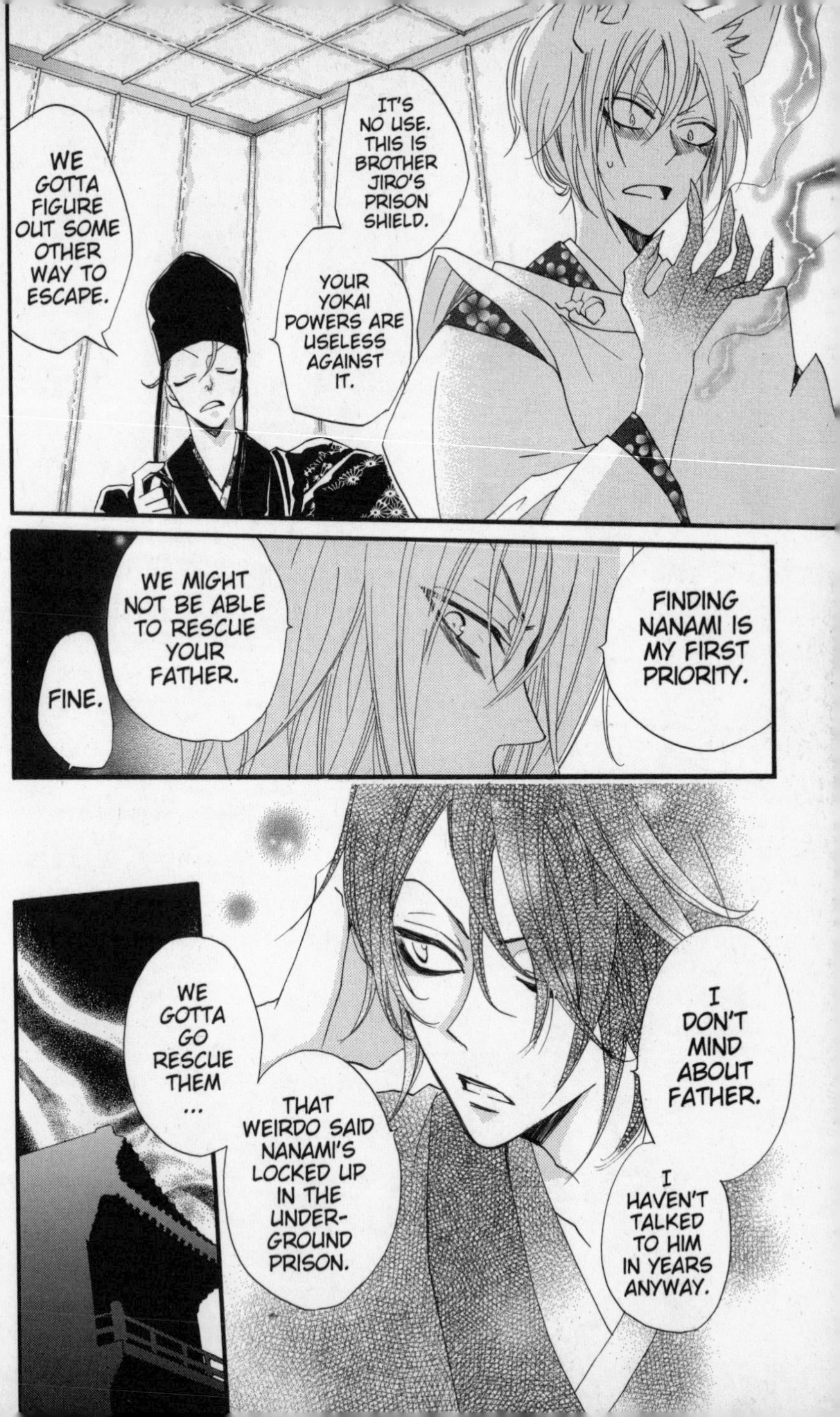
IT'S NO USE. THIS IS BROTHER JIRO'S PRISON SHIELD.
YOUR YOKAI POWERS ARE USELESS AGAINST IT.
WE GOTTA FIGURE OUT SOME OTHER WAY TO ESCAPE.
FINDING NANAMI IS MY FIRST PRIORITY.
WE MIGHT NOT BE ABLE TO RESCUE YOUR FATHER.
FINE.
I DON'T MIND ABOUT FATHER.
I HAVEN'T TALKED TO HIM IN YEARS ANYWAY.
THAT WEIRDO SAID NANAMI'S LOCKED UP IN THE UNDER-GROUND PRISON.
WE GOTTA GO RESCUE THEM ...

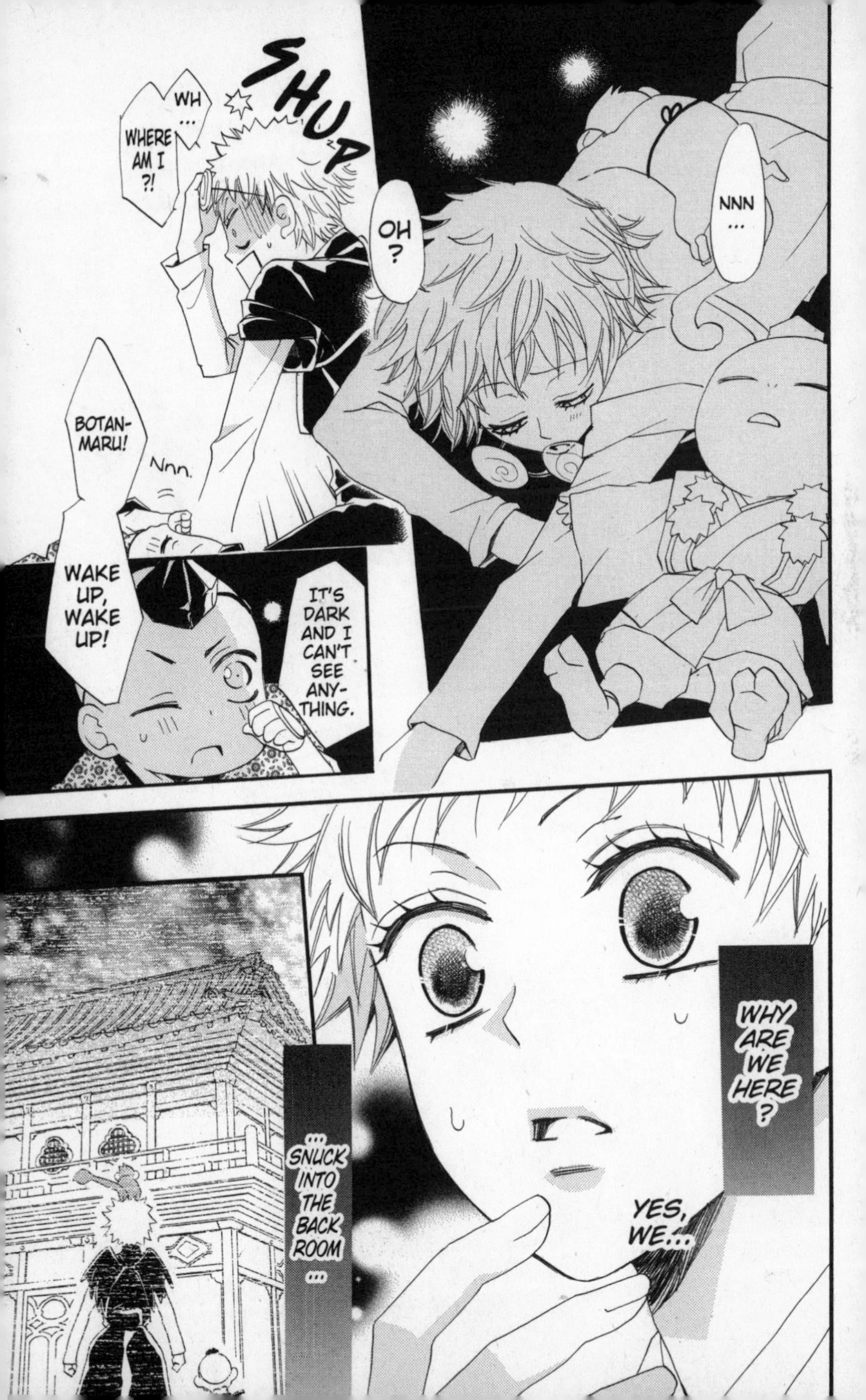
NNN...
OH?
SHUP
WH... WHERE AM I?!
BOTAN-MARU!
Nnn.
WAKE UP, WAKE UP!
IT'S DARK AND I CAN'T SEE ANYTHING.
WHY ARE WE HERE?
YES, WE...
...SNUCK INTO THE BACK ROOM...

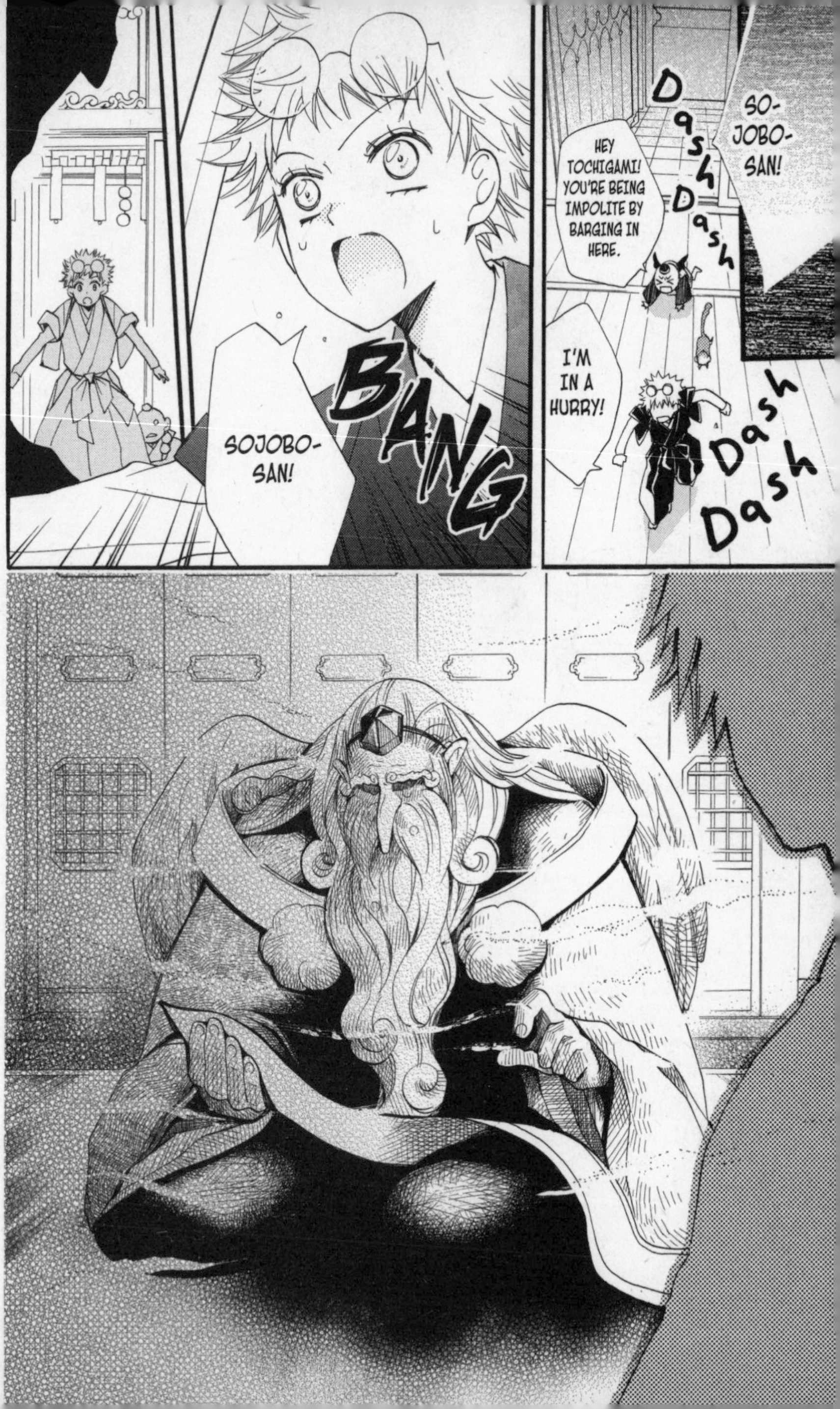
SO-JOBO-SAN!
Dash Dash
HEY TOCHIGAMI! YOU'RE BEING IMPOLITE BY BARGING IN HERE.
Dash Dash
I'M IN A HURRY!
BANG
SOJOBO-SAN!

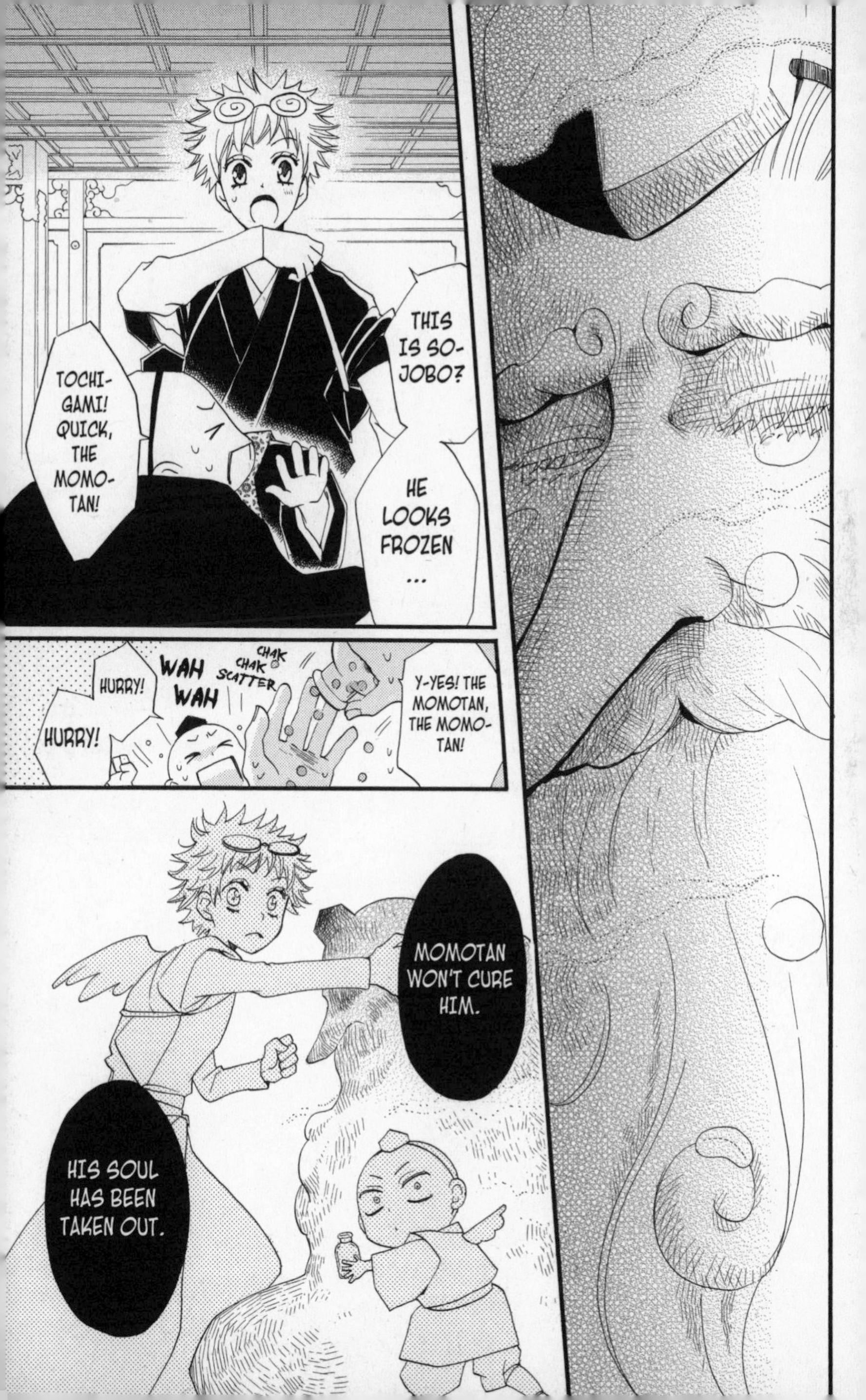
THIS IS SO-JOBO?
TOCHI-GAMI! QUICK, THE MOMO-TAN!
HE LOOKS FROZEN ...
Y-YES! THE MOMOTAN, THE MOMO-TAN!
CHAK CHAK SCATTER
WAH WAH
HURRY!
HURRY!
MOMOTAN WON'T CURE HIM.
HIS SOUL HAS BEEN TAKEN OUT.

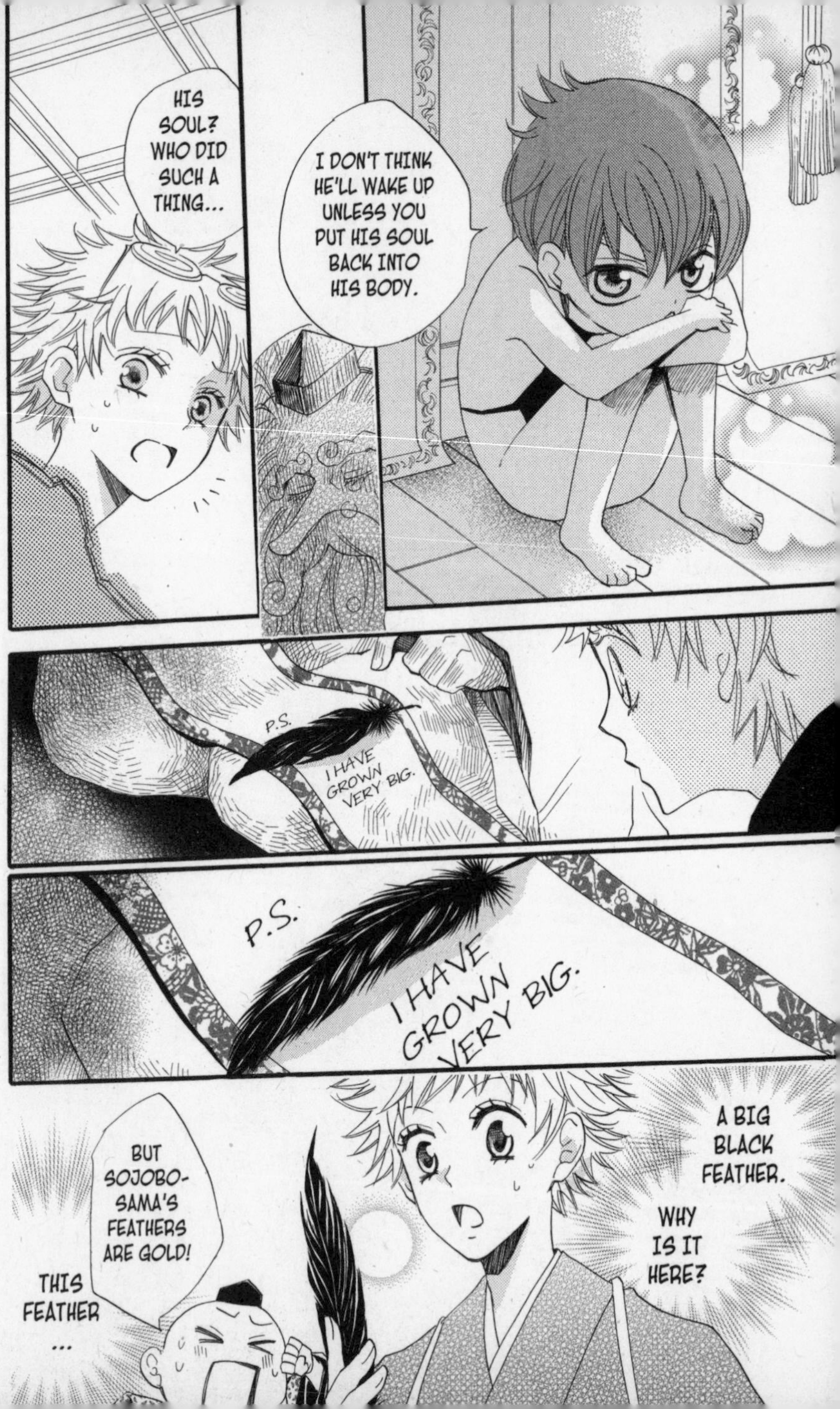
I DON'T THINK HE'LL WAKE UP UNLESS YOU PUT HIS SOUL BACK INTO HIS BODY.
HIS SOUL? WHO DID SUCH A THING...
P.S.
I HAVE GROWN VERY BIG.
P.S.
I HAVE GROWN VERY BIG.
A BIG BLACK FEATHER.
WHY IS IT HERE?
BUT SOJOBO-SAMA'S FEATHERS ARE GOLD!
THIS FEATHER ...

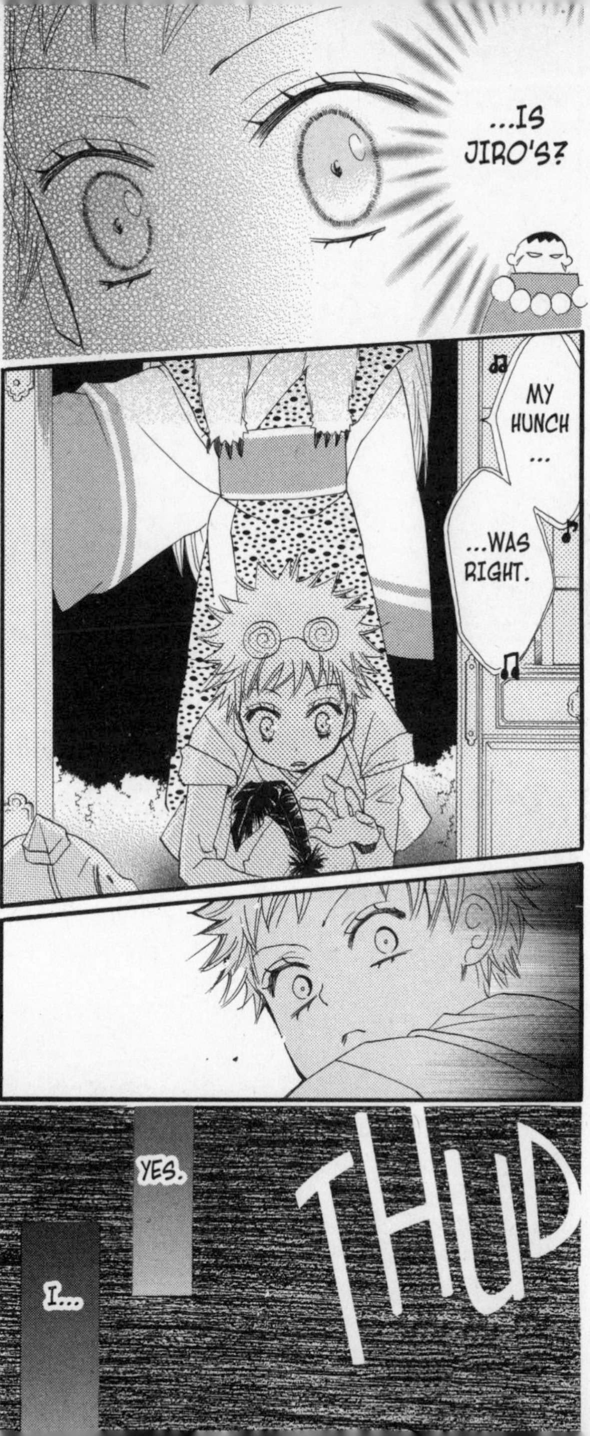
...IS JIRO'S?
MY HUNCH ...
...WAS RIGHT.
THUD
YES.
I...

2

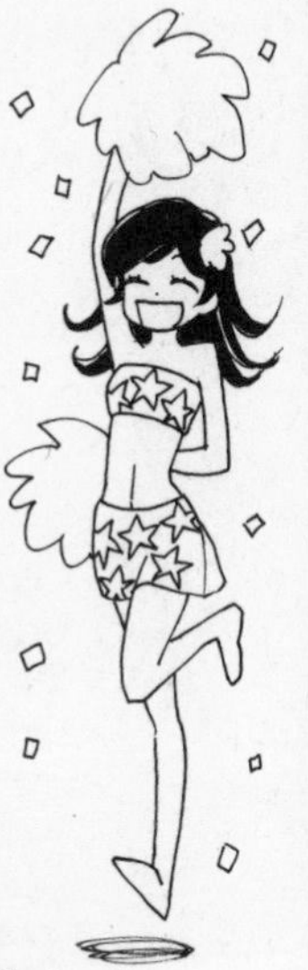

It's hot!
(It's August now.)

But it's winter in the manga. I envy them.

The Kurama arc ends with this volume. My heart aches because I only drew guys.

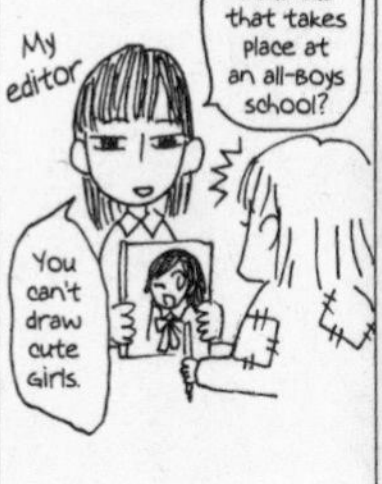
Why don't you draw a manga that takes place at an all-boys school?
My editor
You can't draw cute girls.

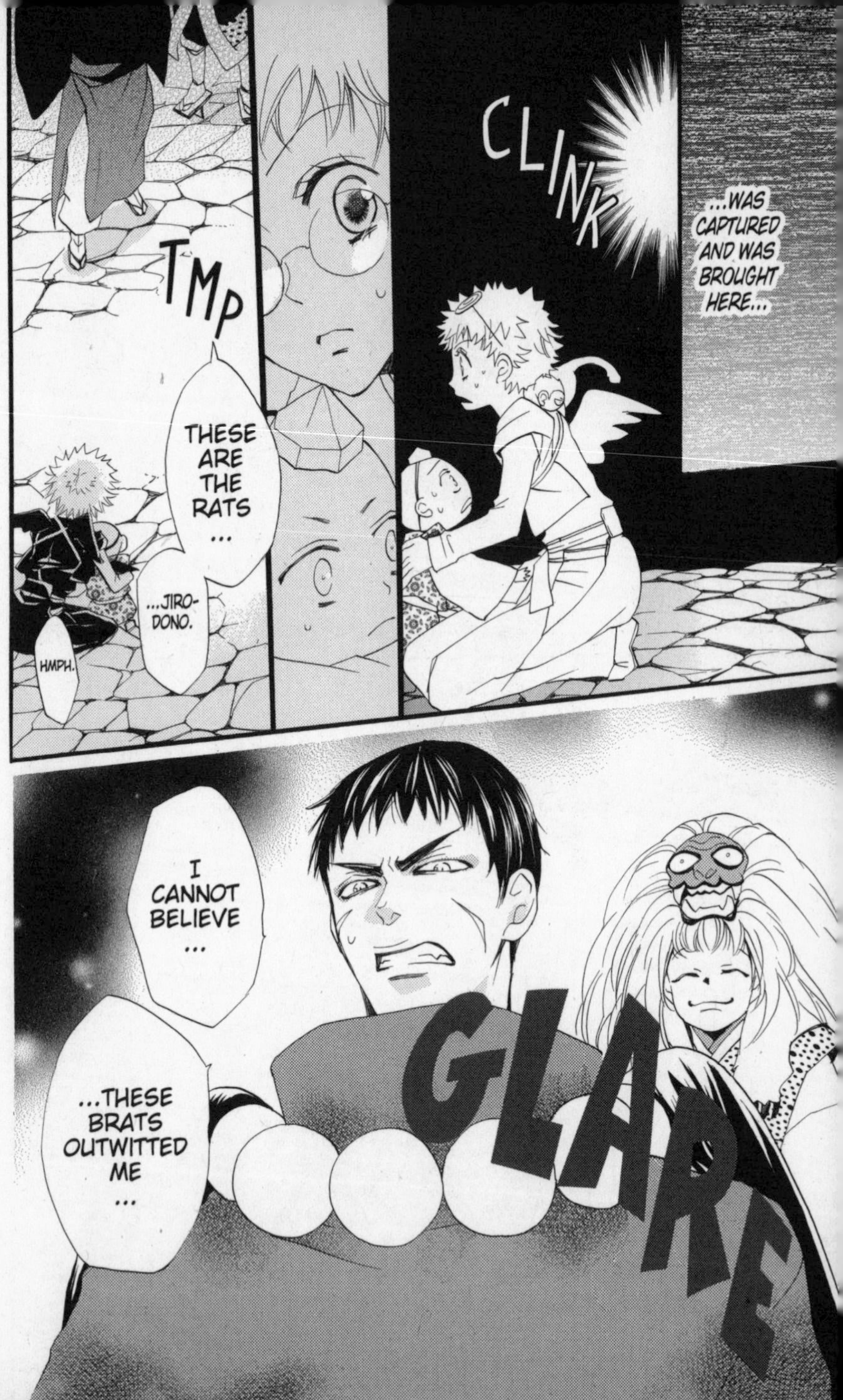
...WAS CAPTURED AND WAS BROUGHT HERE...
CLINK
TMP
THESE ARE THE RATS ...
...JIRO-DONO.
HMPH.
I CANNOT BELIEVE ...
...THESE BRATS OUTWITTED ME ...
GLARE

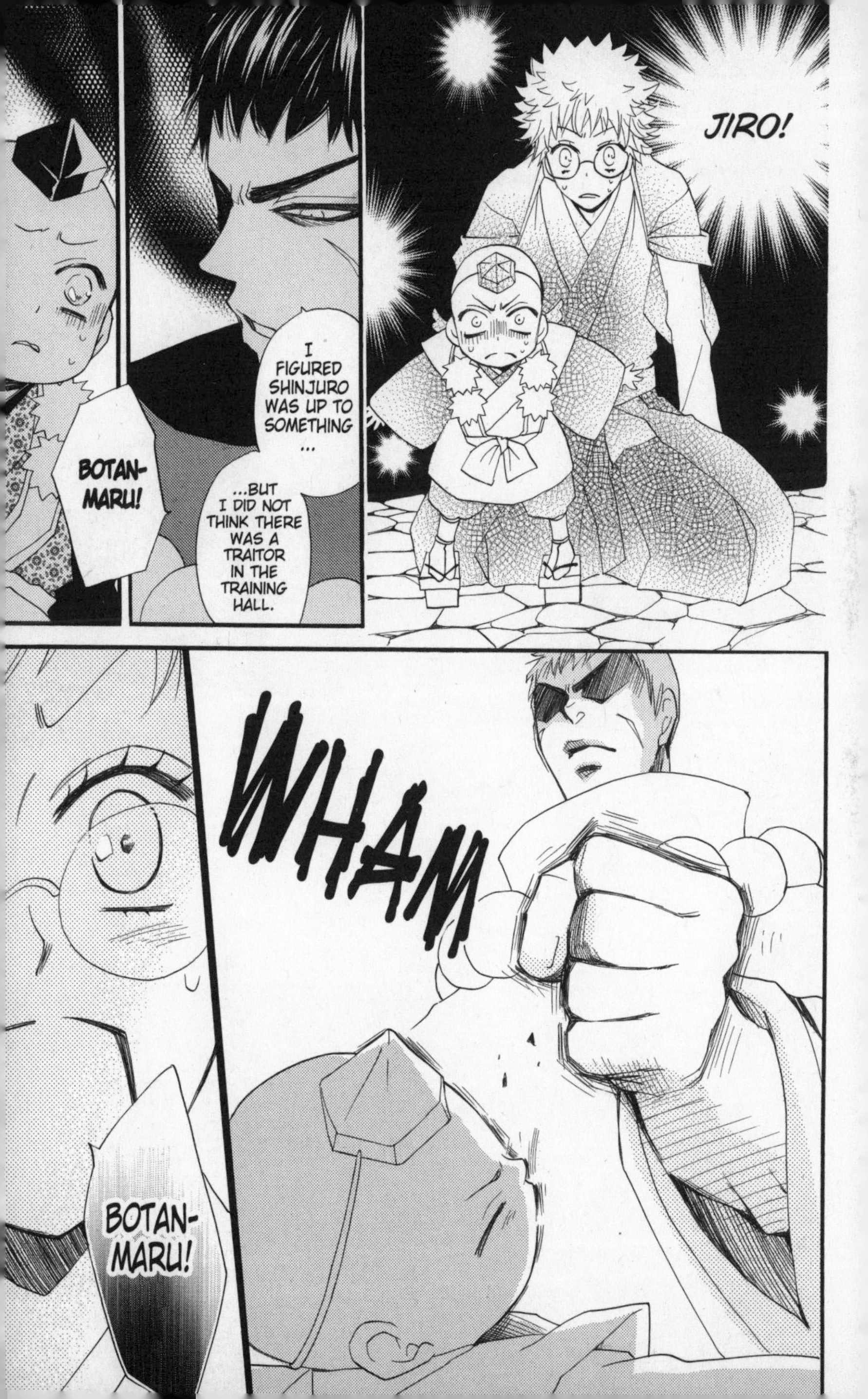
JIRO!
I FIGURED SHINJURO WAS UP TO SOMETHING...
...BUT I DID NOT THINK THERE WAS A TRAITOR IN THE TRAINING HALL.
BOTAN-MARU!
WHAM
BOTAN-MARU!

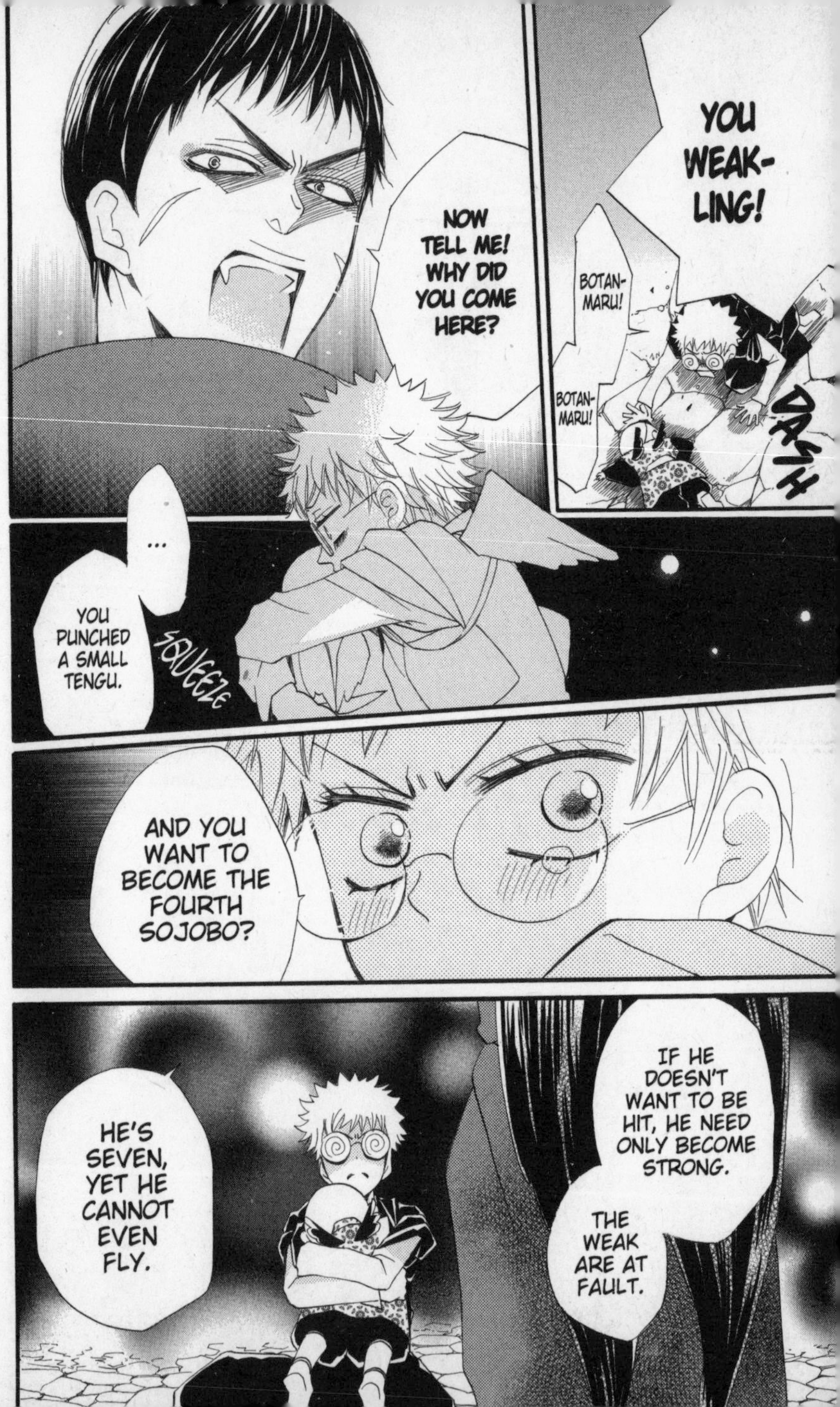
YOU WEAK-LING!
BOTAN-MARU!
BOTAN-MARU!
DASH
NOW TELL ME! WHY DID YOU COME HERE?
...
YOU PUNCHED A SMALL TENGU.
SQUEEZE
AND YOU WANT TO BECOME THE FOURTH SOJOBO?
IF HE DOESN'T WANT TO BE HIT, HE NEED ONLY BECOME STRONG.
THE WEAK ARE AT FAULT.
HE'S SEVEN, YET HE CANNOT EVEN FLY.

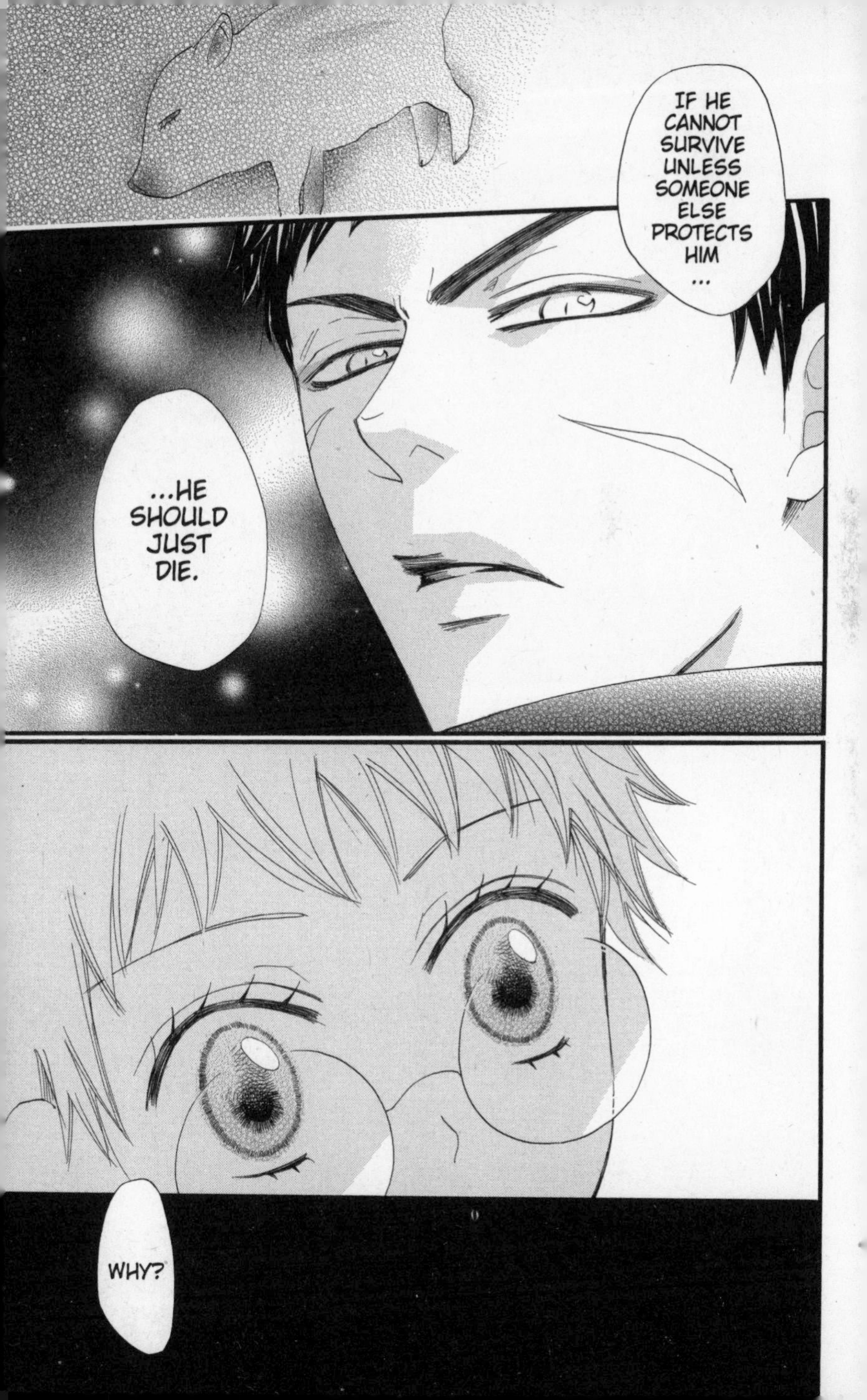
IF HE CANNOT SURVIVE UNLESS SOMEONE ELSE PROTECTS HIM ...
...HE SHOULD JUST DIE.
WHY?

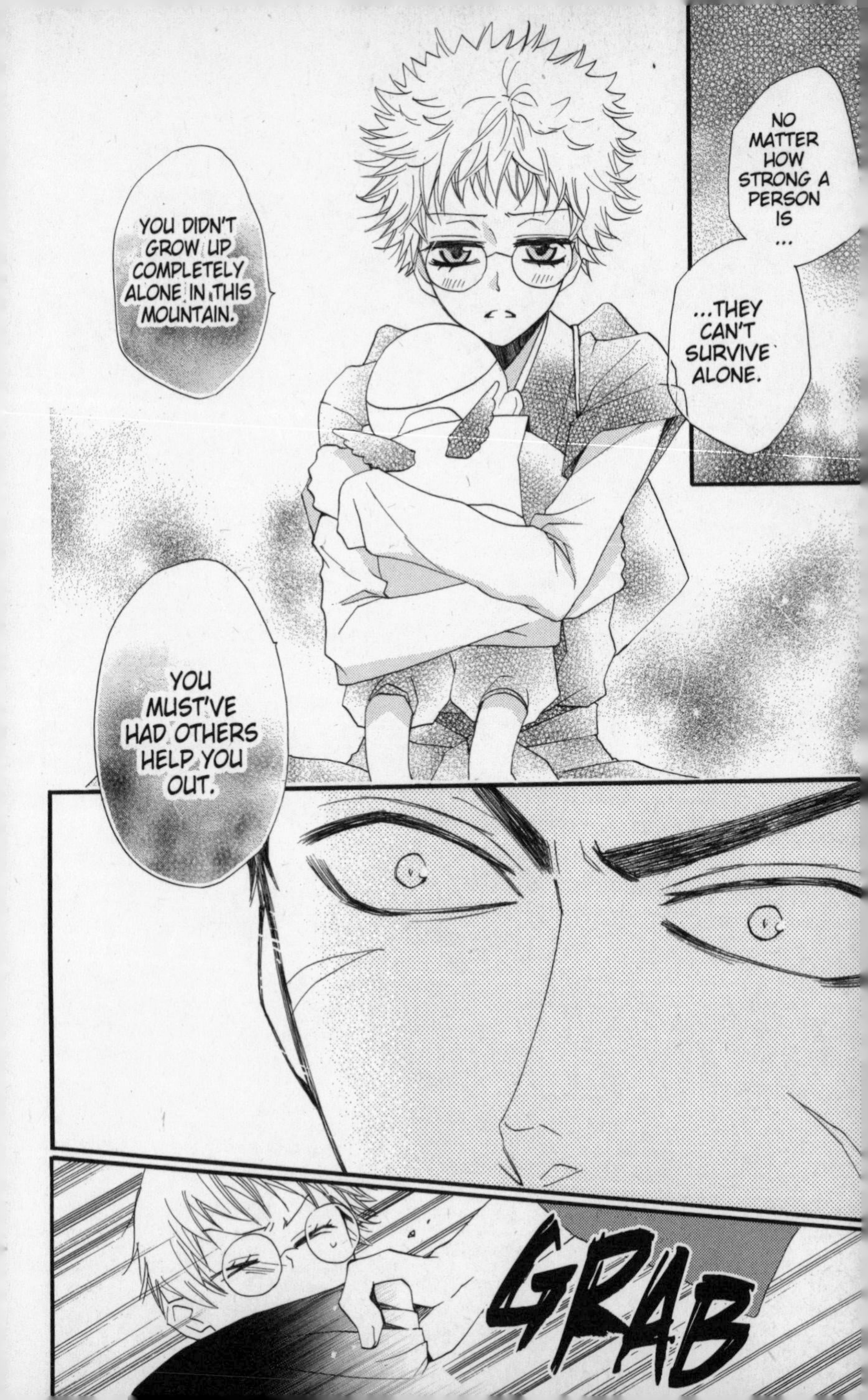
NO MATTER HOW STRONG A PERSON IS...
...THEY CAN'T SURVIVE ALONE.
YOU DIDN'T GROW UP COMPLETELY ALONE IN THIS MOUNTAIN.
YOU MUST'VE HAD OTHERS HELP YOU OUT.
GRAB

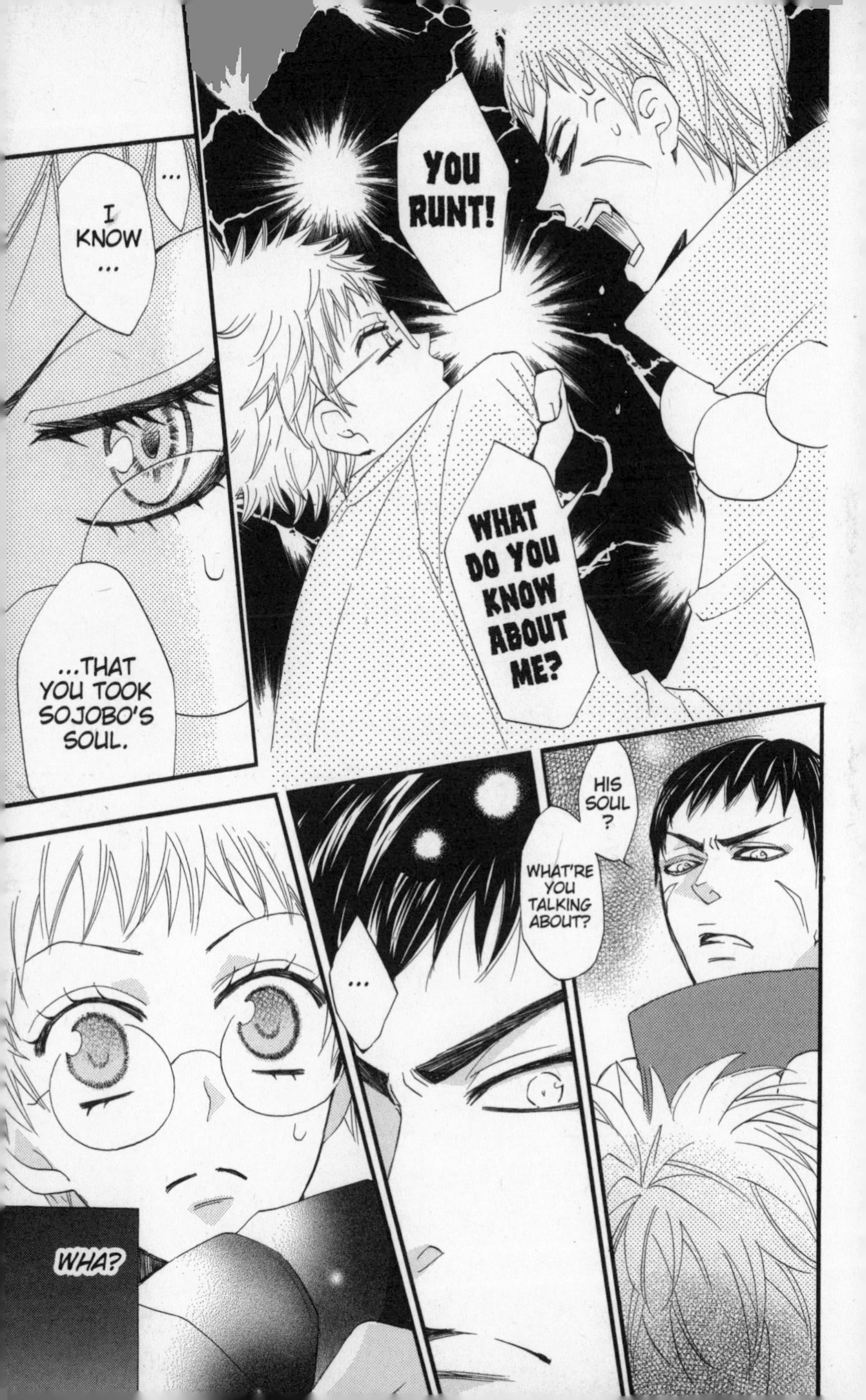
YOU RUNT!
WHAT DO YOU KNOW ABOUT ME?
...
I KNOW ...
...THAT YOU TOOK SOJOBO'S SOUL.
HIS SOUL?
WHAT'RE YOU TALKING ABOUT?
...
WHA?

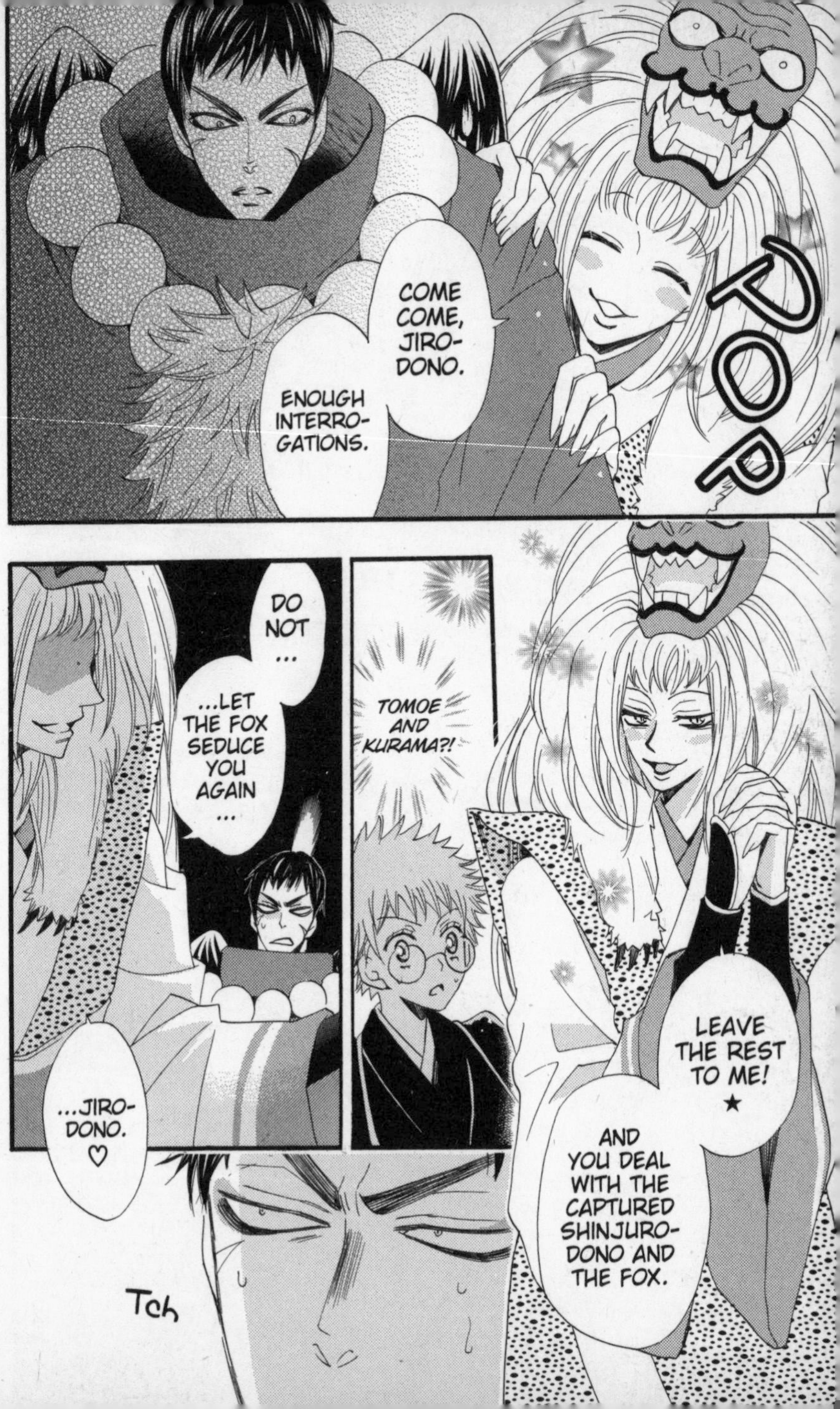
POP
COME COME, JIRO-DONO.
ENOUGH INTERRO-GATIONS.
LEAVE THE REST TO ME! ★
AND YOU DEAL WITH THE CAPTURED SHINJURO-DONO AND THE FOX.
TOMOE AND KURAMA?!
DO NOT ...
...LET THE FOX SEDUCE YOU AGAIN ...
...JIRO-DONO. ♡
Tch

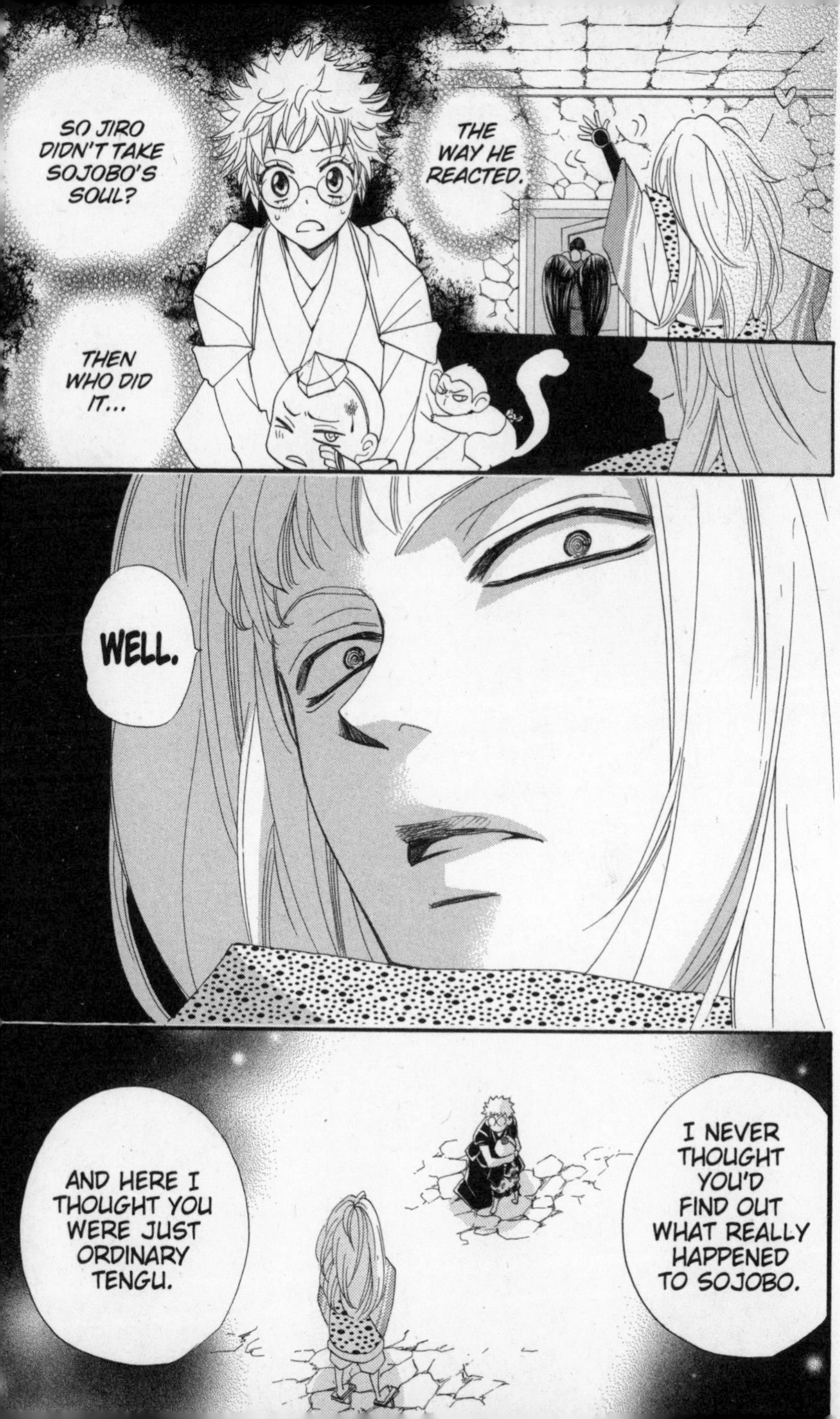
THE WAY HE REACTED.
SO JIRO DIDN'T TAKE SOJOBO'S SOUL?
THEN WHO DID IT...
WELL.
I NEVER THOUGHT YOU'D FIND OUT WHAT REALLY HAPPENED TO SOJOBO.
AND HERE I THOUGHT YOU WERE JUST ORDINARY TENGU.

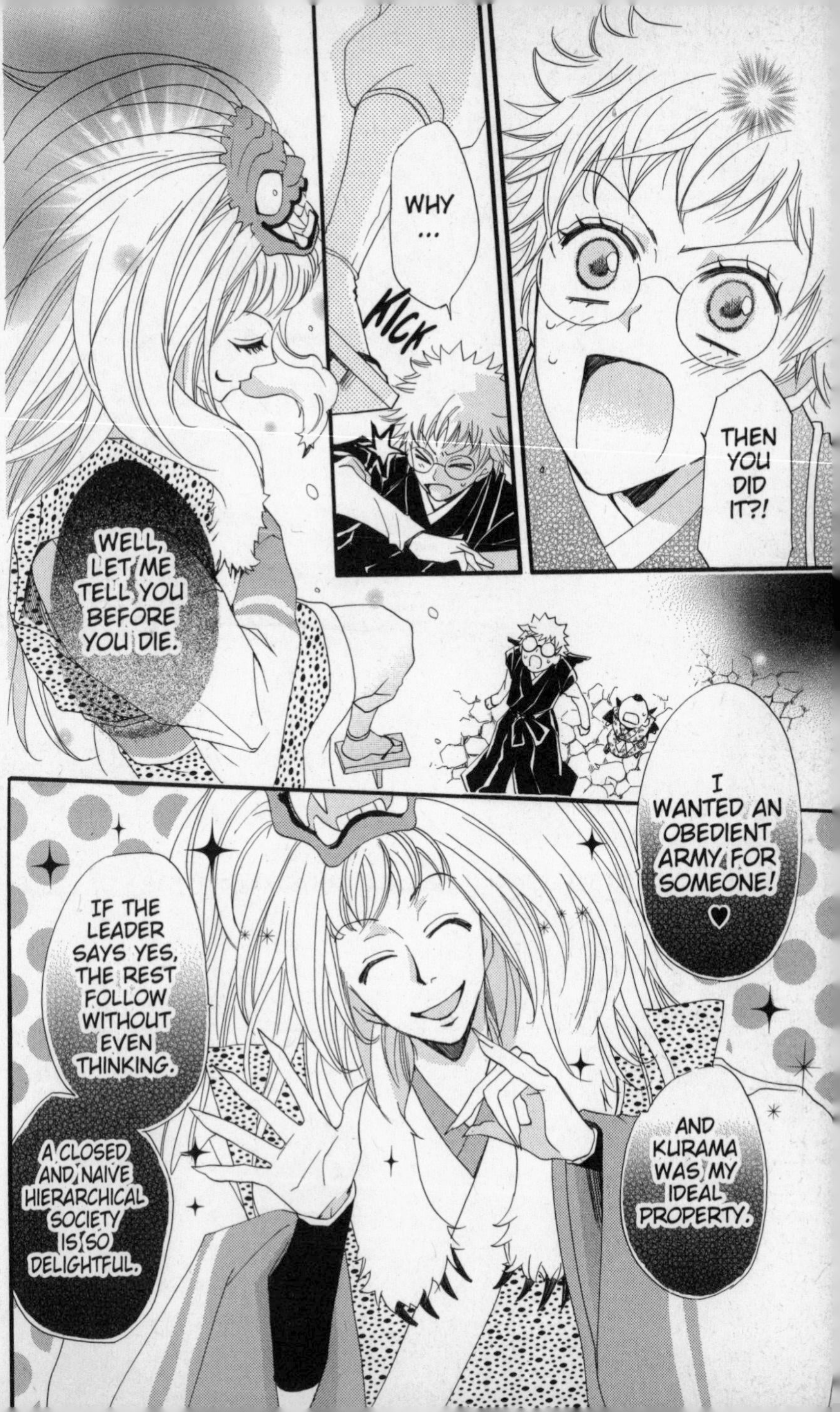
THEN YOU DID IT?!
WHY ...
KICK
WELL, LET ME TELL YOU BEFORE YOU DIE.
I WANTED AN OBEDIENT ARMY FOR SOMEONE! ♥
AND KURAMA WAS MY IDEAL PROPERTY.
IF THE LEADER SAYS YES, THE REST FOLLOW WITHOUT EVEN THINKING.
A CLOSED AND NAIVE HIERARCHICAL SOCIETY IS SO DELIGHTFUL.

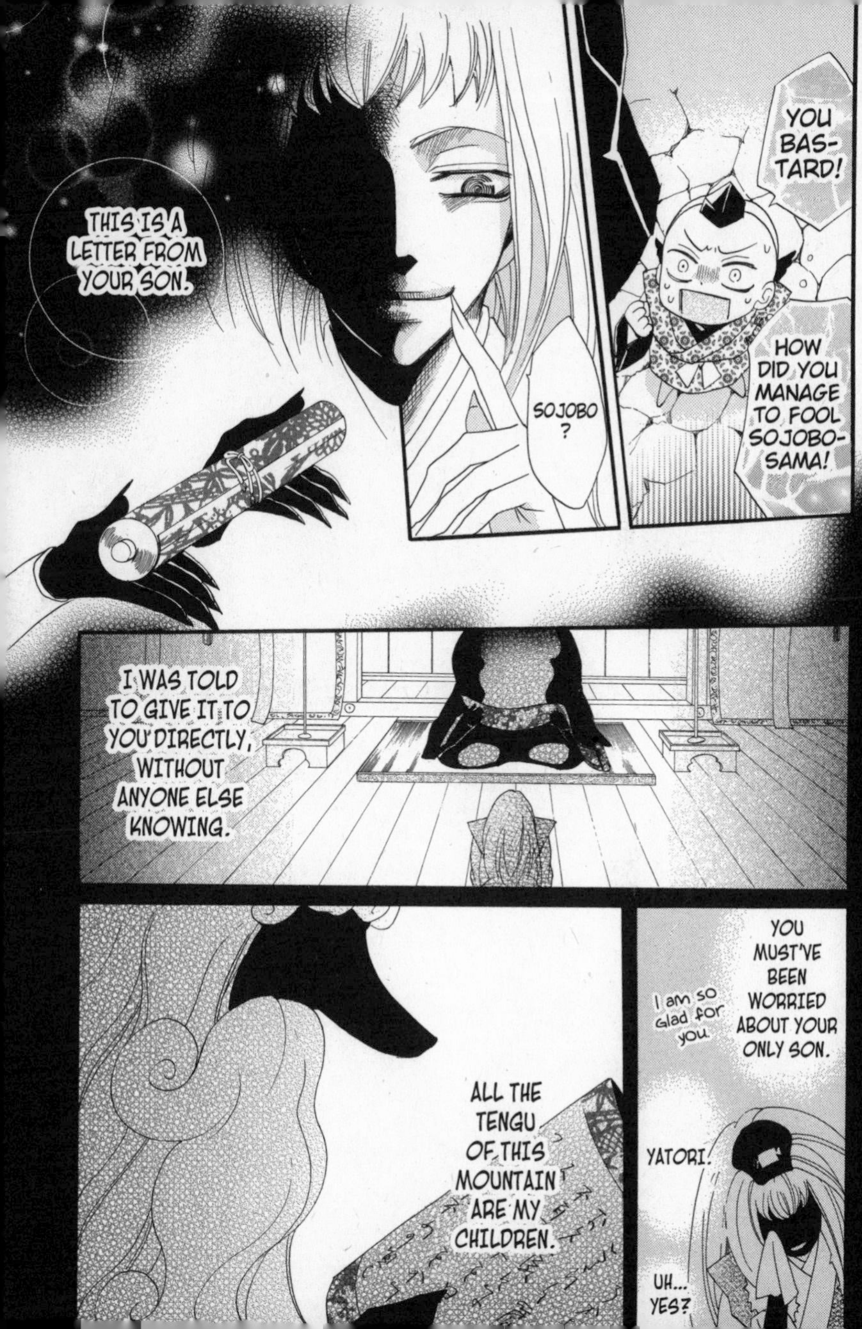
YOU BAS-TARD!
HOW DID YOU MANAGE TO FOOL SOJOBO-SAMA!
SOJOBO?
THIS IS A LETTER FROM YOUR SON.
I WAS TOLD TO GIVE IT TO YOU DIRECTLY, WITHOUT ANYONE ELSE KNOWING.
YOU MUST'VE BEEN WORRIED ABOUT YOUR ONLY SON.
I am so Glad for you.
YATORI!
UH... YES?
ALL THE TENGU OF THIS MOUNTAIN ARE MY CHILDREN.

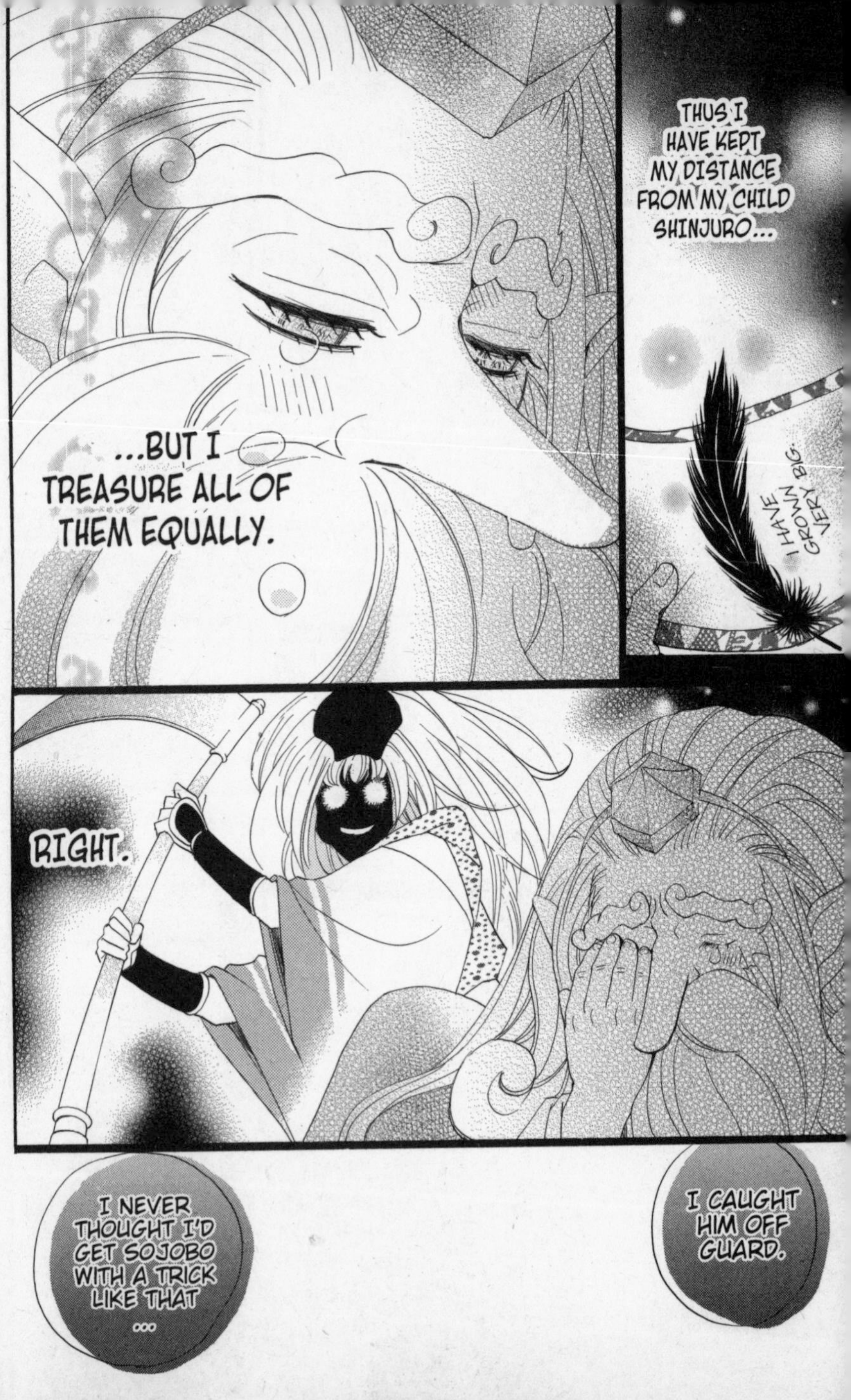
THUS I HAVE KEPT MY DISTANCE FROM MY CHILD SHINJURO...
I HAVE GROWN VERY BIG.
...BUT I TREASURE ALL OF THEM EQUALLY.
RIGHT.
I CAUGHT HIM OFF GUARD.
I NEVER THOUGHT I'D GET SOJOBO WITH A TRICK LIKE THAT...

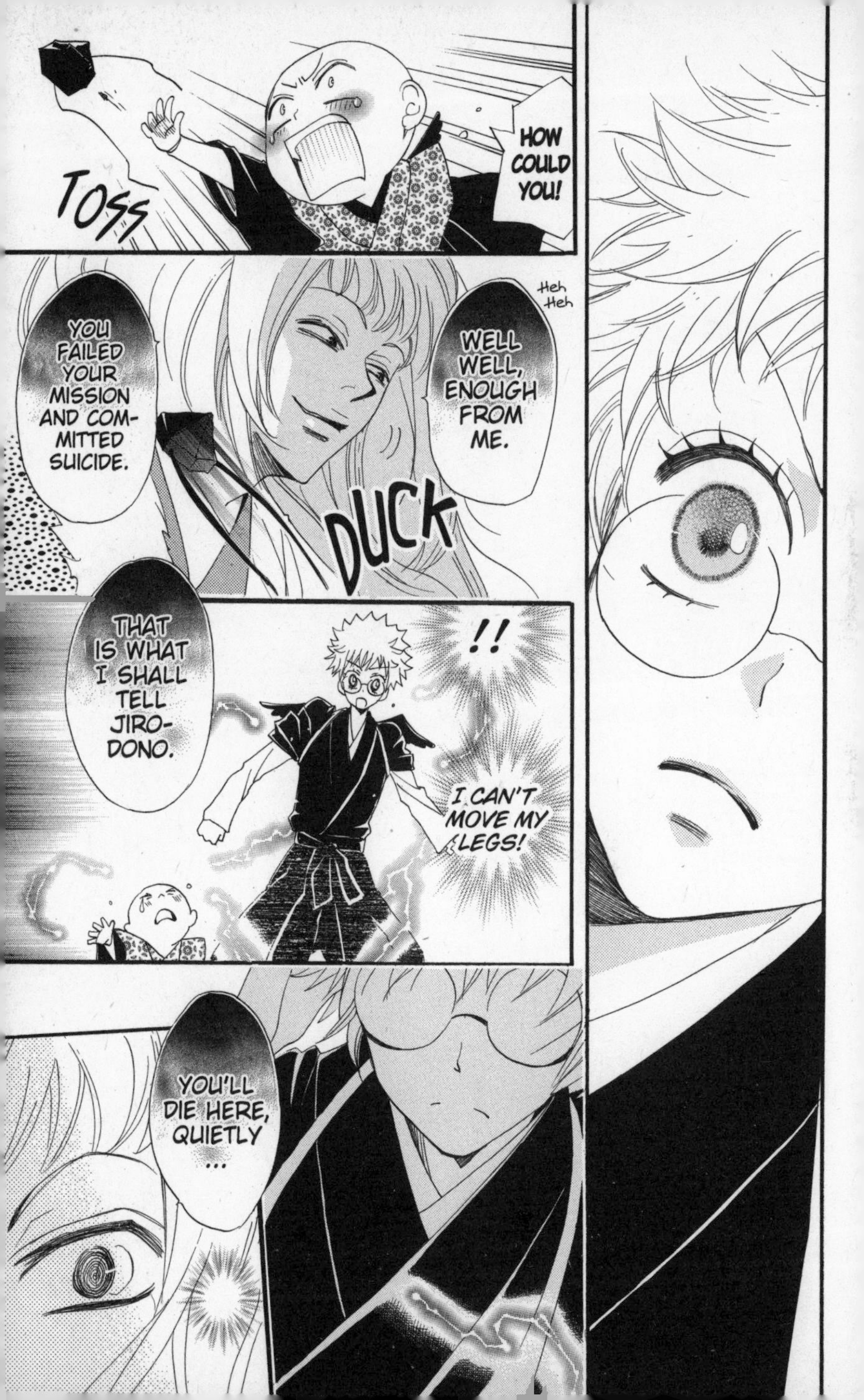
HOW COULD YOU!
TOSS
Heh Heh
WELL WELL, ENOUGH FROM ME.
YOU FAILED YOUR MISSION AND COMMITTED SUICIDE.
DUCK
!!
I CAN'T MOVE MY LEGS!
THAT IS WHAT I SHALL TELL JIRO-DONO.
YOU'LL DIE HERE, QUIETLY ...

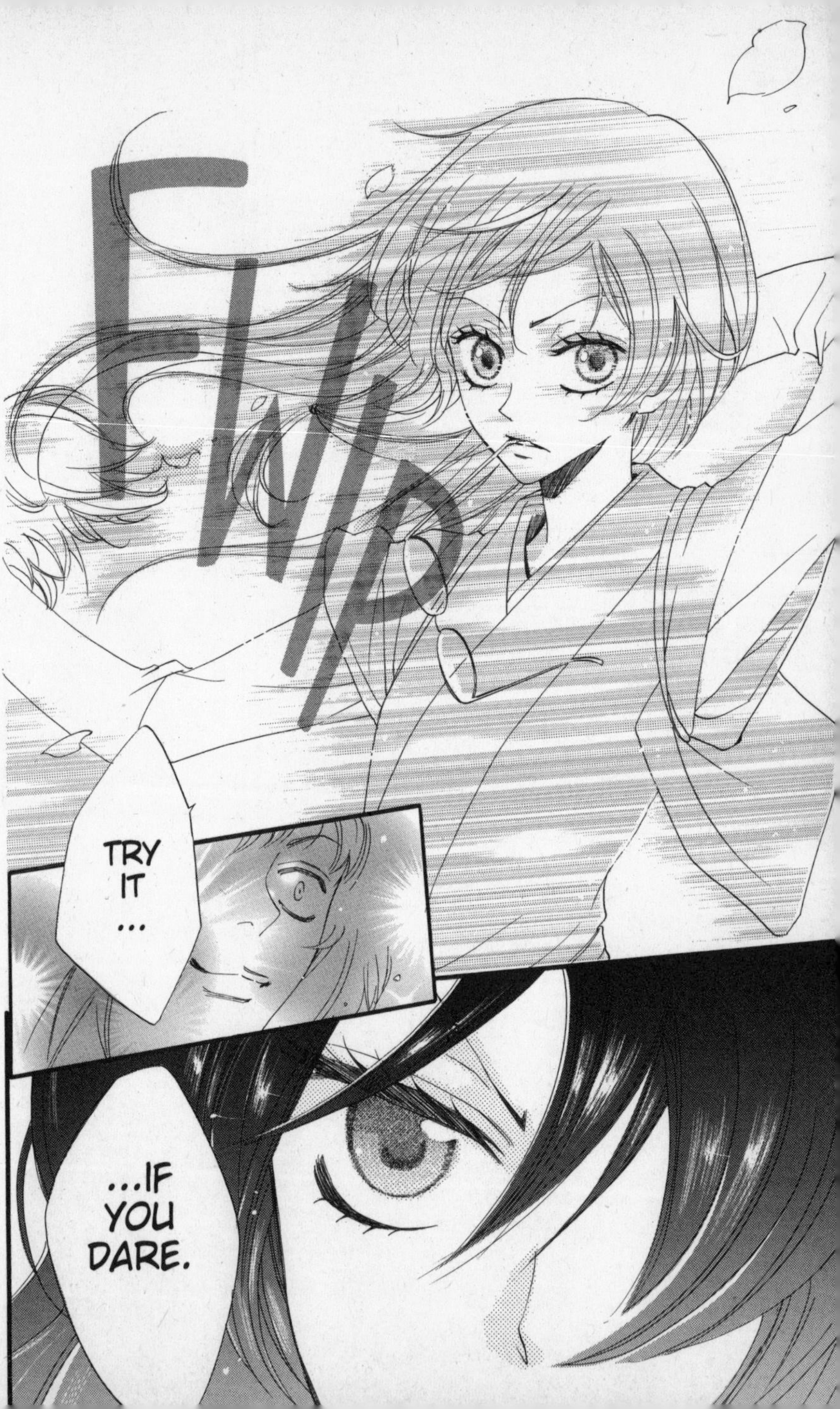
FWIP
TRY IT ...
...IF YOU DARE.

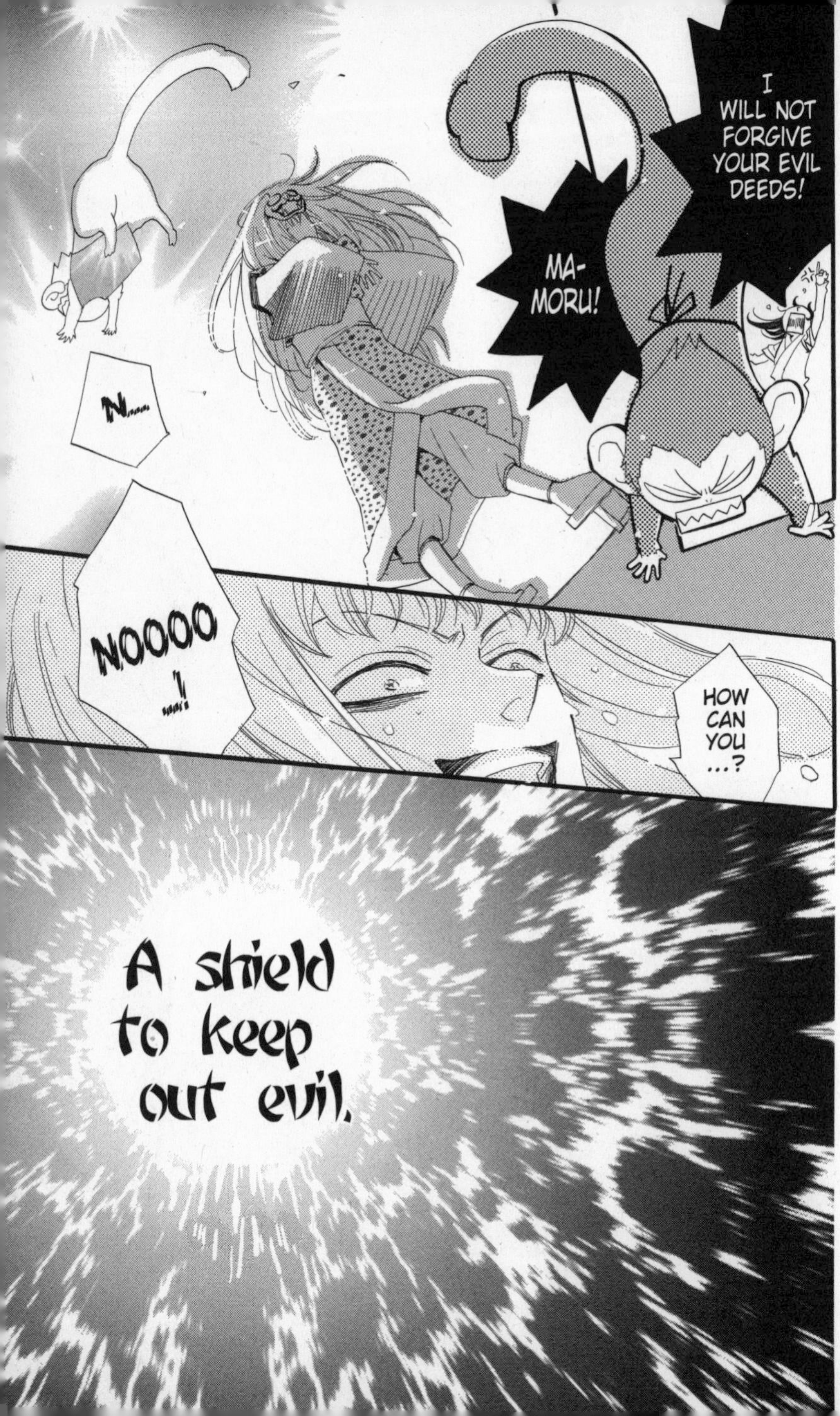

I WILL NOT FORGIVE YOUR EVIL DEEDS!
MA-MORU!
N...
NOOOO...!
HOW CAN YOU...?
A shield to keep out evil.

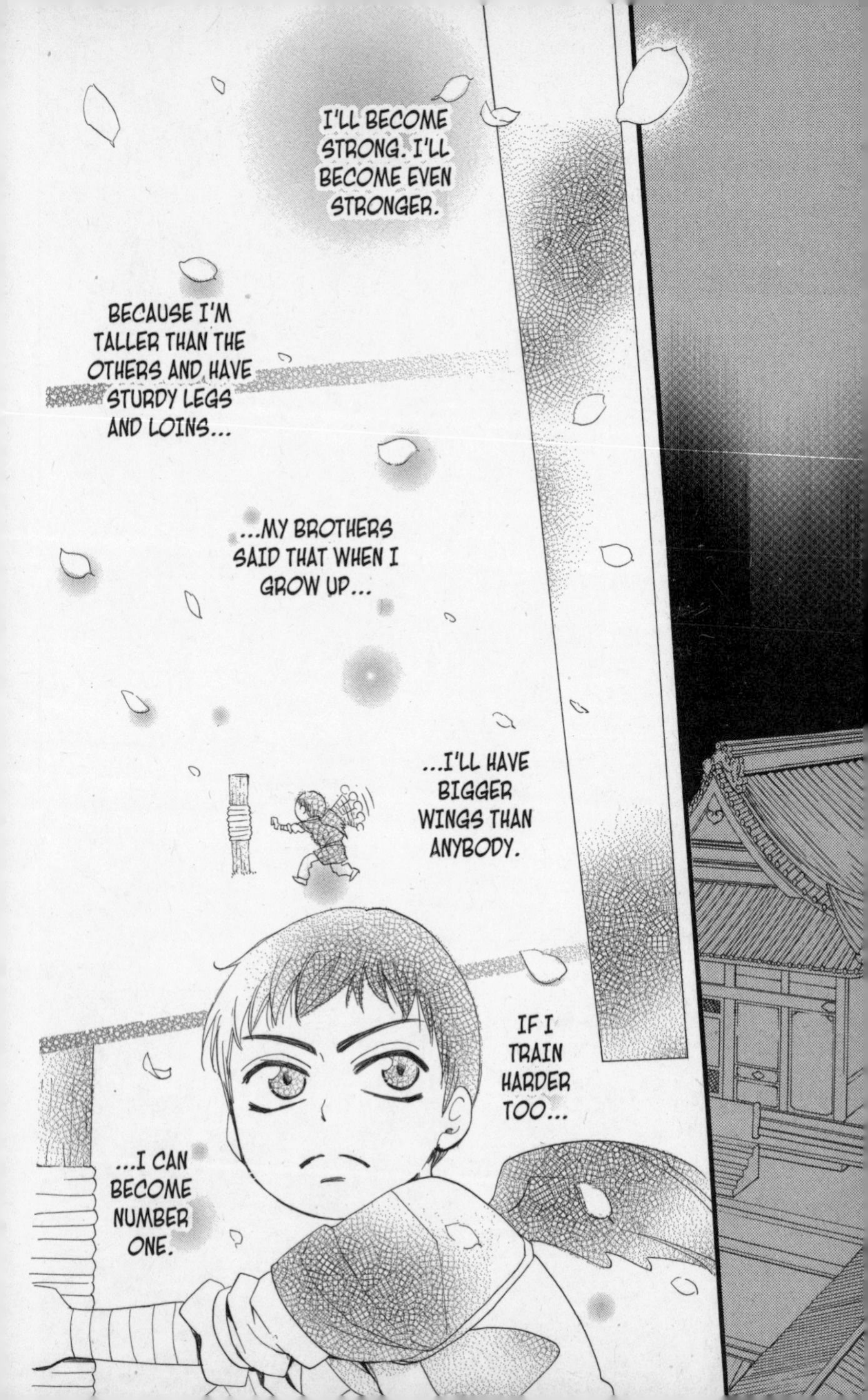
I'LL BECOME STRONG. I'LL BECOME EVEN STRONGER.
BECAUSE I'M TALLER THAN THE OTHERS AND HAVE STURDY LEGS AND LOINS...
...MY BROTHERS SAID THAT WHEN I GROW UP...
...I'LL HAVE BIGGER WINGS THAN ANYBODY.
IF I TRAIN HARDER TOO...
...I CAN BECOME NUMBER ONE.

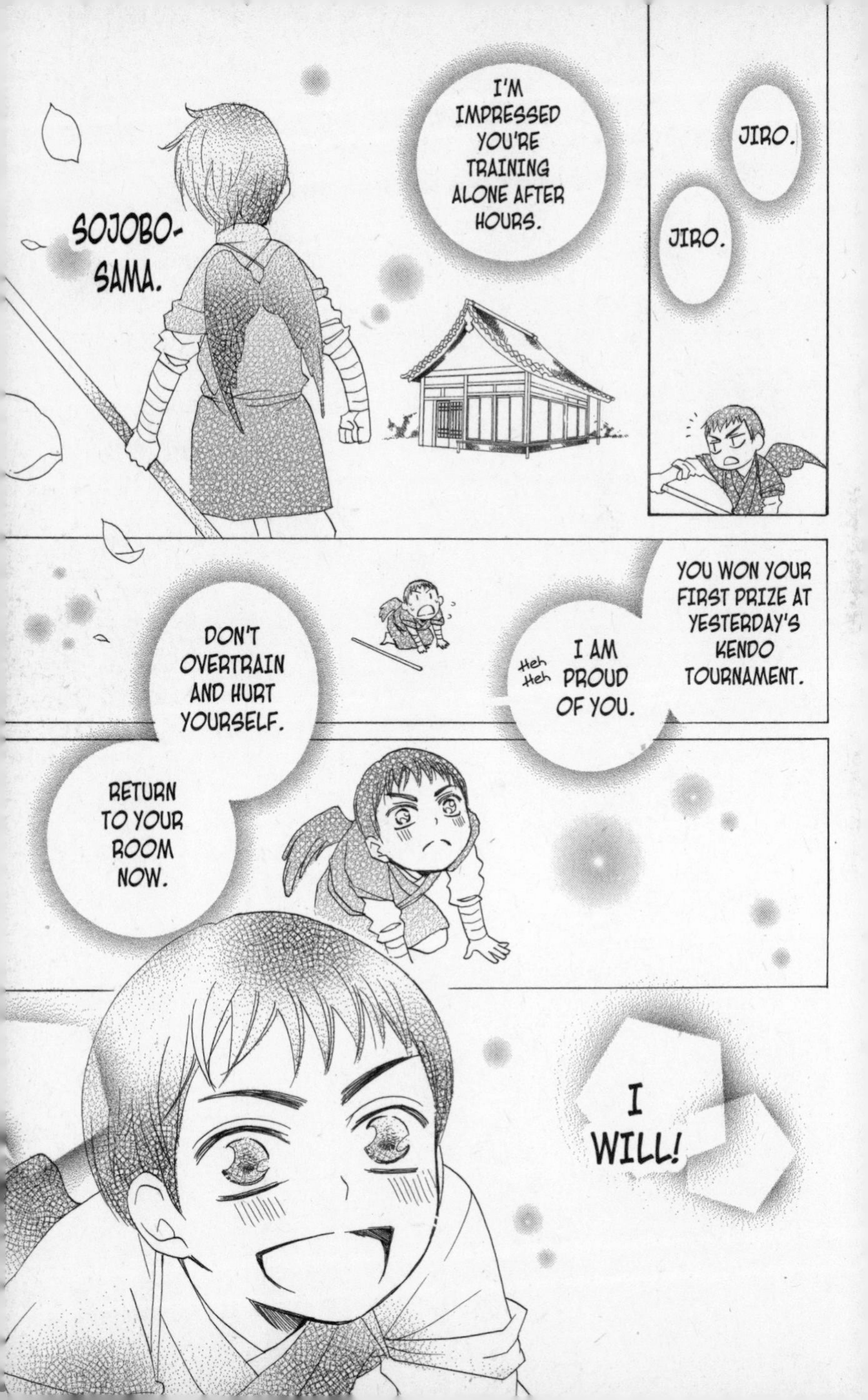
JIRO.
JIRO.
I'M IMPRESSED YOU'RE TRAINING ALONE AFTER HOURS.
SOJOBO-SAMA.
YOU WON YOUR FIRST PRIZE AT YESTERDAY'S KENDO TOURNAMENT.
I AM PROUD OF YOU.
Heh Heh
DON'T OVERTRAIN AND HURT YOURSELF.
RETURN TO YOUR ROOM NOW.
I WILL!

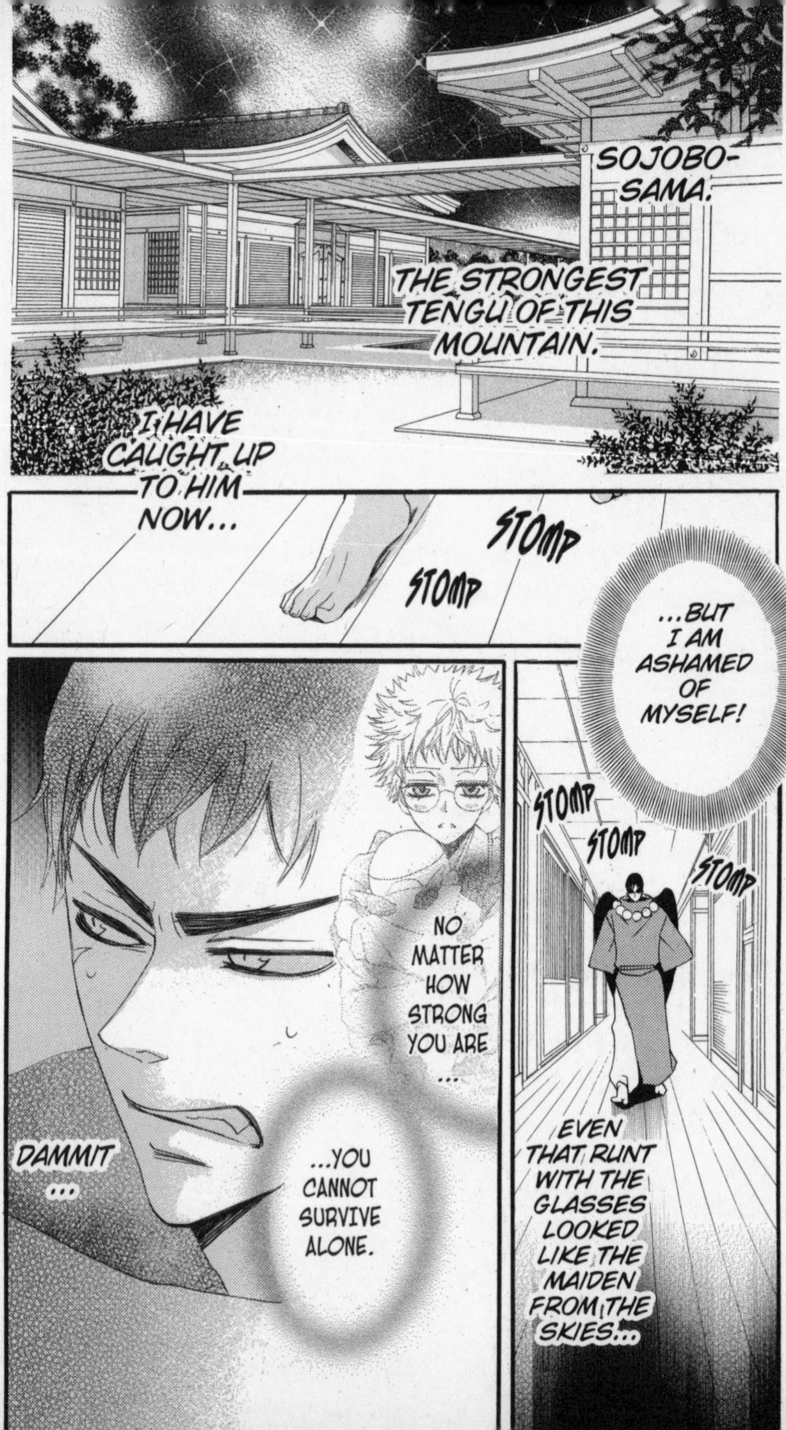
SOJOBO-SAMA.
THE STRONGEST TENGU OF THIS MOUNTAIN.
I HAVE CAUGHT UP TO HIM NOW...
STOMP
STOMP
...BUT I AM ASHAMED OF MYSELF!
STOMP
STOMP
STOMP
EVEN THAT RUNT WITH THE GLASSES LOOKED LIKE THE MAIDEN FROM THE SKIES...
NO MATTER HOW STRONG YOU ARE...
...YOU CANNOT SURVIVE ALONE.
DAMMIT...

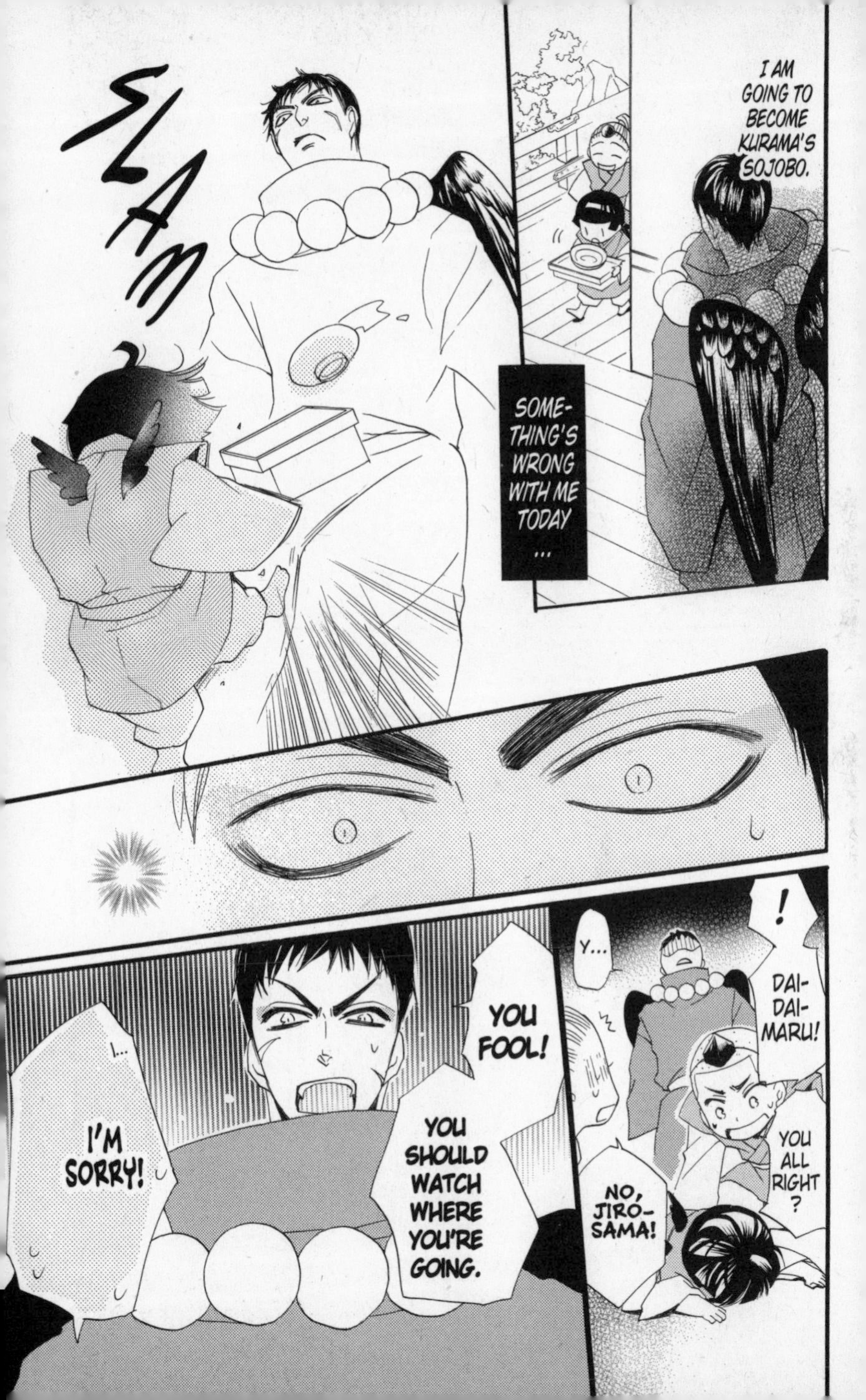
I AM GOING TO BECOME KURAMA'S SOJOBO.
SOME-THING'S WRONG WITH ME TODAY ...
SLAM
!
Y...
DAI-DAIMARU!
YOU ALL RIGHT?
NO, JIRO-SAMA!
YOU FOOL!
YOU SHOULD WATCH WHERE YOU'RE GOING.
I...
I'M SORRY!

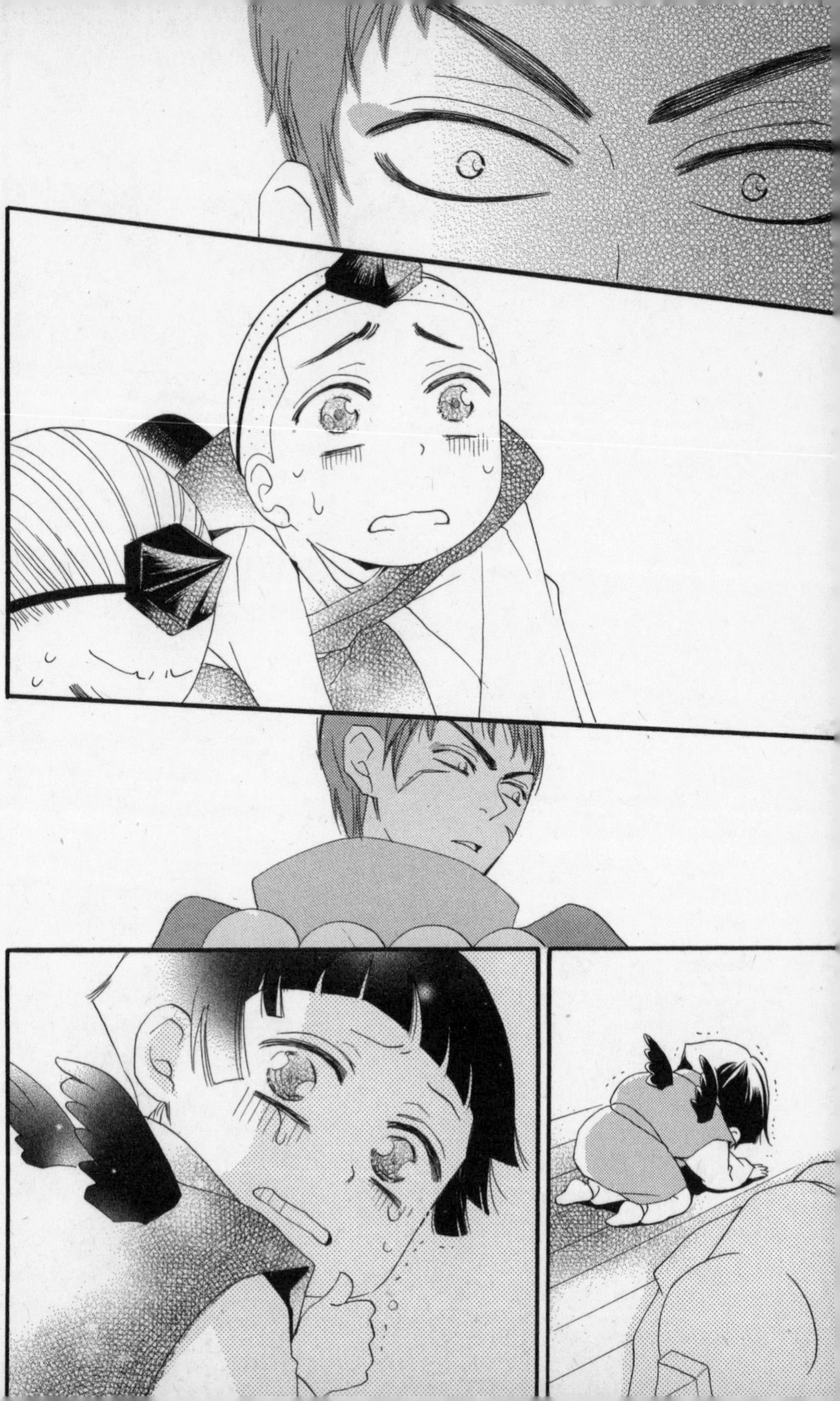

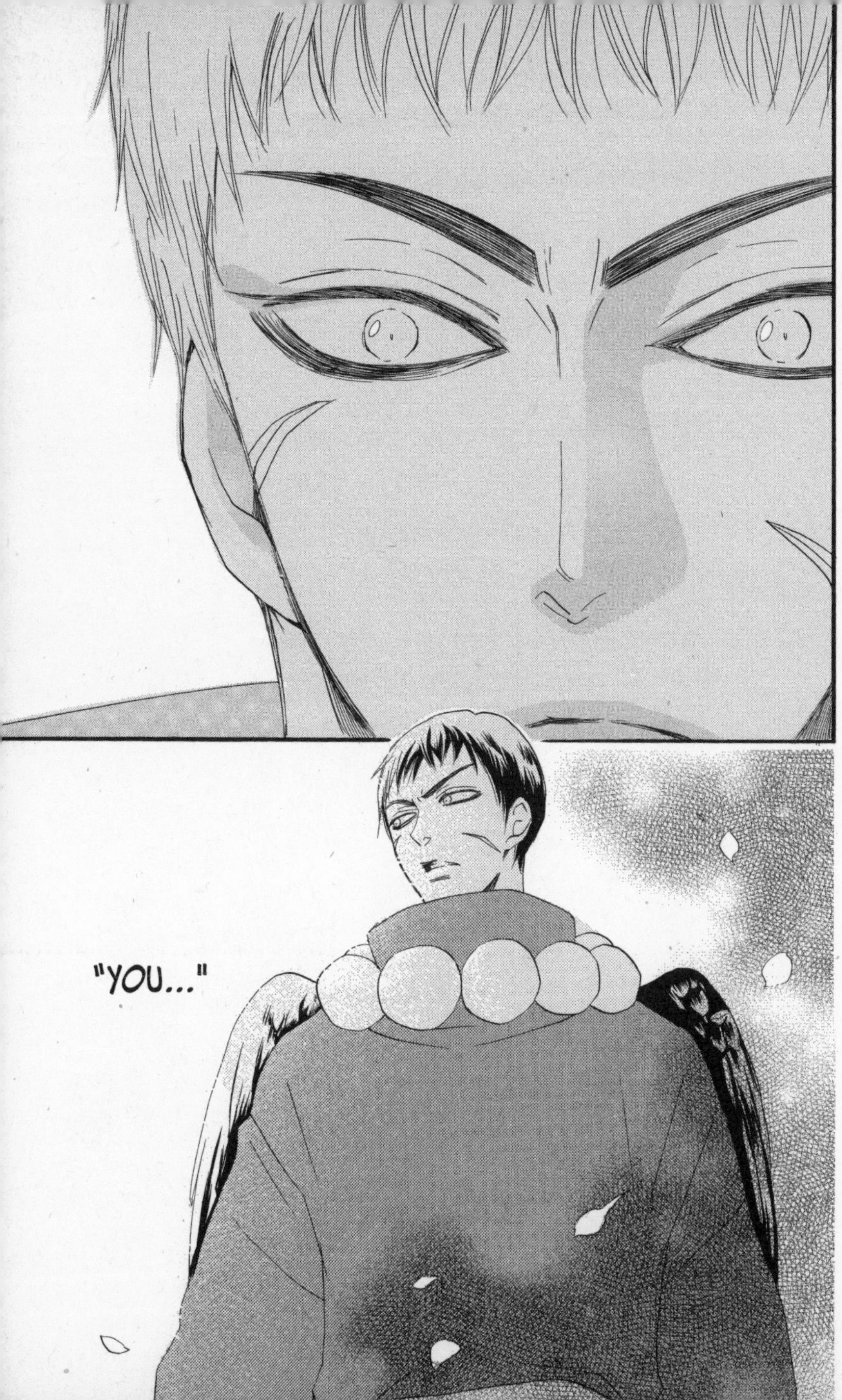
"YOU..."

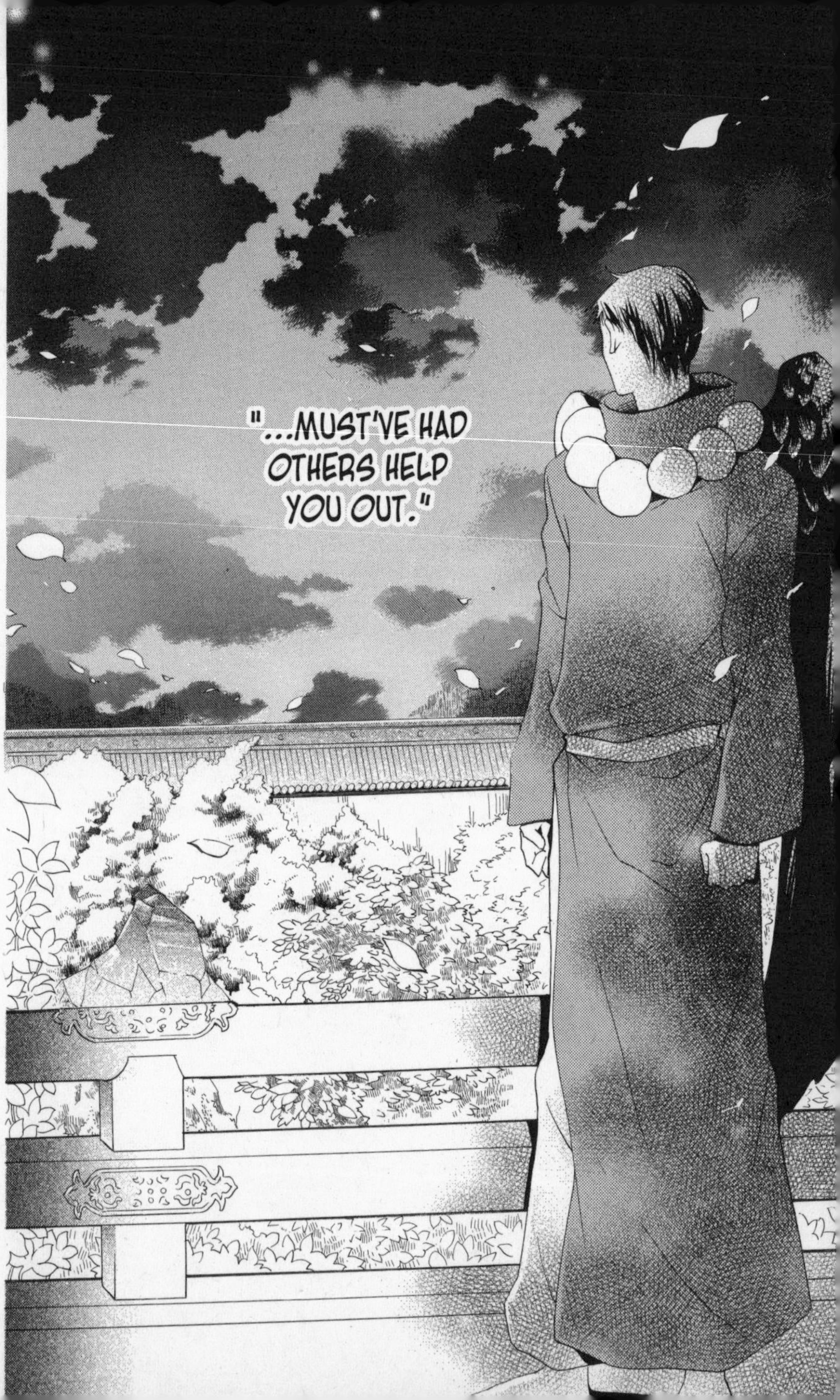
"...MUST'VE HAD OTHERS HELP YOU OUT."

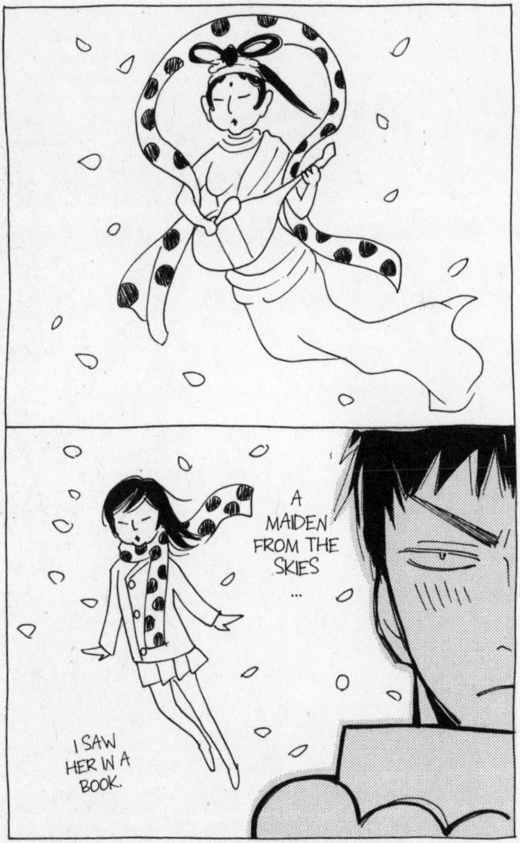
A MAIDEN FROM THE SKIES ...
I SAW HER IN A BOOK.

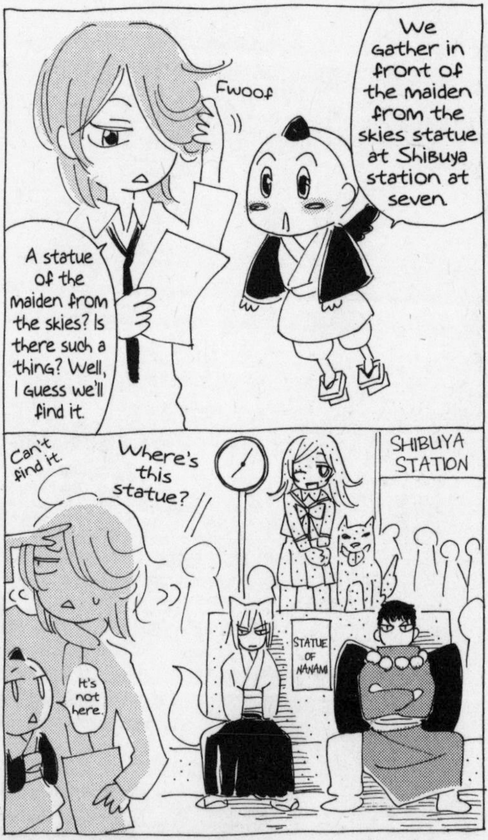
We gather in front of the maiden from the skies statue at Shibuya station at seven.
Fwoof
A statue of the maiden from the skies? Is there such a thing? Well, I guess we'll find it.
SHIBUYA STATION
Where's this statue?
Can't find it.
STATUE OF NANAMI
It's not here.

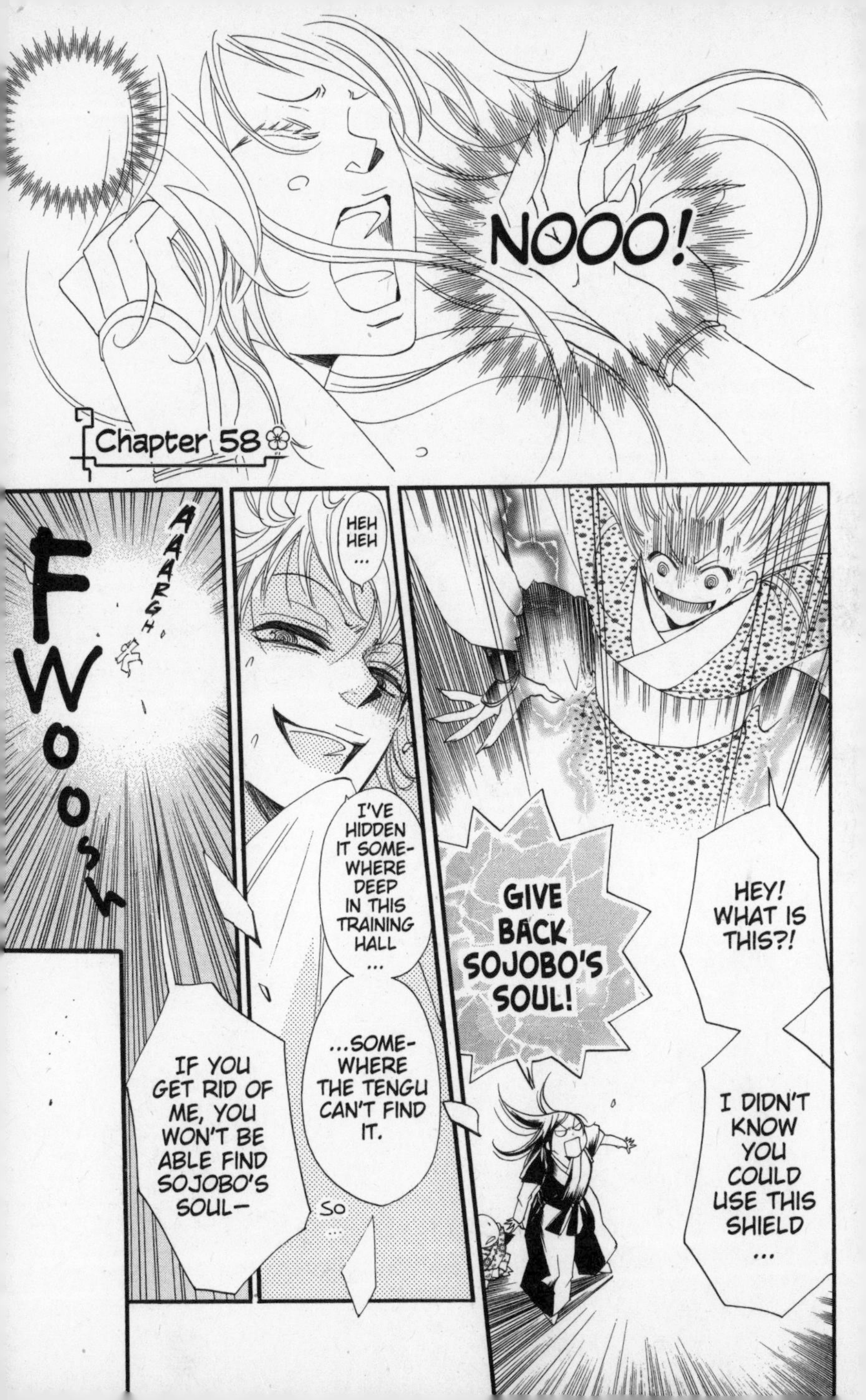
NOOO!
Chapter 58
HEY! WHAT IS THIS?!
I DIDN'T KNOW YOU COULD USE THIS SHIELD...
GIVE BACK SOJOBO'S SOUL!
HEH HEH...
I'VE HIDDEN IT SOME-WHERE DEEP IN THIS TRAINING HALL...
...SOME-WHERE THE TENGU CAN'T FIND IT.
SO...
IF YOU GET RID OF ME, YOU WON'T BE ABLE FIND SOJOBO'S SOUL—
AAARGH
FWOOSH

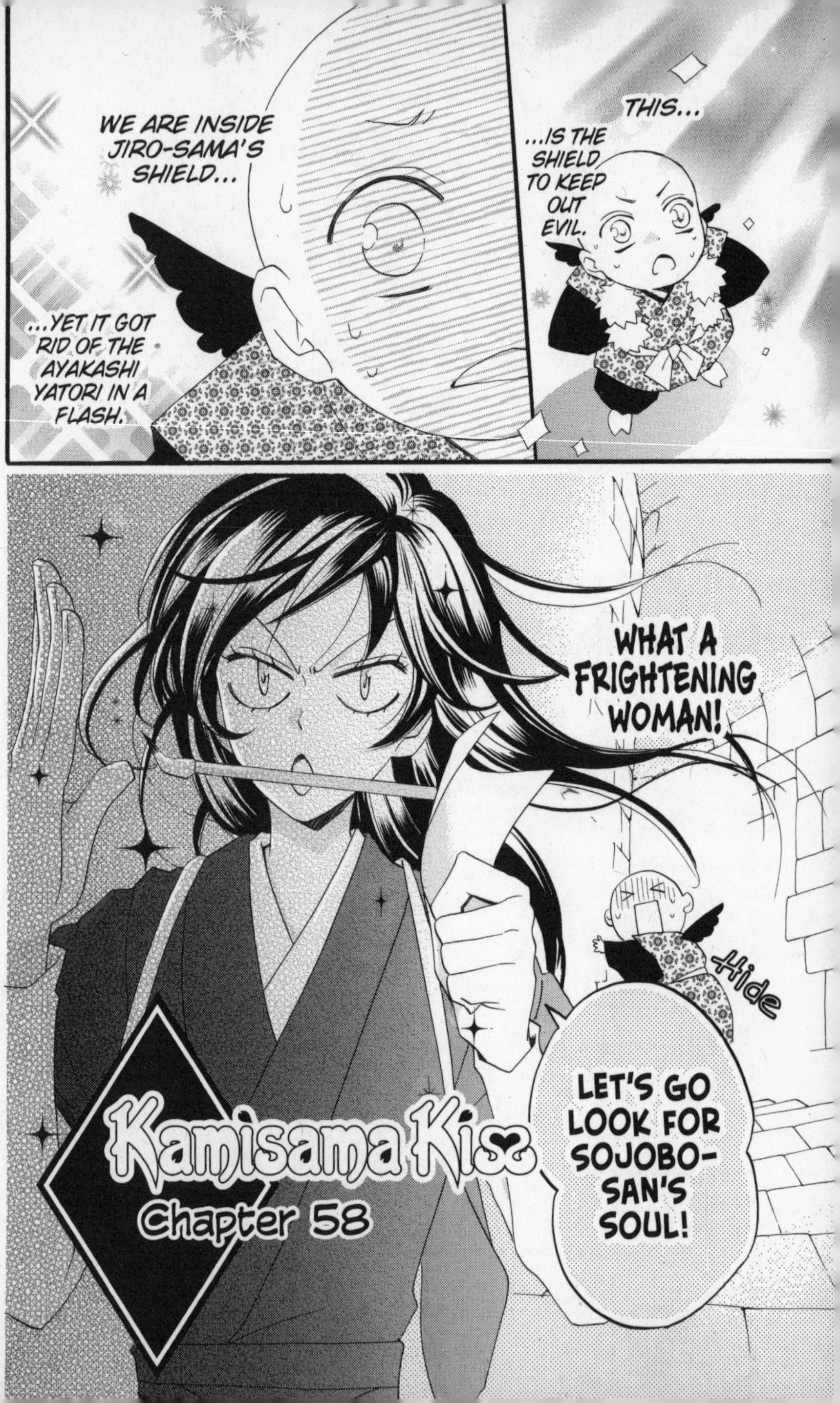
THIS...
...IS THE SHIELD TO KEEP OUT EVIL.
WE ARE INSIDE JIRO-SAMA'S SHIELD...
...YET IT GOT RID OF THE AYAKASHI YATORI IN A FLASH.
WHAT A FRIGHTENING WOMAN!
Hide
LET'S GO LOOK FOR SOJOBO-SAN'S SOUL!
Kamisama Kiss
Chapter 58

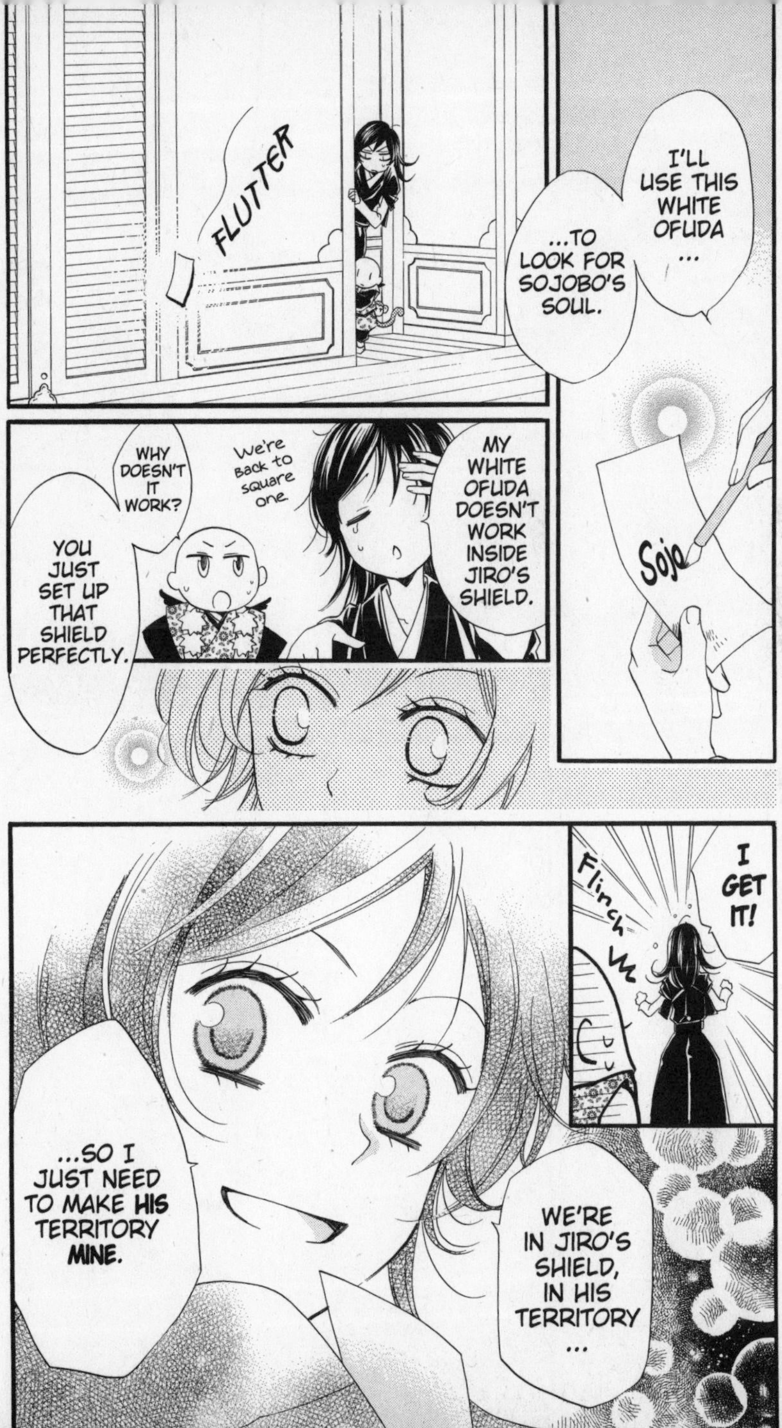
I'LL USE THIS WHITE OFUDA ...
...TO LOOK FOR SOJOBO'S SOUL.
Sojo
FLUTTER
MY WHITE OFUDA DOESN'T WORK INSIDE JIRO'S SHIELD.
We're back to square one.
WHY DOESN'T IT WORK?
YOU JUST SET UP THAT SHIELD PERFECTLY.
I GET IT!
Flinch
WE'RE IN JIRO'S SHIELD, IN HIS TERRITORY ...
...SO I JUST NEED TO MAKE **HIS** TERRITORY **MINE**.

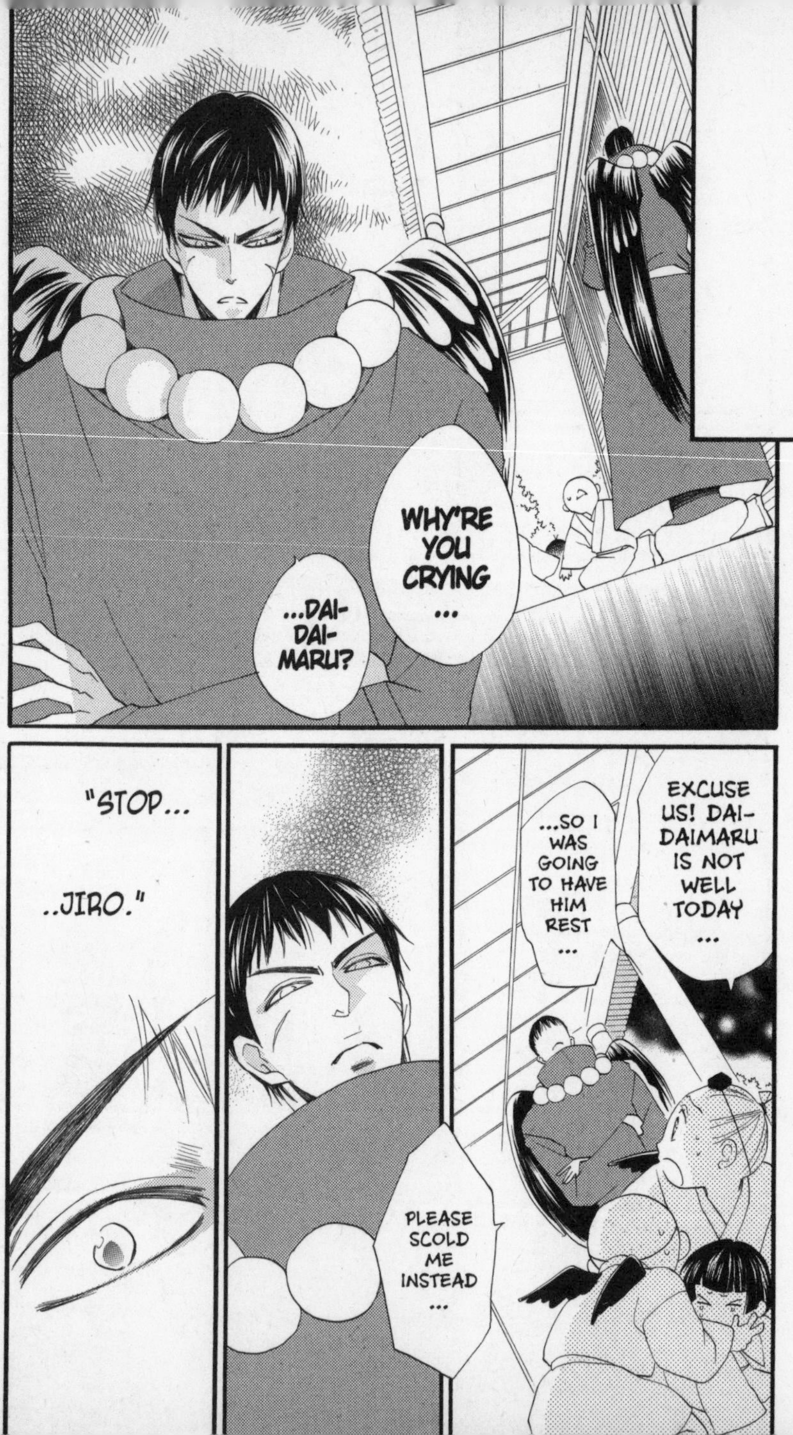
WHY'RE YOU CRYING ...
...DAI-DAIMARU?
EXCUSE US! DAI-DAIMARU IS NOT WELL TODAY ...
...SO I WAS GOING TO HAVE HIM REST ...
PLEASE SCOLD ME INSTEAD ...
"STOP...
..JIRO."

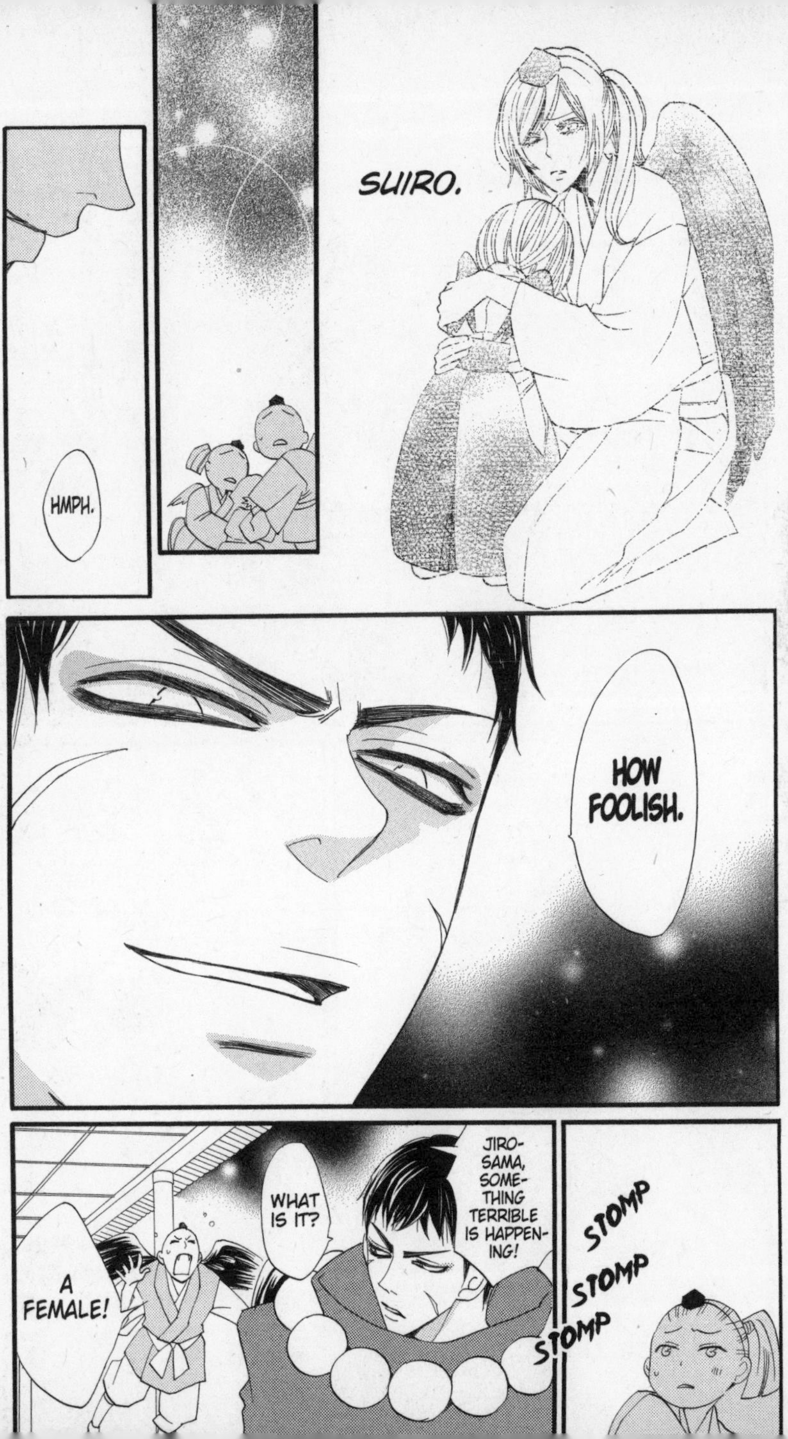
SUIRO.
HMPH.
HOW FOOLISH.
STOMP
STOMP
STOMP
JIRO-SAMA, SOMETHING TERRIBLE IS HAPPENING!
WHAT IS IT?
A FEMALE!

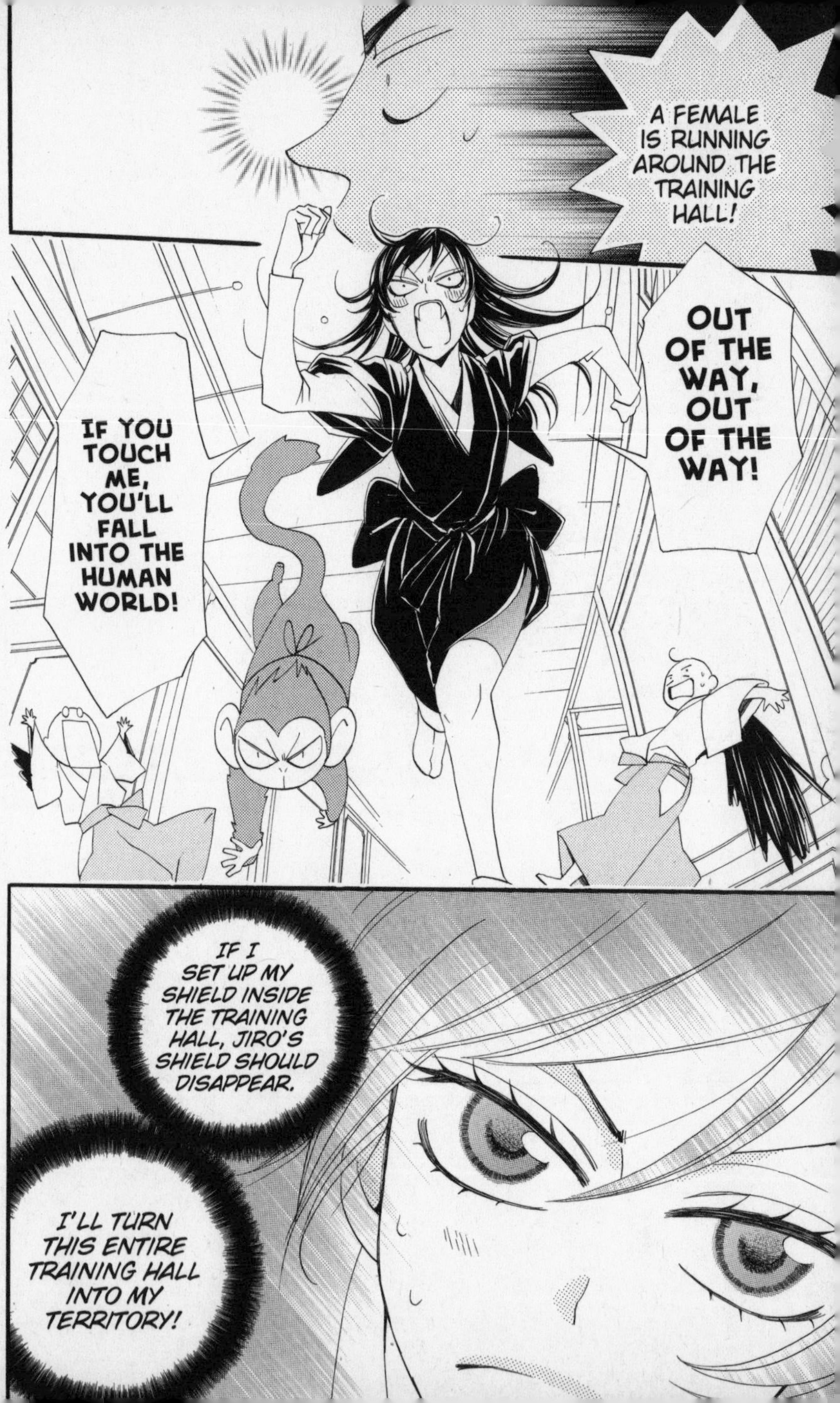
A FEMALE IS RUNNING AROUND THE TRAINING HALL!
OUT OF THE WAY, OUT OF THE WAY!
IF YOU TOUCH ME, YOU'LL FALL INTO THE HUMAN WORLD!
IF I SET UP MY SHIELD INSIDE THE TRAINING HALL, JIRO'S SHIELD SHOULD DISAPPEAR.
I'LL TURN THIS ENTIRE TRAINING HALL INTO MY TERRITORY!

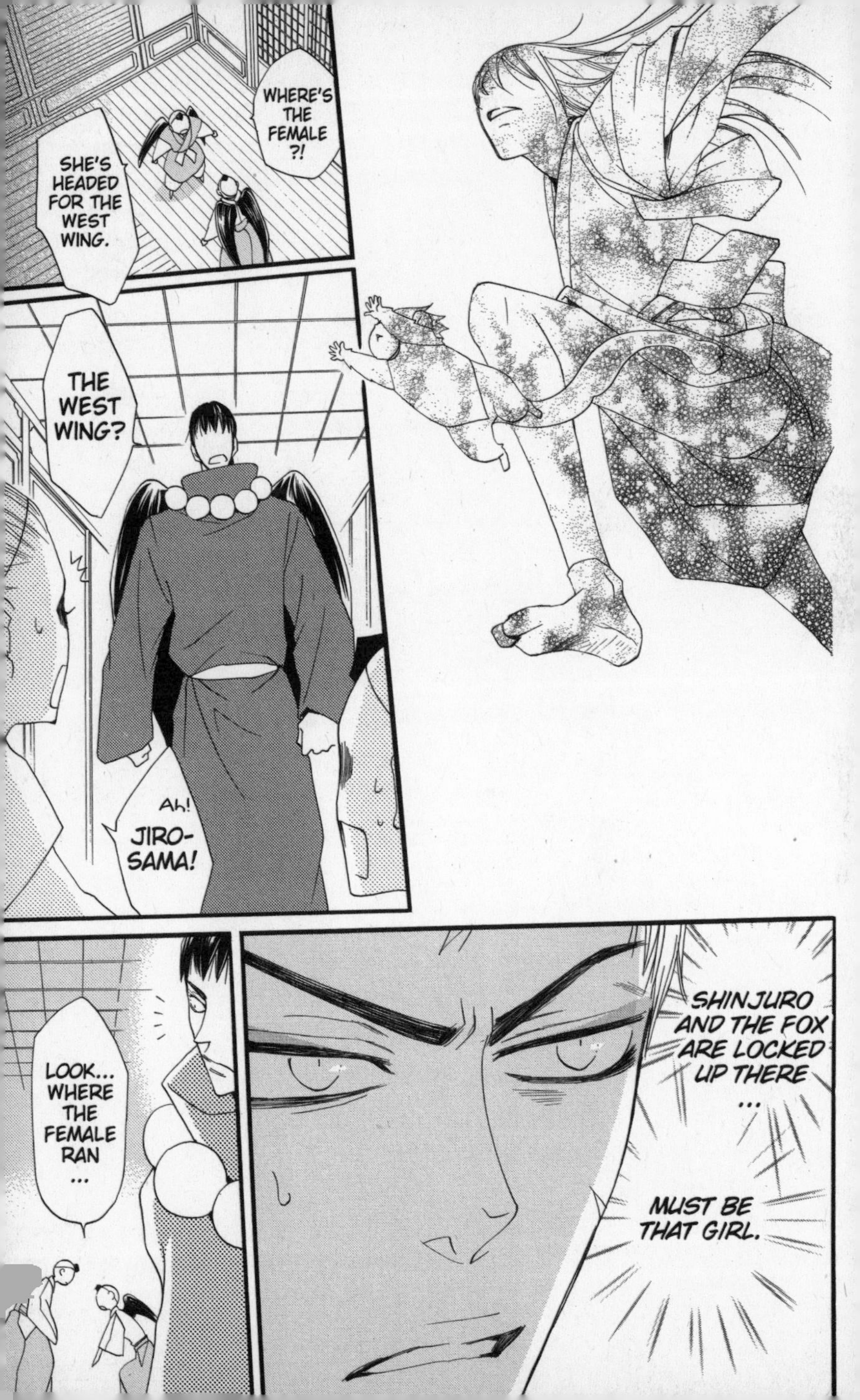
WHERE'S THE FEMALE?!
SHE'S HEADED FOR THE WEST WING.
THE WEST WING?
Ah! JIRO-SAMA!
SHINJURO AND THE FOX ARE LOCKED UP THERE...
MUST BE THAT GIRL.
LOOK... WHERE THE FEMALE RAN...

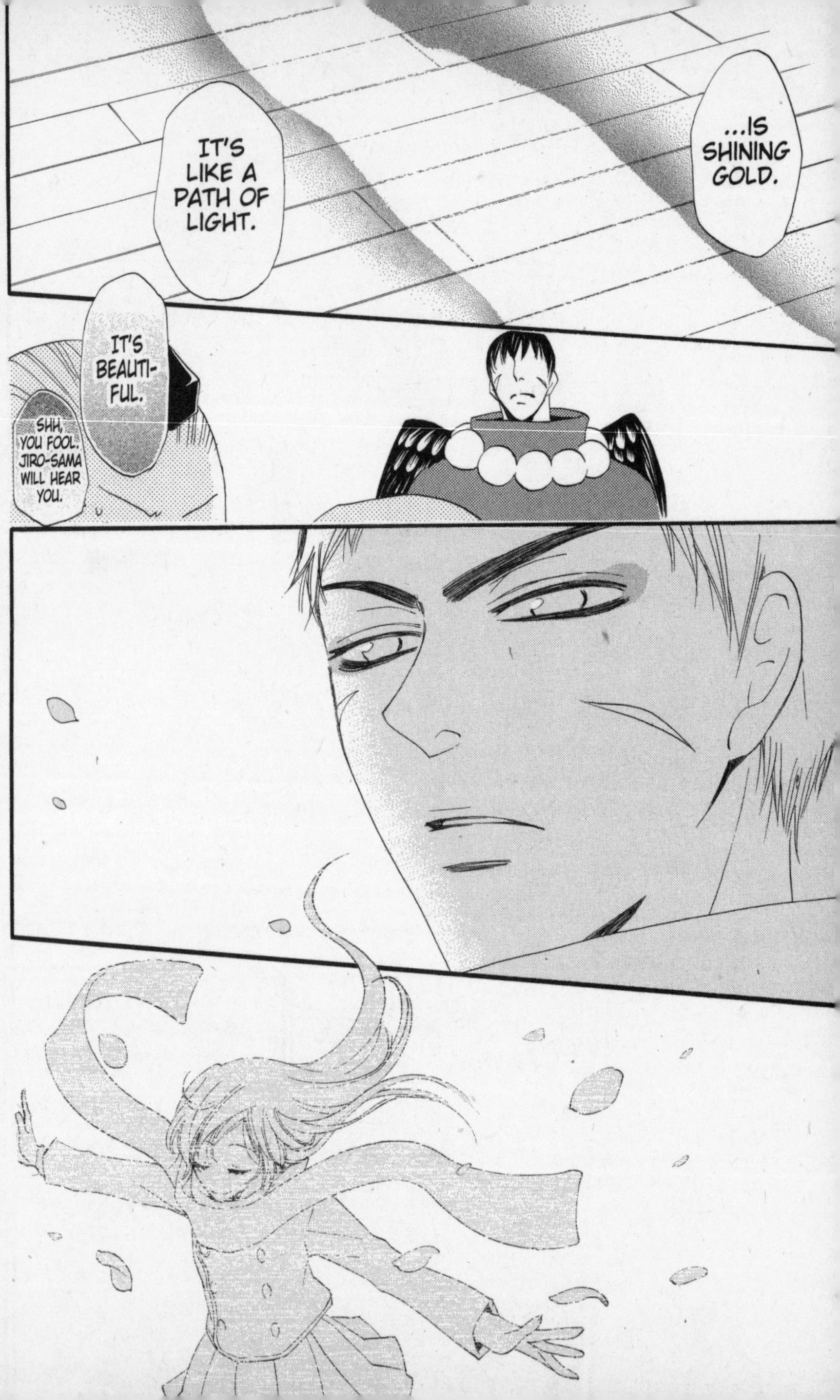
...IS SHINING GOLD.
IT'S LIKE A PATH OF LIGHT.
IT'S BEAUTIFUL.
SHH, YOU FOOL. JIRO-SAMA WILL HEAR YOU.

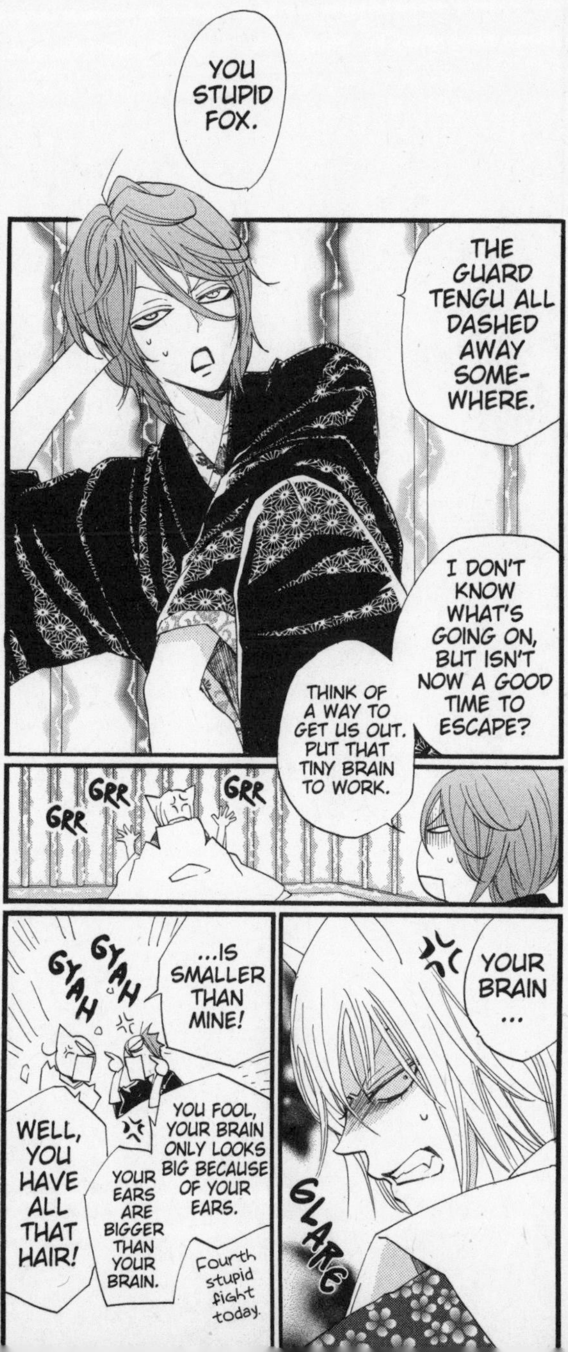
YOU STUPID FOX.
THE GUARD TENGU ALL DASHED AWAY SOME-WHERE.
I DON'T KNOW WHAT'S GOING ON, BUT ISN'T NOW A GOOD TIME TO ESCAPE?
THINK OF A WAY TO GET US OUT. PUT THAT TINY BRAIN TO WORK.
GRR
GRR
GRR
YOUR BRAIN...
GLARG
...IS SMALLER THAN MINE!
GYAH
GYAH
YOU FOOL, YOUR BRAIN ONLY LOOKS BIG BECAUSE OF YOUR EARS.
WELL, YOU HAVE ALL THAT HAIR!
YOUR EARS ARE BIGGER THAN YOUR BRAIN.
Fourth stupid fight today.

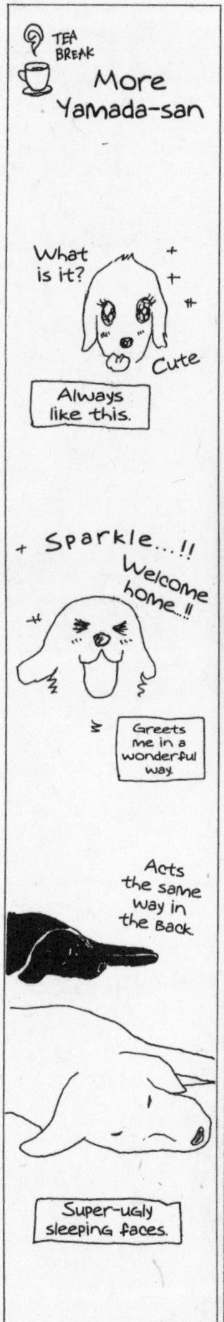
TEA BREAK
More Yamada-san
What is it?
Cute
Always like this.
Sparkle...!!
Welcome home...!!
Greets me in a wonderful way.
Acts the same way in the Back.
Super-ugly sleeping faces.

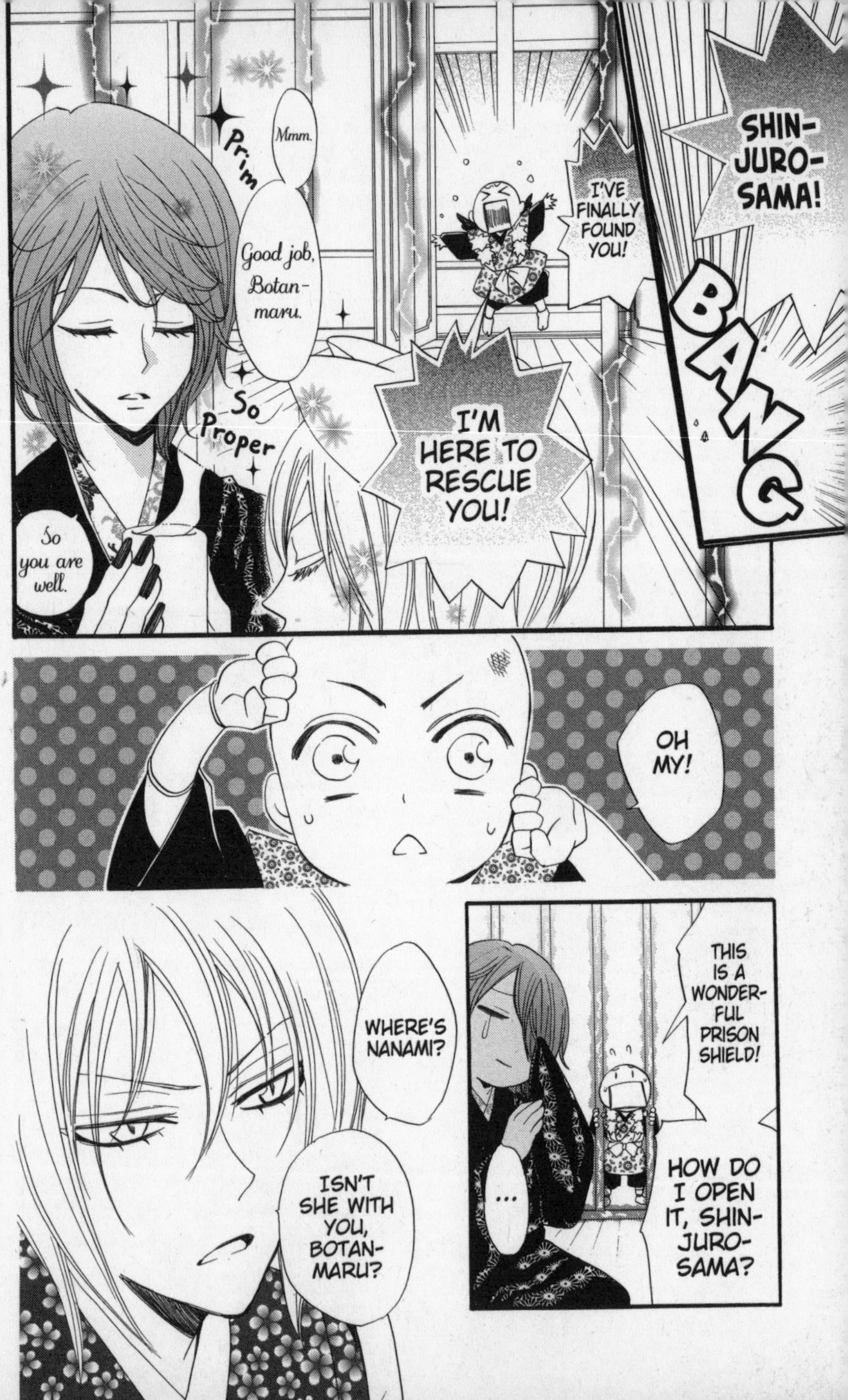
SHIN-JURO-SAMA!
BANG
I'VE FINALLY FOUND YOU!
I'M HERE TO RESCUE YOU!
Mmm.
Prim
Good job, Botan-maru.
So Proper
So you are well.
OH MY!
THIS IS A WONDERFUL PRISON SHIELD!
HOW DO I OPEN IT, SHIN-JURO-SAMA?
...
WHERE'S NANAMI?
ISN'T SHE WITH YOU, BOTAN-MARU?

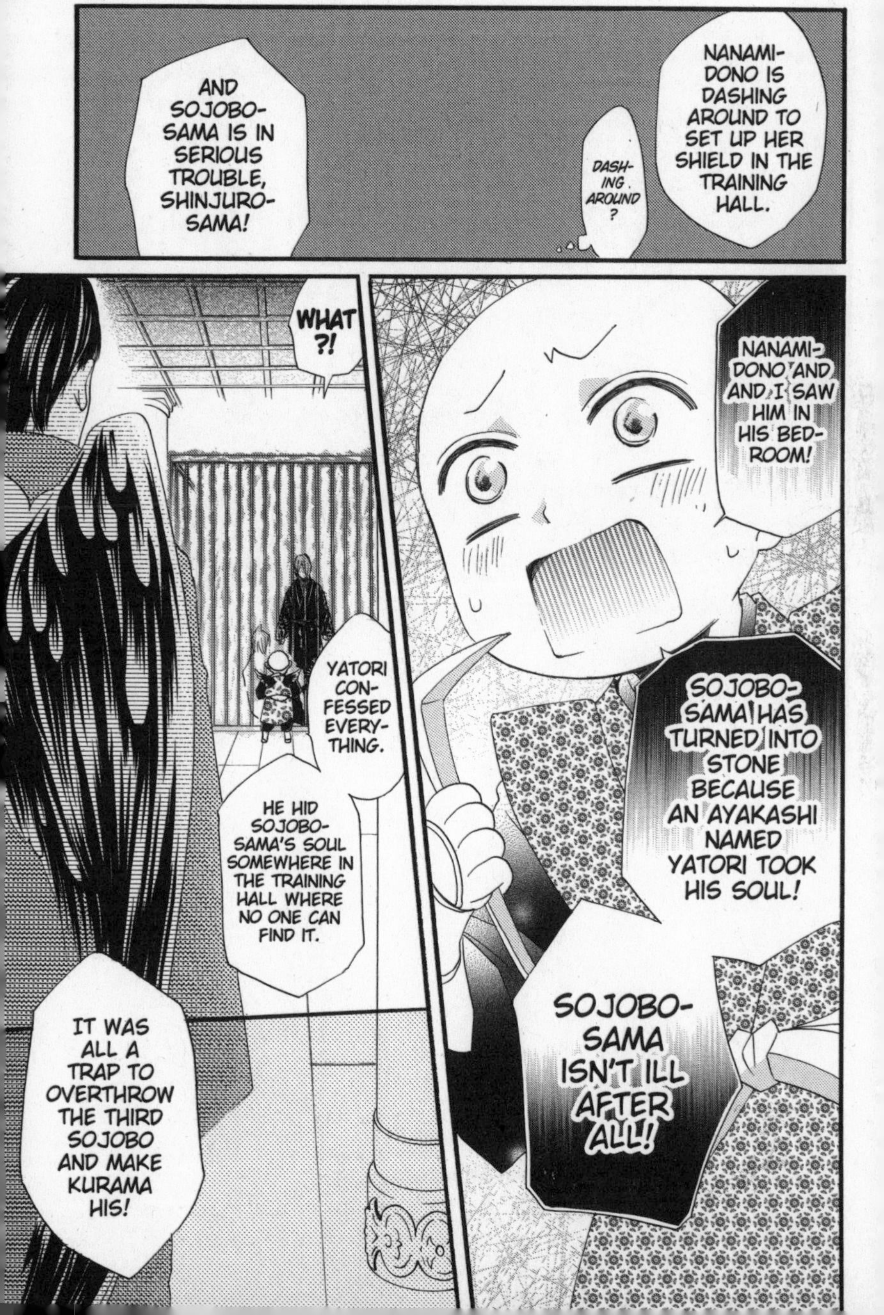
NANAMI-DONO IS DASHING AROUND TO SET UP HER SHIELD IN THE TRAINING HALL.
DASHING AROUND?
AND SOJOBO-SAMA IS IN SERIOUS TROUBLE, SHINJURO-SAMA!
NANAMI-DONO AND AND I SAW HIM IN HIS BEDROOM!
SOJOBO-SAMA HAS TURNED INTO STONE BECAUSE AN AYAKASHI NAMED YATORI TOOK HIS SOUL!
SOJOBO-SAMA ISN'T ILL AFTER ALL!
WHAT?!
YATORI CONFESSED EVERYTHING.
HE HID SOJOBO-SAMA'S SOUL SOMEWHERE IN THE TRAINING HALL WHERE NO ONE CAN FIND IT.
IT WAS ALL A TRAP TO OVERTHROW THE THIRD SOJOBO AND MAKE KURAMA HIS!

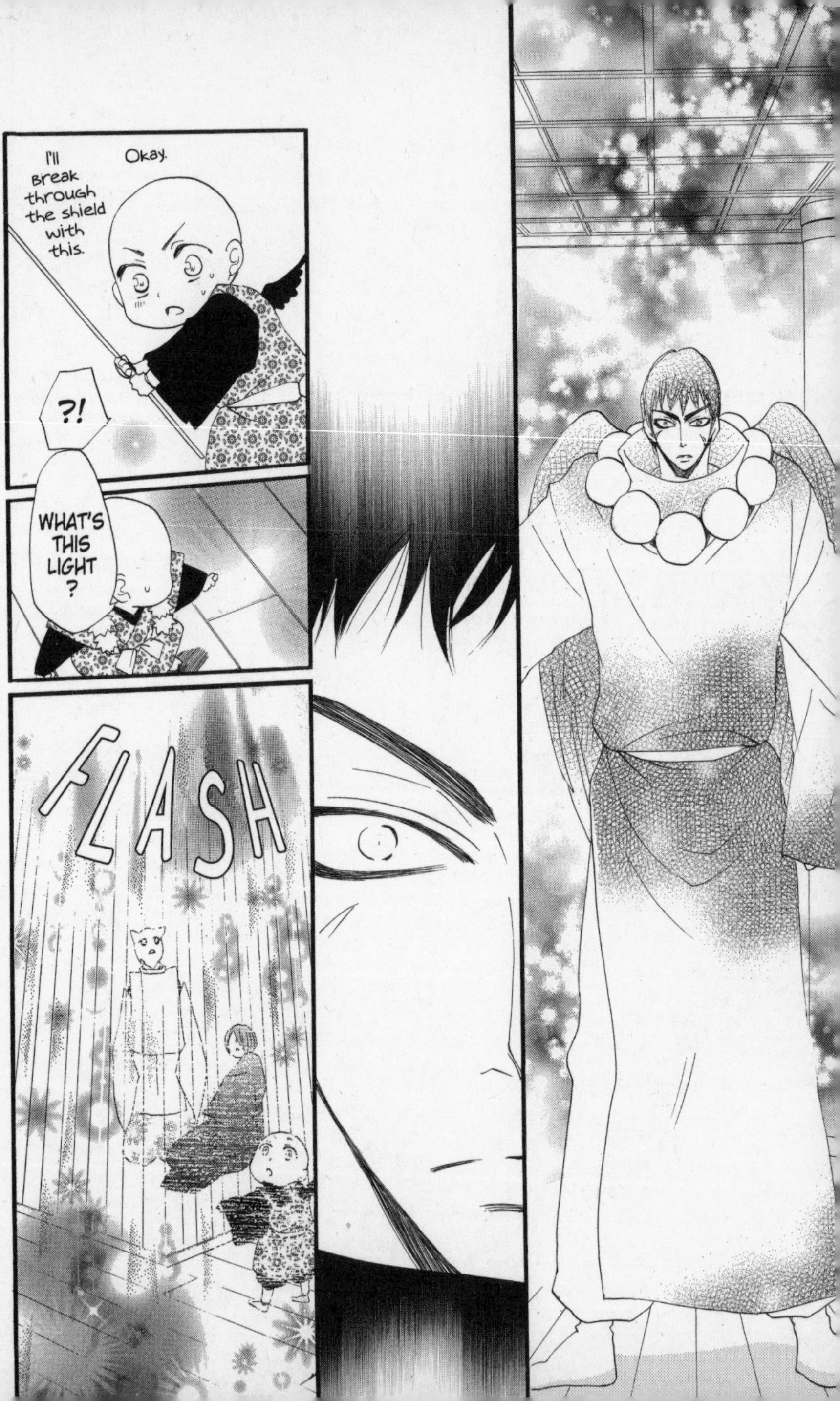
Okay.
I'll break through the shield with this.
?!
WHAT'S THIS LIGHT?
FLASH

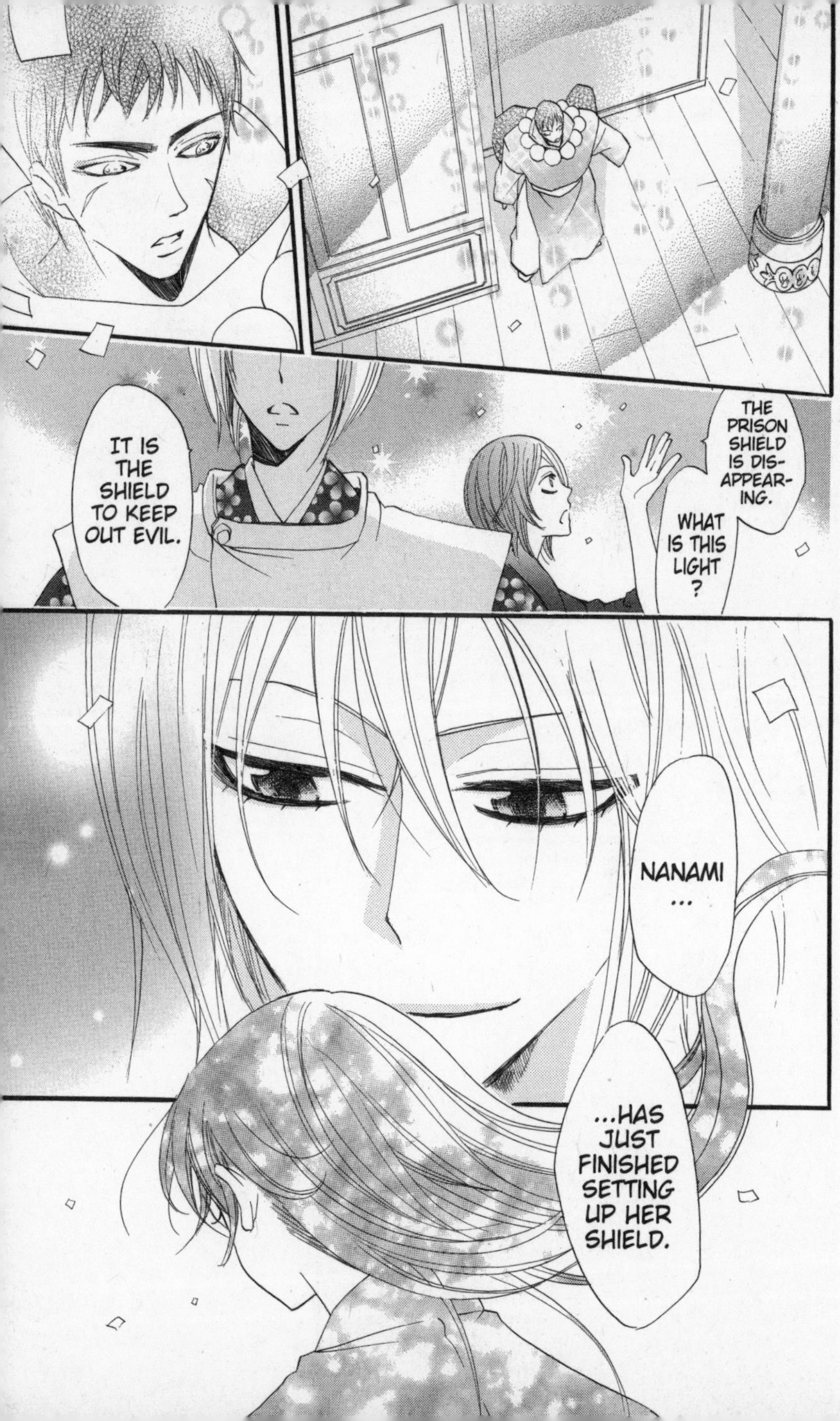
THE PRISON SHIELD IS DIS-APPEAR-ING.
WHAT IS THIS LIGHT ?
IT IS THE SHIELD TO KEEP OUT EVIL.
NANAMI ...
...HAS JUST FINISHED SETTING UP HER SHIELD.

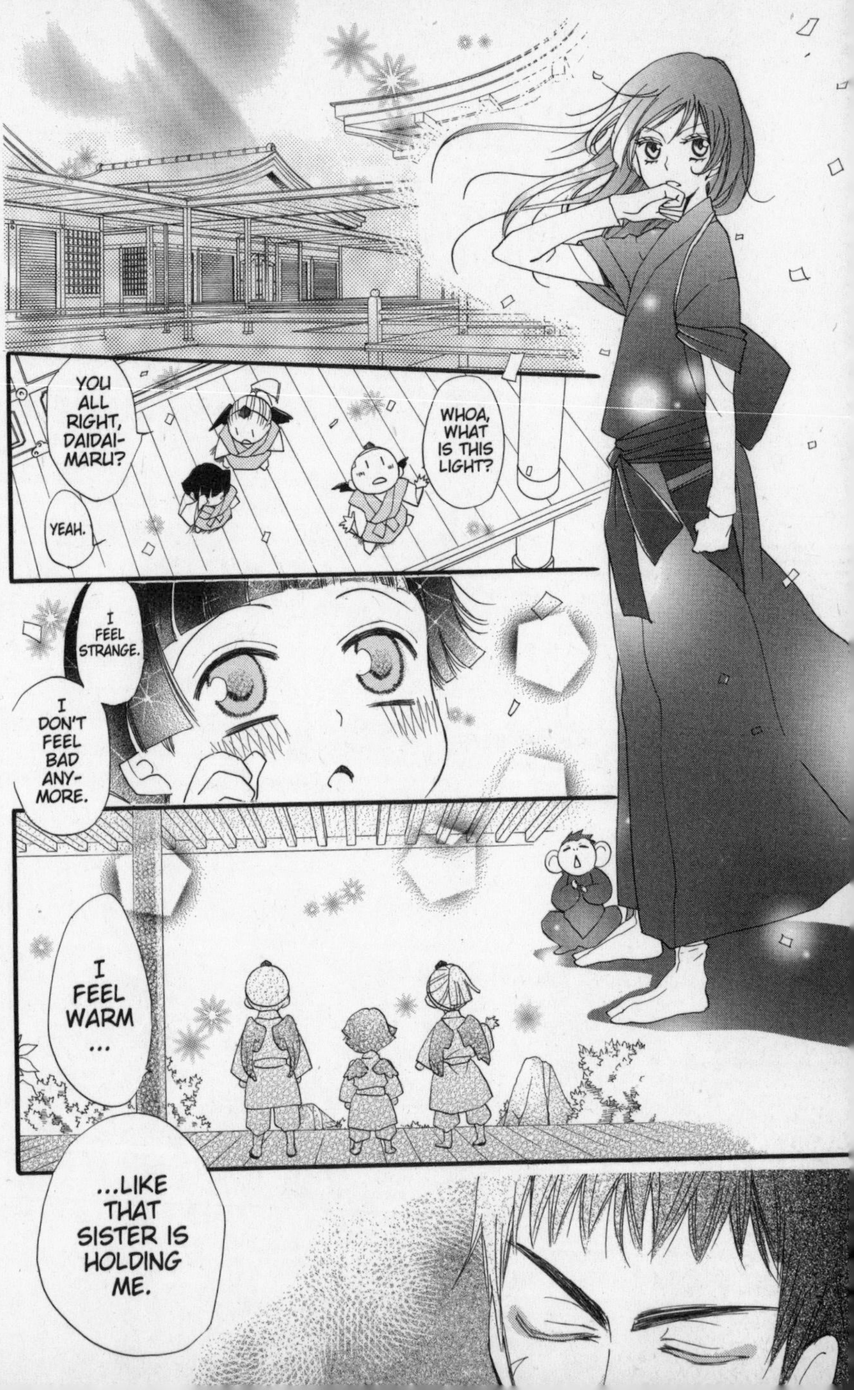
WHOA, WHAT IS THIS LIGHT?
YOU ALL RIGHT, DAIDAI-MARU?
YEAH.
I FEEL STRANGE.
I DON'T FEEL BAD ANY-MORE.
I FEEL WARM ...
...LIKE THAT SISTER IS HOLDING ME.

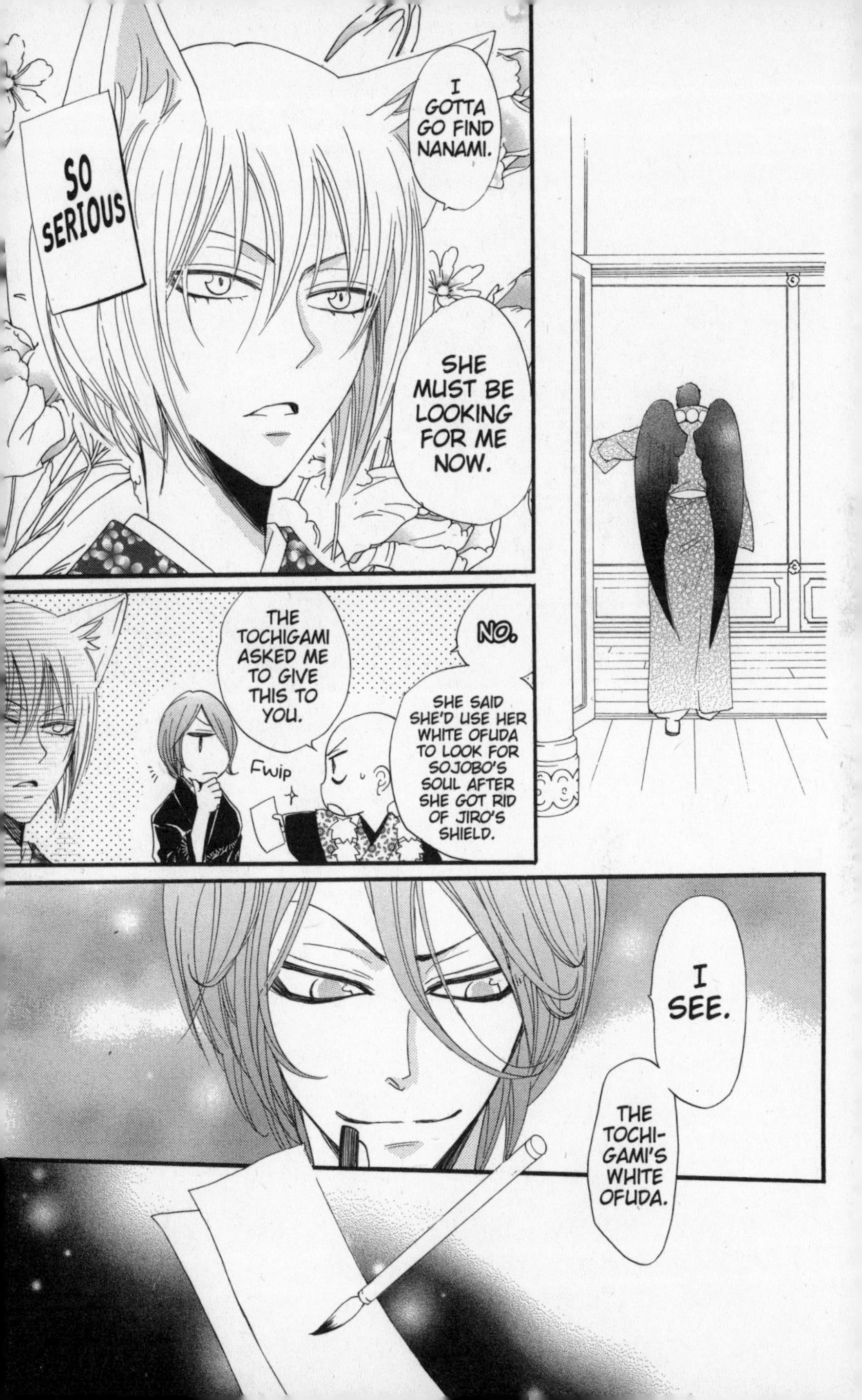
I GOTTA GO FIND NANAMI.
SO SERIOUS
SHE MUST BE LOOKING FOR ME NOW.
NO.
SHE SAID SHE'D USE HER WHITE OFUDA TO LOOK FOR SOJOBO'S SOUL AFTER SHE GOT RID OF JIRO'S SHIELD.
THE TOCHIGAMI ASKED ME TO GIVE THIS TO YOU.
Fwip
I SEE.
THE TOCHI-GAMI'S WHITE OFUDA.

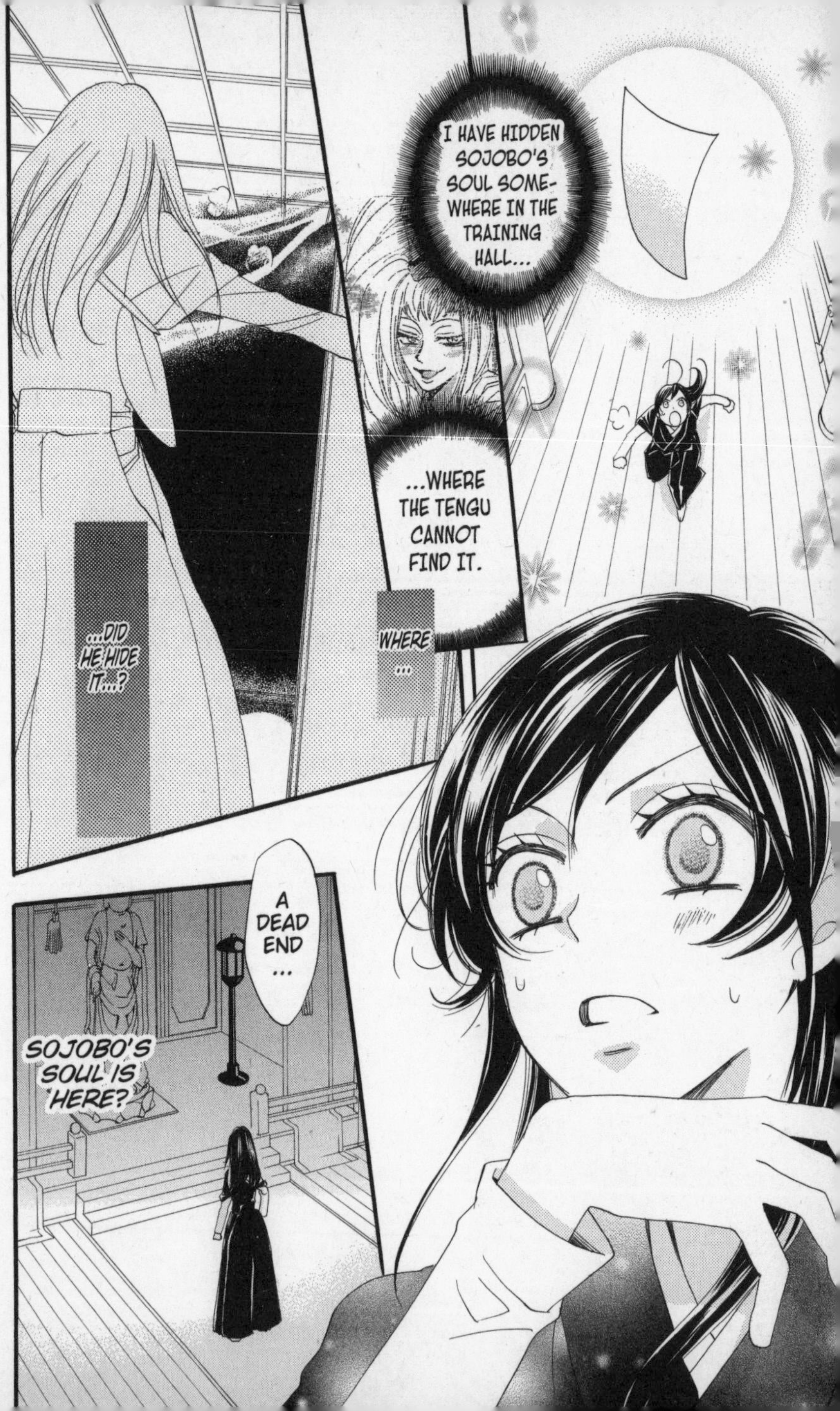
I HAVE HIDDEN SOJOBO'S SOUL SOME-WHERE IN THE TRAINING HALL...
...WHERE THE TENGU CANNOT FIND IT.
WHERE ...
...DID HE HIDE IT...?
A DEAD END ...
SOJOBO'S SOUL IS HERE?

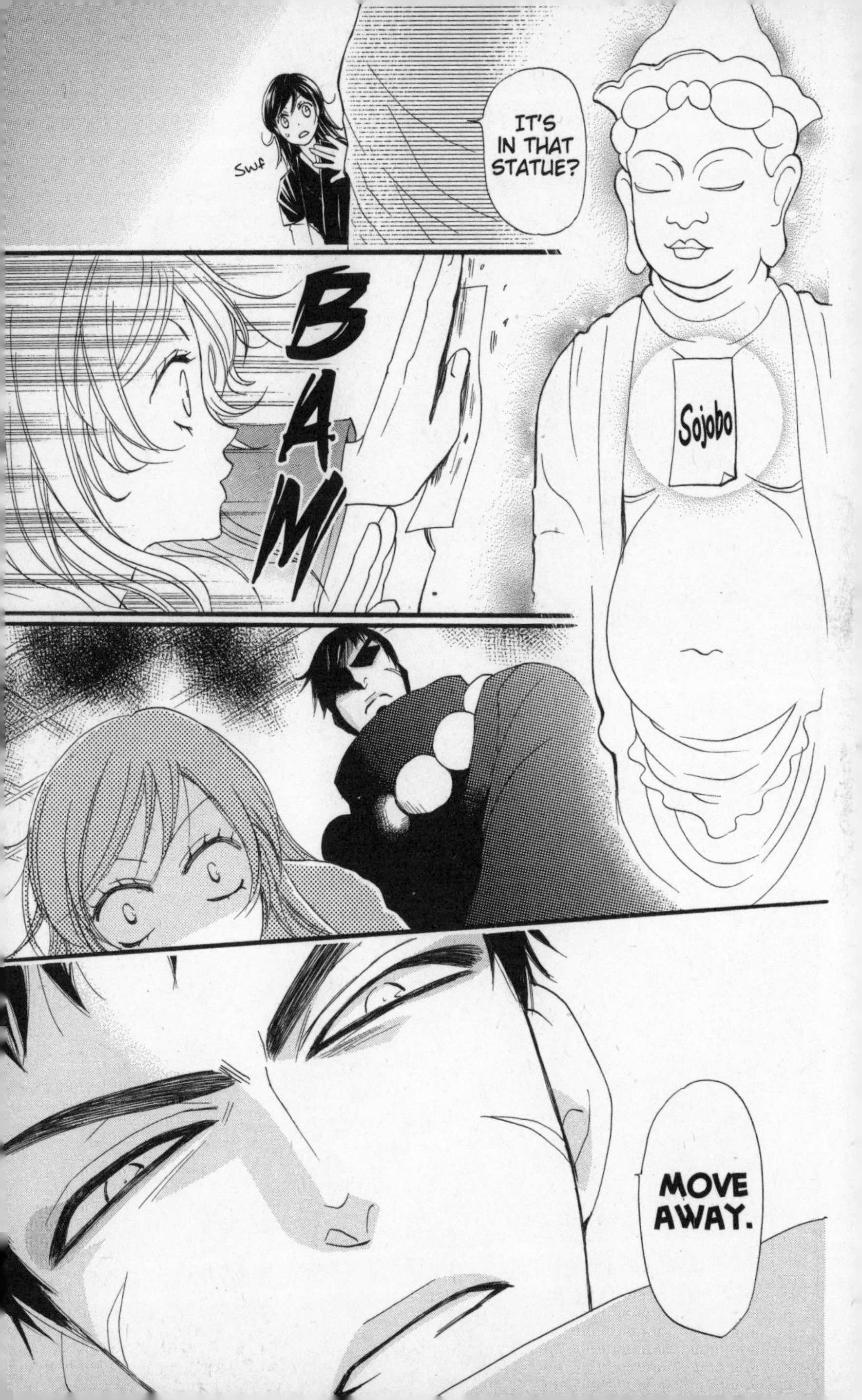
Sojobo
IT'S IN THAT STATUE?
Swf
BAM
MOVE AWAY.

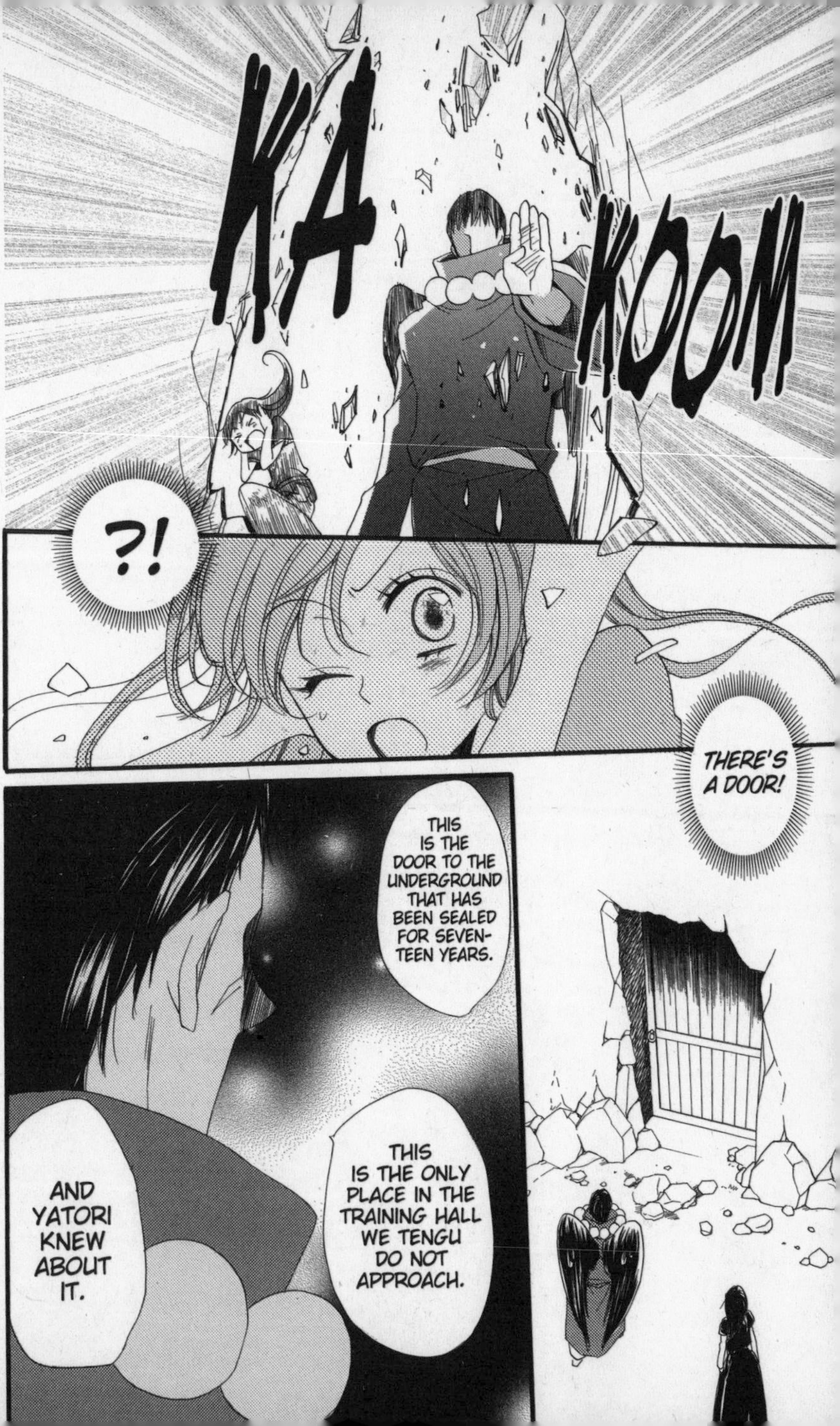
KA
KOOM
?!
THERE'S A DOOR!
THIS IS THE DOOR TO THE UNDERGROUND THAT HAS BEEN SEALED FOR SEVEN-TEEN YEARS.
THIS IS THE ONLY PLACE IN THE TRAINING HALL WE TENGU DO NOT APPROACH.
AND YATORI KNEW ABOUT IT.

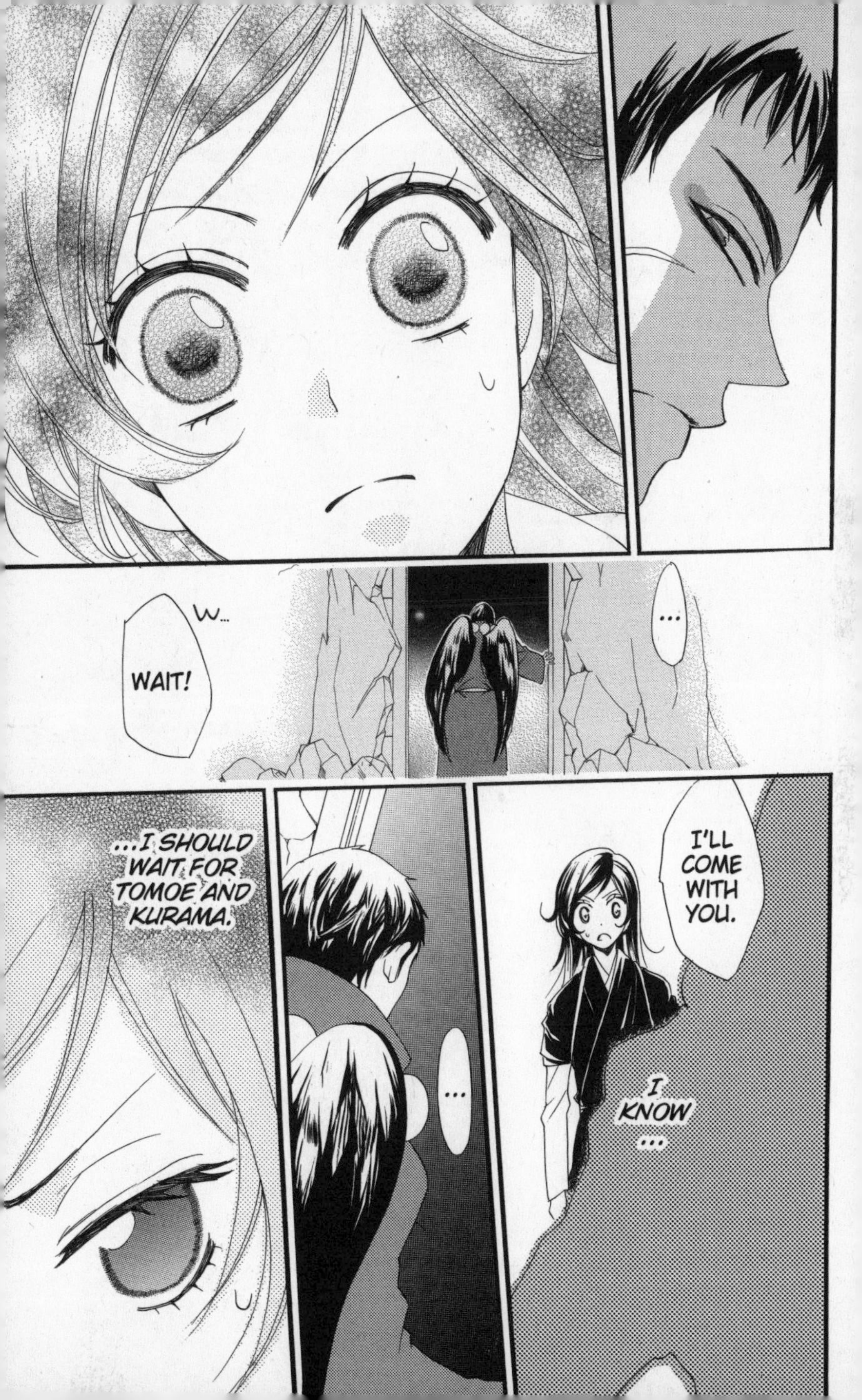
...
W...
WAIT!
I'LL COME WITH YOU.
I KNOW...
...
...I SHOULD WAIT FOR TOMOE AND KURAMA.

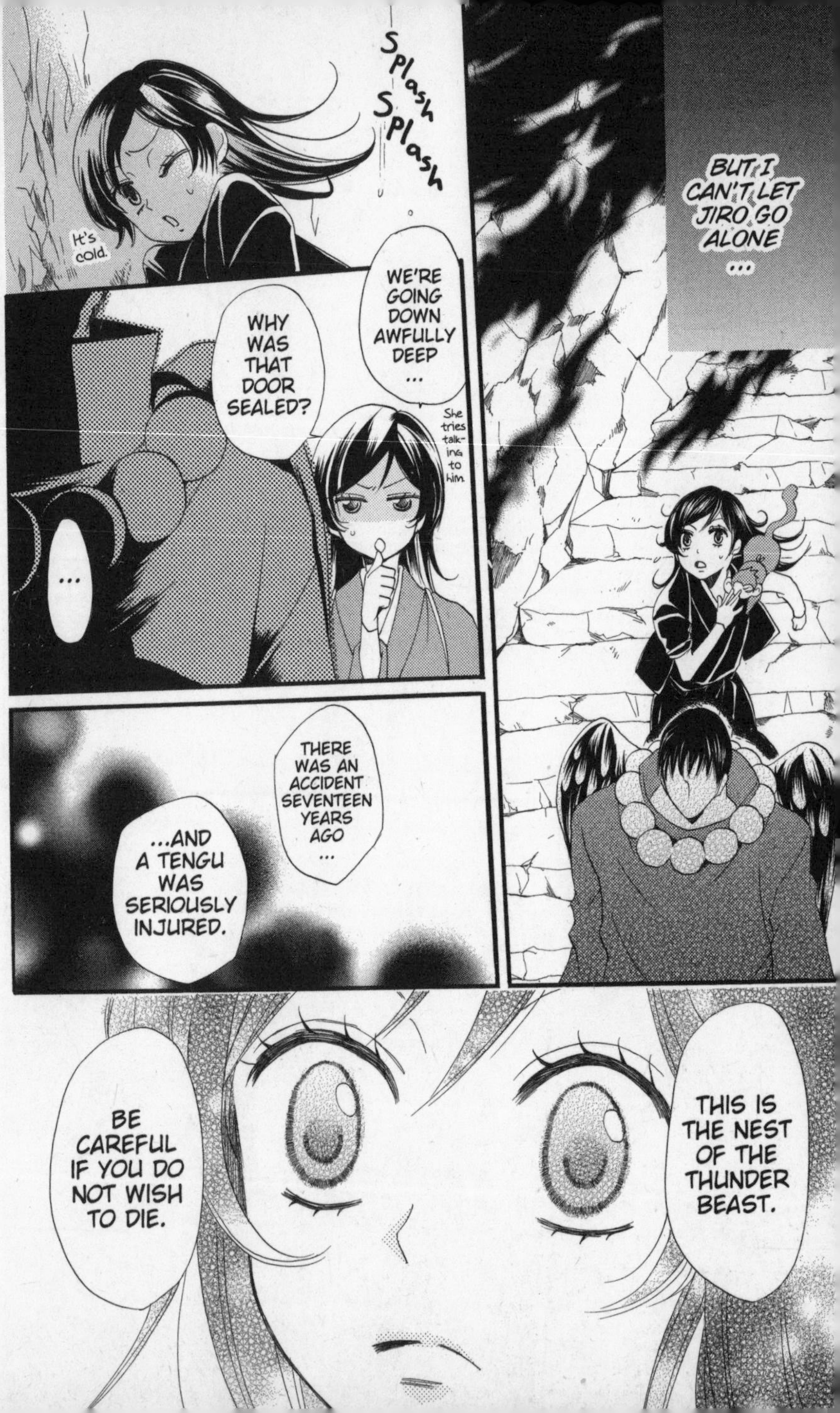

BUT I CAN'T LET JIRO GO ALONE ...
Splash Splash
It's cold.
WE'RE GOING DOWN AWFULLY DEEP ...
She tries talking to him.
WHY WAS THAT DOOR SEALED?
...
THERE WAS AN ACCIDENT SEVENTEEN YEARS AGO ...
...AND A TENGU WAS SERIOUSLY INJURED.
THIS IS THE NEST OF THE THUNDER BEAST.
BE CAREFUL IF YOU DO NOT WISH TO DIE.

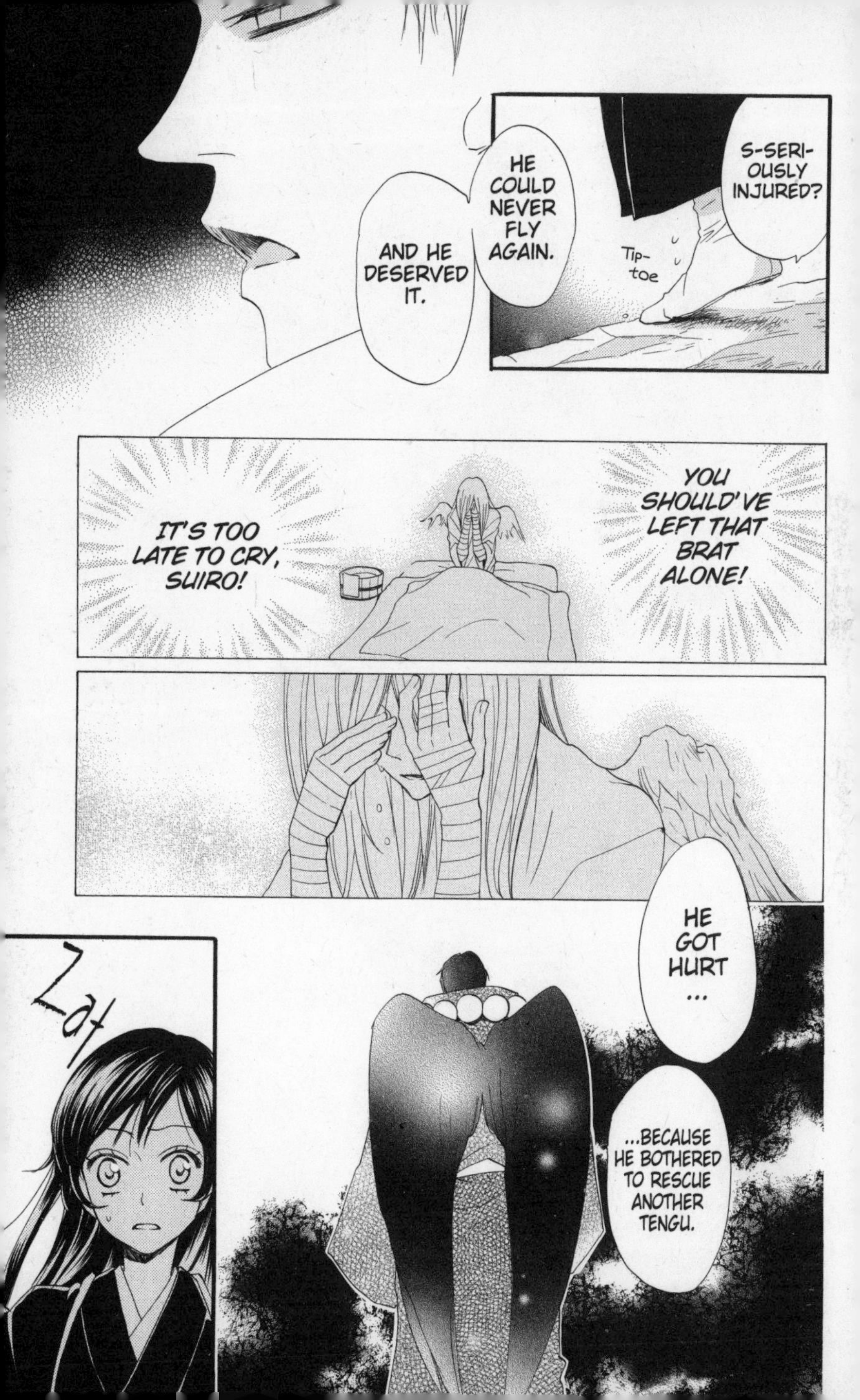
S-SERIOUSLY INJURED?
Tip-toe
HE COULD NEVER FLY AGAIN.
AND HE DESERVED IT.
YOU SHOULD'VE LEFT THAT BRAT ALONE!
IT'S TOO LATE TO CRY, SUIRO!
HE GOT HURT...
...BECAUSE HE BOTHERED TO RESCUE ANOTHER TENGU.
Zat

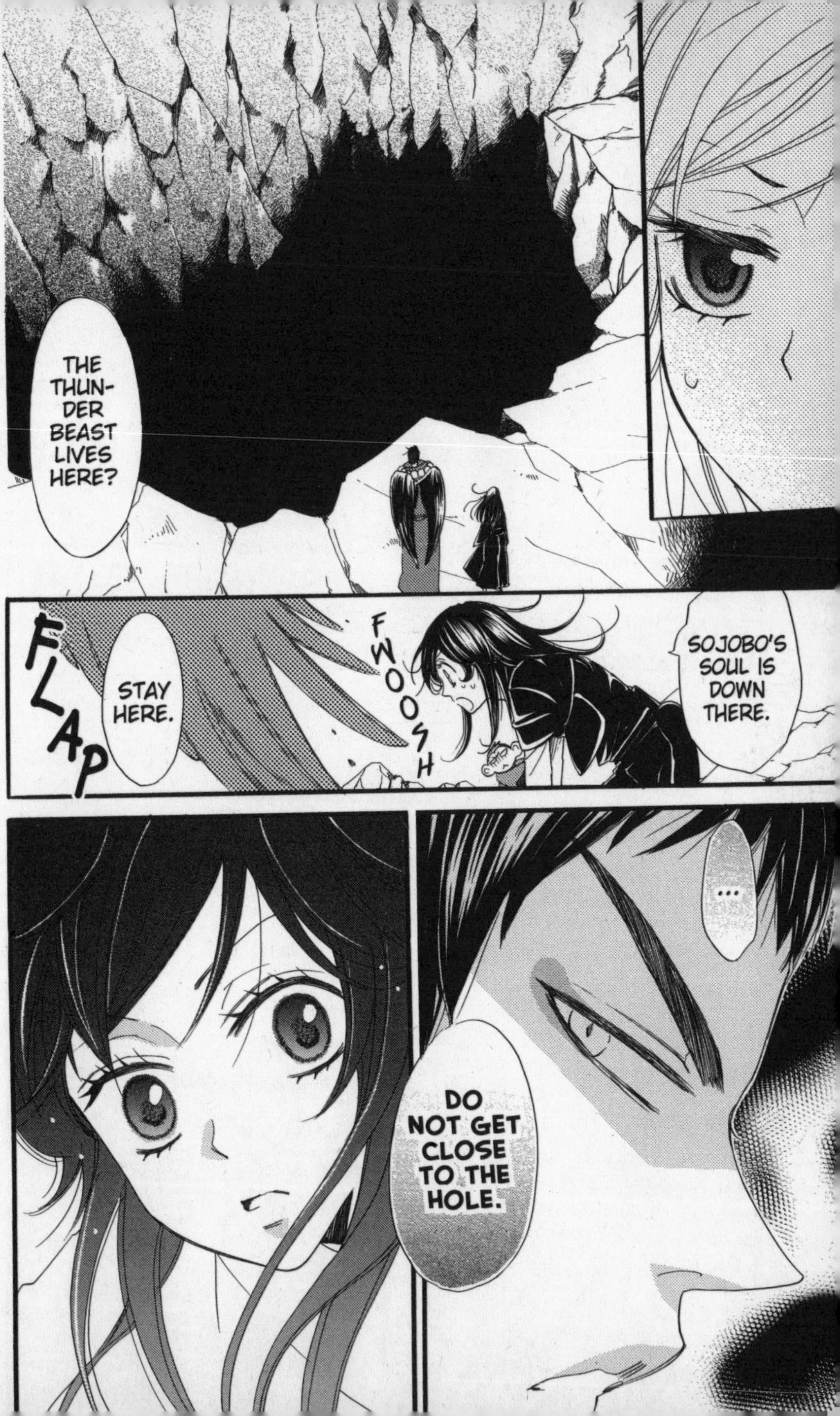
THE THUNDER-DER BEAST LIVES HERE?
SOJOBO'S SOUL IS DOWN THERE.
FWOOSH
STAY HERE.
FLAP
...
DO NOT GET CLOSE TO THE HOLE.

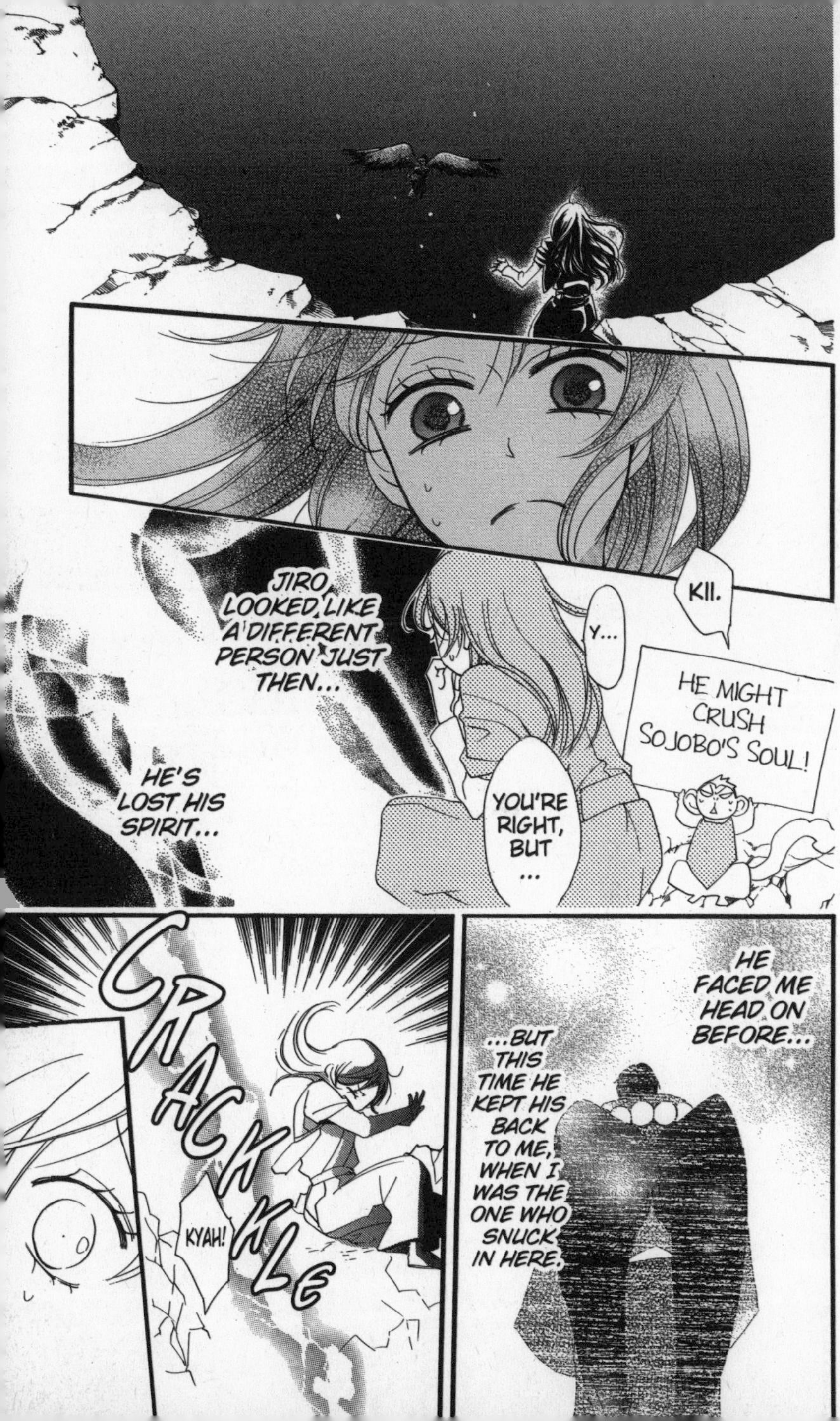
KII.
Y...
HE MIGHT CRUSH SOJOBO'S SOUL!
JIRO LOOKED LIKE A DIFFERENT PERSON JUST THEN...
YOU'RE RIGHT, BUT ...
HE'S LOST HIS SPIRIT...
HE FACED ME HEAD ON BEFORE...
...BUT THIS TIME HE KEPT HIS BACK TO ME, WHEN I WAS THE ONE WHO SNUCK IN HERE.
CRACKLE
KYAH!

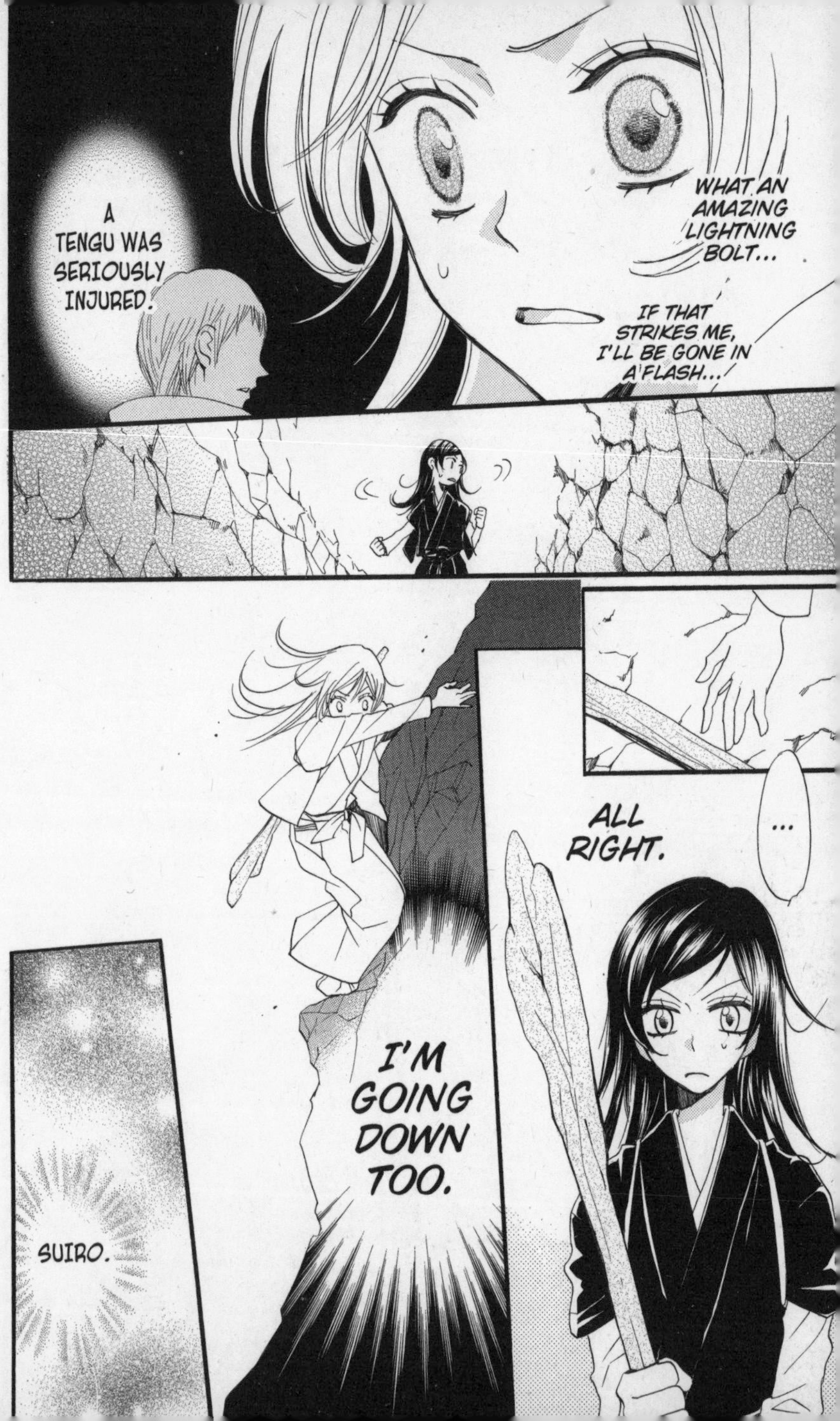
WHAT AN AMAZING LIGHTNING BOLT...
IF THAT STRIKES ME, I'LL BE GONE IN A FLASH...
A TENGU WAS SERIOUSLY INJURED.
...
ALL RIGHT.
I'M GOING DOWN TOO.
SUIRO.

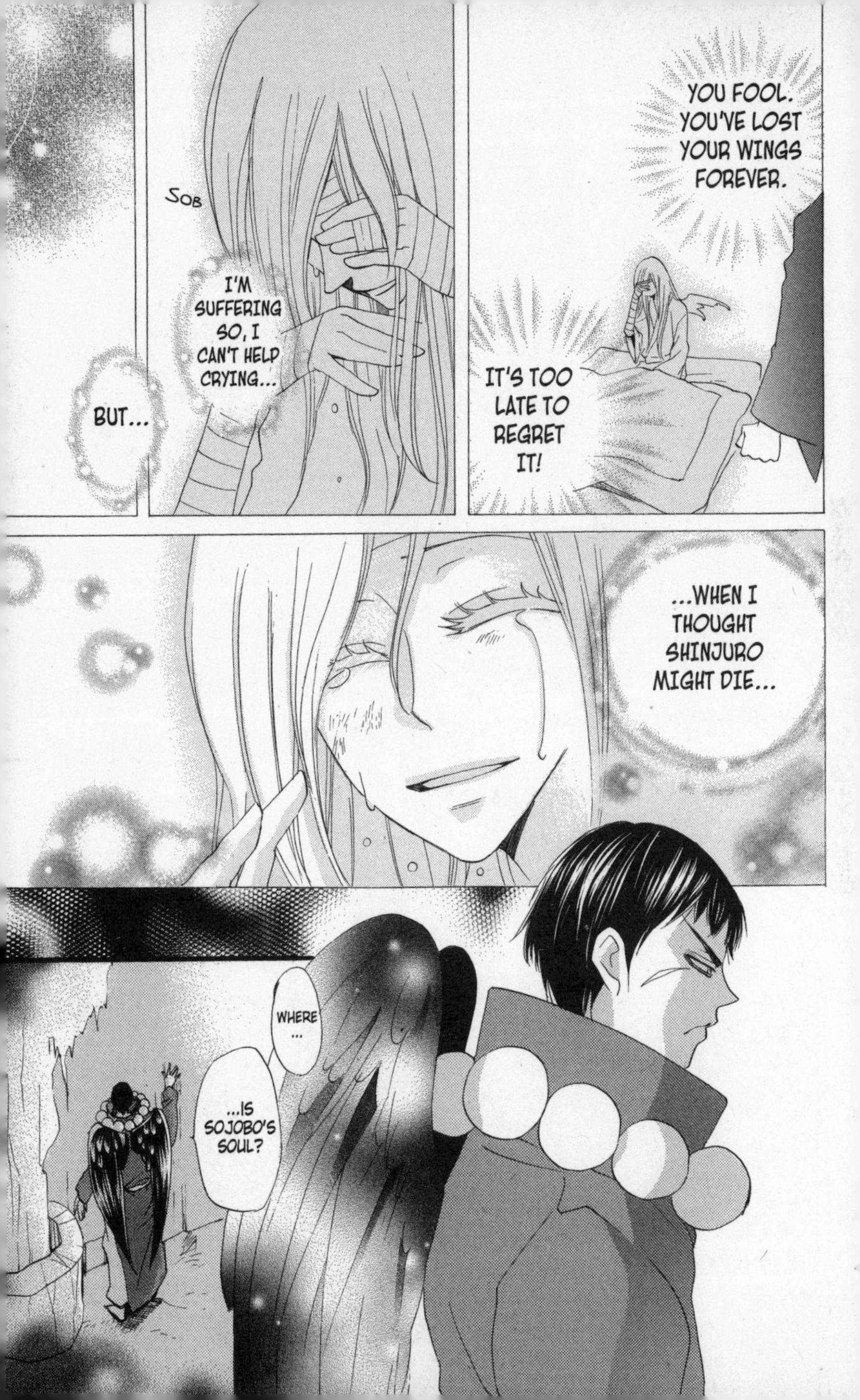
YOU FOOL. YOU'VE LOST YOUR WINGS FOREVER.
IT'S TOO LATE TO REGRET IT!
SOB
I'M SUFFERING SO, I CAN'T HELP CRYING...
BUT...
...WHEN I THOUGHT SHINJURO MIGHT DIE...
WHERE ...
...IS SOJOBO'S SOUL?

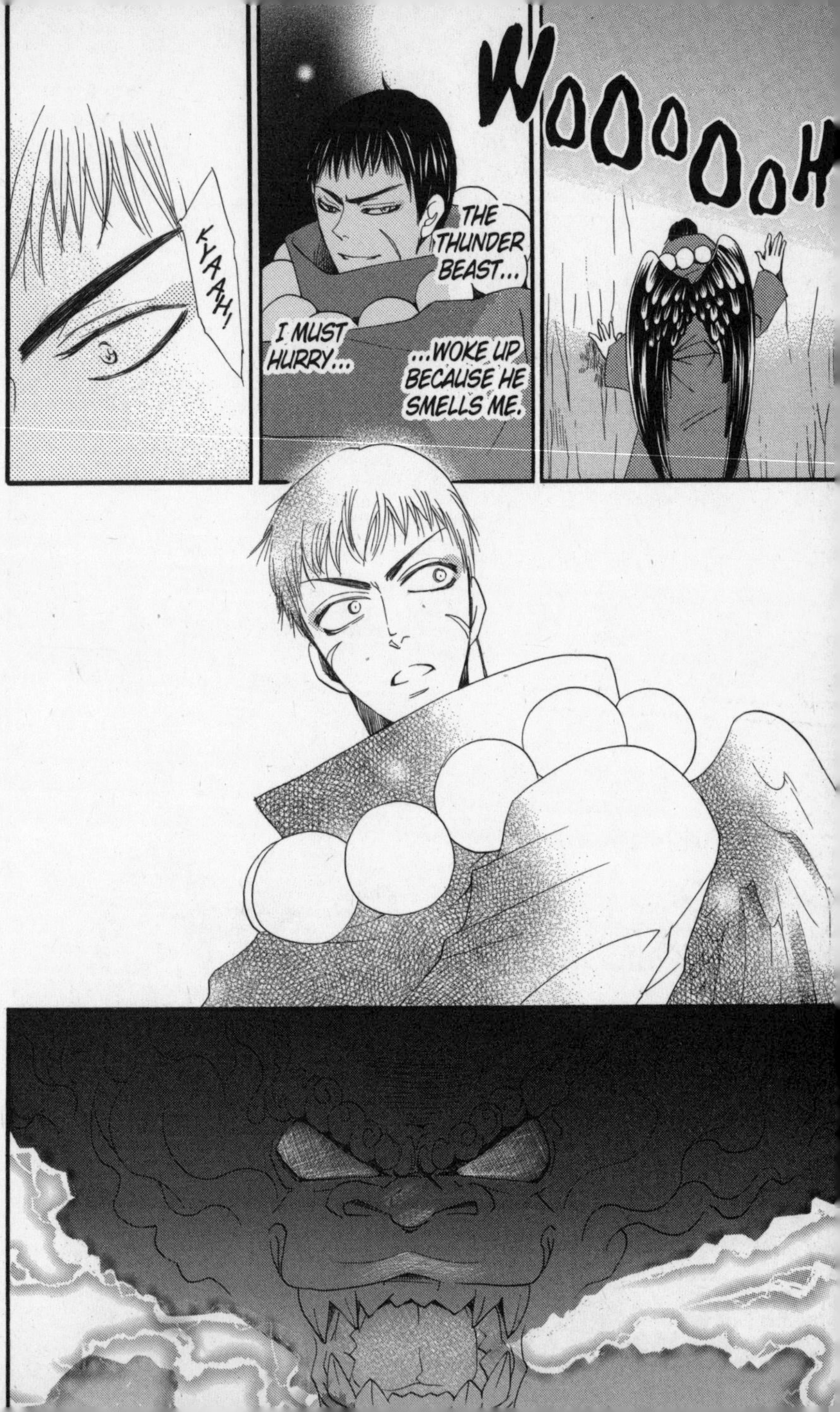
WOOOOOH
THE THUNDER BEAST...
...WOKE UP BECAUSE HE SMELLS ME.
I MUST HURRY...
KYAAH!

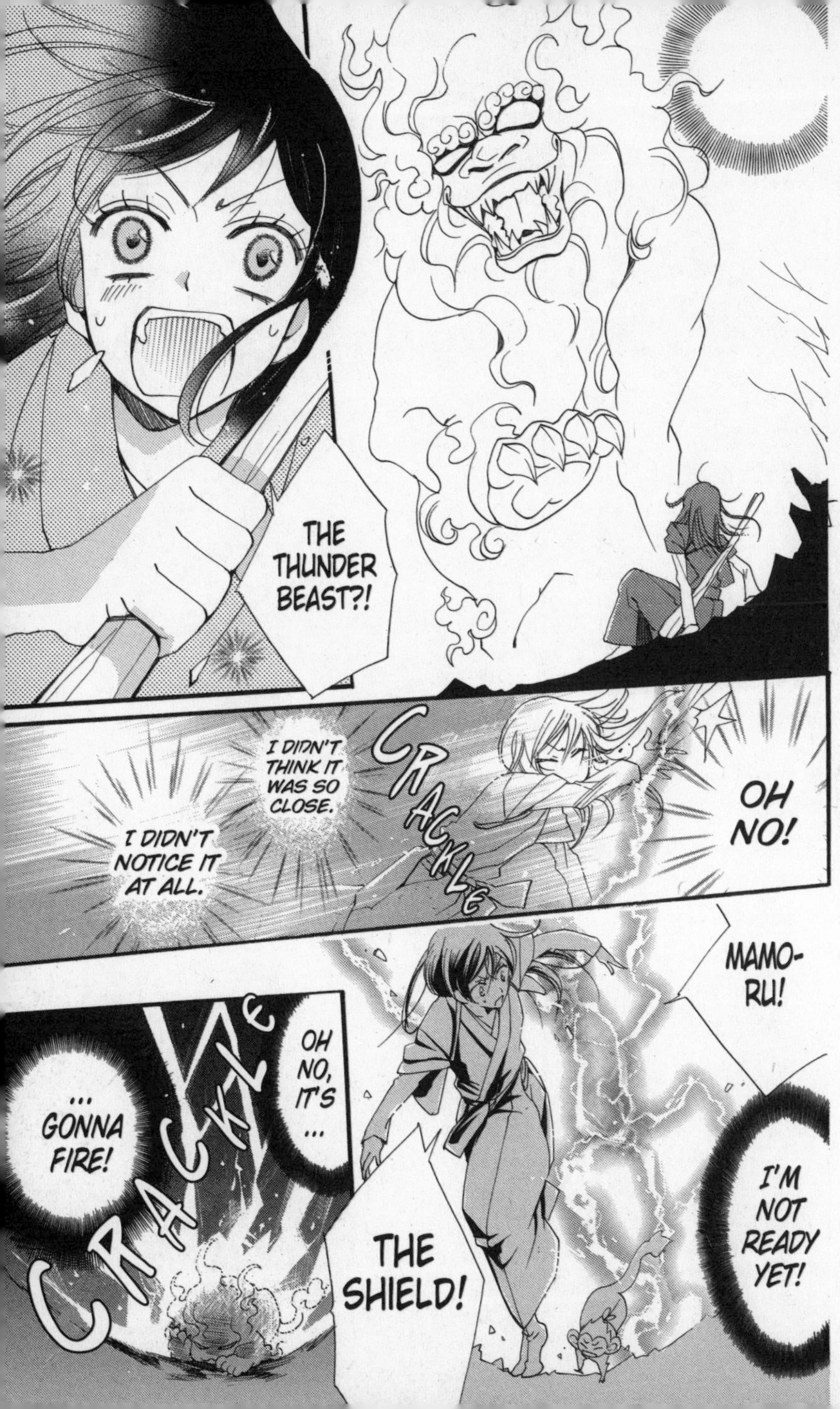
THE THUNDER BEAST?!
OH NO!
CRACKLE
I DIDN'T THINK IT WAS SO CLOSE.
I DIDN'T NOTICE IT AT ALL.
MAMO-RU!
I'M NOT READY YET!
THE SHIELD!
OH NO, IT'S ...
... GONNA FIRE!
CRACKLE

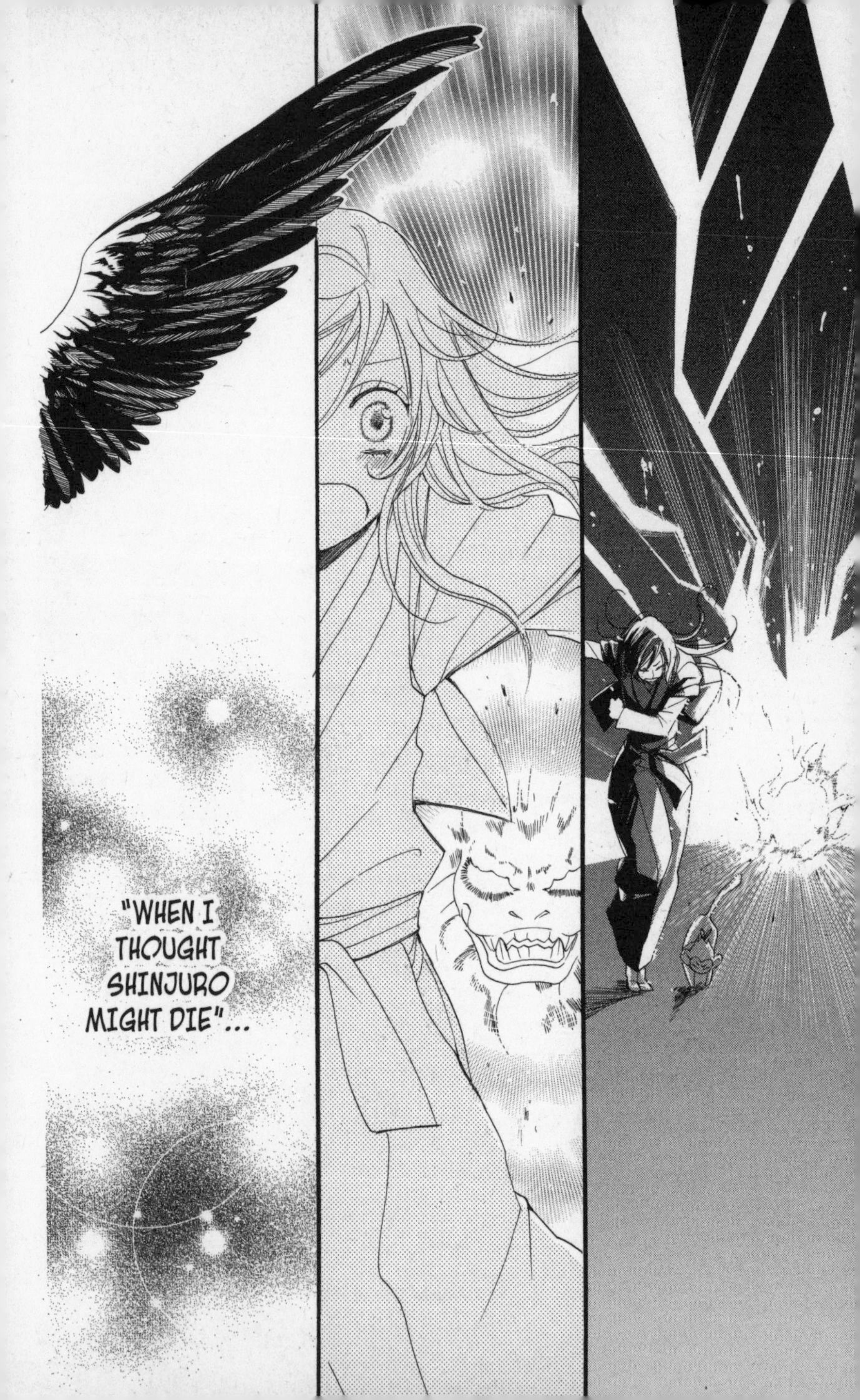
"WHEN I THOUGHT SHINJURO MIGHT DIE"...

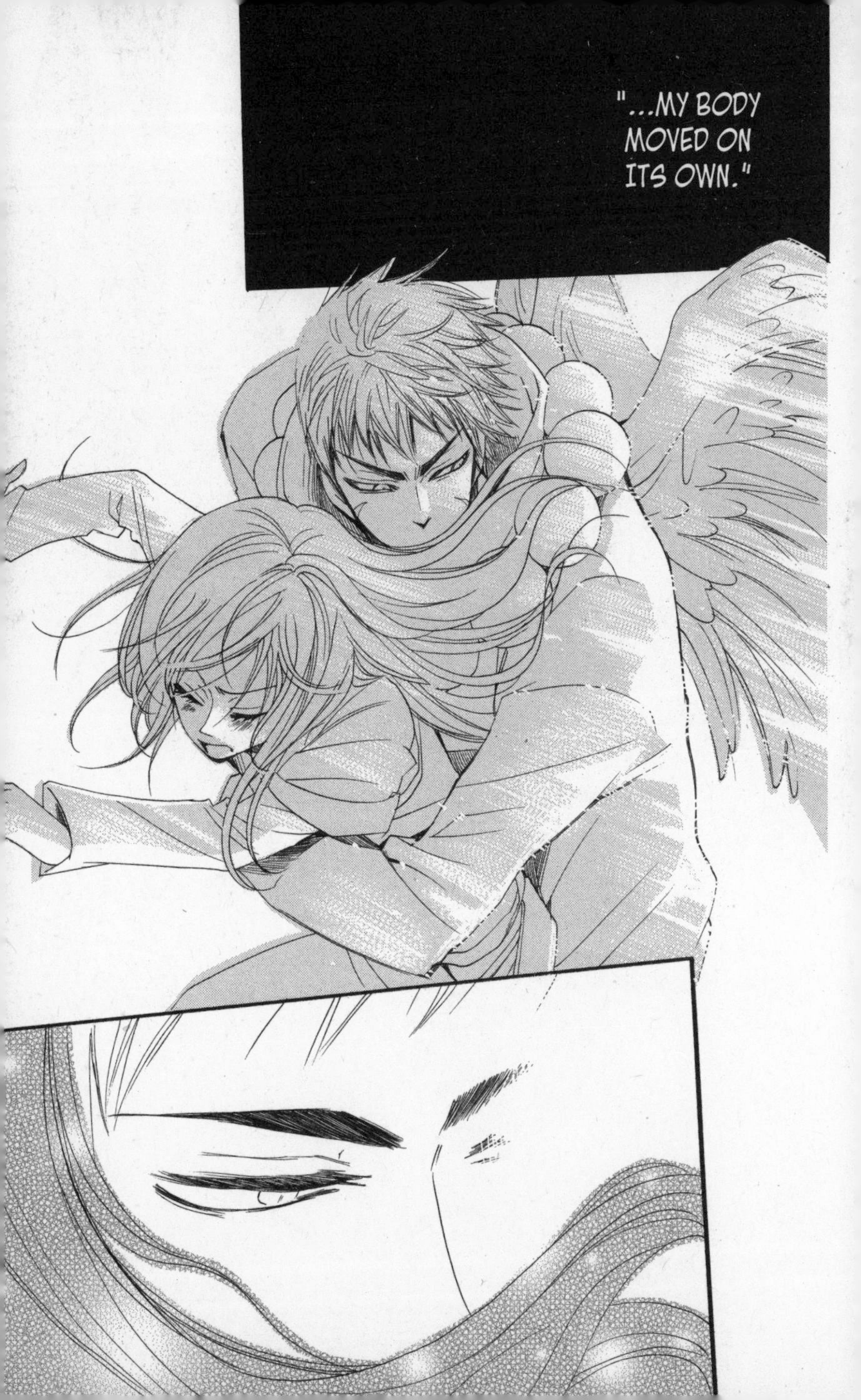
"...MY BODY MOVED ON ITS OWN."

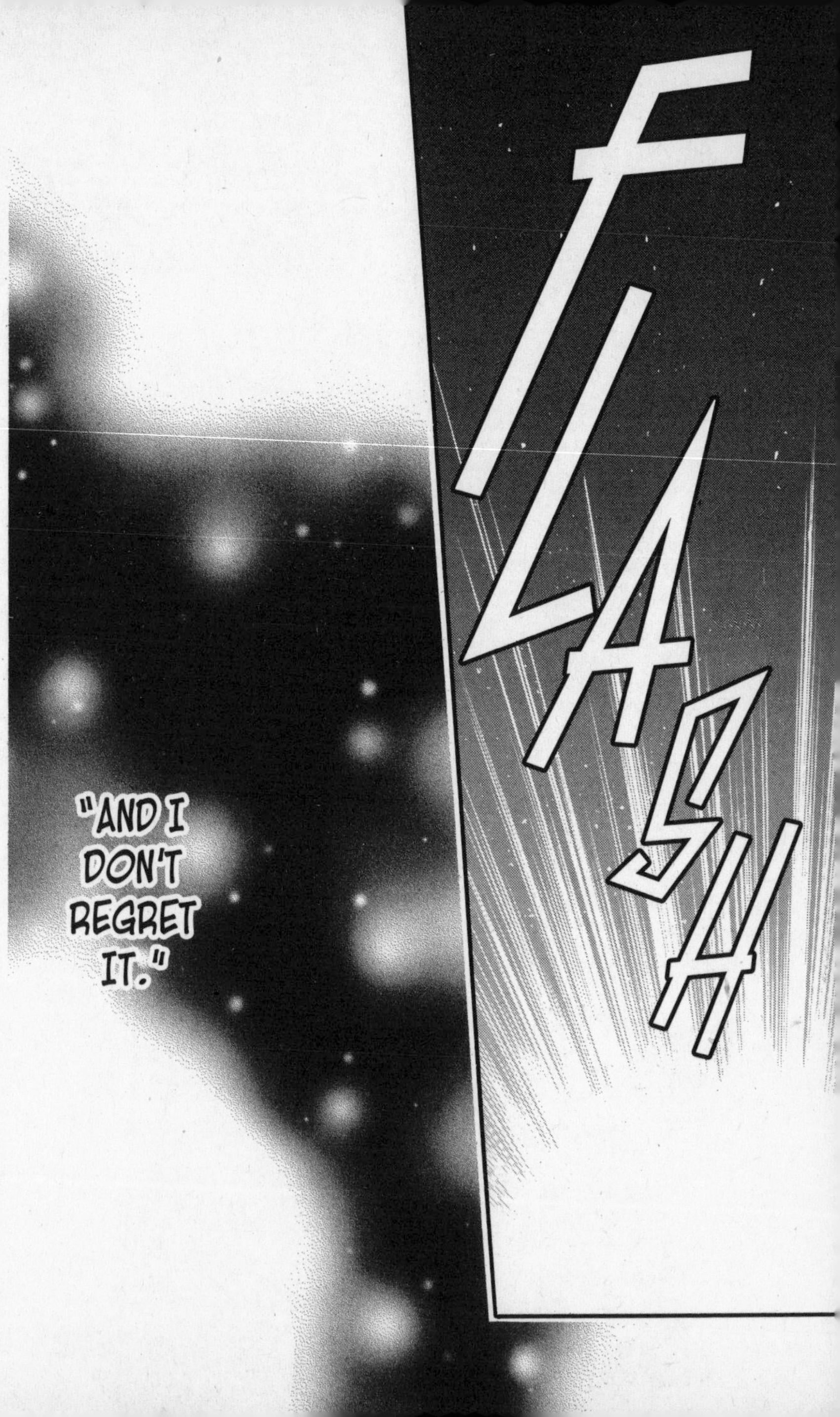
FLASH
"AND I DON'T REGRET IT."

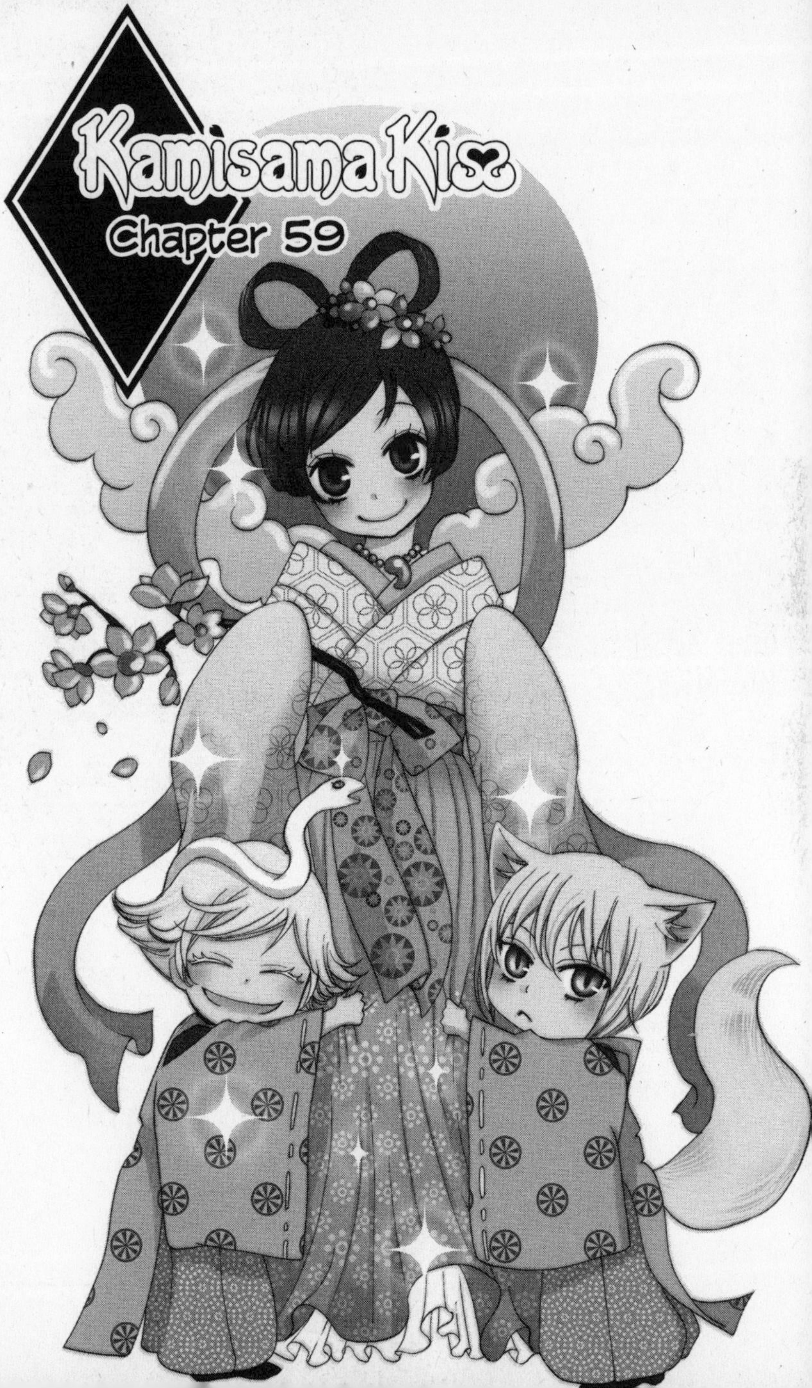
Kamisama Kiss
Chapter 59

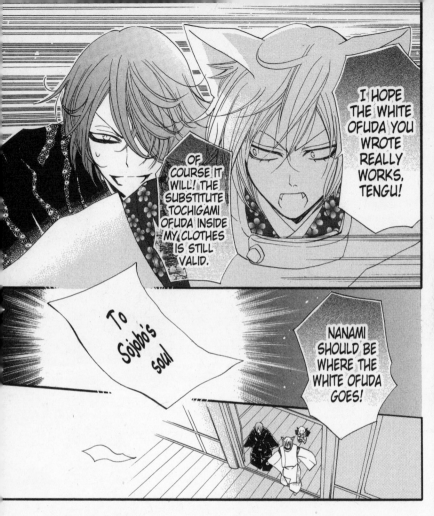

I HOPE THE WHITE OFUDA YOU WROTE REALLY WORKS, TENGU!
OF COURSE IT WILL! THE SUBSTITUTE TOCHIGAMI OFUDA INSIDE MY CLOTHES IS STILL VALID.
NANAMI SHOULD BE WHERE THE WHITE OFUDA GOES!
To Sojobo's soul

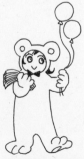

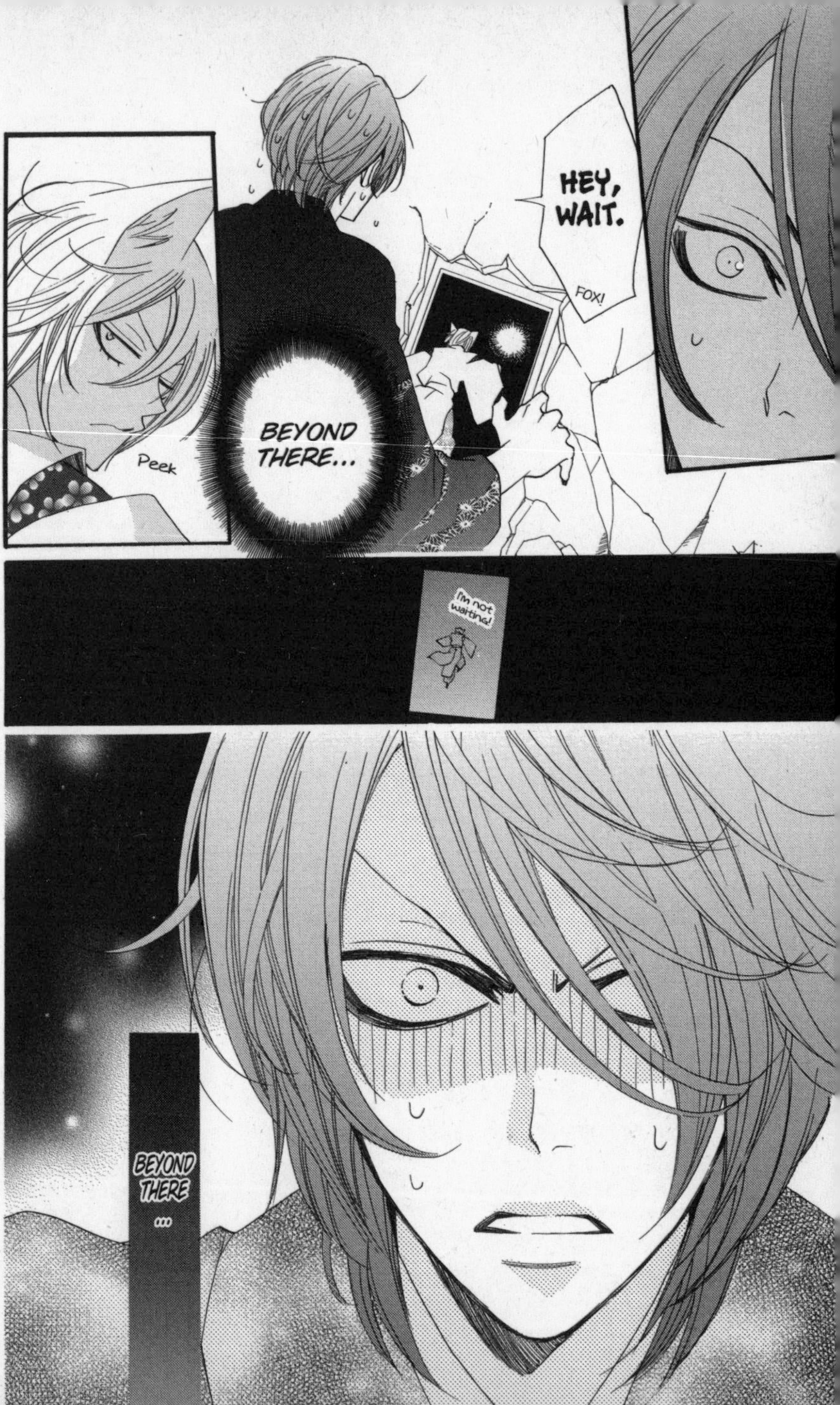
HEY, WAIT.
FOX!
BEYOND THERE...
Peek
I'm not waiting!
BEYOND THERE...

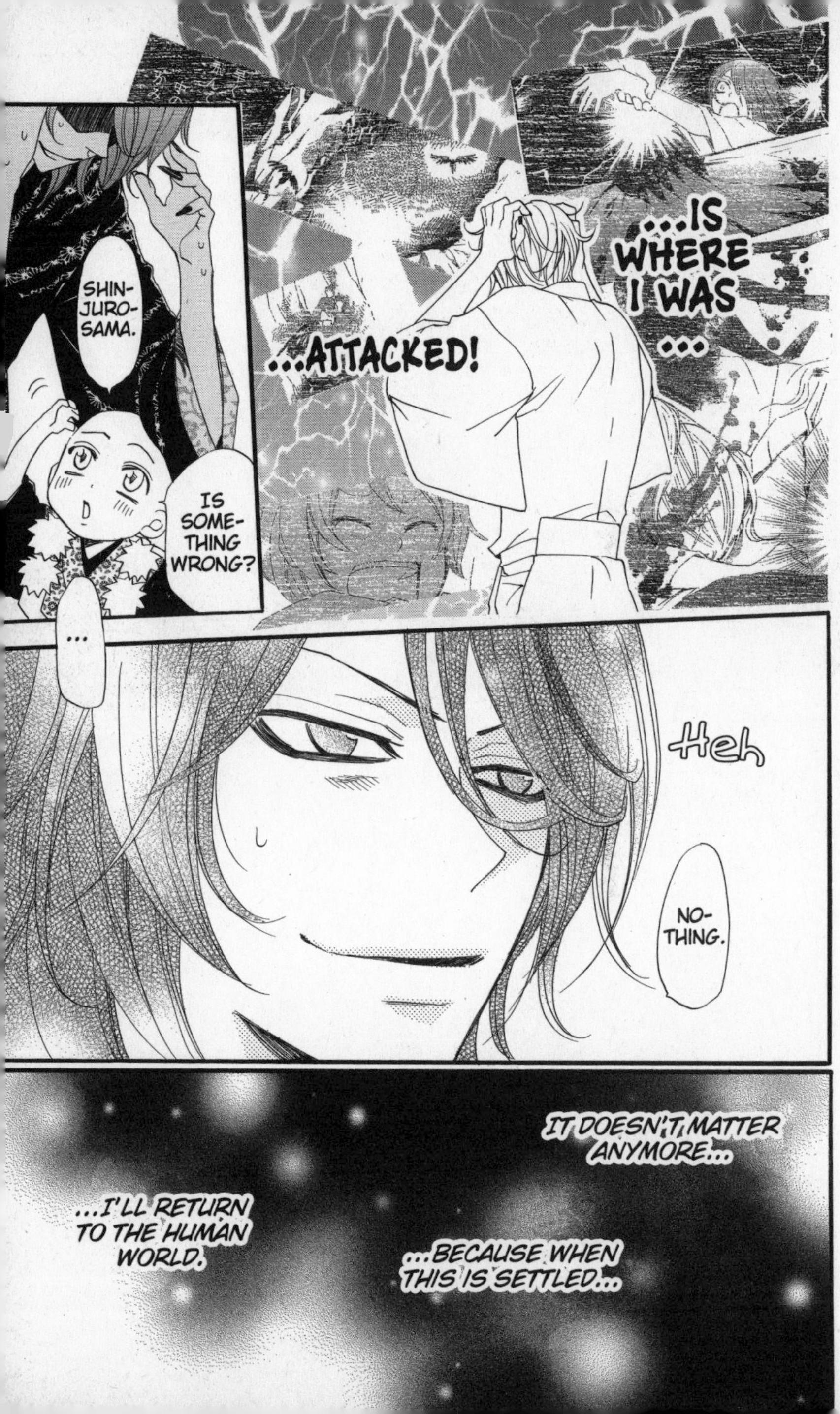
...IS WHERE I WAS...
...ATTACKED!
SHIN-JURO-SAMA.
IS SOMETHING WRONG?
...
Heh
NO-THING.
IT DOESN'T MATTER ANYMORE...
...BECAUSE WHEN THIS IS SETTLED...
...I'LL RETURN TO THE HUMAN WORLD.

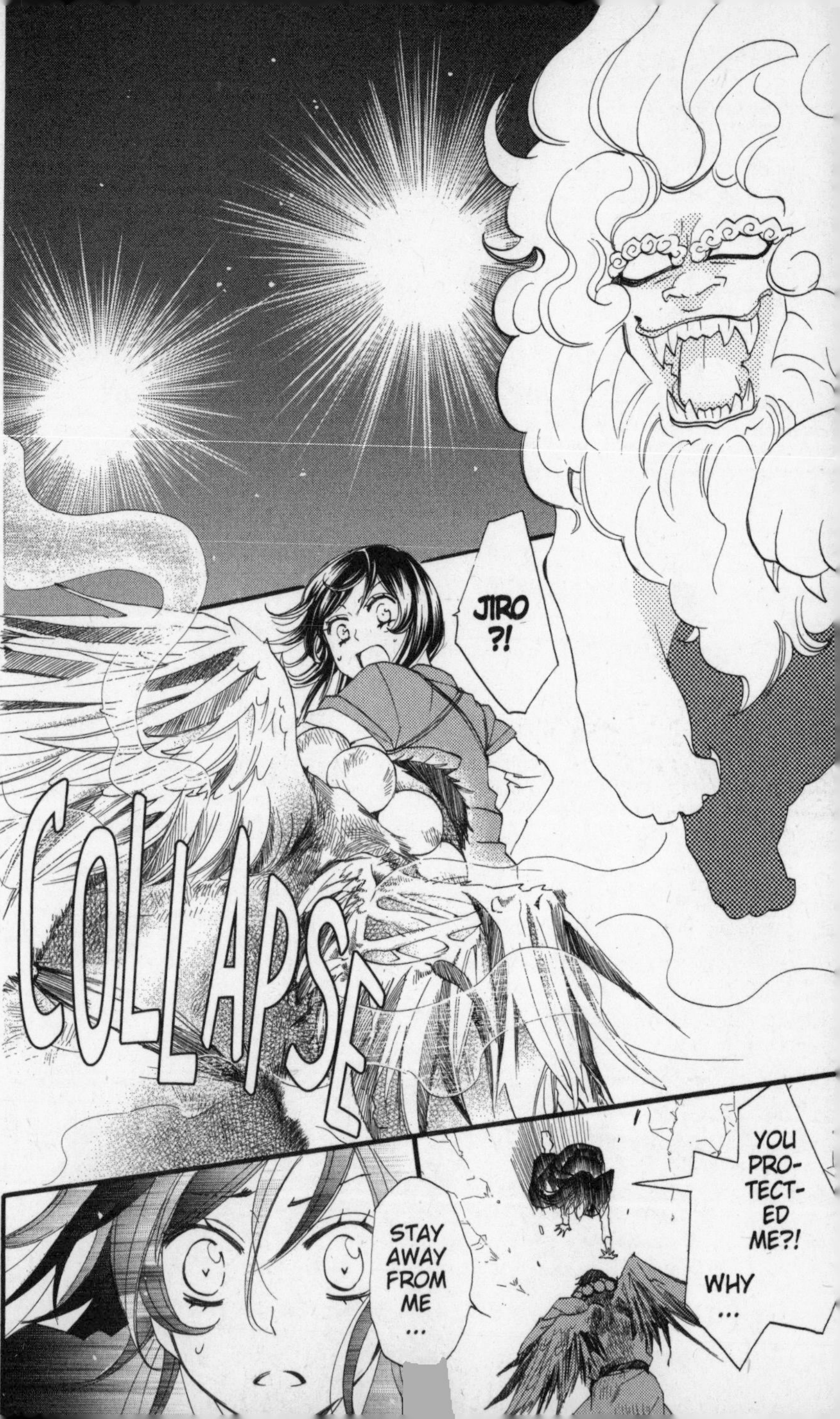
JIRO ?!
COLLAPSE
YOU PROTECTED ME?!
WHY ...
STAY AWAY FROM ME ...

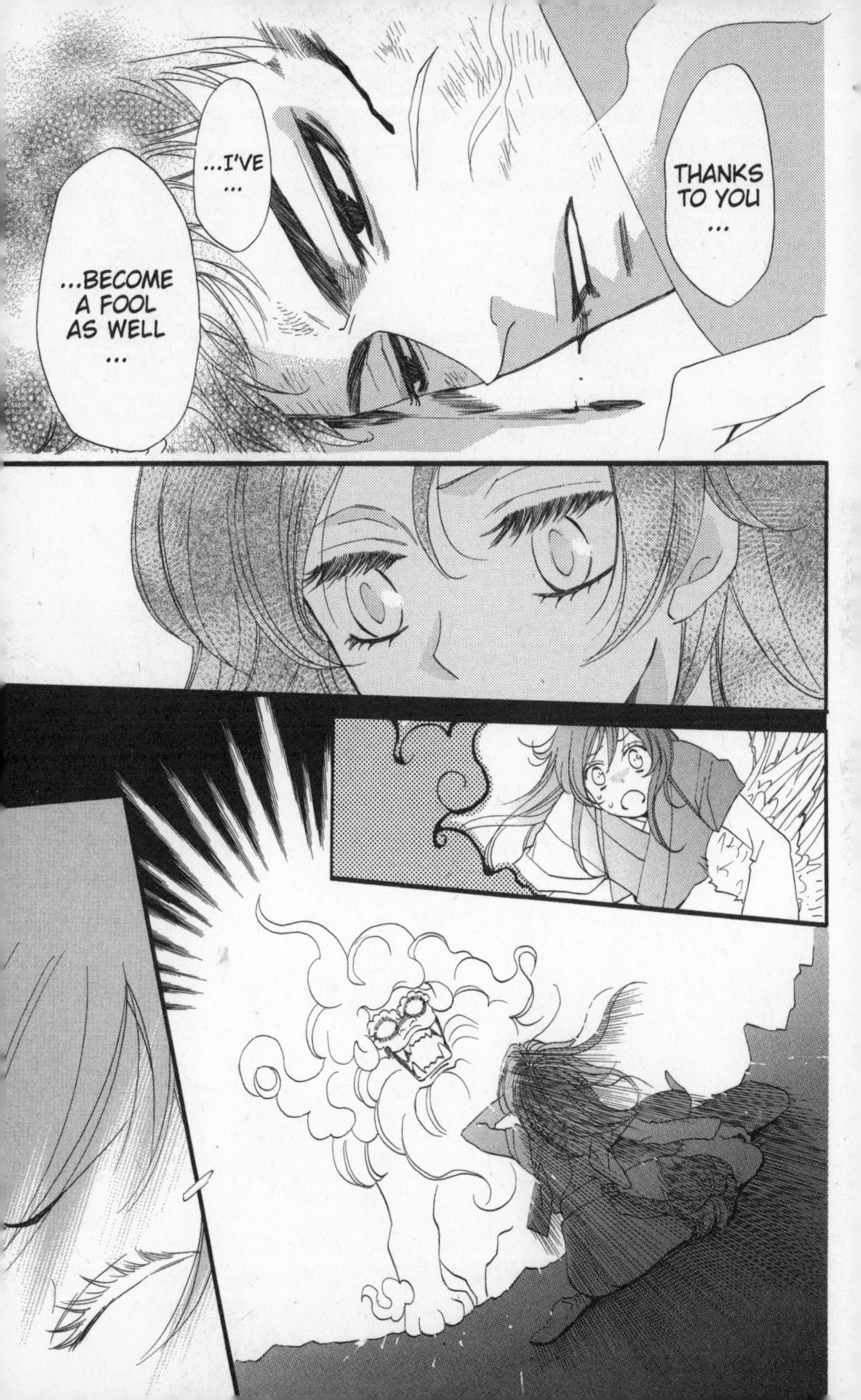
THANKS TO YOU ...
...I'VE ...
...BECOME A FOOL AS WELL ...

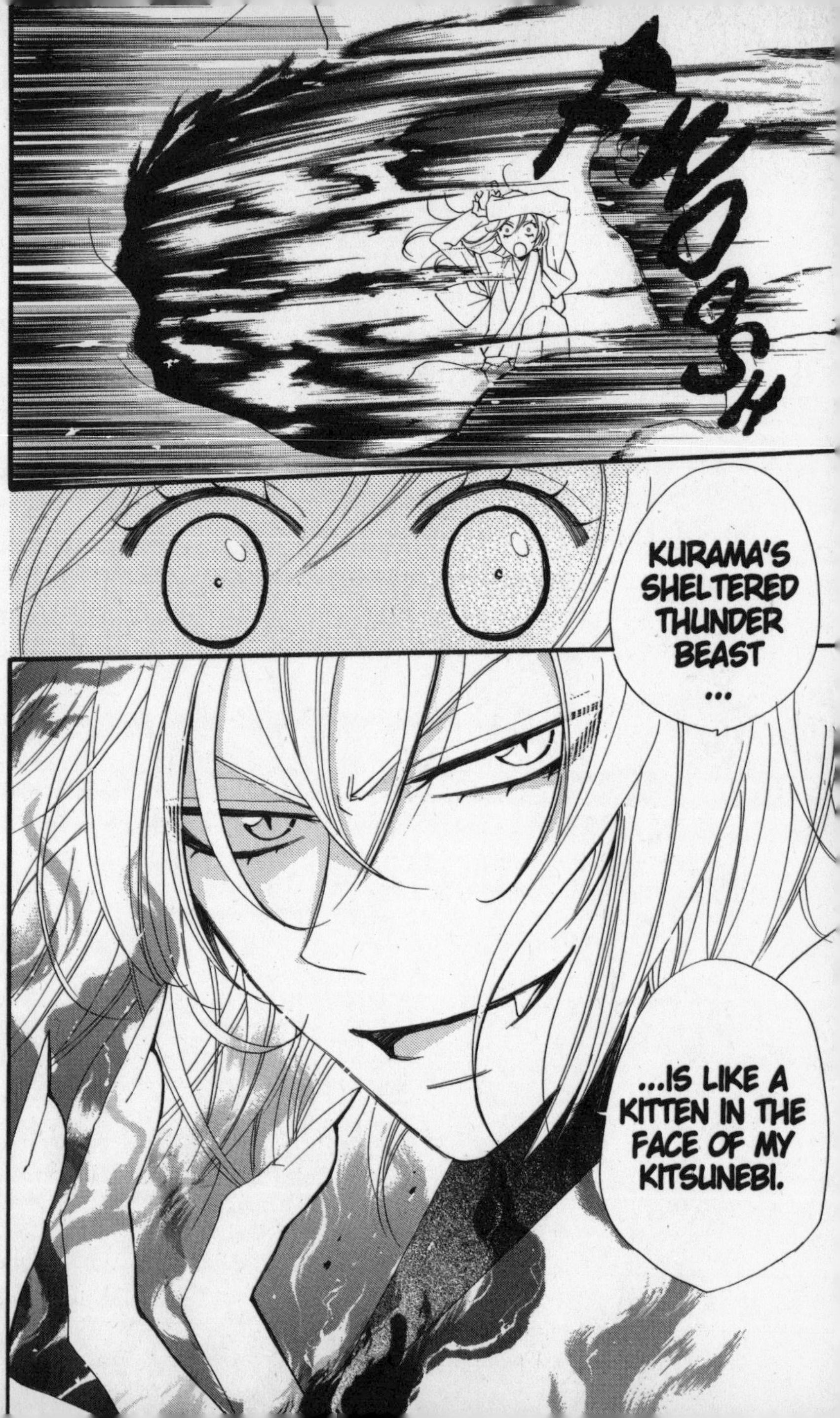
FWOOSH
KURAMA'S SHELTERED THUNDER BEAST ...
...IS LIKE A KITTEN IN THE FACE OF MY KITSUNEBI.

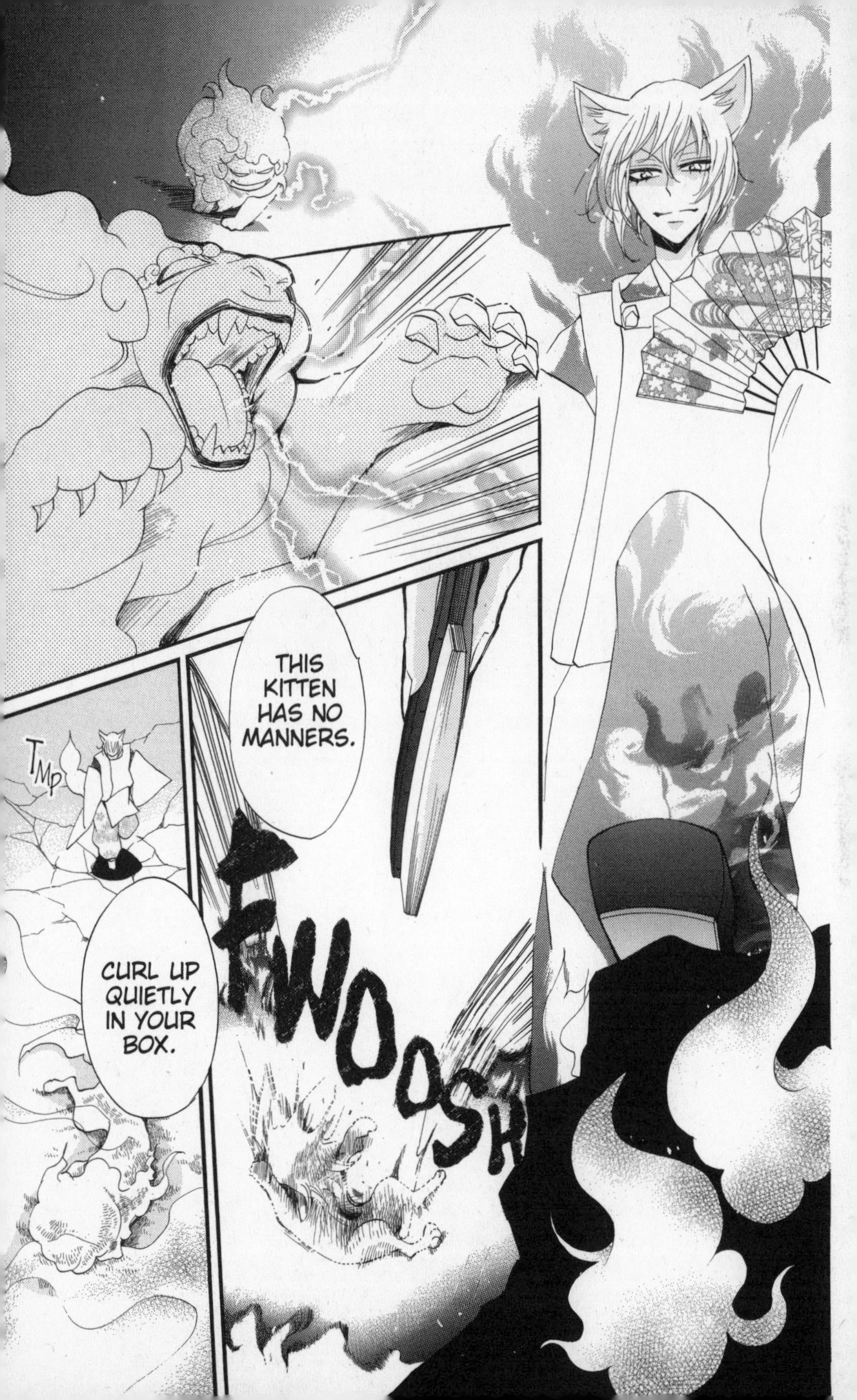
THIS KITTEN HAS NO MANNERS.
FWOOSH
TMP
CURL UP QUIETLY IN YOUR BOX.

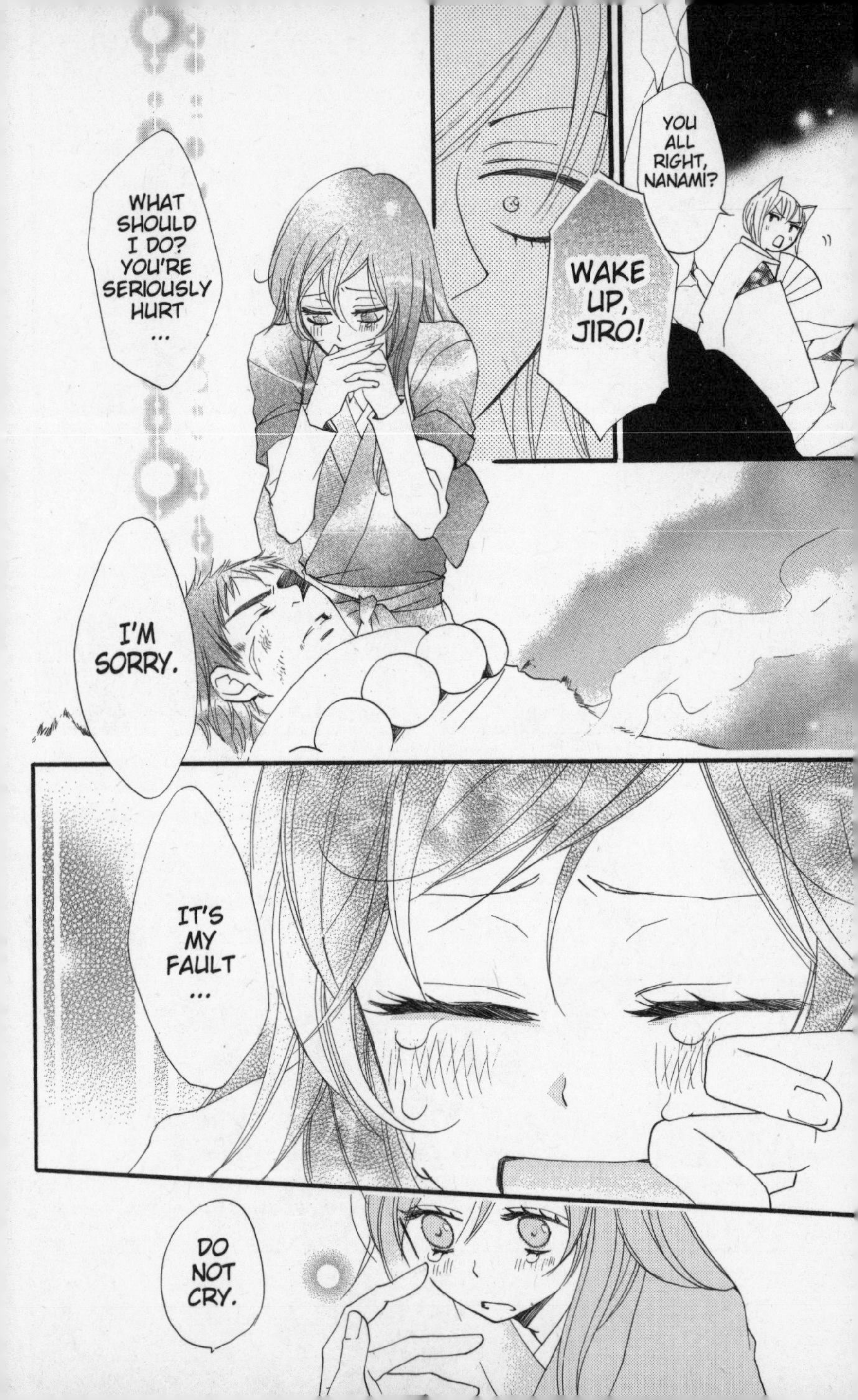

YOU ALL RIGHT, NANAMI?
WAKE UP, JIRO!
WHAT SHOULD I DO? YOU'RE SERIOUSLY HURT ...
I'M SORRY.
IT'S MY FAULT ...
DO NOT CRY.

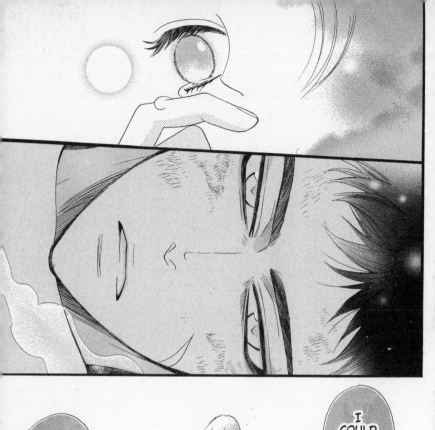

I COULD NOT BEAR ...

...HAVING THE WOMAN I LOVE DIE IN FRONT OF MY EYES.

THAT'S ALL.

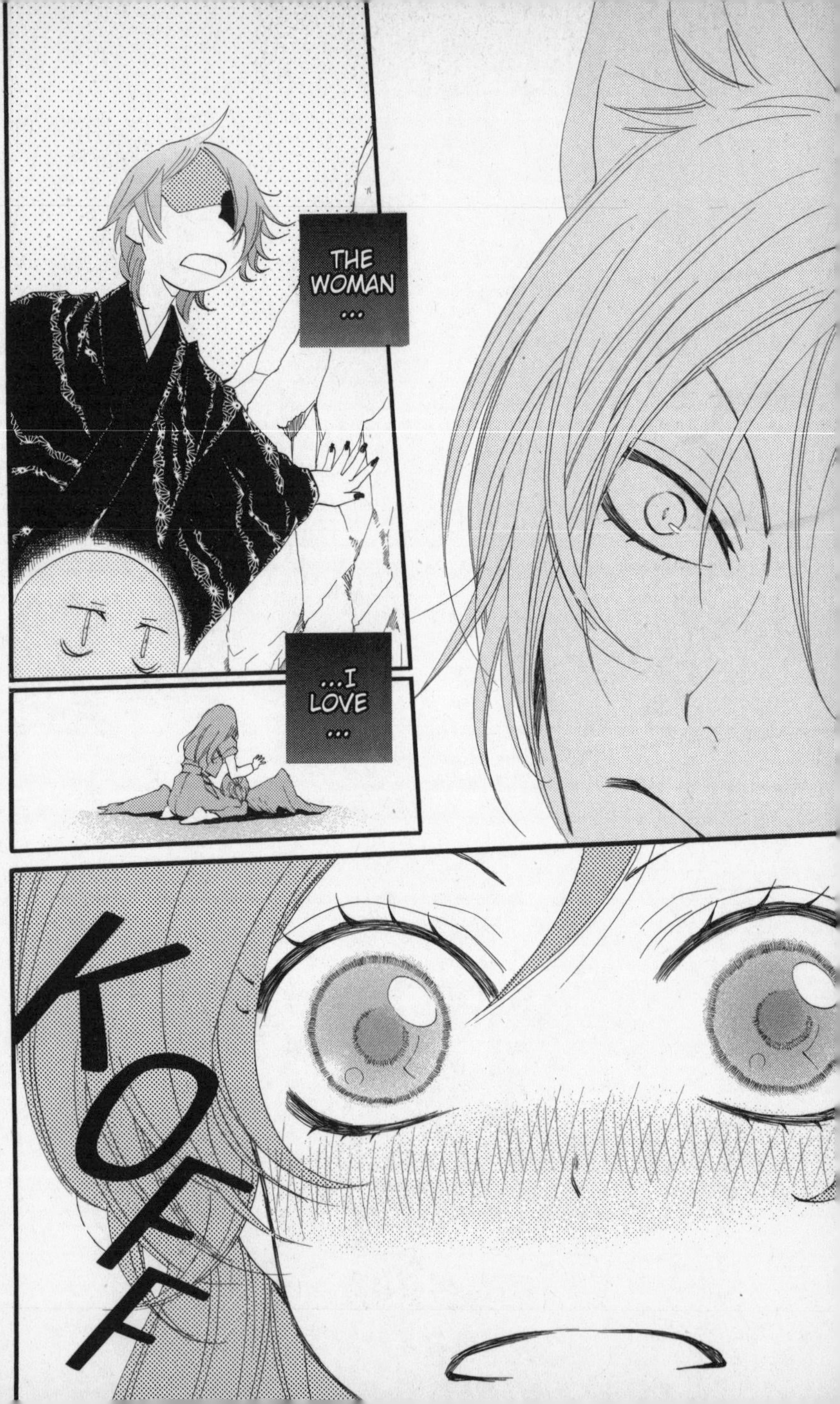
THE WOMAN ...
...I LOVE ...
KOFF

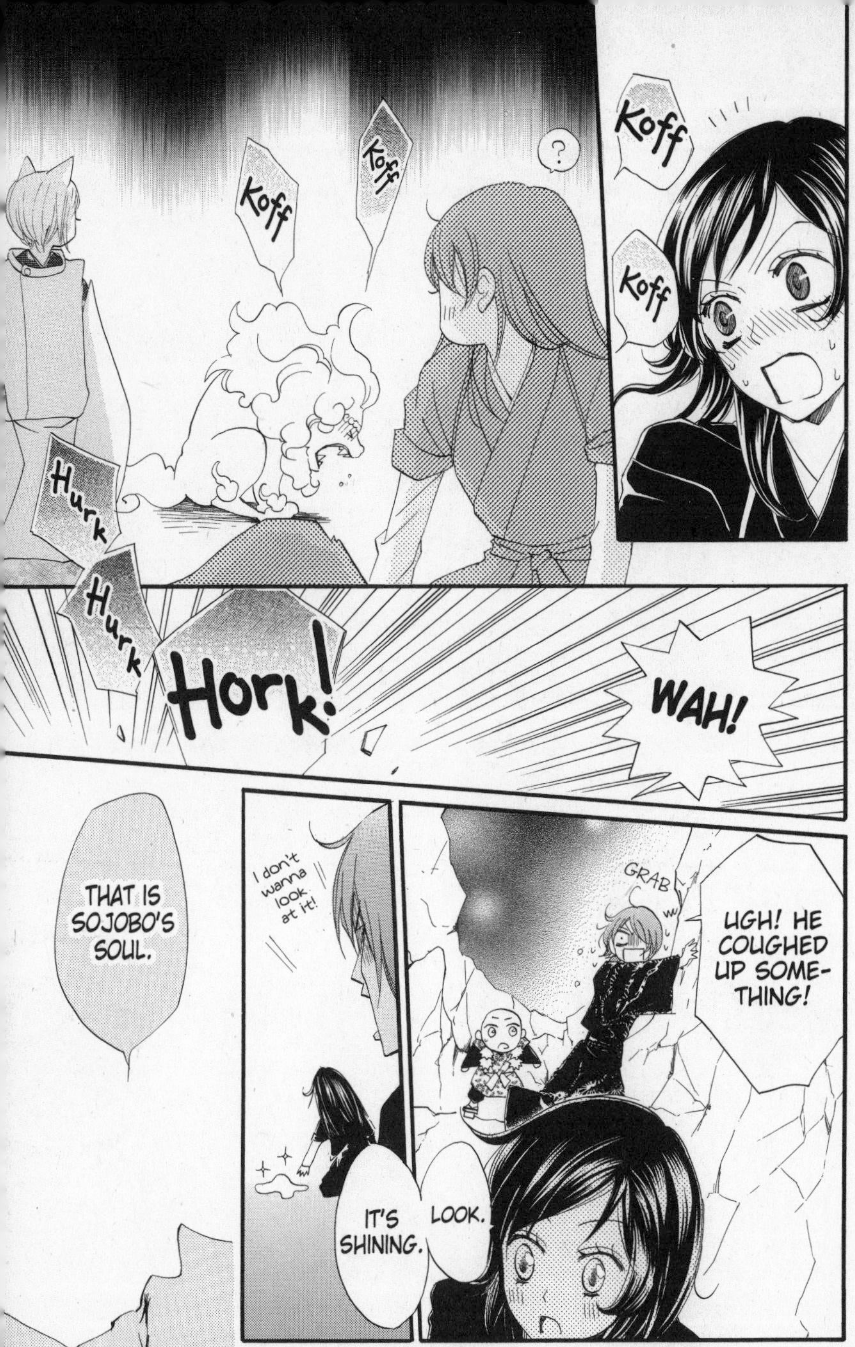

Koff
Koff
?
Koff
Koff
Hurk
Hurk
Hork!
WAH!
GRAB
UGH! HE COUGHED UP SOME-THING!
LOOK.
I don't wanna look at it!
IT'S SHINING.
THAT IS SOJOBO'S SOUL.

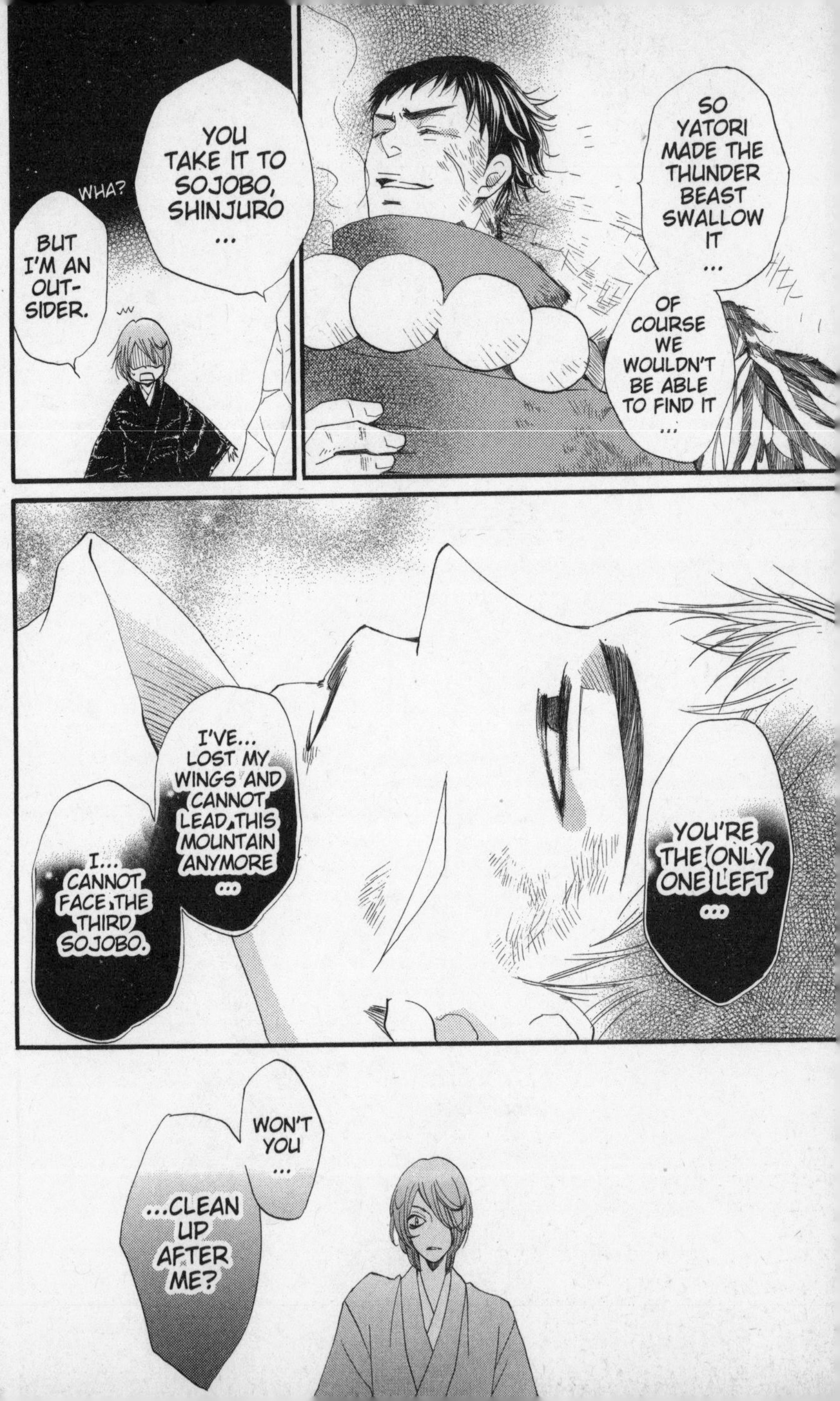
SO YATORI MADE THE THUNDER BEAST SWALLOW IT ...
OF COURSE WE WOULDN'T BE ABLE TO FIND IT ...
YOU TAKE IT TO SOJOBO, SHINJURO ...
WHA?
BUT I'M AN OUT-SIDER.
YOU'RE THE ONLY ONE LEFT ...
I'VE... LOST MY WINGS AND CANNOT LEAD THIS MOUNTAIN ANYMORE ...
I... CANNOT FACE THE THIRD SOJOBO.
WON'T YOU ...
...CLEAN UP AFTER ME?

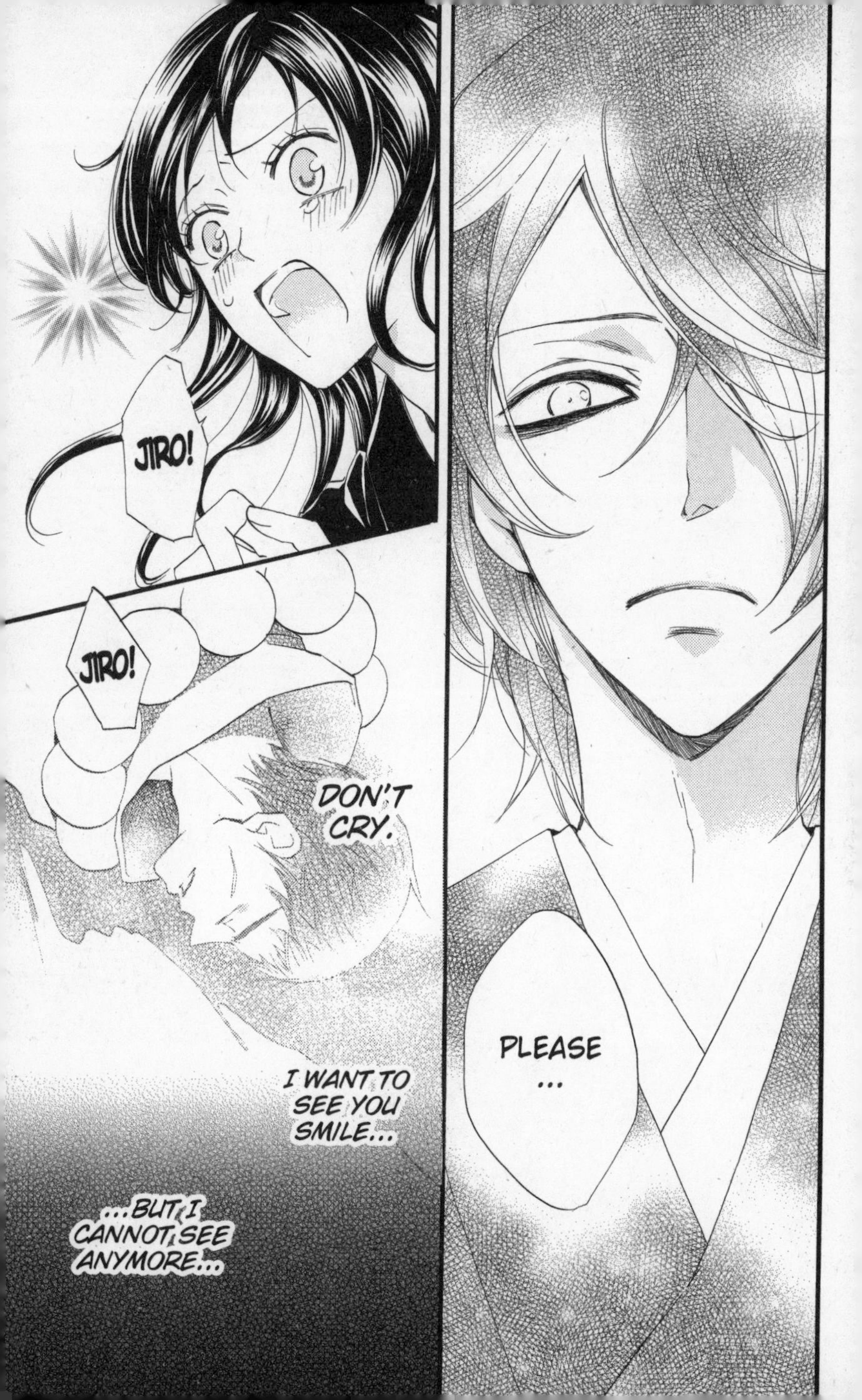
PLEASE ...
JIRO!
JIRO!
DON'T CRY.
I WANT TO SEE YOU SMILE...
...BUT I CANNOT SEE ANYMORE...

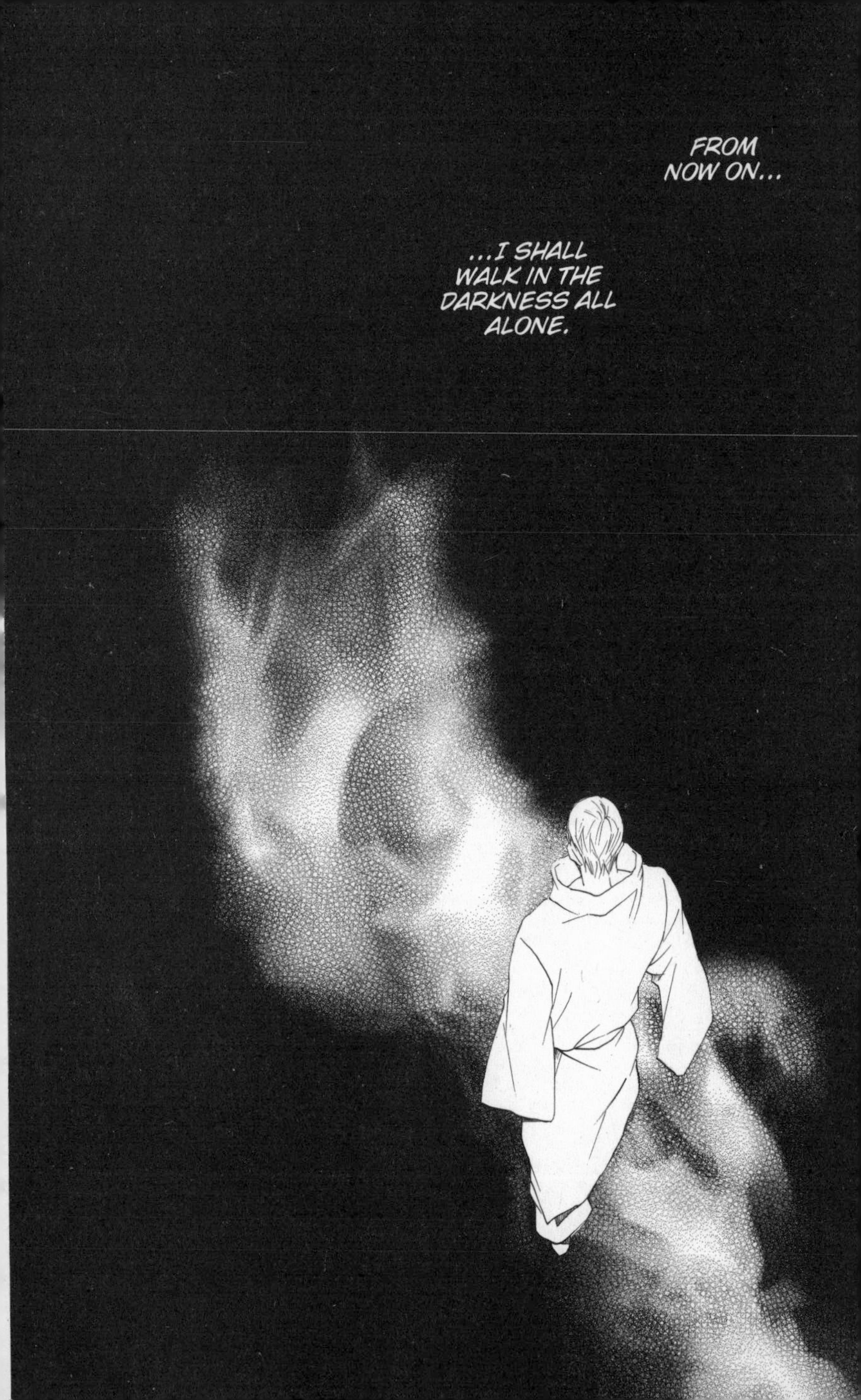
FROM NOW ON...
...I SHALL WALK IN THE DARKNESS ALL ALONE.

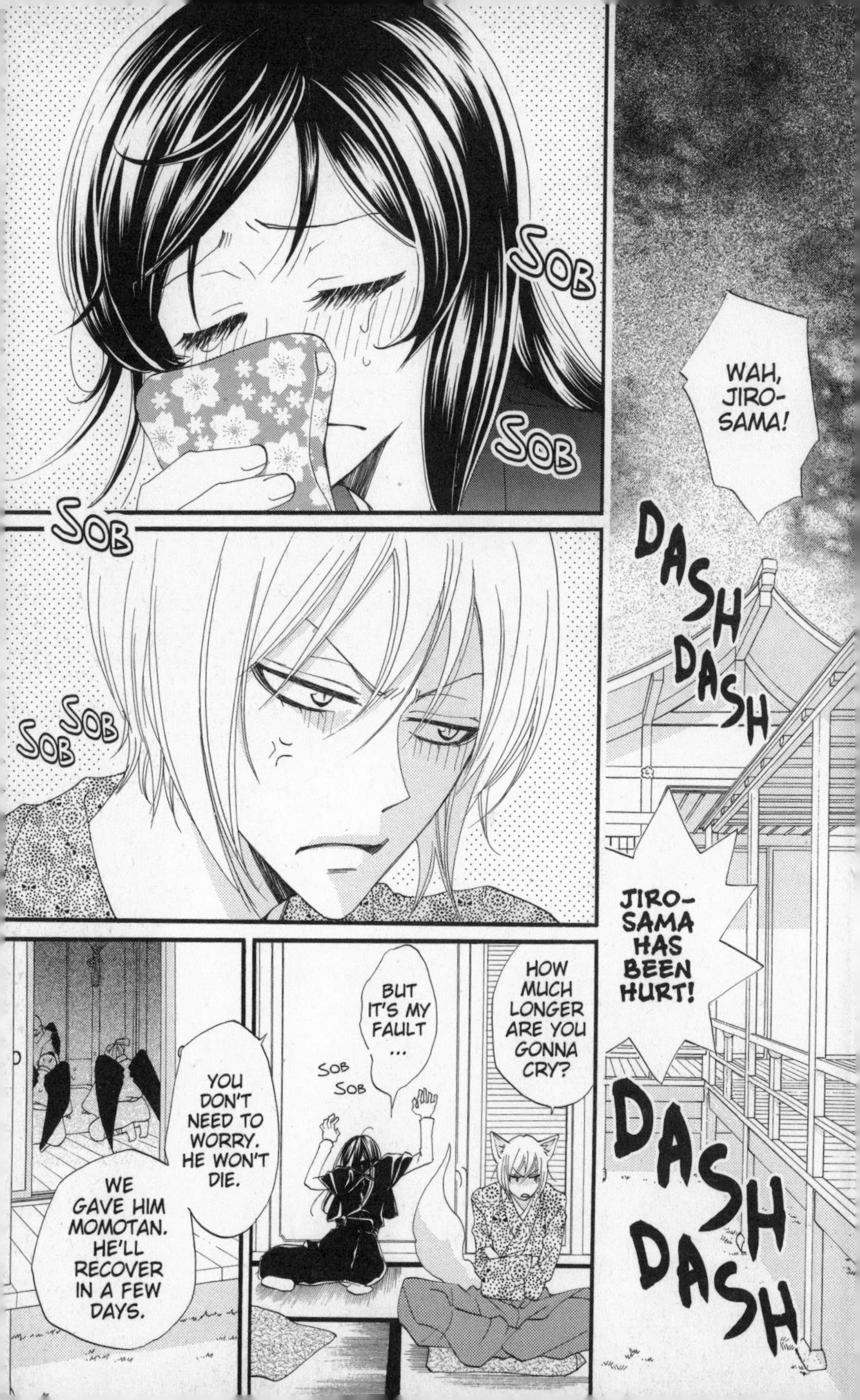
WAH, JIRO-SAMA!
DASH DASH
JIRO-SAMA HAS BEEN HURT!
DASH DASH
SOB
SOB
SOB
SOB SOB
HOW MUCH LONGER ARE YOU GONNA CRY?
BUT IT'S MY FAULT...
SOB SOB
YOU DON'T NEED TO WORRY. HE WON'T DIE.
WE GAVE HIM MOMOTAN. HE'LL RECOVER IN A FEW DAYS.

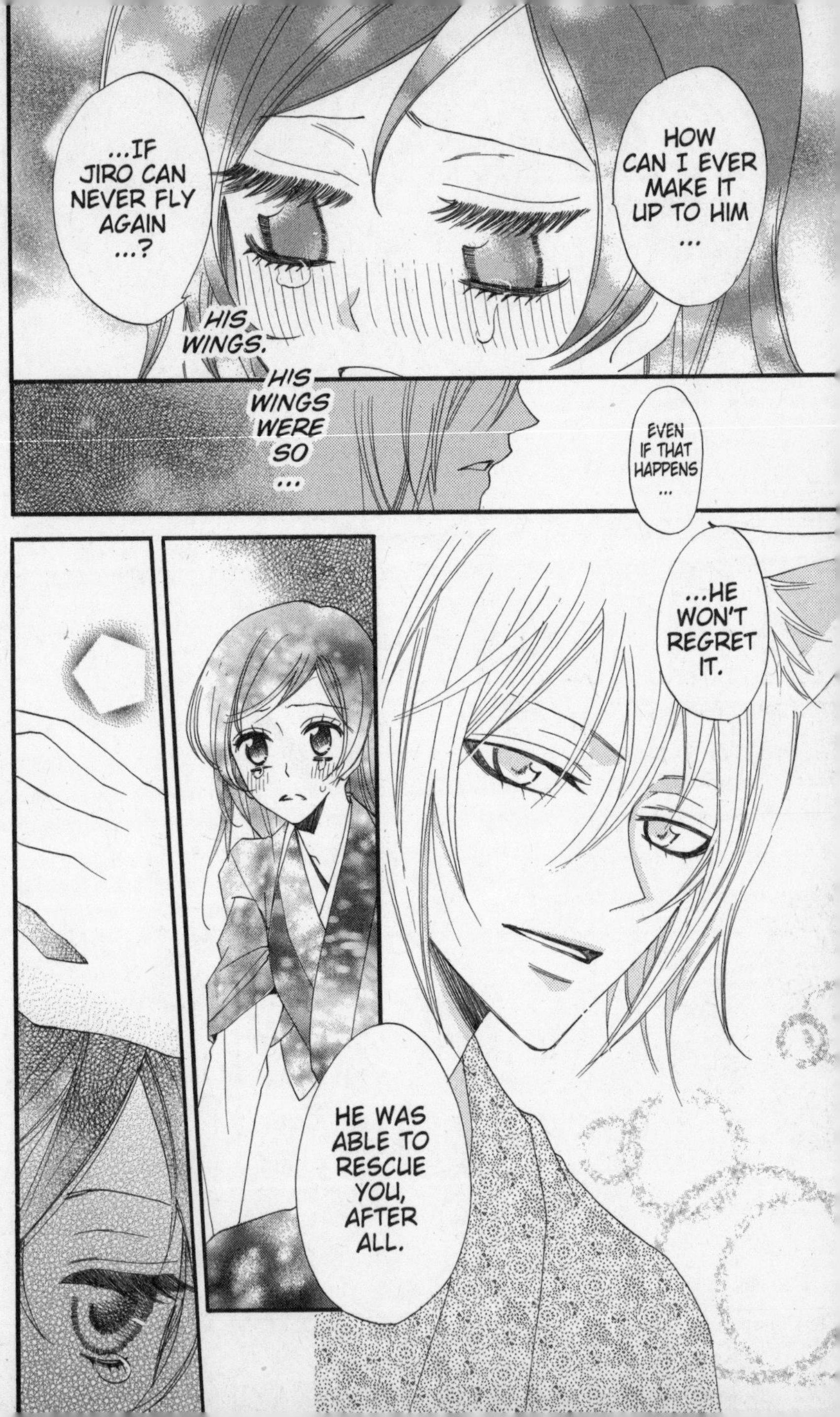
HOW CAN I EVER MAKE IT UP TO HIM ...
...IF JIRO CAN NEVER FLY AGAIN ...?
HIS WINGS.
HIS WINGS WERE SO ...
EVEN IF THAT HAPPENS ...
...HE WON'T REGRET IT.
HE WAS ABLE TO RESCUE YOU, AFTER ALL.

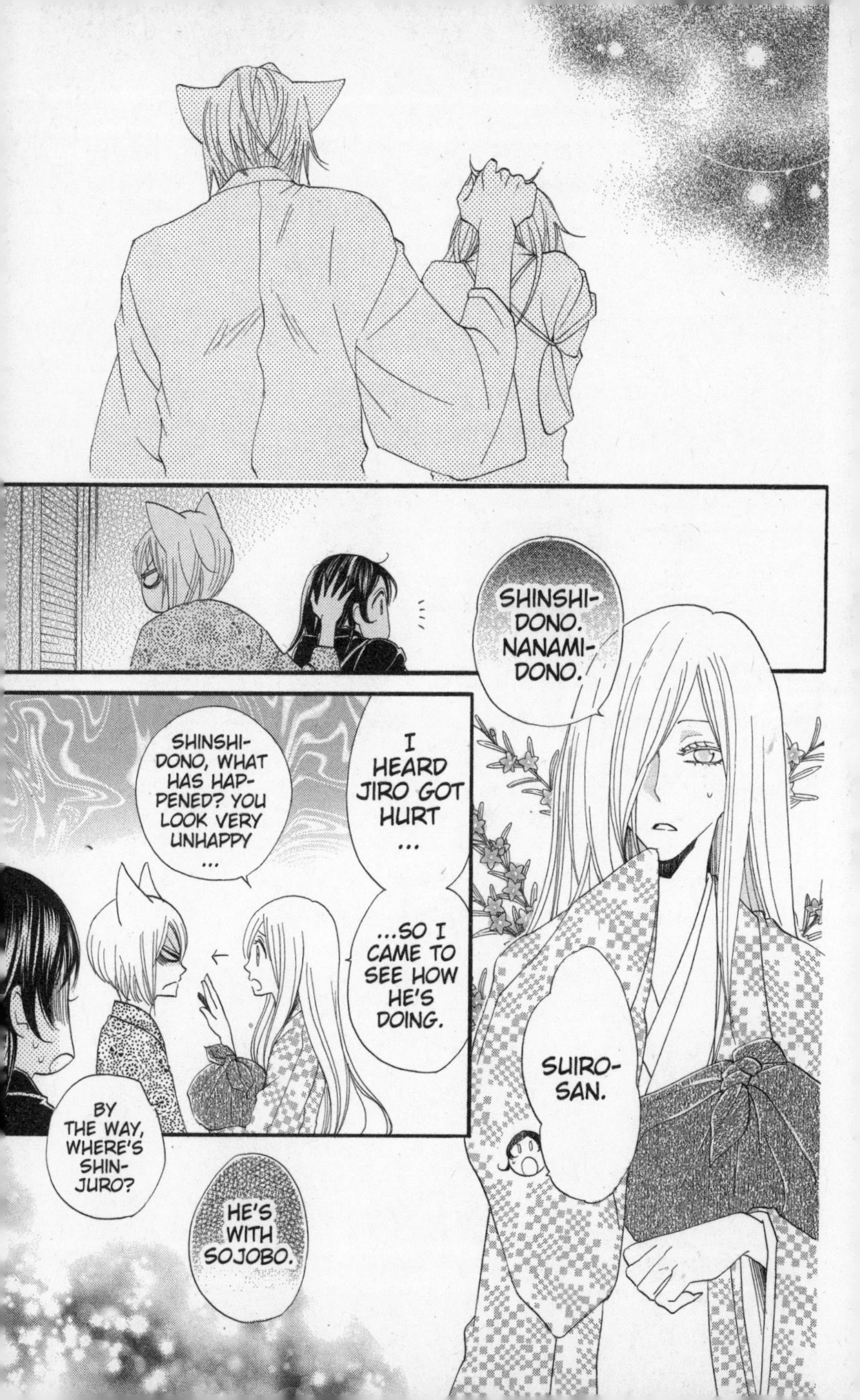
SHINSHI-DONO. NANAMI-DONO.
SUIRO-SAN.
I HEARD JIRO GOT HURT ...
...SO I CAME TO SEE HOW HE'S DOING.
SHINSHI-DONO, WHAT HAS HAPPENED? YOU LOOK VERY UNHAPPY ...
BY THE WAY, WHERE'S SHINJURO?
HE'S WITH SOJOBO.

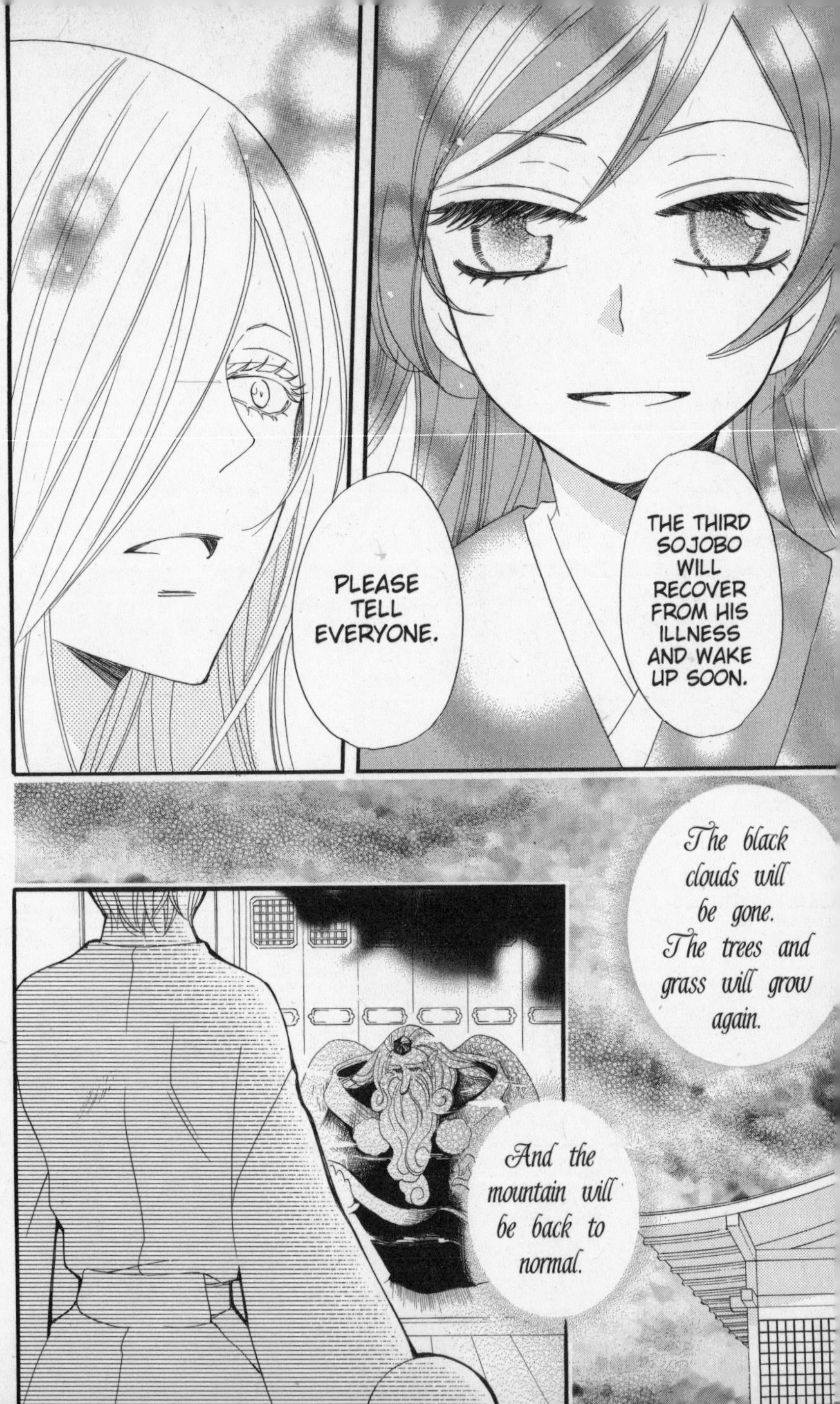
THE THIRD SOJOBO WILL RECOVER FROM HIS ILLNESS AND WAKE UP SOON.
PLEASE TELL EVERYONE.
The black clouds will be gone. The trees and grass will grow again.
And the mountain will be back to normal.

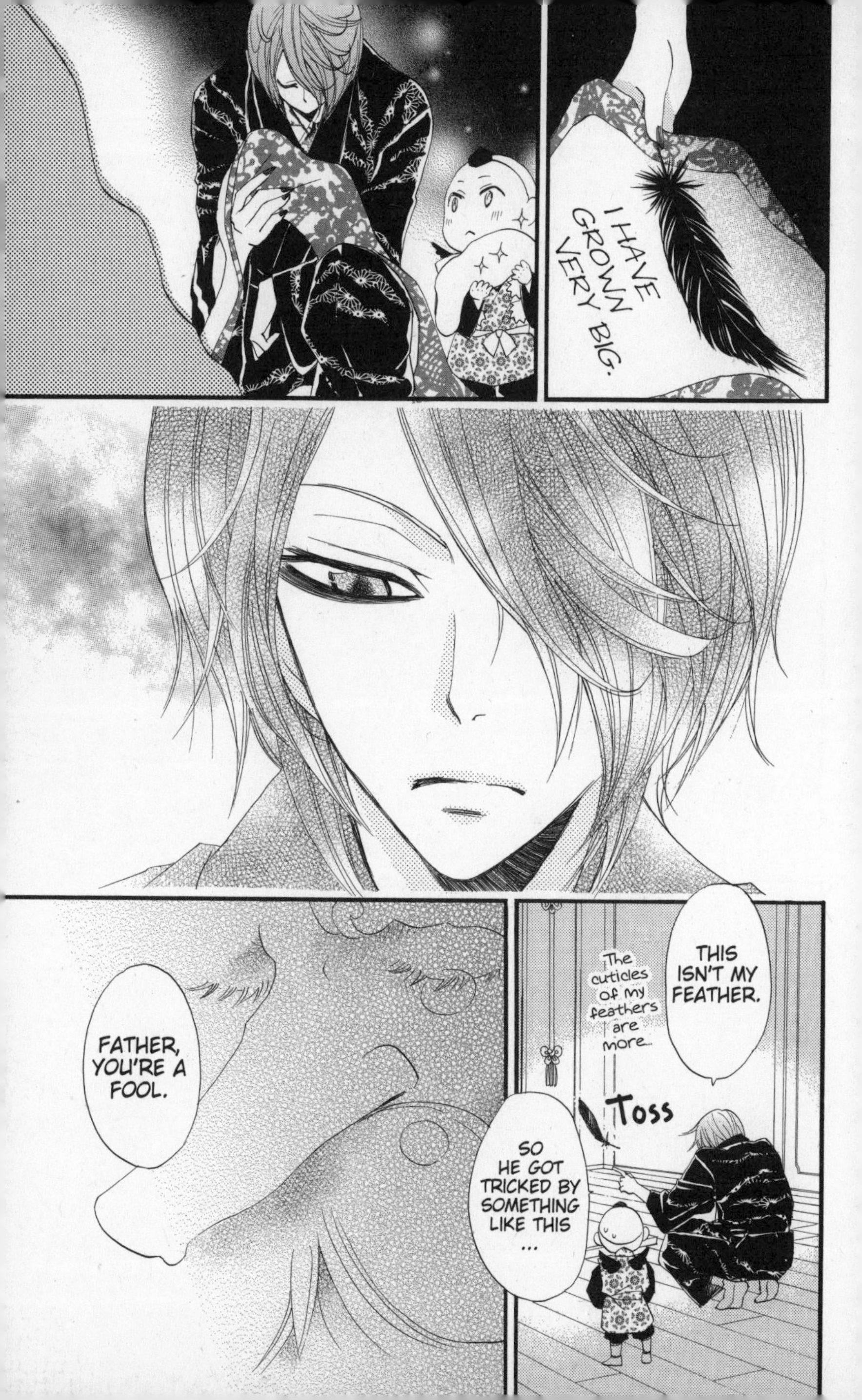
I HAVE GROWN VERY BIG.
THIS ISN'T MY FEATHER.
The cuticles of my feathers are more...
Toss
SO HE GOT TRICKED BY SOMETHING LIKE THIS ...
FATHER, YOU'RE A FOOL.

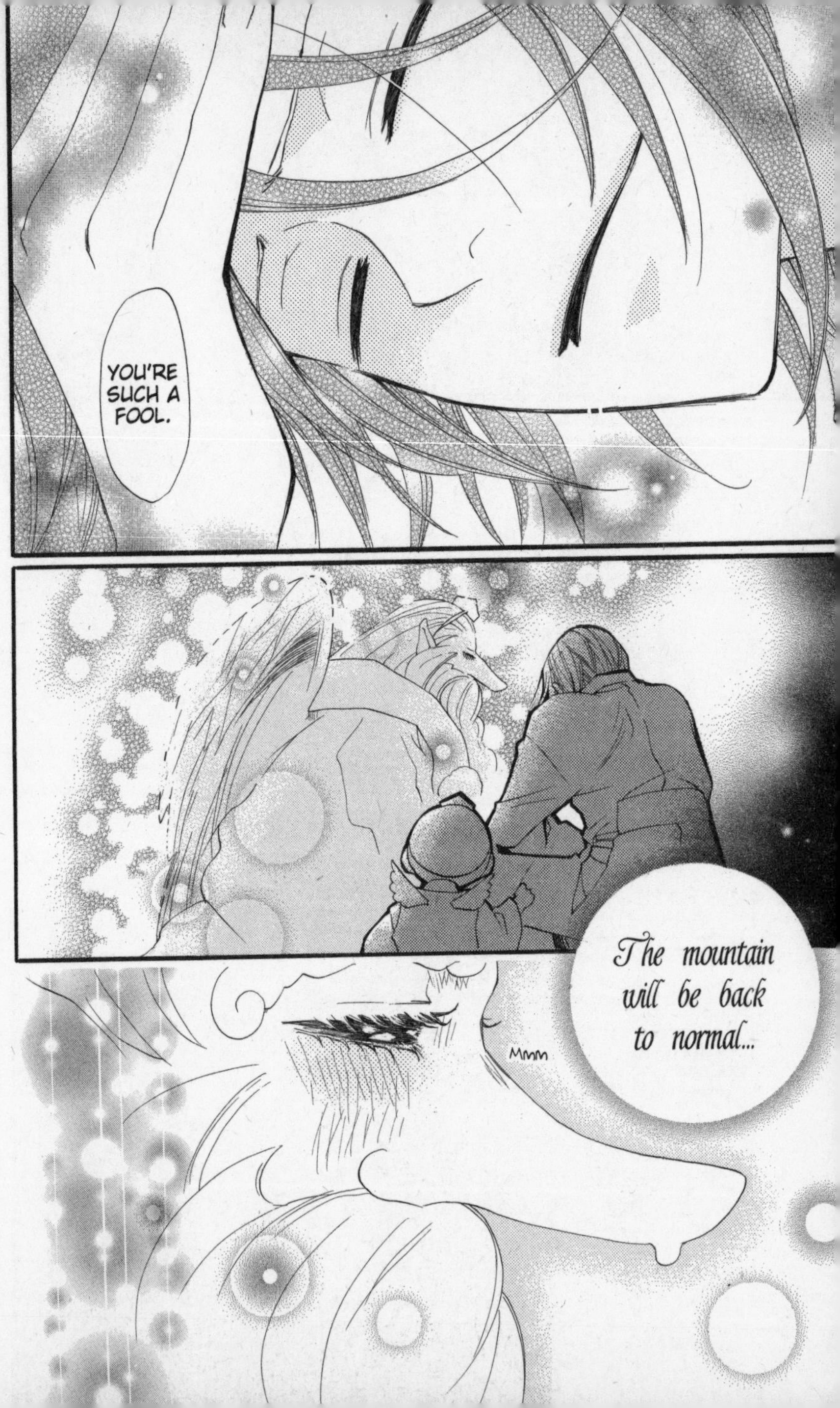
YOU'RE SUCH A FOOL.
The mountain will be back to normal...
Mmm

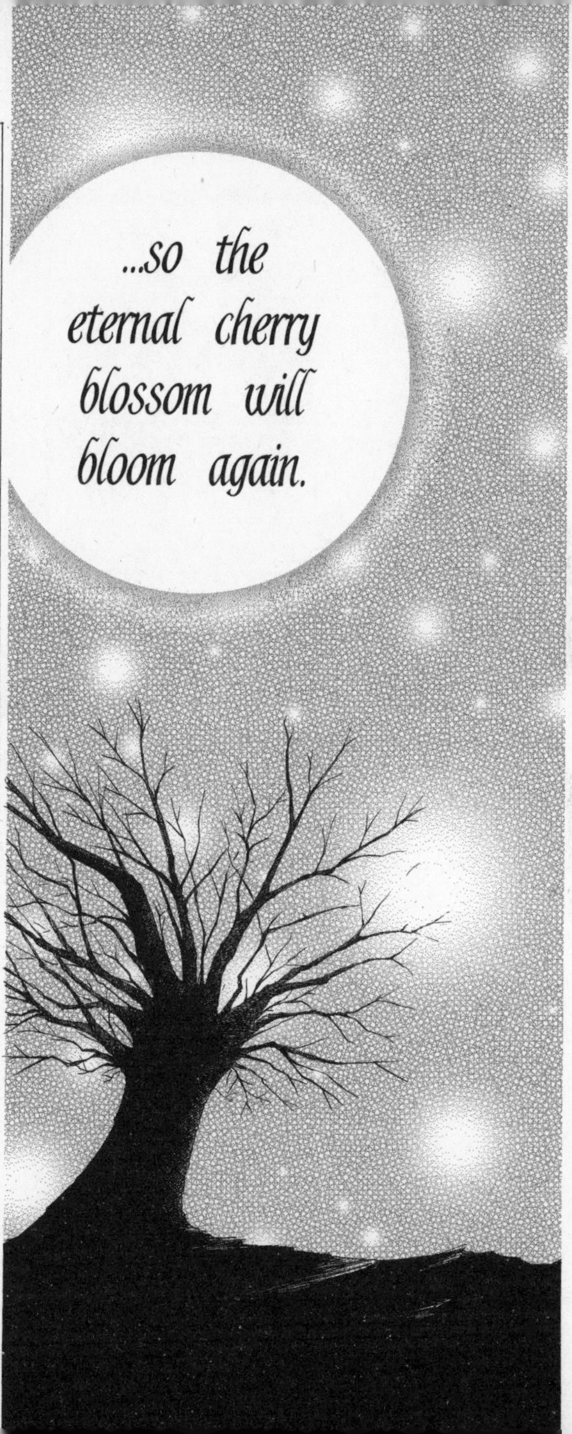
...so the eternal cherry blossom will bloom again.

4

I like manga. I love drawing and reading it.

If I could draw the manga I love just the way I want to, I might be called to heaven from happiness. I want to be called to heaven soon. (In a good way.)

I'm weak-willed, but I'm continuing to write in my diary.

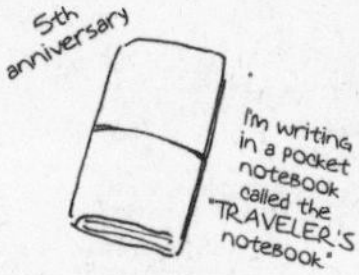
5th anniversary
I'm writing in a pocket notebook called the "TRAVELER'S notebook"

Writing seems to help me keep my heart in balance, and I don't find it bothersome. The two secrets(?) are

I don't have to write every day.

I don't have to write down every single thing that happens.

It's made me realize that I tend to shoulder things much more than I thought (smile) I'll live in a more carefree way

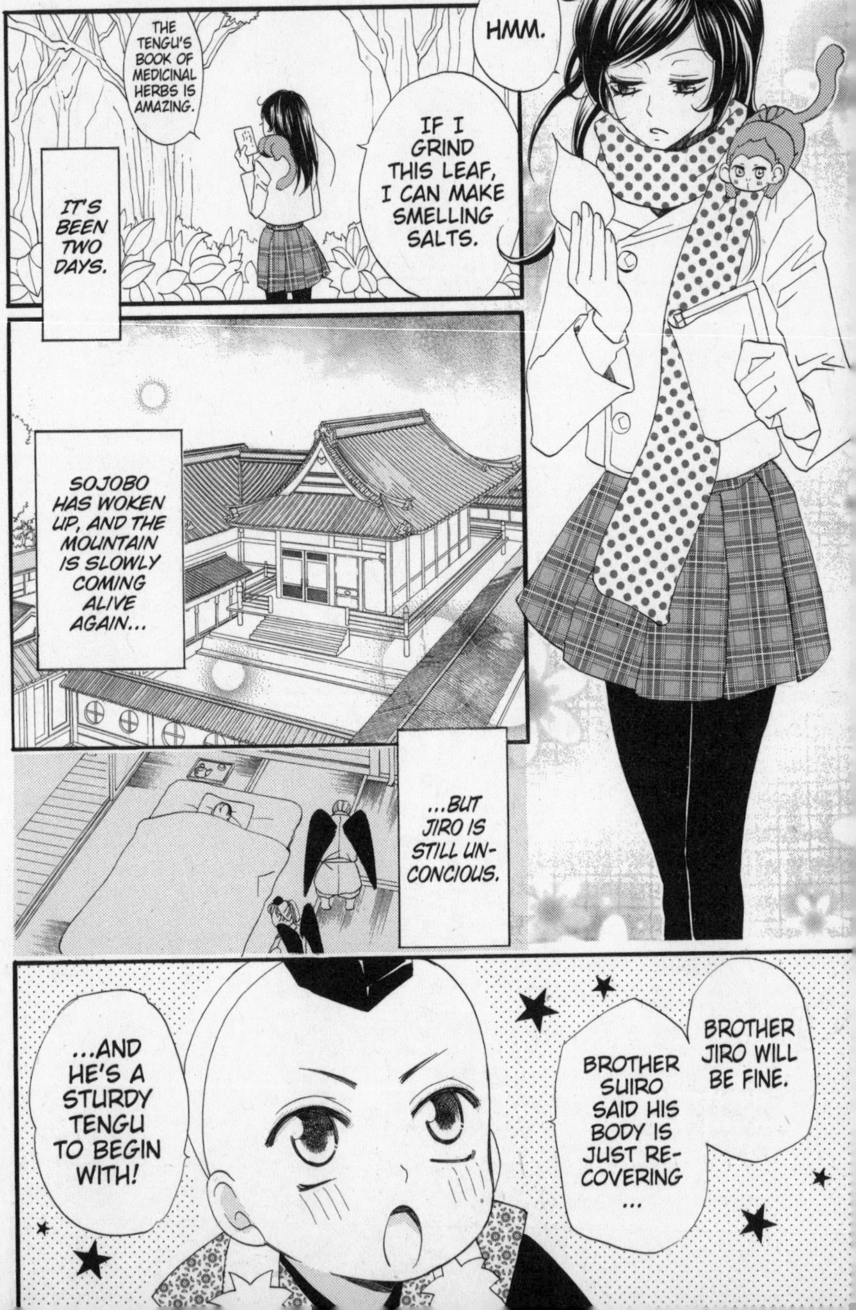
HMM.
IF I GRIND THIS LEAF, I CAN MAKE SMELLING SALTS.
THE TENGU'S BOOK OF MEDICINAL HERBS IS AMAZING.
IT'S BEEN TWO DAYS.
SOJOBO HAS WOKEN UP, AND THE MOUNTAIN IS SLOWLY COMING ALIVE AGAIN...
...BUT JIRO IS STILL UN-CONCIOUS.
BROTHER JIRO WILL BE FINE.
BROTHER SUIRO SAID HIS BODY IS JUST RE-COVERING ...
...AND HE'S A STURDY TENGU TO BEGIN WITH!

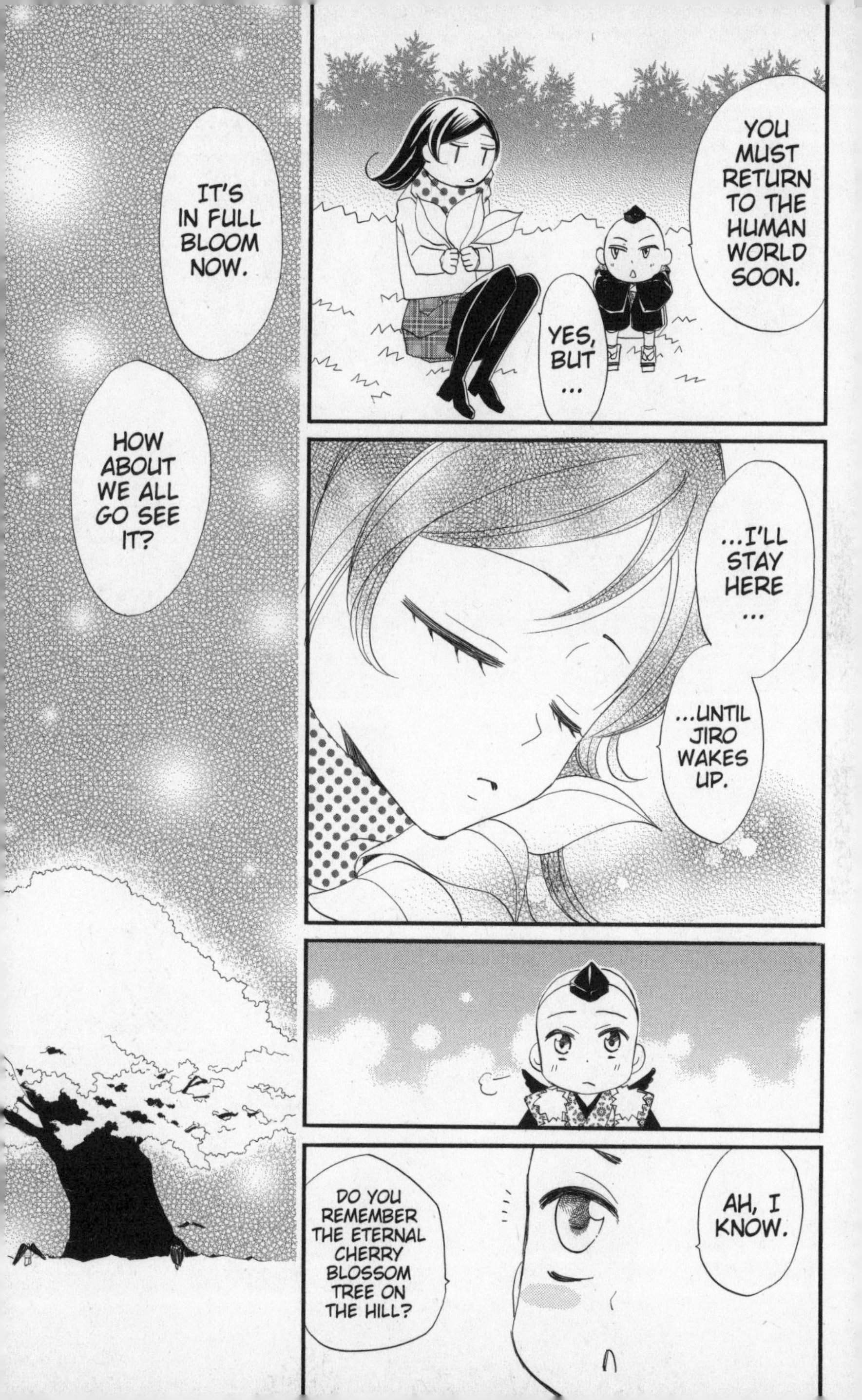
YOU MUST RETURN TO THE HUMAN WORLD SOON.
YES, BUT ...
...I'LL STAY HERE ...
...UNTIL JIRO WAKES UP.
AH, I KNOW.
DO YOU REMEMBER THE ETERNAL CHERRY BLOSSOM TREE ON THE HILL?
IT'S IN FULL BLOOM NOW.
HOW ABOUT WE ALL GO SEE IT?

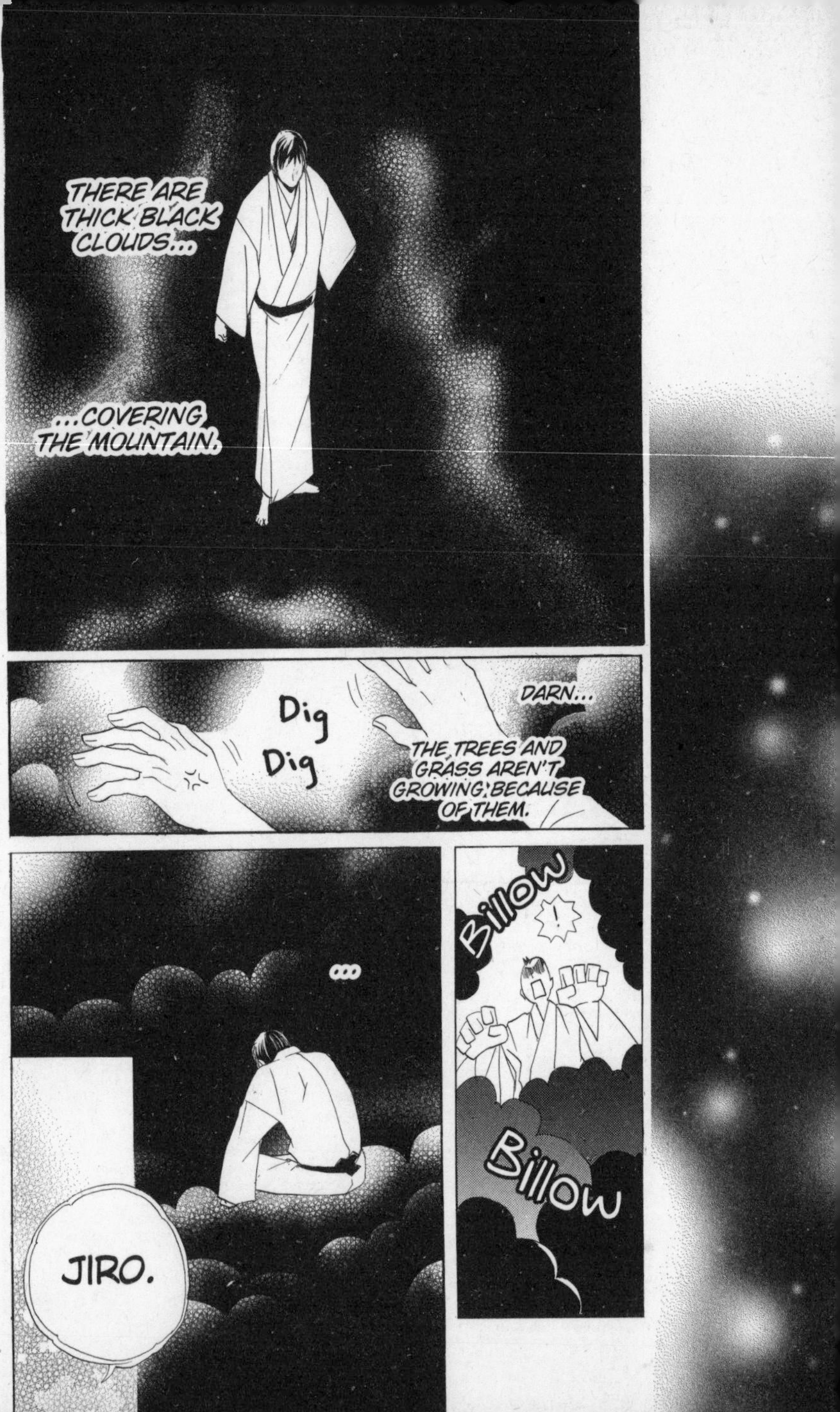
THERE ARE THICK BLACK CLOUDS...
...COVERING THE MOUNTAIN.
DARN...
THE TREES AND GRASS AREN'T GROWING BECAUSE OF THEM.
Dig
Dig
Billow
!
Billow
...
JIRO.

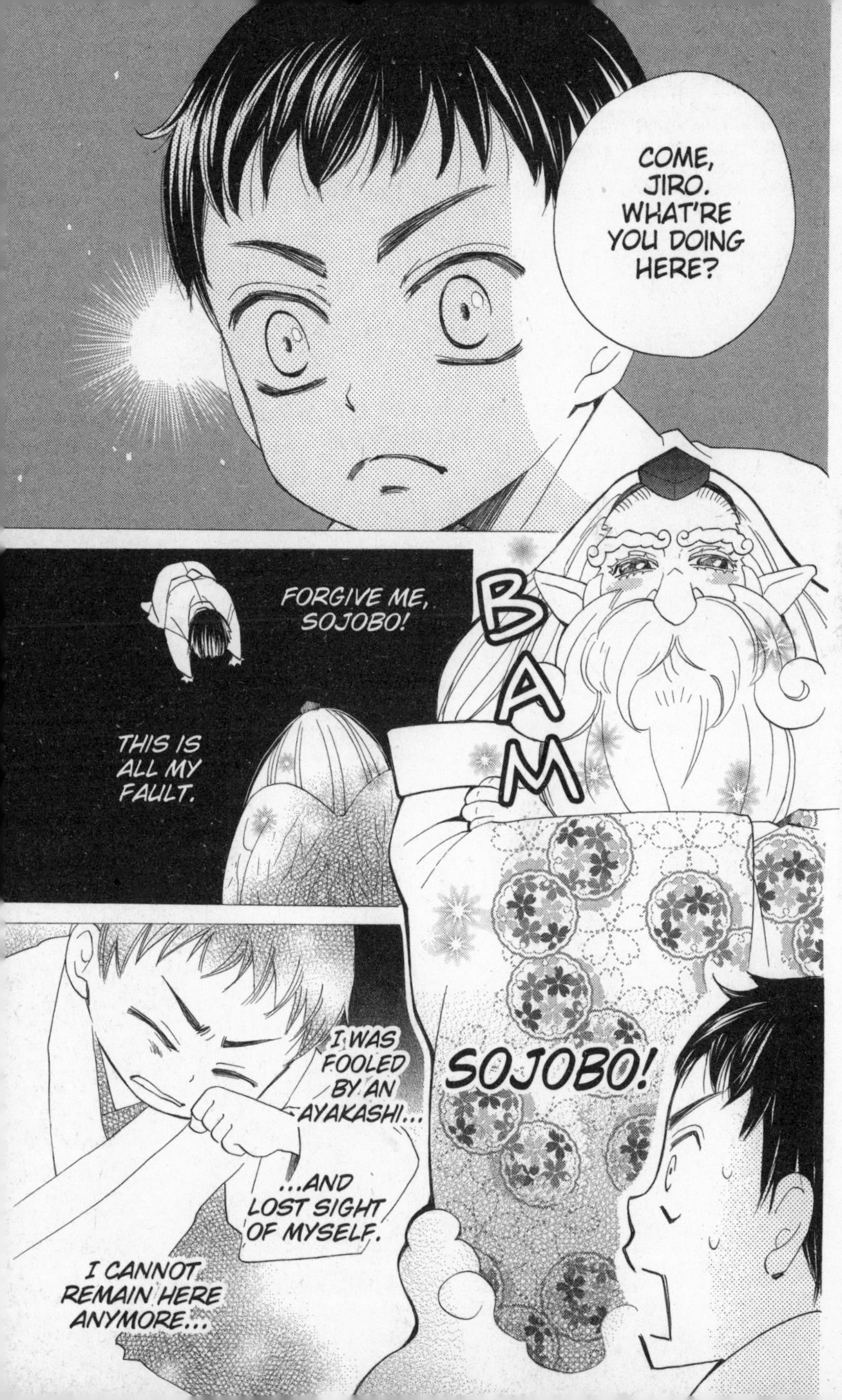
COME, JIRO. WHAT'RE YOU DOING HERE?
BAM
FORGIVE ME, SOJOBO!
THIS IS ALL MY FAULT.
SOJOBO!
I WAS FOOLED BY AN AYAKASHI...
...AND LOST SIGHT OF MYSELF.
I CANNOT REMAIN HERE ANYMORE...

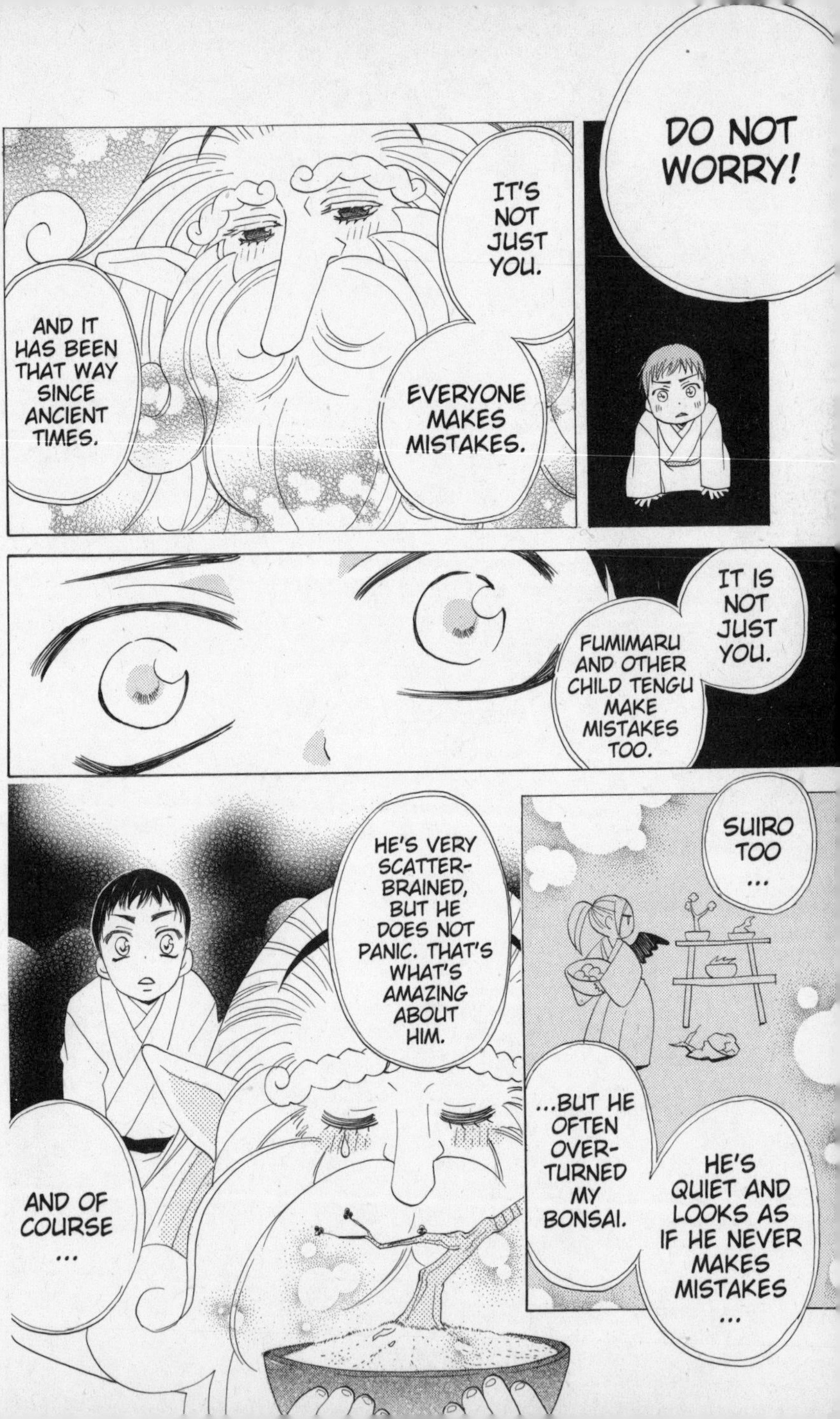
DO NOT WORRY!
IT'S NOT JUST YOU.
EVERYONE MAKES MISTAKES.
AND IT HAS BEEN THAT WAY SINCE ANCIENT TIMES.
IT IS NOT JUST YOU.
FUMIMARU AND OTHER CHILD TENGU MAKE MISTAKES TOO.
SUIRO TOO ...
HE'S QUIET AND LOOKS AS IF HE NEVER MAKES MISTAKES ...
...BUT HE OFTEN OVER-TURNED MY BONSAI.
HE'S VERY SCATTER-BRAINED, BUT HE DOES NOT PANIC. THAT'S WHAT'S AMAZING ABOUT HIM.
AND OF COURSE ...

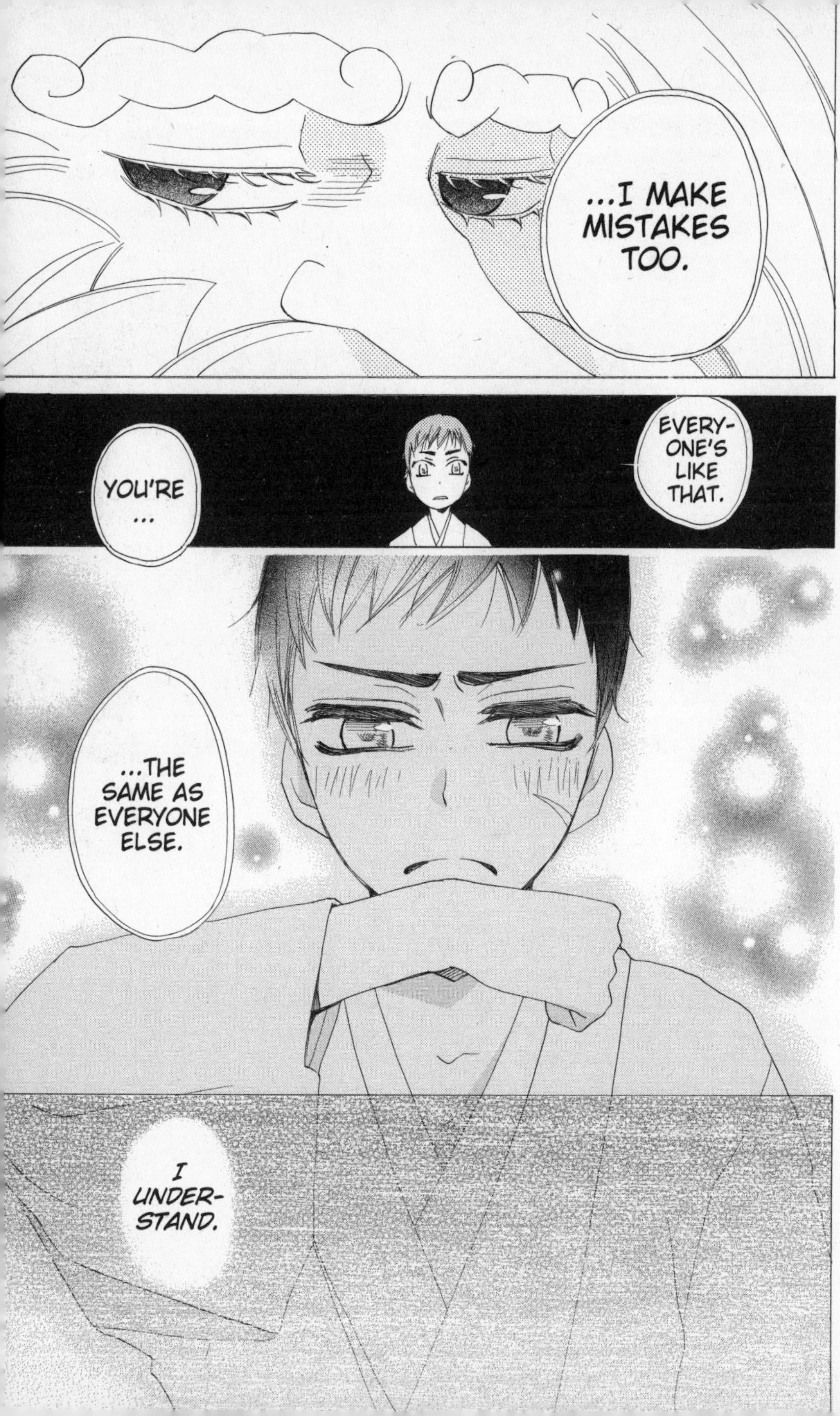
...I MAKE MISTAKES TOO.
EVERY-ONE'S LIKE THAT.
YOU'RE ...
...THE SAME AS EVERYONE ELSE.
I UNDER-STAND.

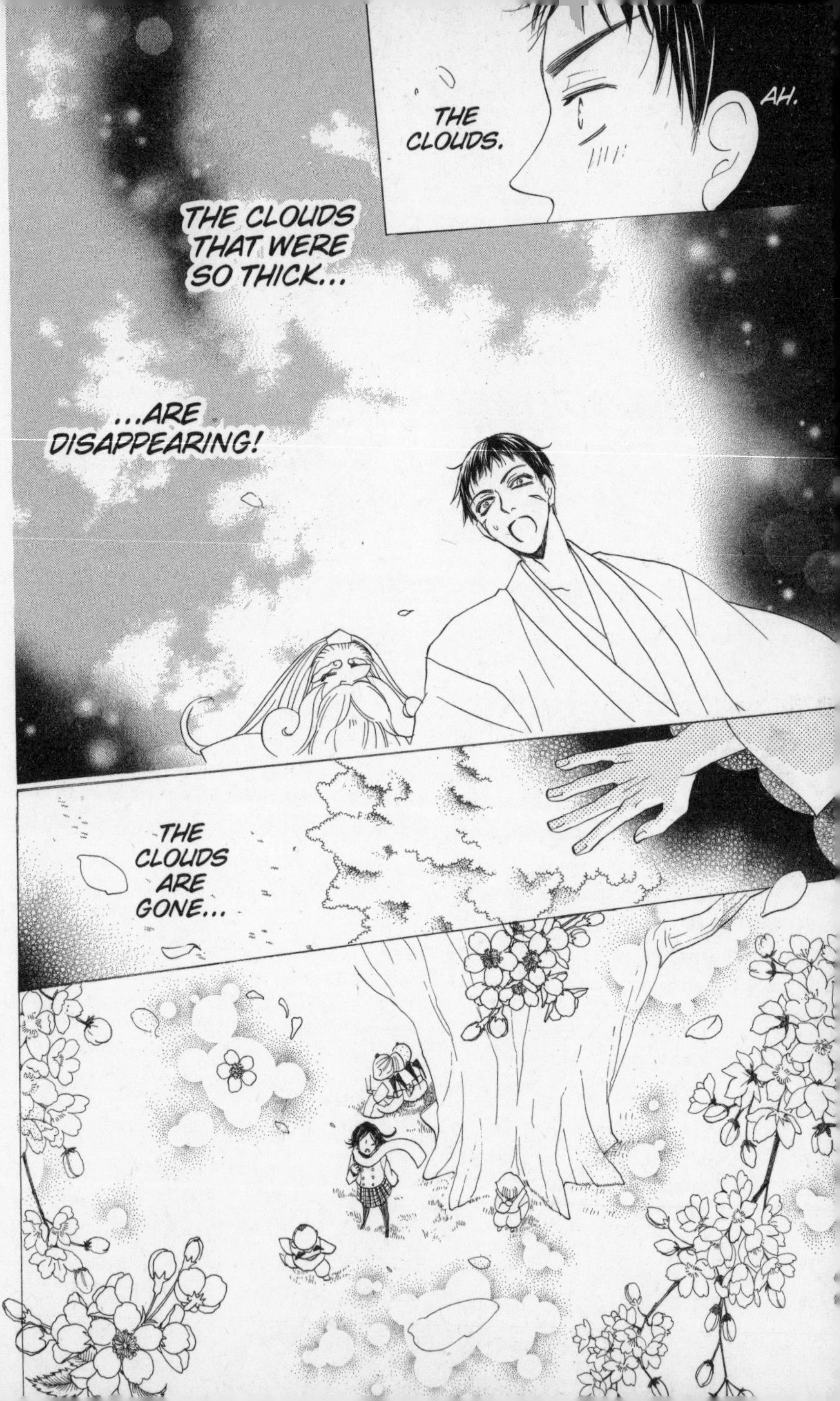
AH.
THE CLOUDS.
THE CLOUDS THAT WERE SO THICK...
...ARE DISAPPEARING!
THE CLOUDS ARE GONE...

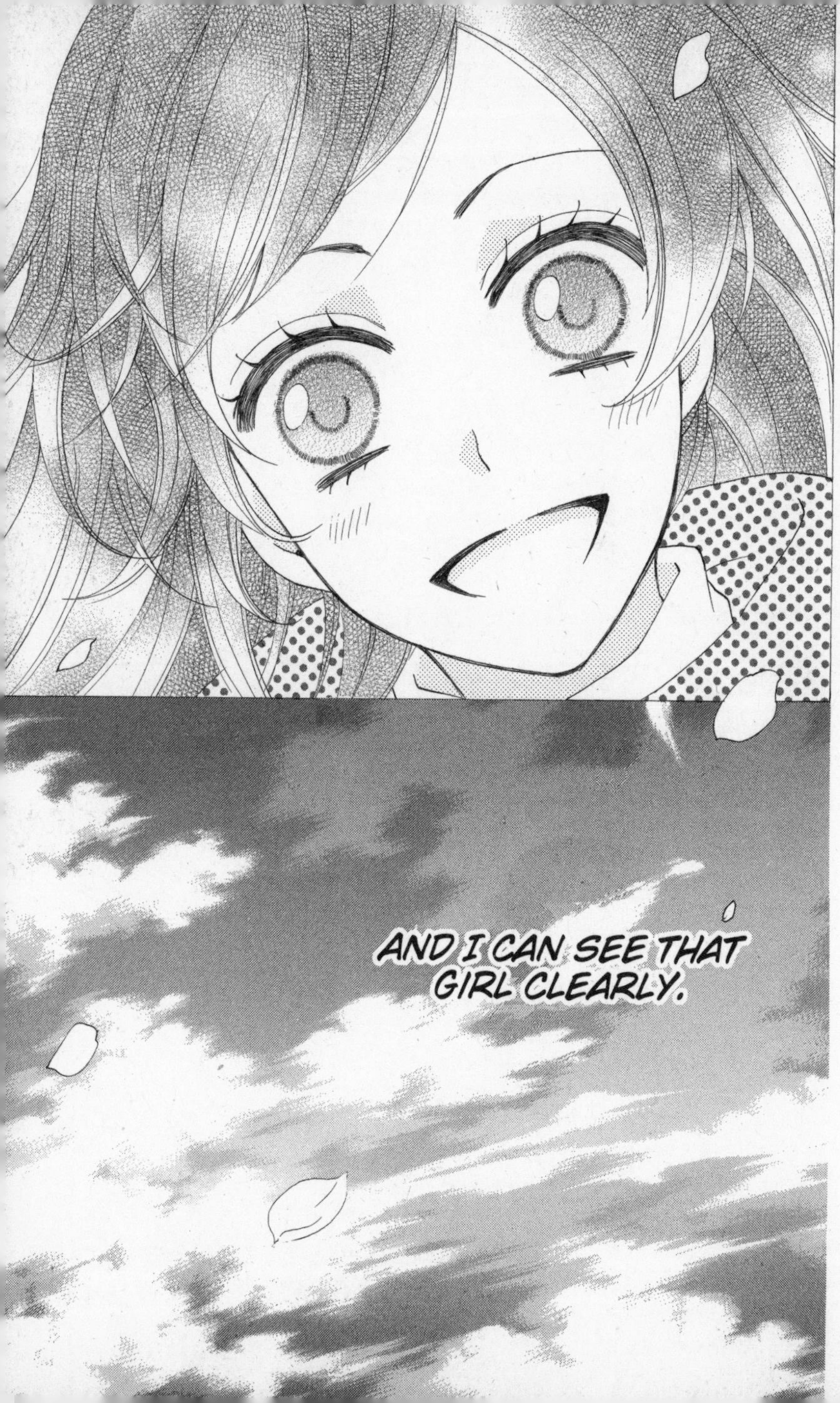
AND I CAN SEE THAT GIRL CLEARLY.

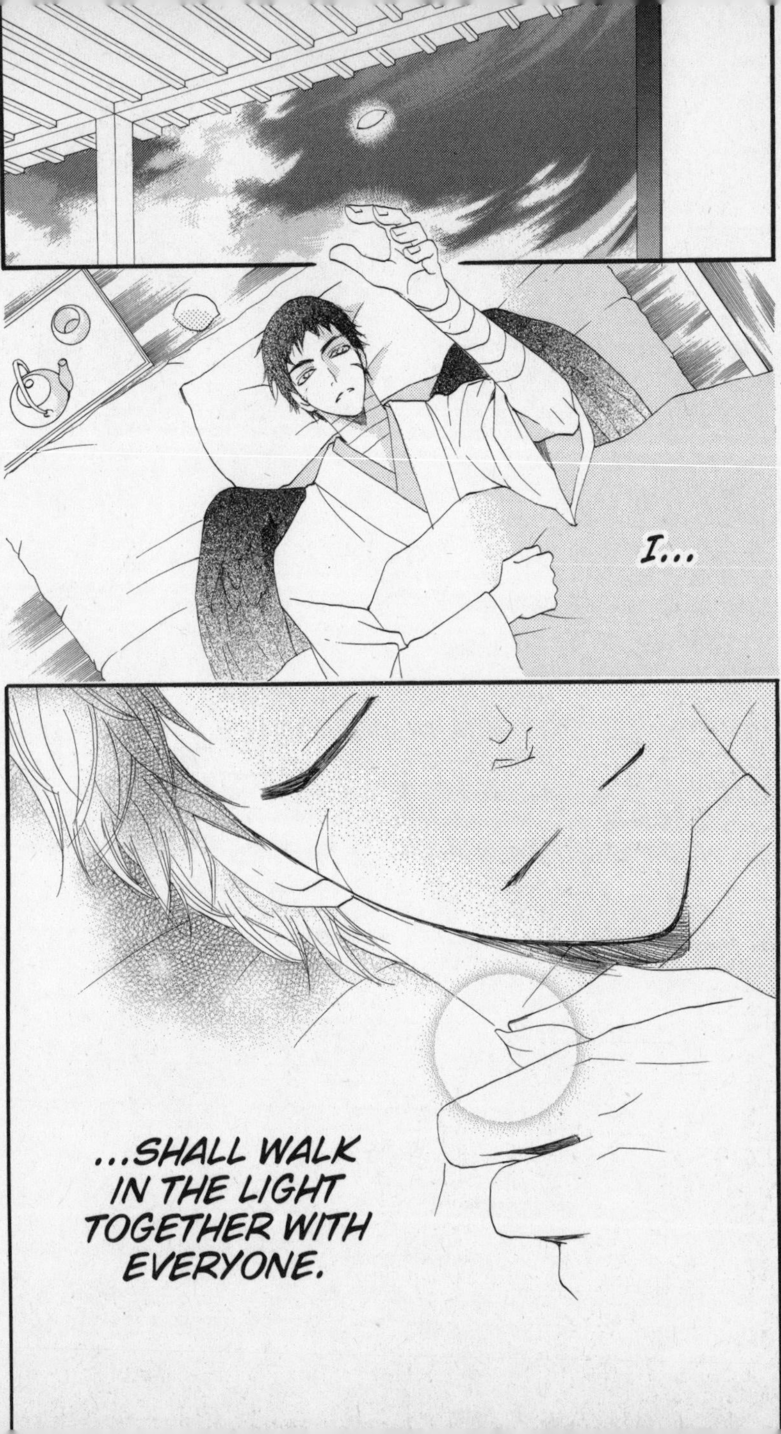
I...
...SHALL WALK IN THE LIGHT TOGETHER WITH EVERYONE.

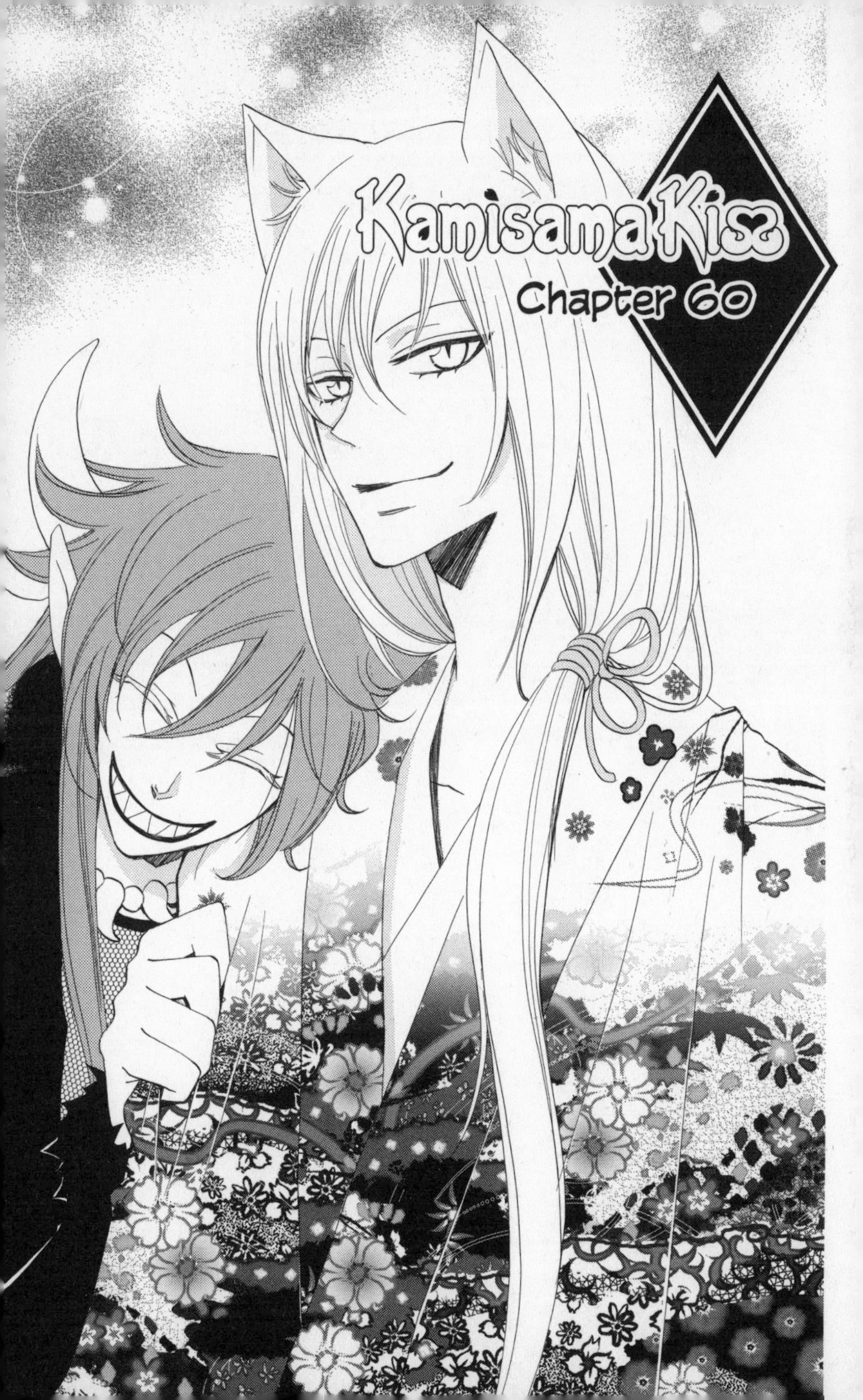
Kamisama Kiss
Chapter 60

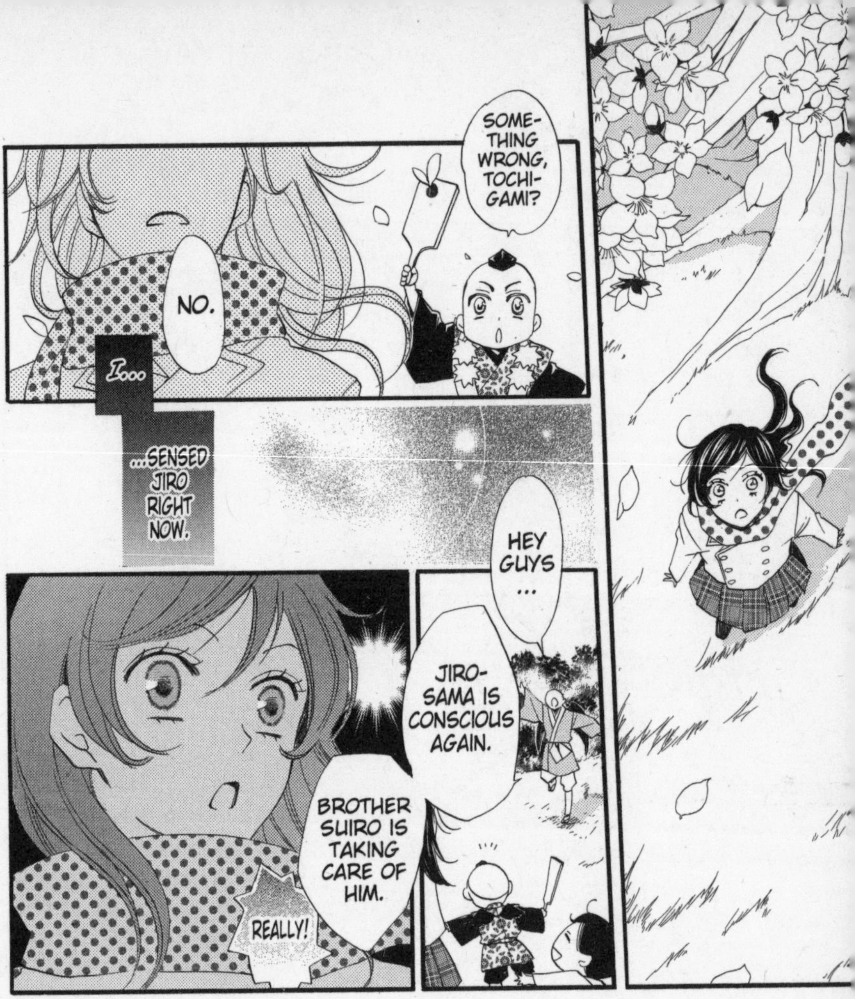
SOME-THING WRONG, TOCHI-GAMI?
NO.
I...
...SENSED JIRO RIGHT NOW.
HEY GUYS...
JIRO-SAMA IS CONSCIOUS AGAIN.
BROTHER SUIRO IS TAKING CARE OF HIM.
REALLY!

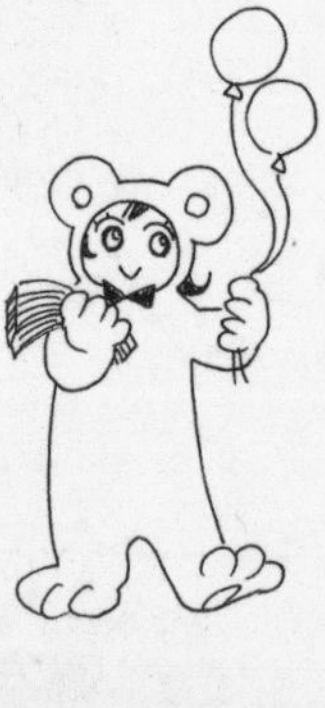

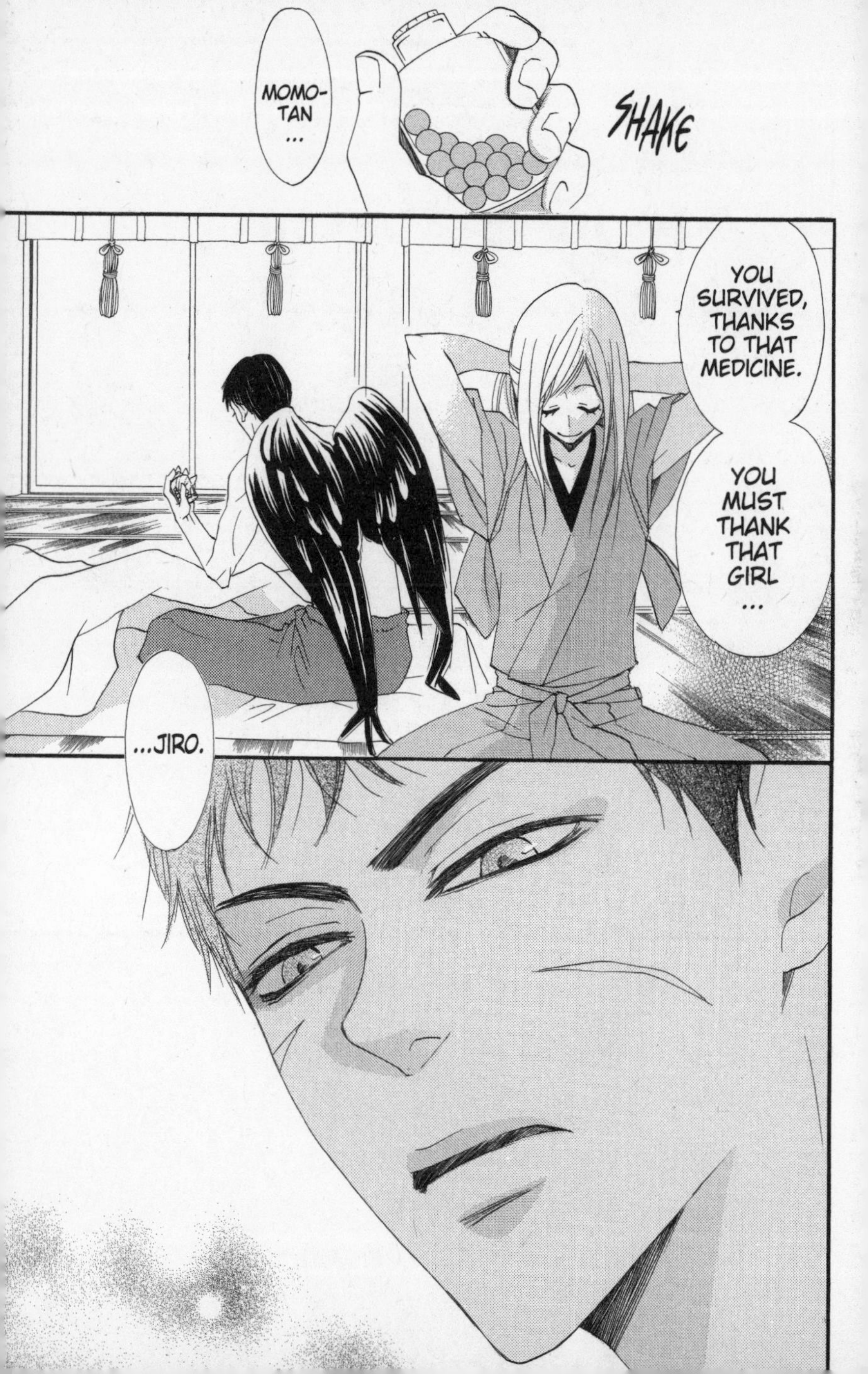
SHAKE
MOMO-TAN ...
YOU SURVIVED, THANKS TO THAT MEDICINE.
YOU MUST THANK THAT GIRL ...
...JIRO.

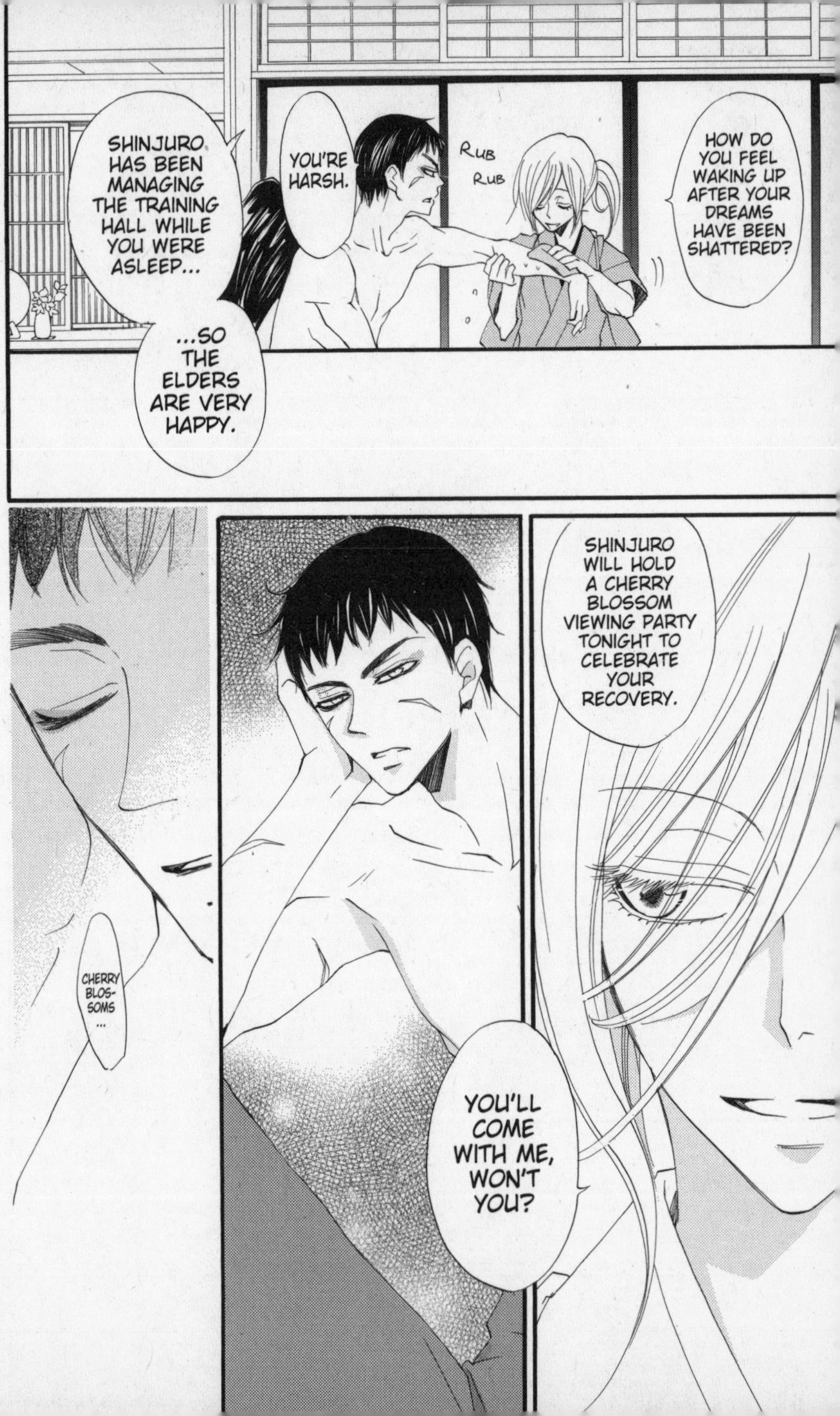
HOW DO YOU FEEL WAKING UP AFTER YOUR DREAMS HAVE BEEN SHATTERED?
RUB RUB
YOU'RE HARSH.
SHINJURO HAS BEEN MANAGING THE TRAINING HALL WHILE YOU WERE ASLEEP...
...SO THE ELDERS ARE VERY HAPPY.
SHINJURO WILL HOLD A CHERRY BLOSSOM VIEWING PARTY TONIGHT TO CELEBRATE YOUR RECOVERY.
YOU'LL COME WITH ME, WON'T YOU?
CHERRY BLOS-SOMS...

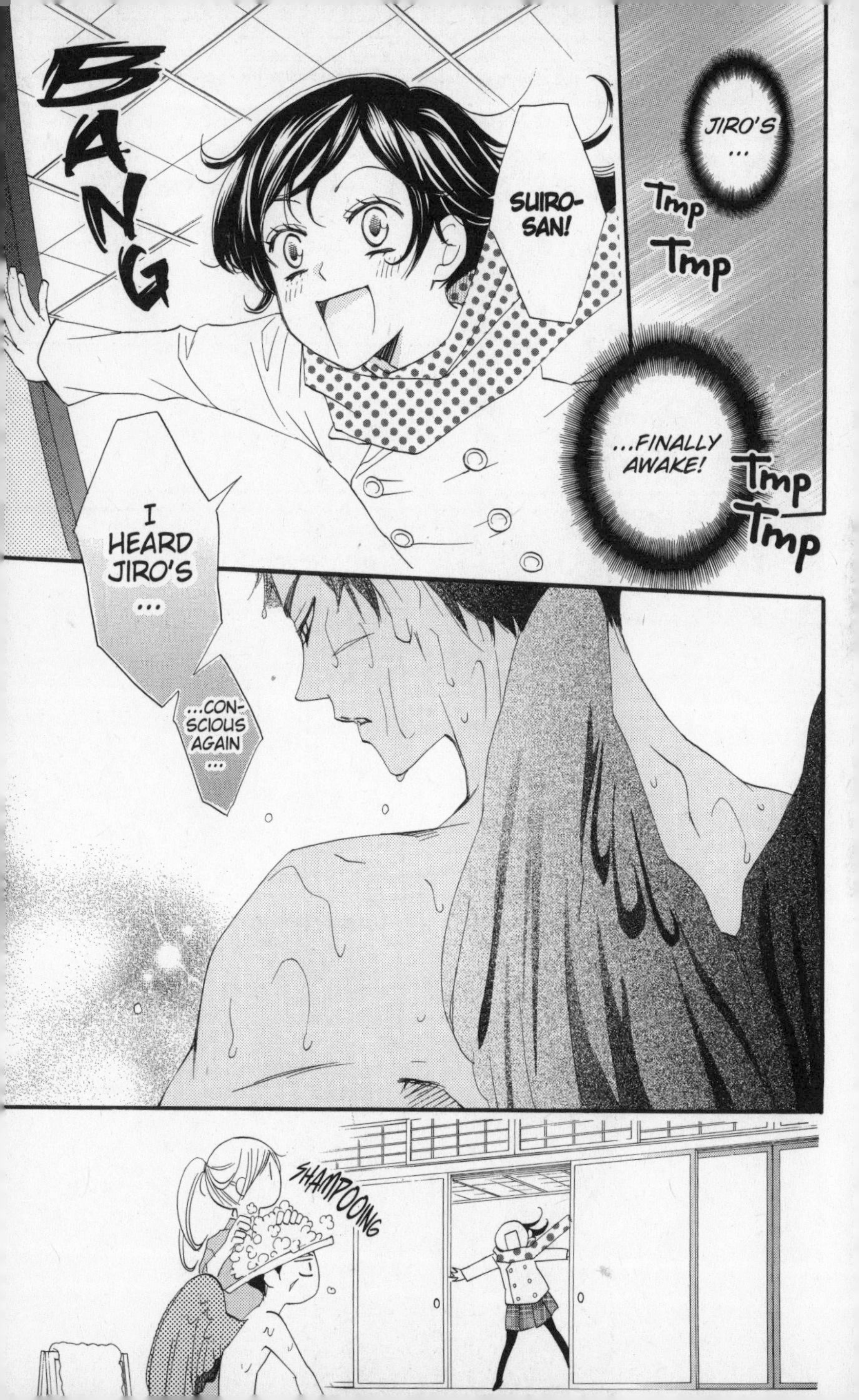
JIRO'S ...
Tmp Tmp
...FINALLY AWAKE!
Tmp Tmp
BANG
SUIRO-SAN!
I HEARD JIRO'S ...
...CON-SCIOUS AGAIN ...
SHAMPOOING

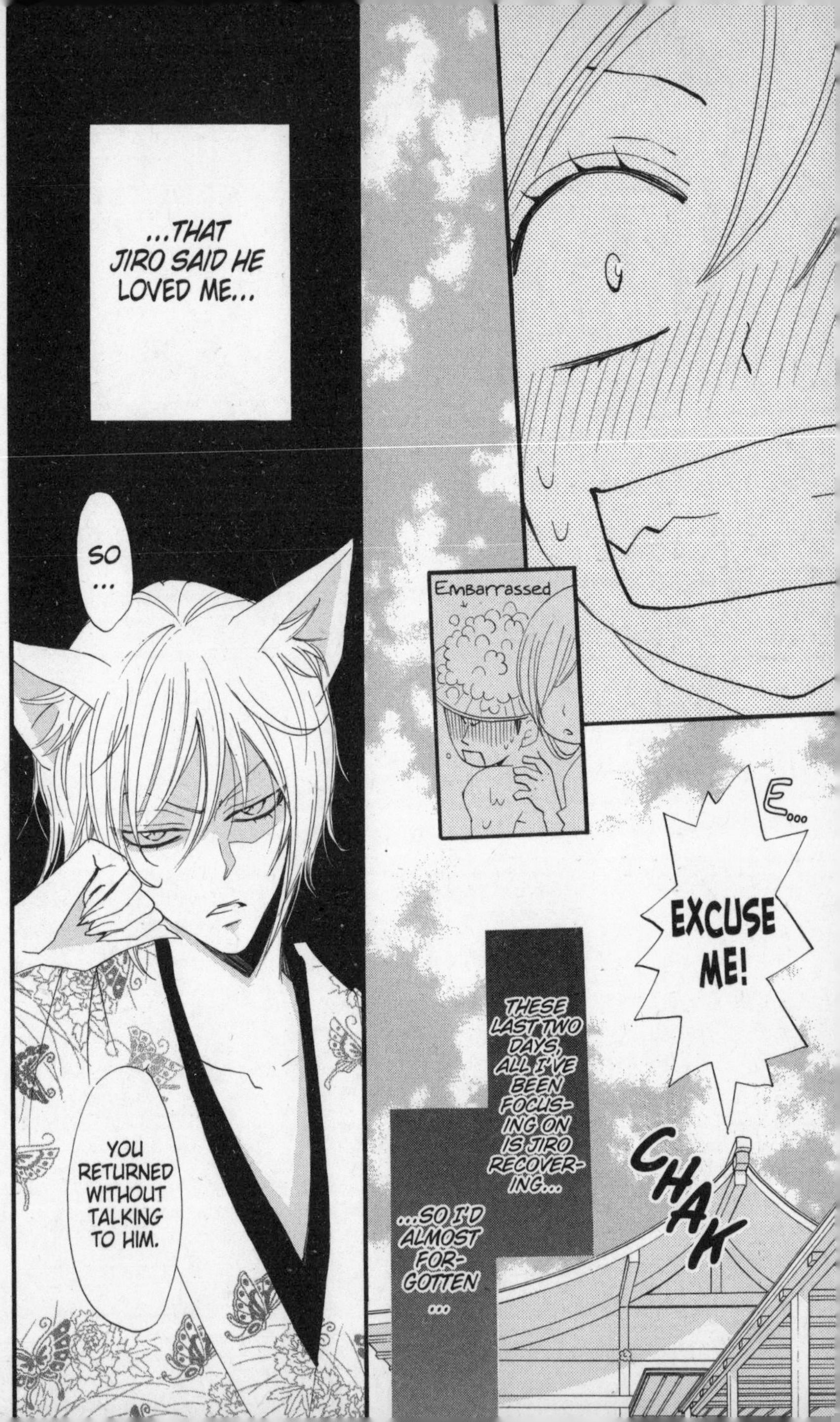
Embarrassed
E...
EXCUSE ME!
CHAK
THESE LAST TWO DAYS, ALL I'VE BEEN FOCUS-ING ON IS JIRO RECOVER-ING...
...SO I'D ALMOST FOR-GOTTEN...
...THAT JIRO SAID HE LOVED ME...
SO...
YOU RETURNED WITHOUT TALKING TO HIM.

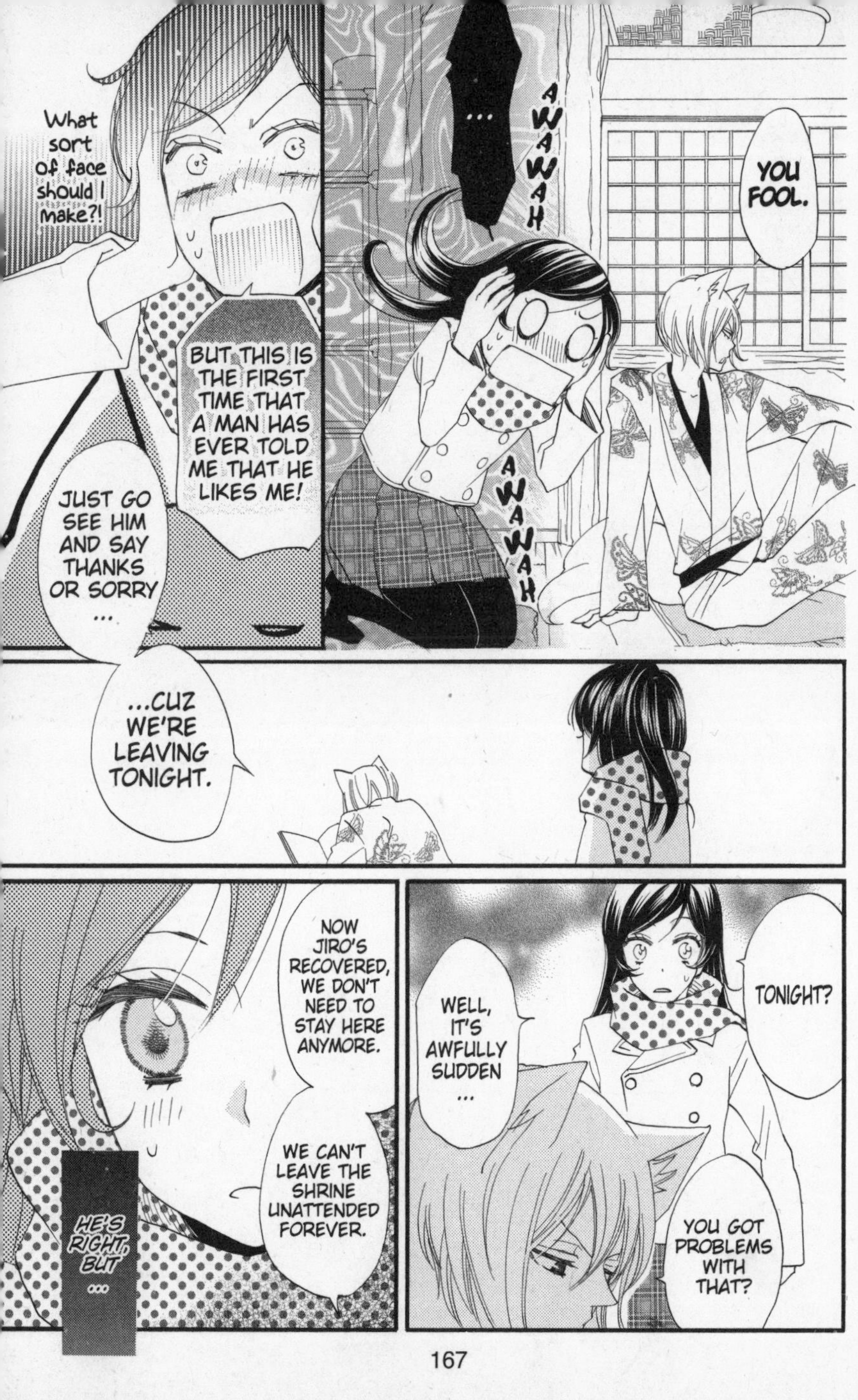
YOU FOOL.
AWAWAH
...
AWAWAH
What sort of face should I make?!
BUT THIS IS THE FIRST TIME THAT A MAN HAS EVER TOLD ME THAT HE LIKES ME!
JUST GO SEE HIM AND SAY THANKS OR SORRY ...
...CUZ WE'RE LEAVING TONIGHT.
TONIGHT?
WELL, IT'S AWFULLY SUDDEN ...
YOU GOT PROBLEMS WITH THAT?
NOW JIRO'S RECOVERED, WE DON'T NEED TO STAY HERE ANYMORE.
WE CAN'T LEAVE THE SHRINE UNATTENDED FOREVER.
HE'S RIGHT, BUT ...

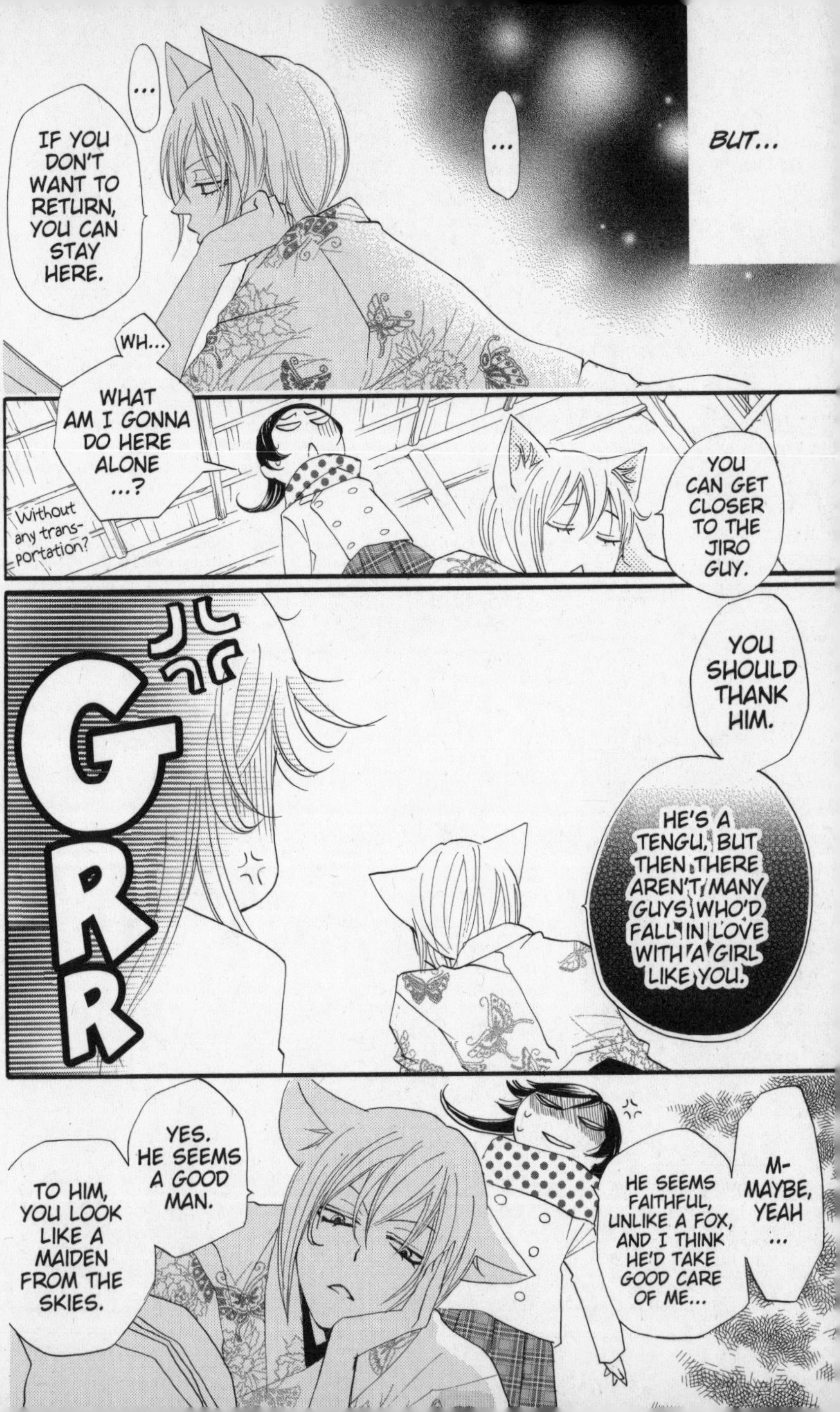
BUT...
...
...
IF YOU DON'T WANT TO RETURN, YOU CAN STAY HERE.
WH...
WHAT AM I GONNA DO HERE ALONE ...?
Without any transportation?
YOU CAN GET CLOSER TO THE JIRO GUY.
YOU SHOULD THANK HIM.
HE'S A TENGU, BUT THEN THERE AREN'T MANY GUYS WHO'D FALL IN LOVE WITH A GIRL LIKE YOU.
GRR
M-MAYBE, YEAH ...
HE SEEMS FAITHFUL, UNLIKE A FOX, AND I THINK HE'D TAKE GOOD CARE OF ME...
YES. HE SEEMS A GOOD MAN.
TO HIM, YOU LOOK LIKE A MAIDEN FROM THE SKIES.

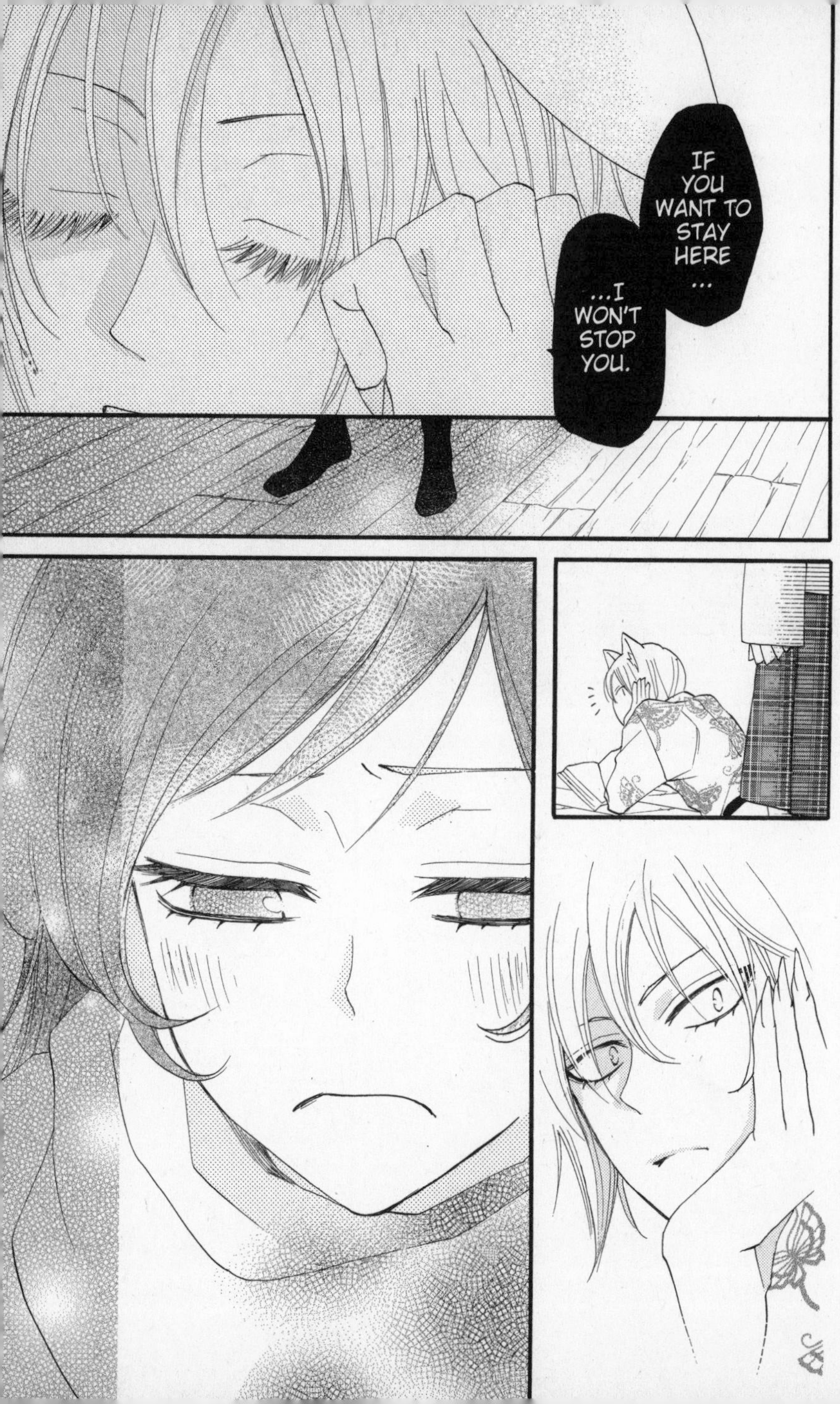
IF YOU WANT TO STAY HERE...
...I WON'T STOP YOU.

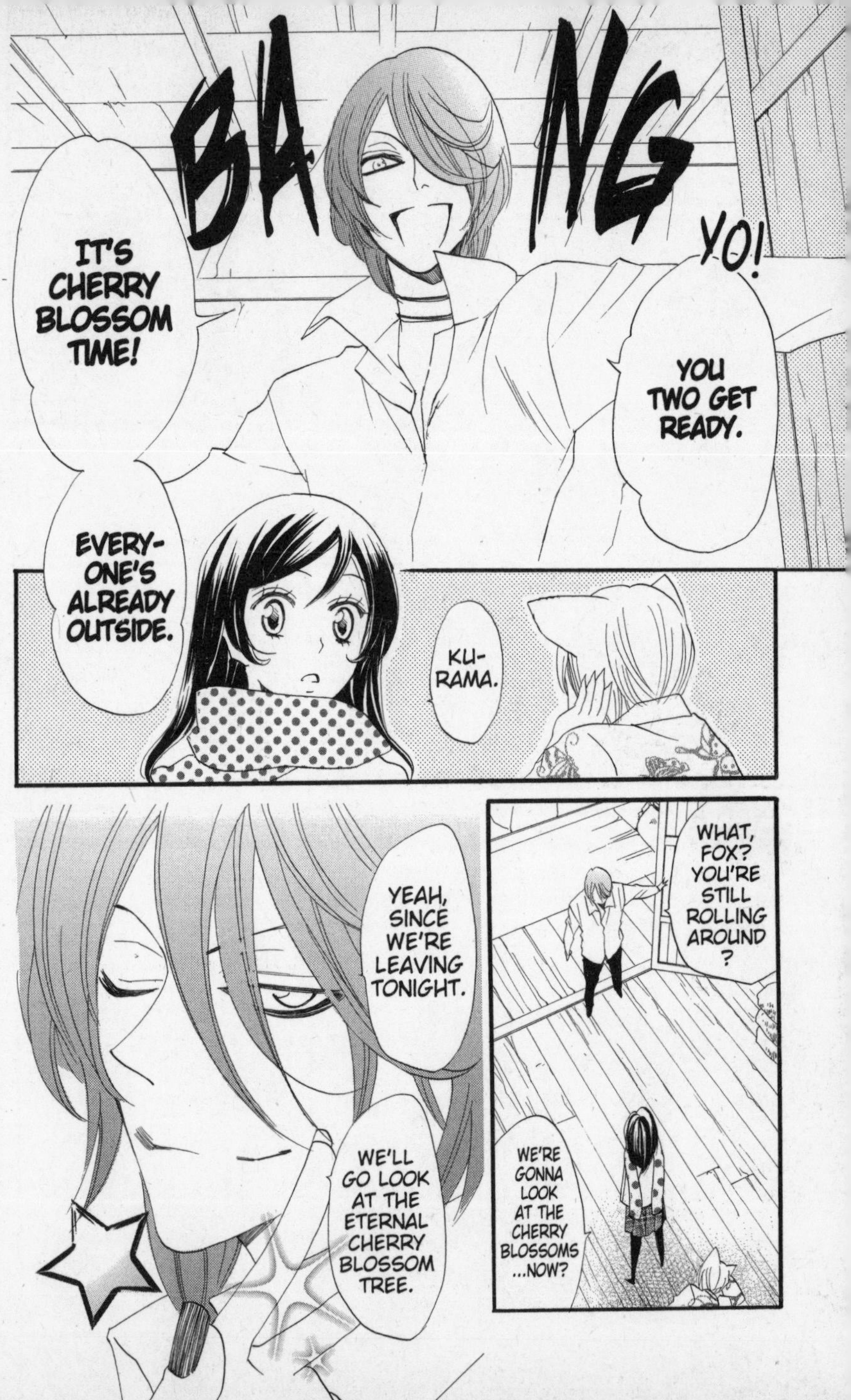
BANG
YO!
YOU TWO GET READY.
IT'S CHERRY BLOSSOM TIME!
EVERY-ONE'S ALREADY OUTSIDE.
KU-RAMA.
WHAT, FOX? YOU'RE STILL ROLLING AROUND?
WE'RE GONNA LOOK AT THE CHERRY BLOSSOMS ...NOW?
YEAH, SINCE WE'RE LEAVING TONIGHT.
WE'LL GO LOOK AT THE ETERNAL CHERRY BLOSSOM TREE.

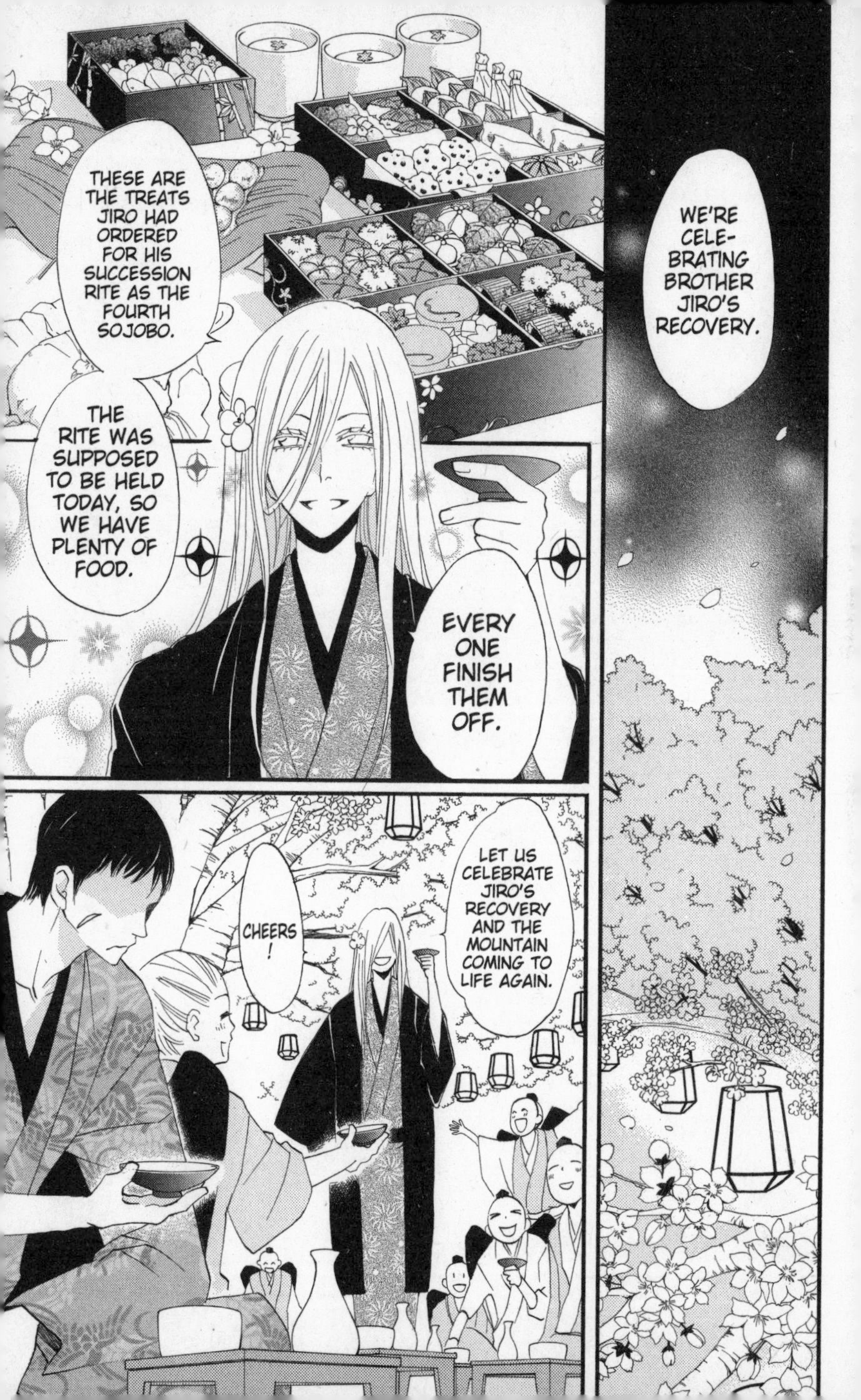
WE'RE CELE-BRATING BROTHER JIRO'S RECOVERY.
THESE ARE THE TREATS JIRO HAD ORDERED FOR HIS SUCCESSION RITE AS THE FOURTH SOJOBO.
THE RITE WAS SUPPOSED TO BE HELD TODAY, SO WE HAVE PLENTY OF FOOD.
EVERY ONE FINISH THEM OFF.
LET US CELEBRATE JIRO'S RECOVERY AND THE MOUNTAIN COMING TO LIFE AGAIN.
CHEERS!

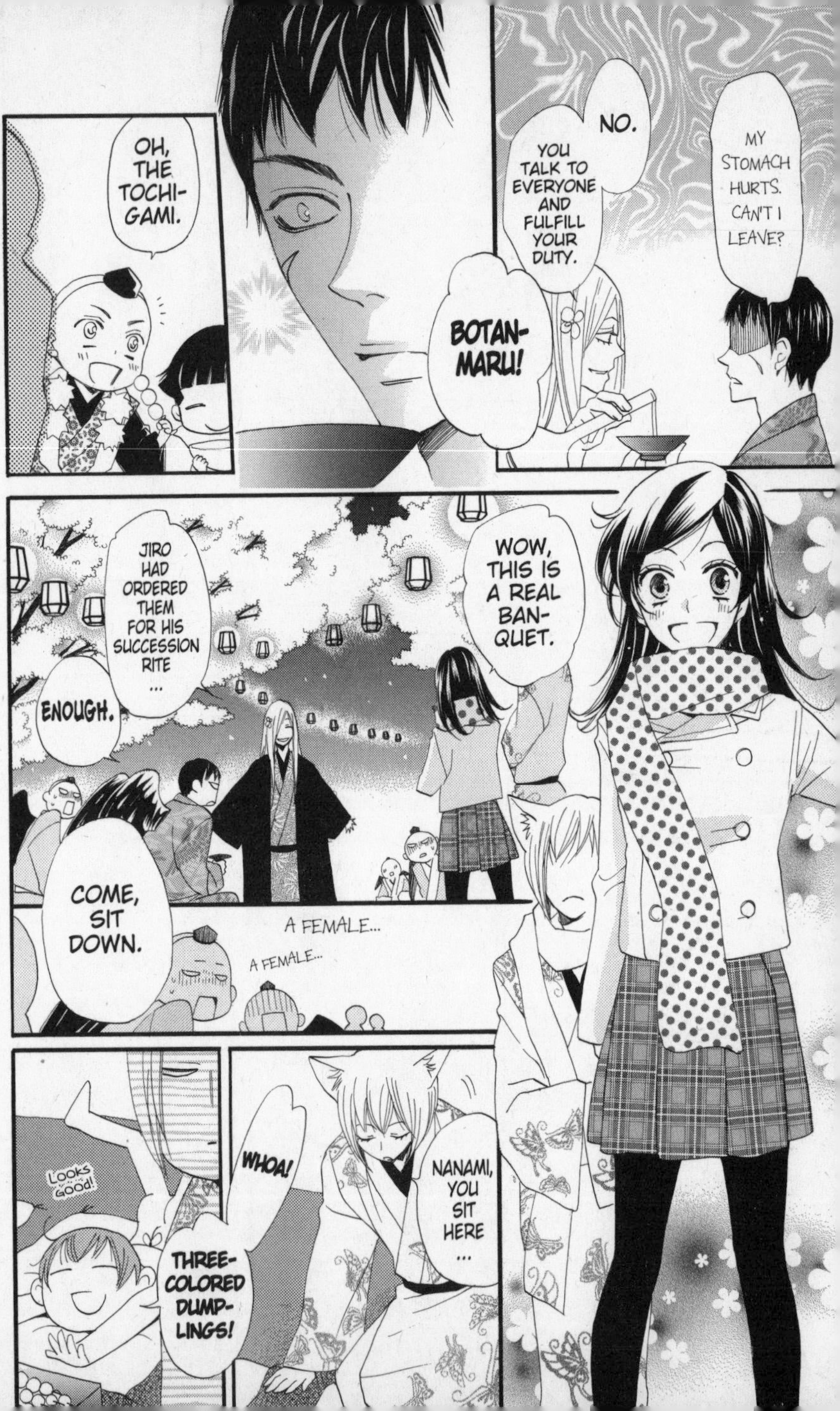
MY STOMACH HURTS. CAN'T I LEAVE?
NO.
YOU TALK TO EVERYONE AND FULFILL YOUR DUTY.
BOTAN-MARU!
OH, THE TOCHI-GAMI.
WOW, THIS IS A REAL BAN-QUET.
JIRO HAD ORDERED THEM FOR HIS SUCCESSION RITE ...
ENOUGH.
COME, SIT DOWN.
A FEMALE...
A FEMALE...
NANAMI, YOU SIT HERE ...
WHOA!
THREE-COLORED DUMP-LINGS!
Looks Good!

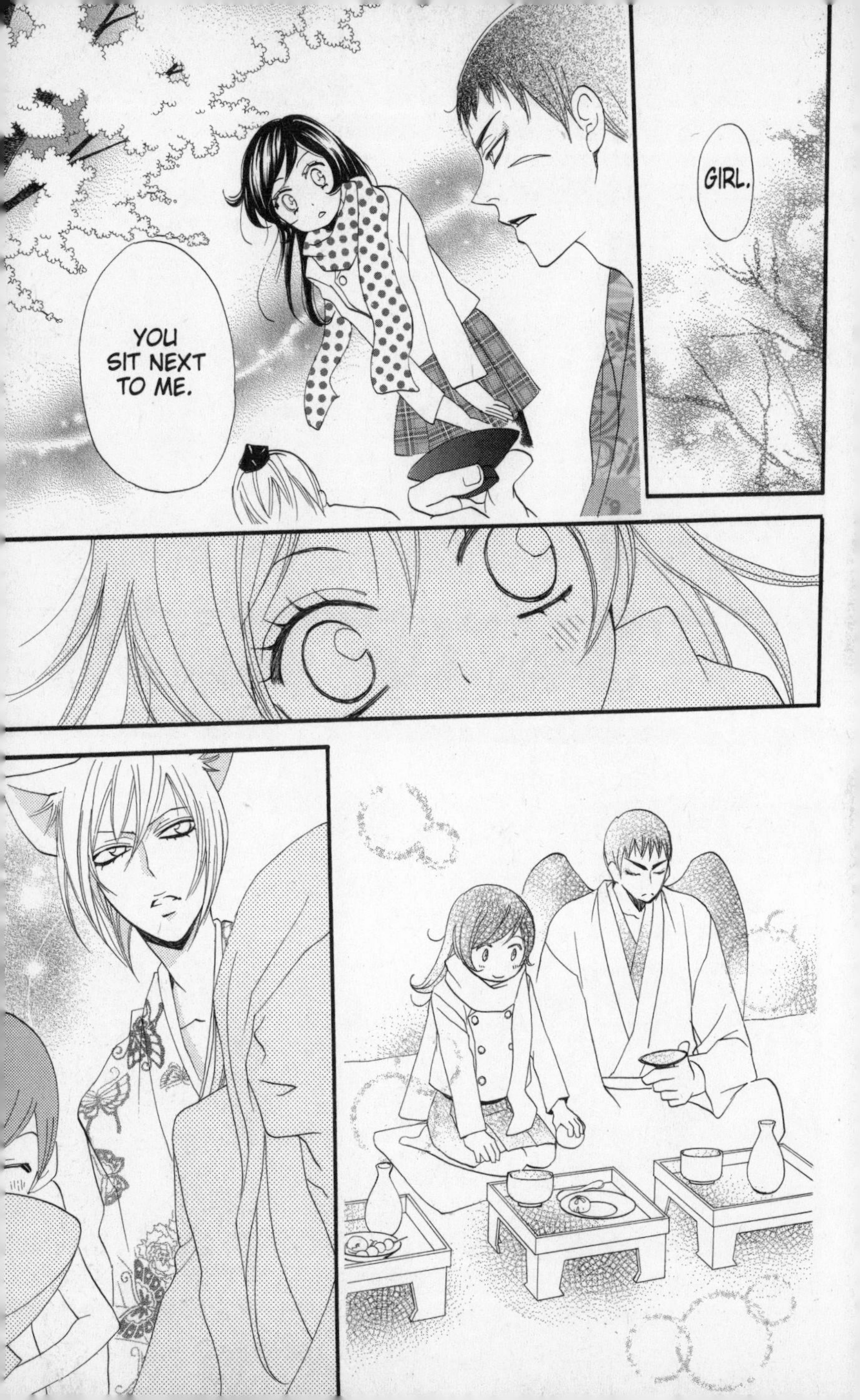
GIRL.
YOU SIT NEXT TO ME.

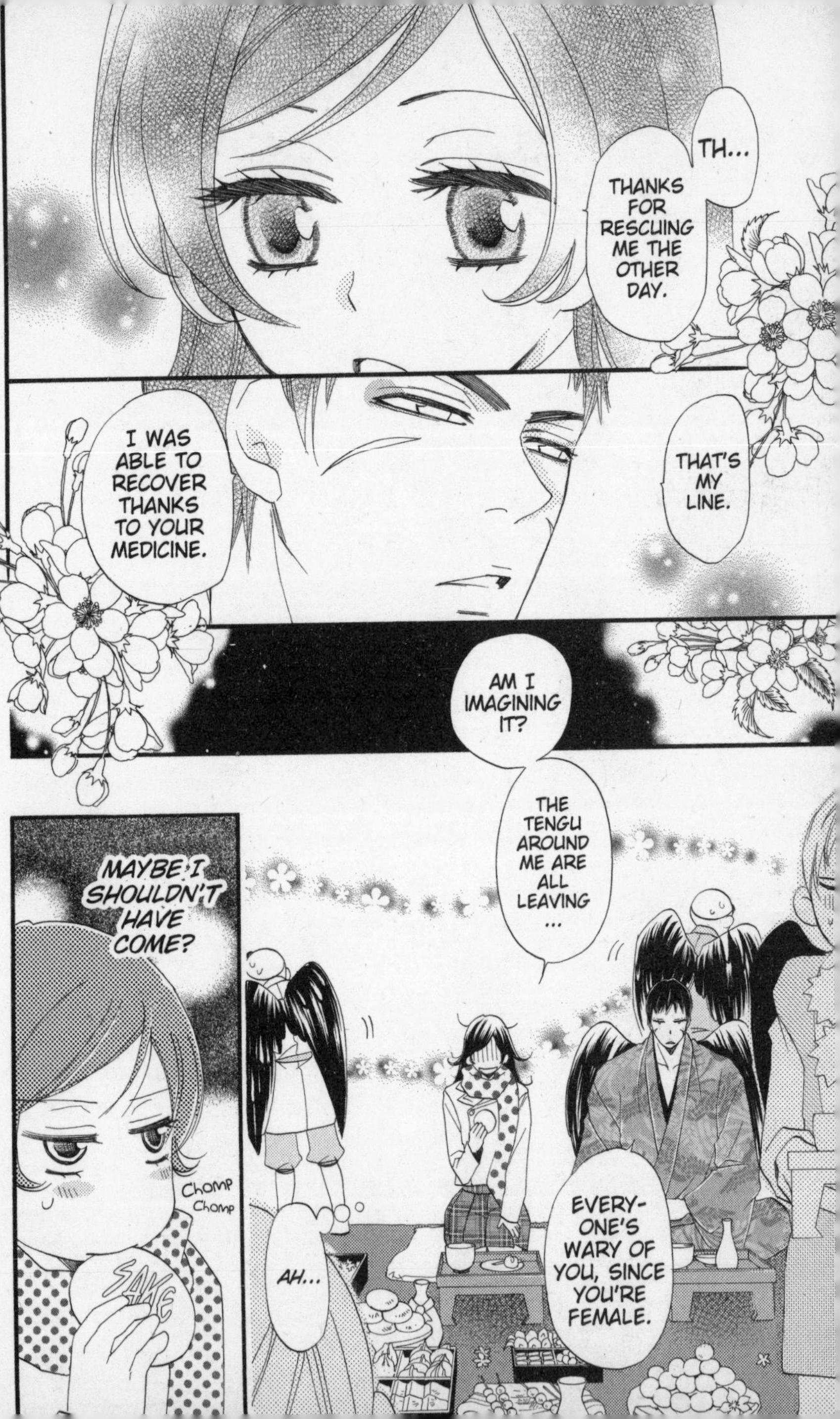
TH...
THANKS FOR RESCUING ME THE OTHER DAY.
THAT'S MY LINE.
I WAS ABLE TO RECOVER THANKS TO YOUR MEDICINE.
AM I IMAGINING IT?
THE TENGU AROUND ME ARE ALL LEAVING...
EVERY-ONE'S WARY OF YOU, SINCE YOU'RE FEMALE.
AH...
MAYBE I SHOULDN'T HAVE COME?
Chomp Chomp
SAKE

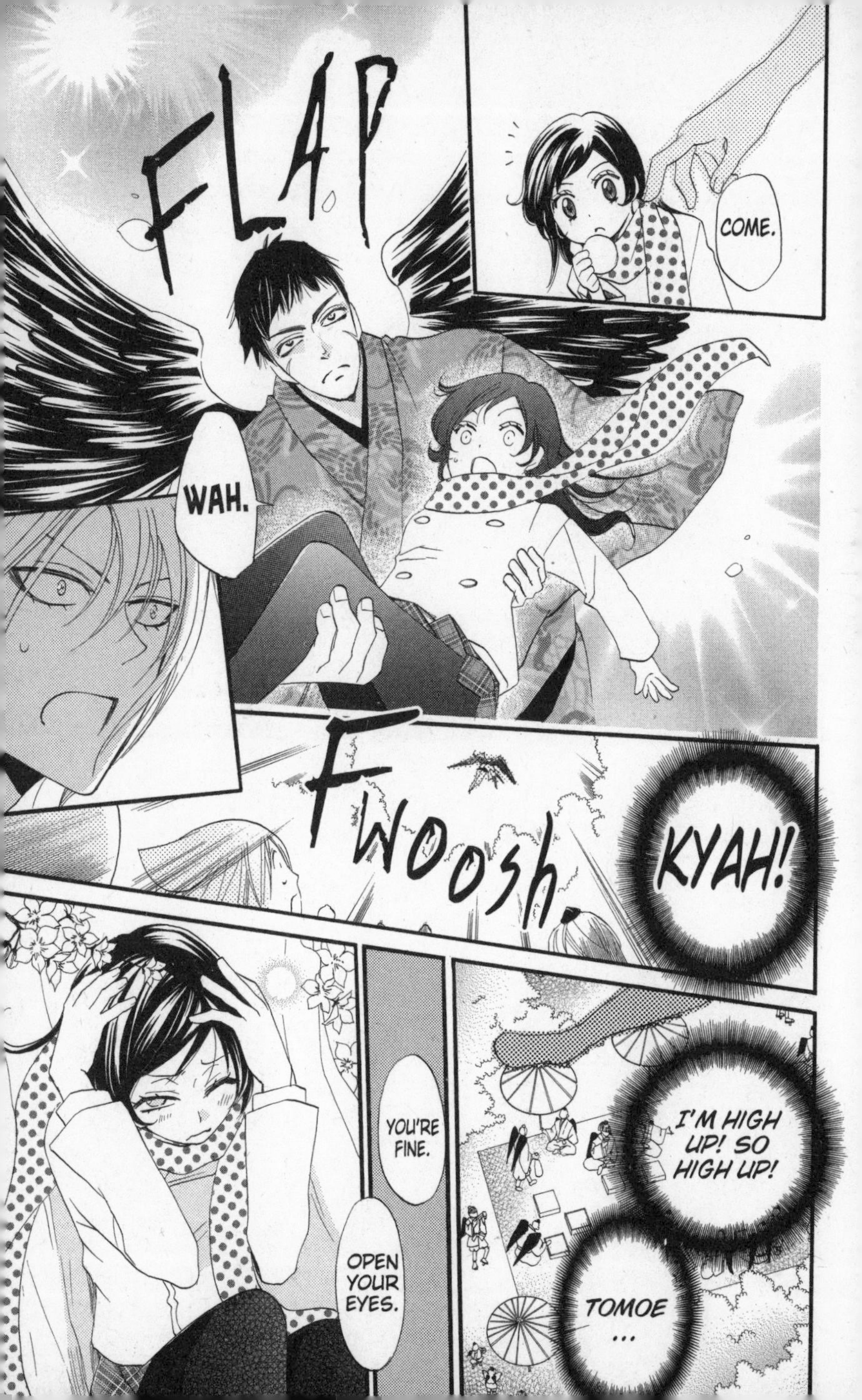
COME.
FLAP
WAH.
KYAH!
FWOOSH
I'M HIGH UP! SO HIGH UP!
TOMOE ...
YOU'RE FINE.
OPEN YOUR EYES.

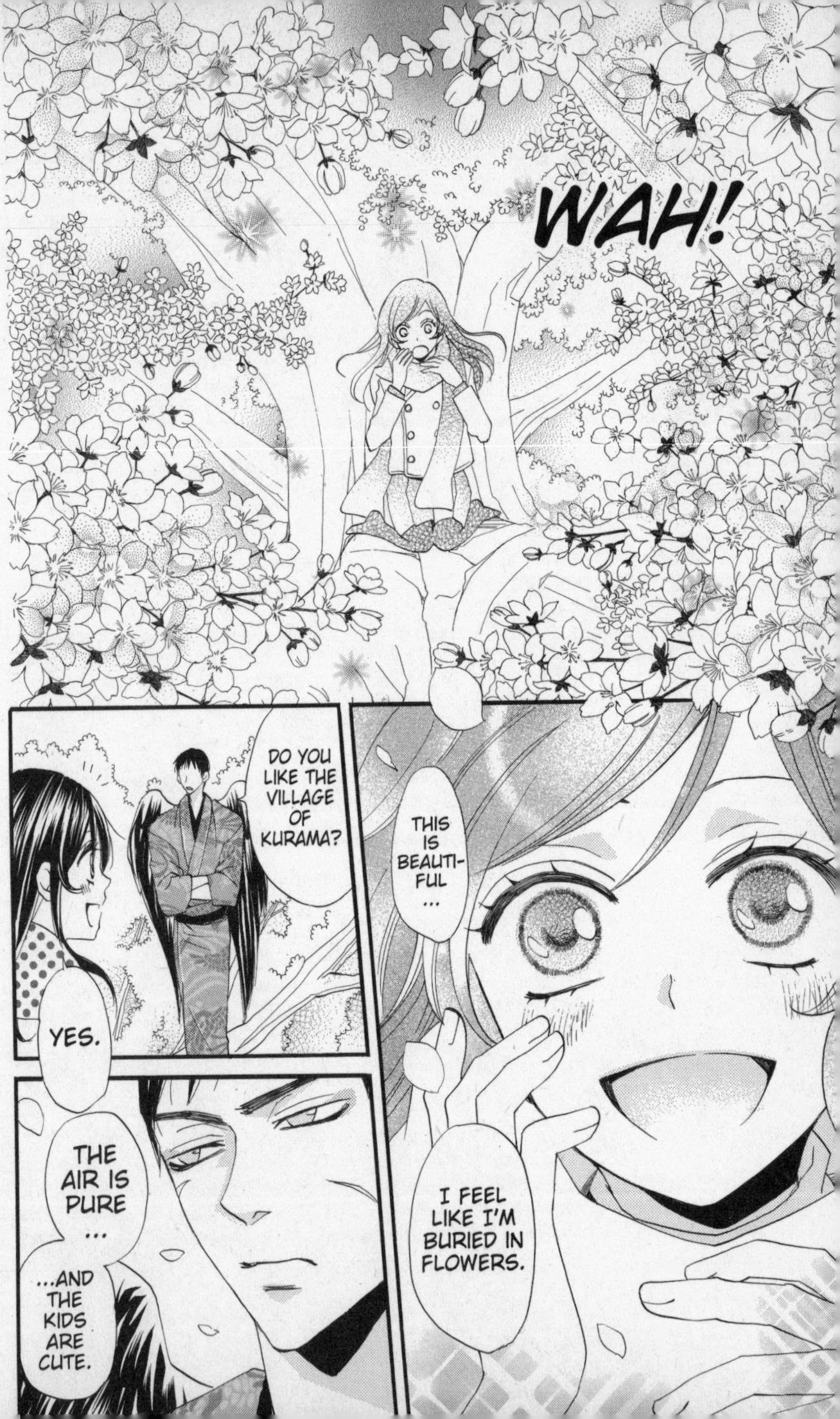
WAH!
THIS IS BEAUTIFUL...
I FEEL LIKE I'M BURIED IN FLOWERS.
DO YOU LIKE THE VILLAGE OF KURAMA?
YES.
THE AIR IS PURE...
...AND THE KIDS ARE CUTE.

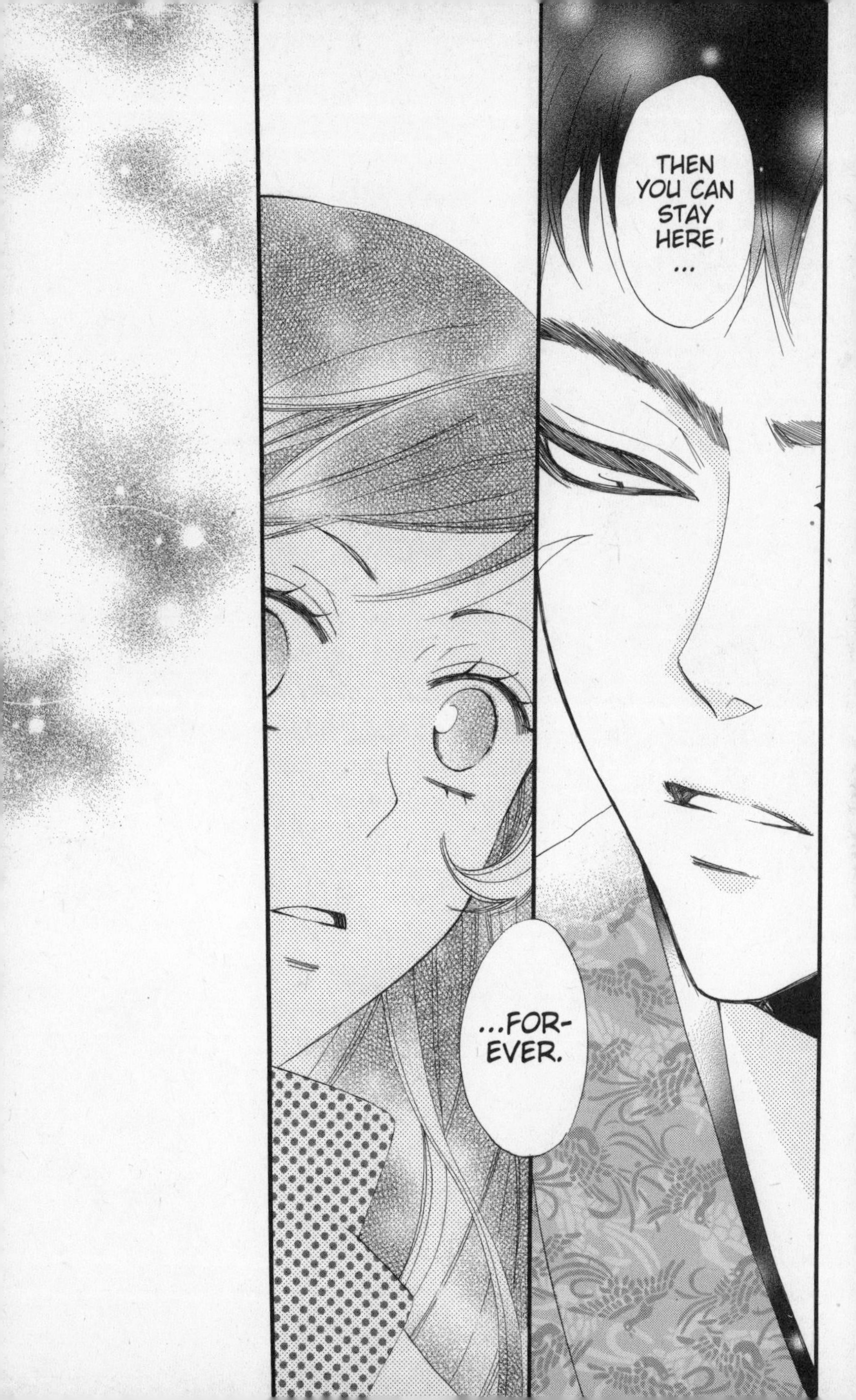
THEN YOU CAN STAY HERE ...
...FOR-EVER.

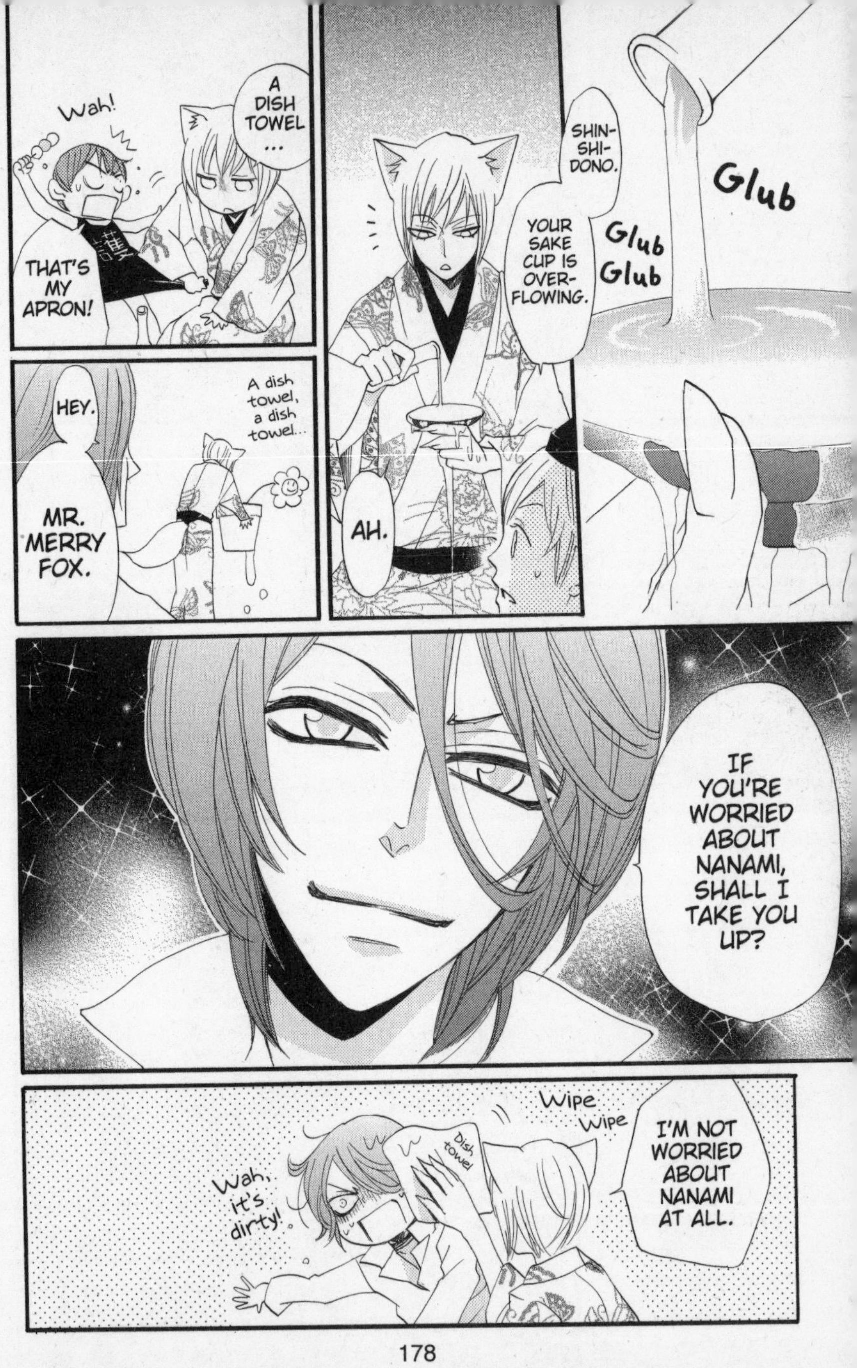
Glub
Glub Glub
SHIN-SHI-DONO.
YOUR SAKE CUP IS OVER-FLOWING.
AH.
A DISH TOWEL ...
Wah!
THAT'S MY APRON!
A dish towel, a dish towel...
HEY.
MR. MERRY FOX.
IF YOU'RE WORRIED ABOUT NANAMI, SHALL I TAKE YOU UP?
I'M NOT WORRIED ABOUT NANAMI AT ALL.
Wipe Wipe
Dish towel
Wah, it's dirty!

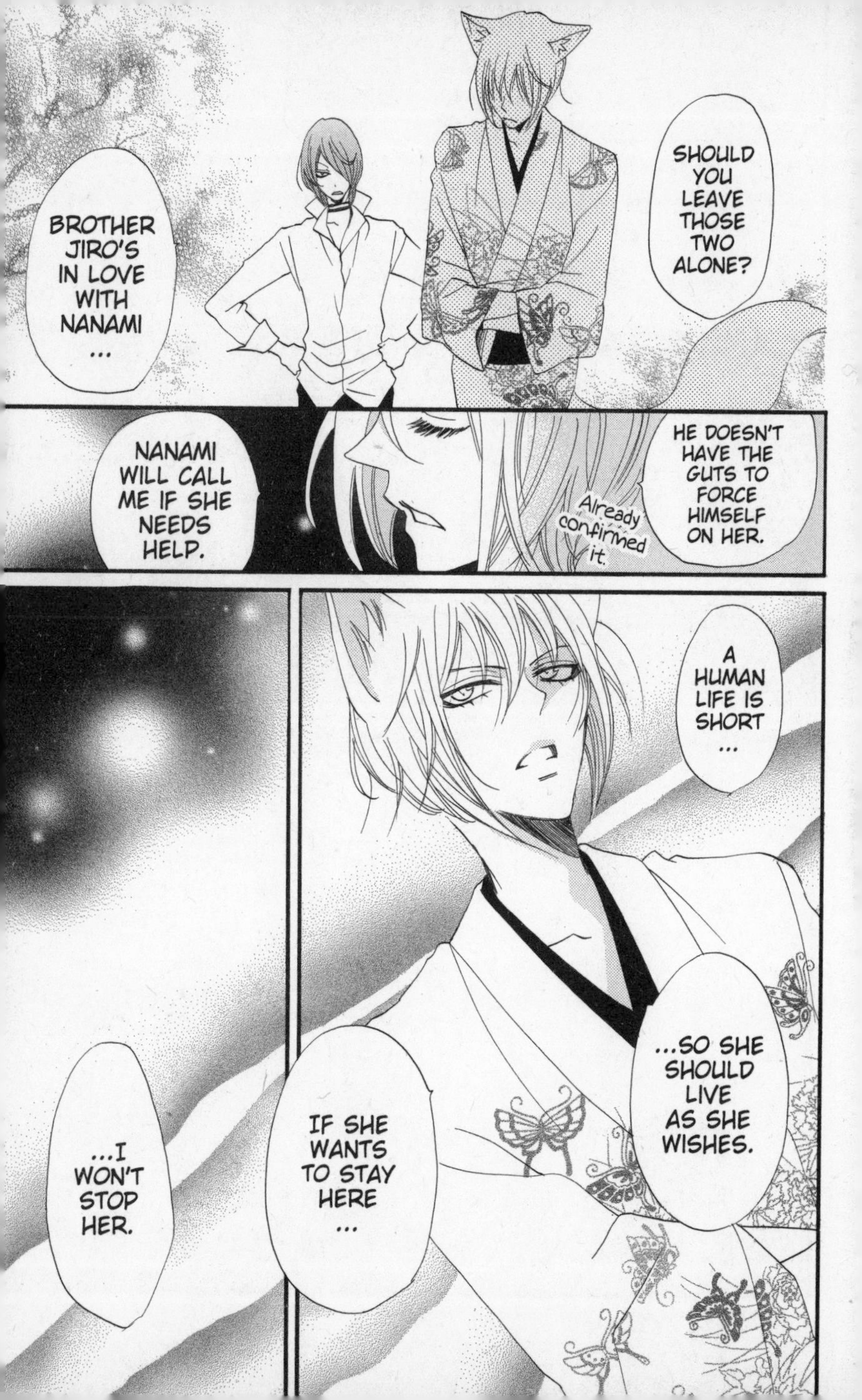
SHOULD YOU LEAVE THOSE TWO ALONE?
BROTHER JIRO'S IN LOVE WITH NANAMI ...
HE DOESN'T HAVE THE GUTS TO FORCE HIMSELF ON HER.
Already confirmed it.
NANAMI WILL CALL ME IF SHE NEEDS HELP.
A HUMAN LIFE IS SHORT ...
...SO SHE SHOULD LIVE AS SHE WISHES.
IF SHE WANTS TO STAY HERE ...
...I WON'T STOP HER.

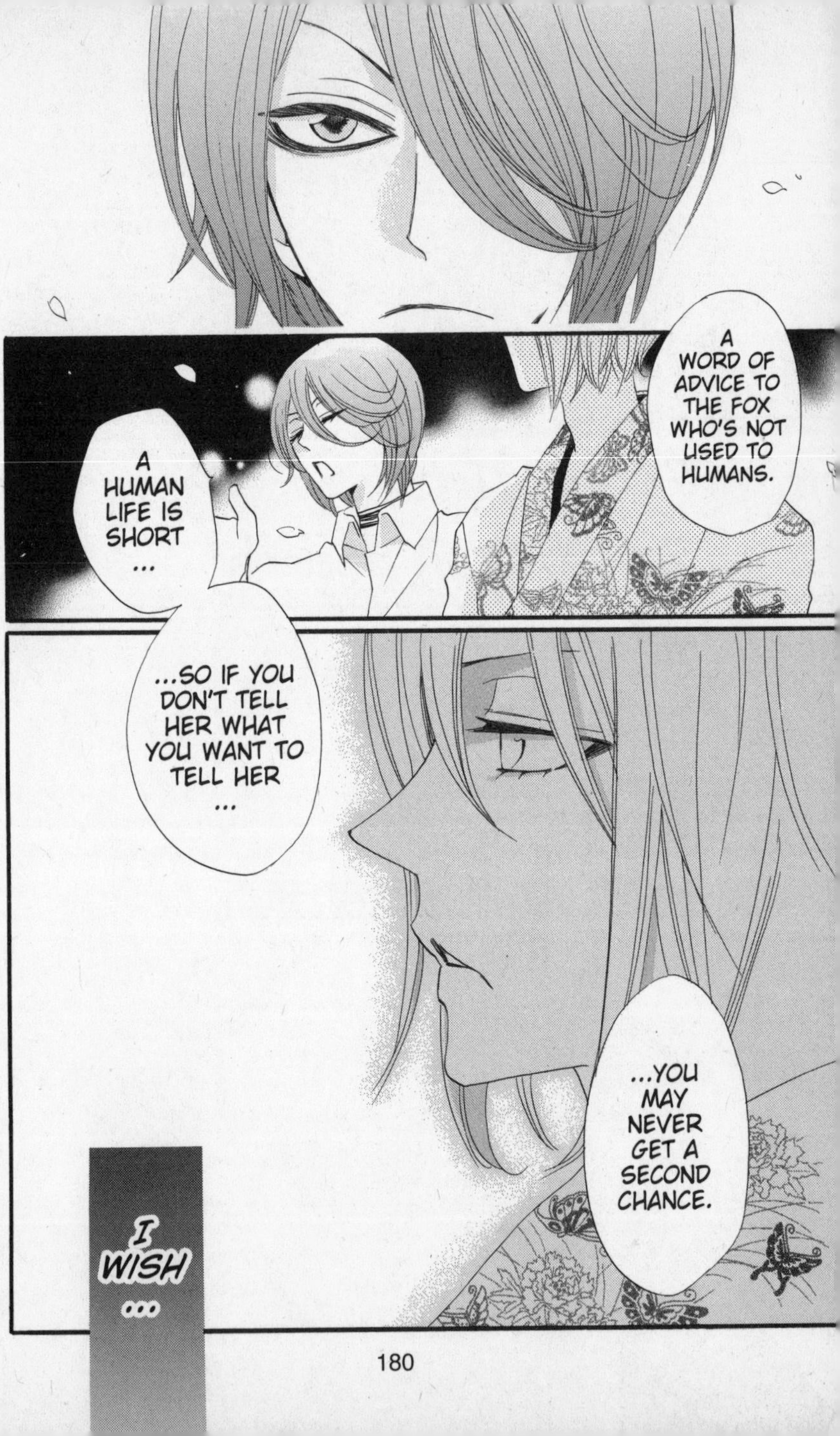
A WORD OF ADVICE TO THE FOX WHO'S NOT USED TO HUMANS.
A HUMAN LIFE IS SHORT...
...SO IF YOU DON'T TELL HER WHAT YOU WANT TO TELL HER...
...YOU MAY NEVER GET A SECOND CHANCE.
I WISH...

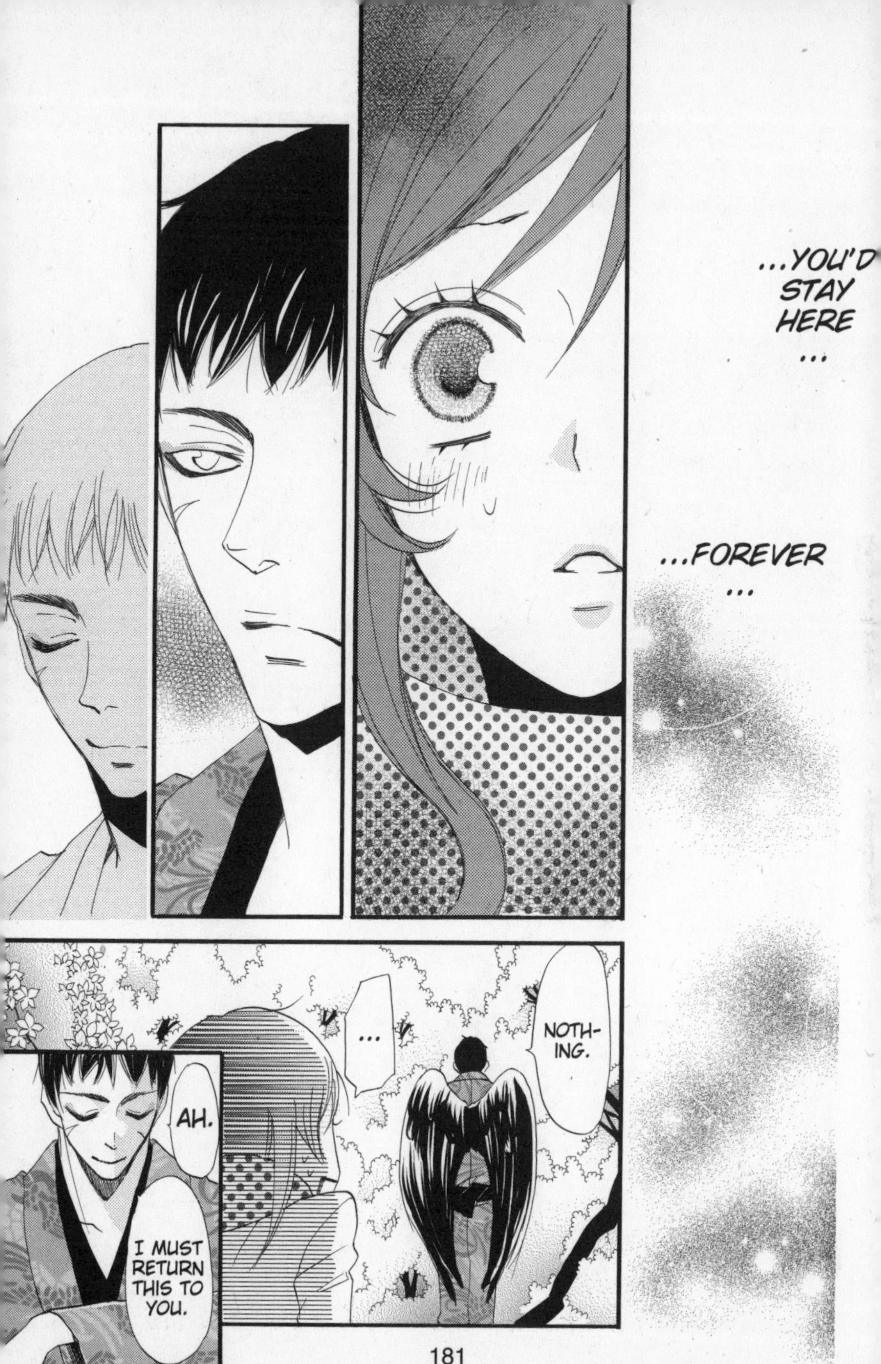
...YOU'D STAY HERE ...
...FOREVER ...
NOTH- ING.
...
AH.
I MUST RETURN THIS TO YOU.

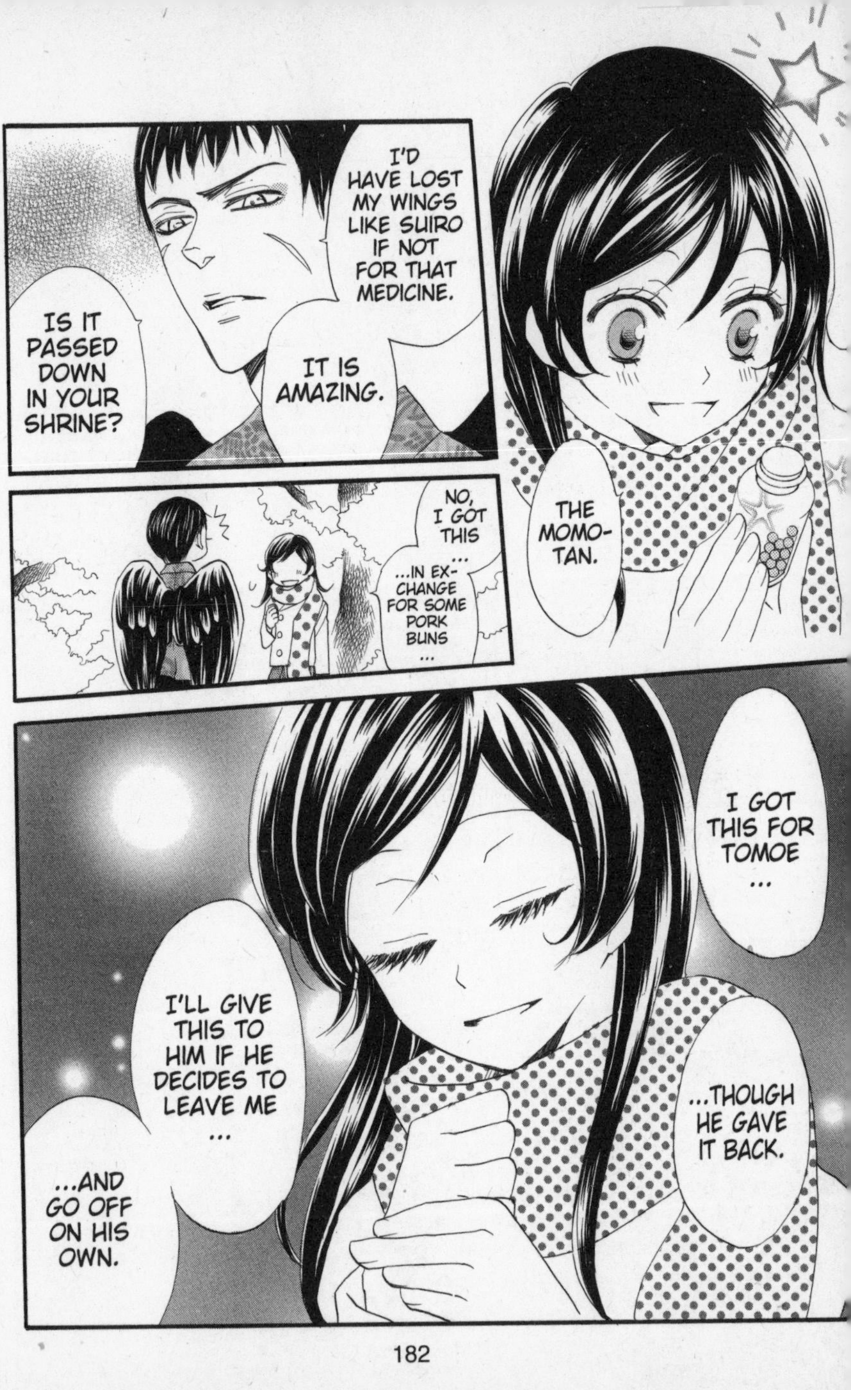
THE MOMO-TAN.
I'D HAVE LOST MY WINGS LIKE SUIRO IF NOT FOR THAT MEDICINE.
IT IS AMAZING.
IS IT PASSED DOWN IN YOUR SHRINE?
NO, I GOT THIS ...
...IN EX-CHANGE FOR SOME PORK BUNS ...
I GOT THIS FOR TOMOE ...
...THOUGH HE GAVE IT BACK.
I'LL GIVE THIS TO HIM IF HE DECIDES TO LEAVE ME ...
...AND GO OFF ON HIS OWN.

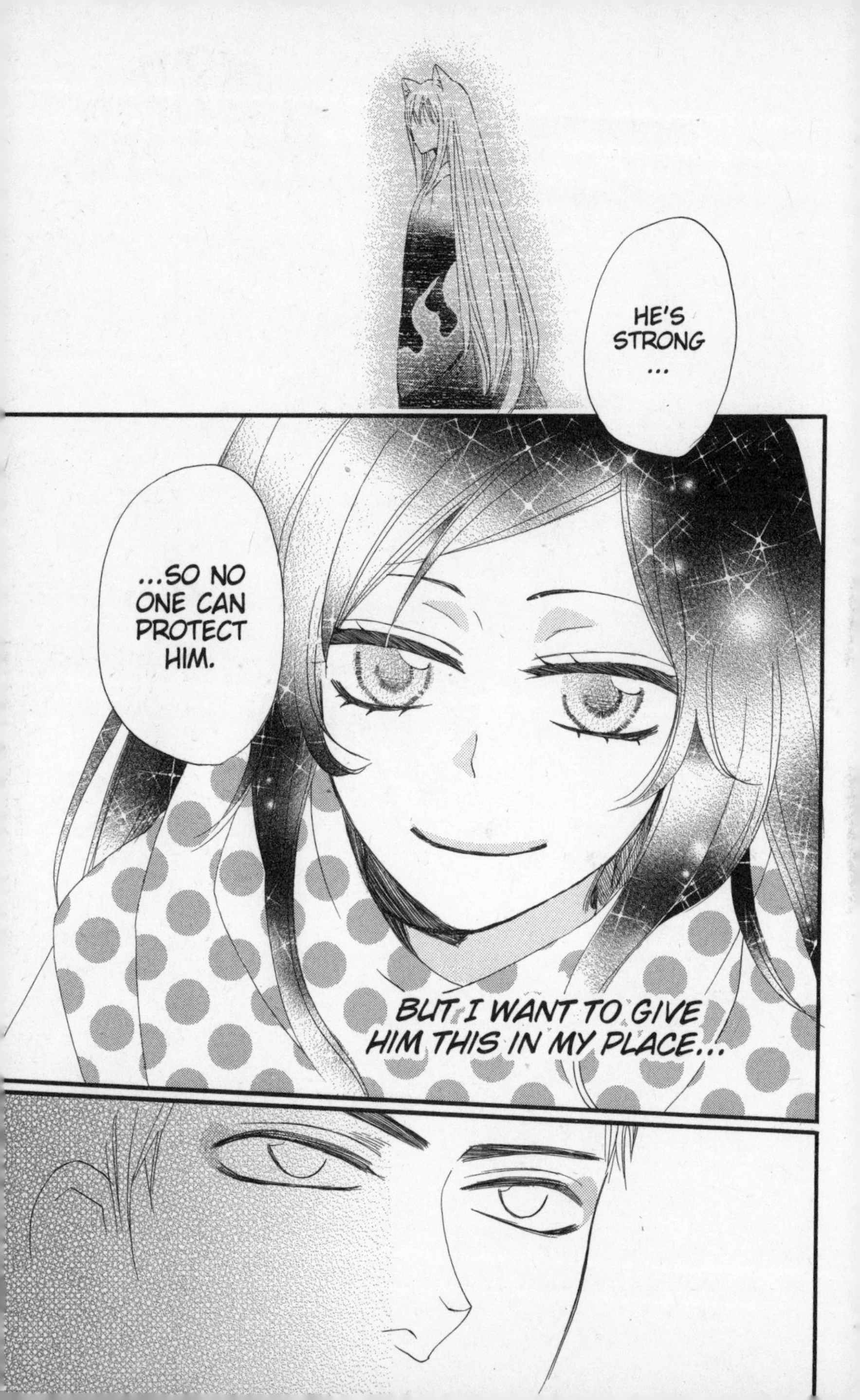
HE'S STRONG ...
...SO NO ONE CAN PROTECT HIM.
BUT I WANT TO GIVE HIM THIS IN MY PLACE...

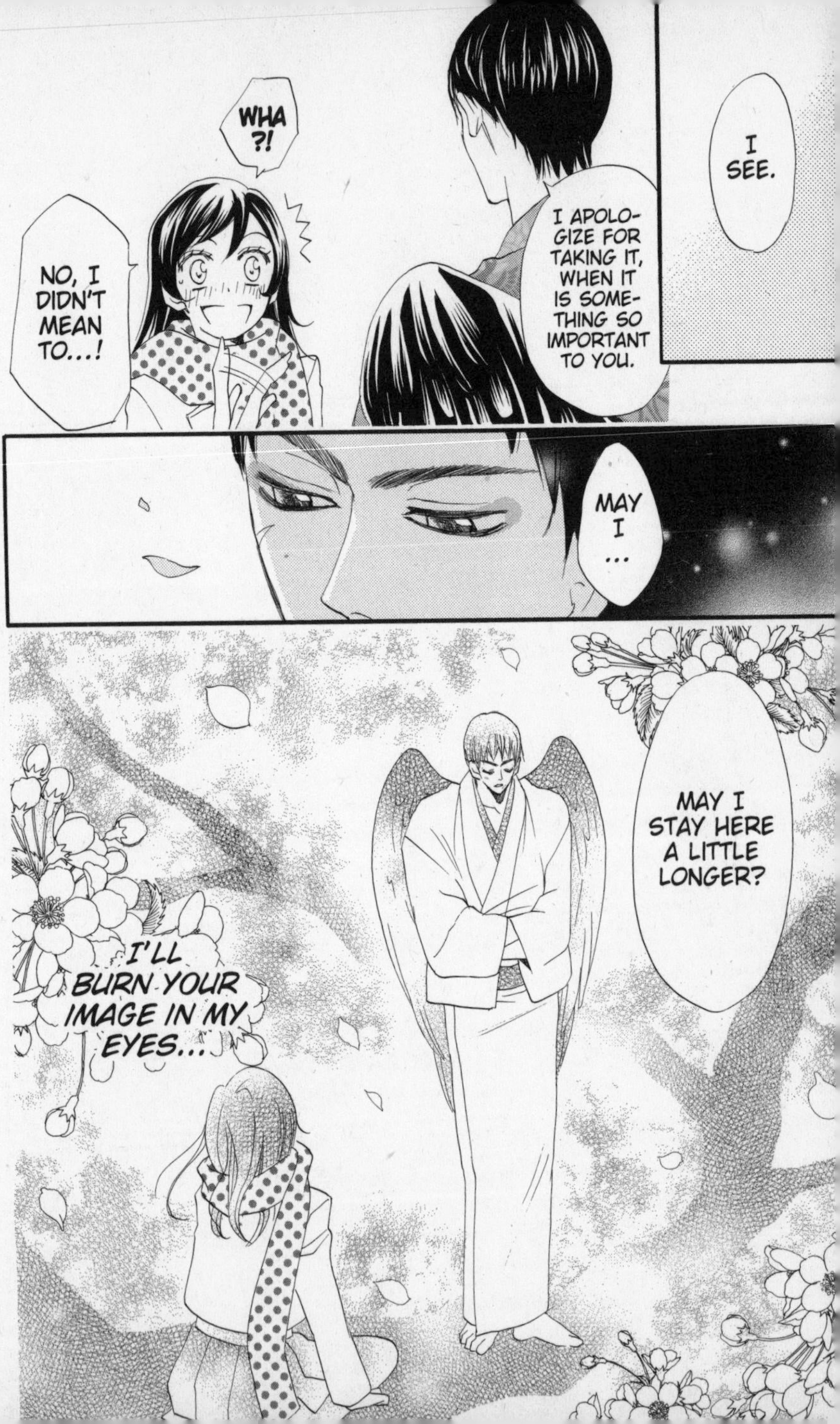
I SEE.
I APOLOGIZE FOR TAKING IT, WHEN IT IS SOMETHING SO IMPORTANT TO YOU.
WHA ?!
NO, I DIDN'T MEAN TO...!
MAY I ...
MAY I STAY HERE A LITTLE LONGER?
I'LL BURN YOUR IMAGE IN MY EYES...

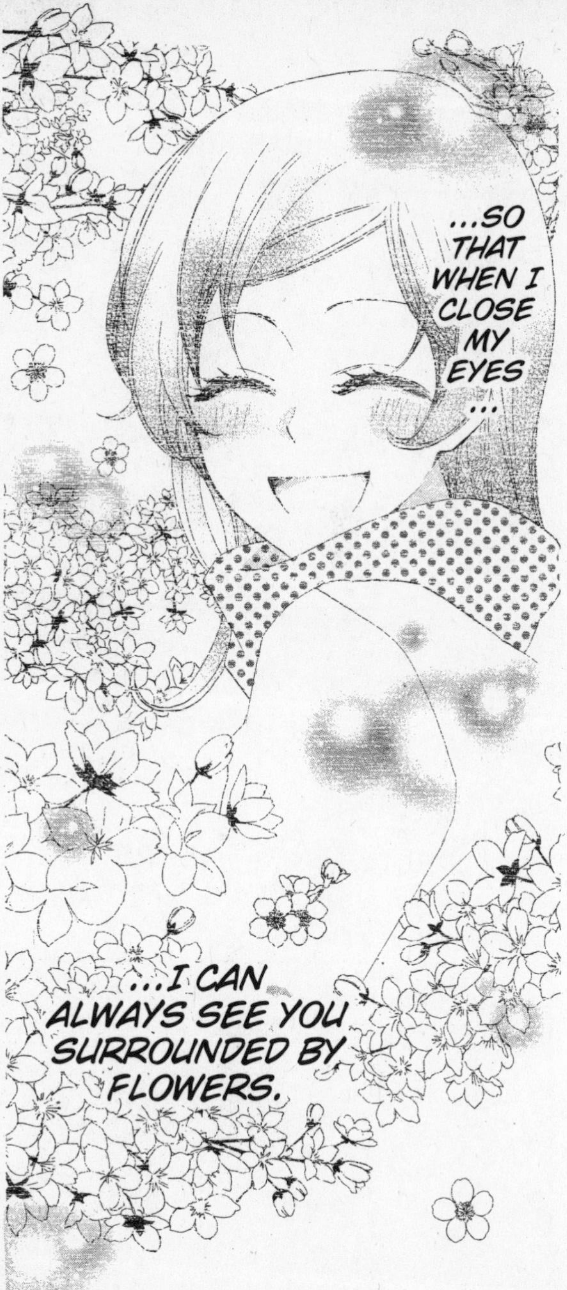
...SO THAT WHEN I CLOSE MY EYES ...
...I CAN ALWAYS SEE YOU SURROUNDED BY FLOWERS.

5

Thank you for reading this far!

People who've been reading this series, people who've picked up this series for the first time, I'll be happy if you enjoyed reading volume 10. And I'll be really, really happy if you read volume 11 as well.

If you have any comments, please let me know. ☺

Julietta Suzuki

c/o Shojo Beat
VIZ Media, LLC
P.O. Box 77010
San Francisco
CA 94107

I write a blog, and I twitter as well. ✿

http://suzuju.jugem.jp/ My BLOG

Please come take a look. ✿

Well well! I pray that we'll be able to meet again!

Juli

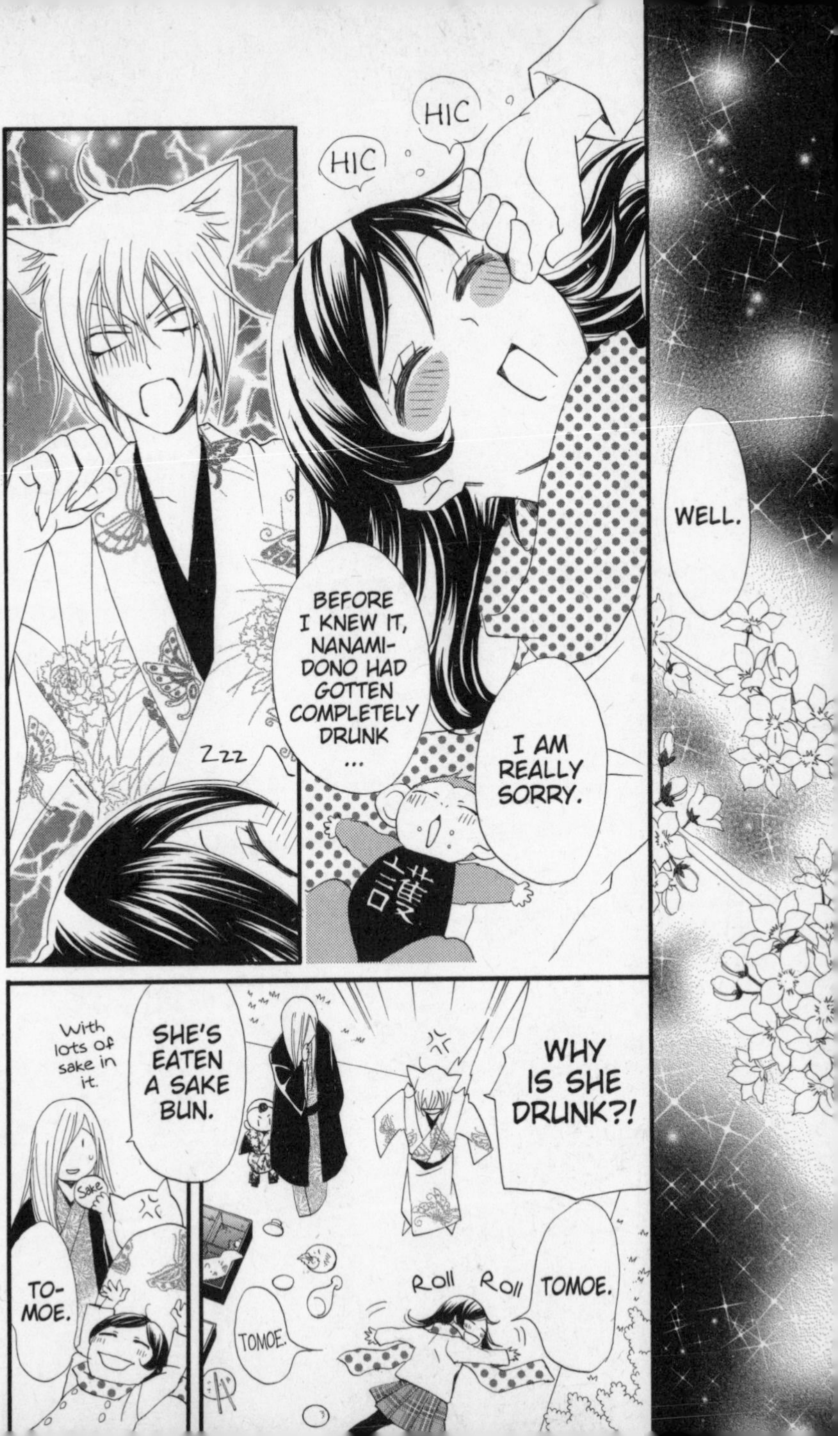
WELL.
HIC
HIC
BEFORE I KNEW IT, NANAMI-DONO HAD GOTTEN COMPLETELY DRUNK ...
I AM REALLY SORRY.
Zzz
WHY IS SHE DRUNK?!
SHE'S EATEN A SAKE BUN.
With lots of sake in it.
TOMOE.
Roll Roll
TOMOE.
Sake
TO-MOE.

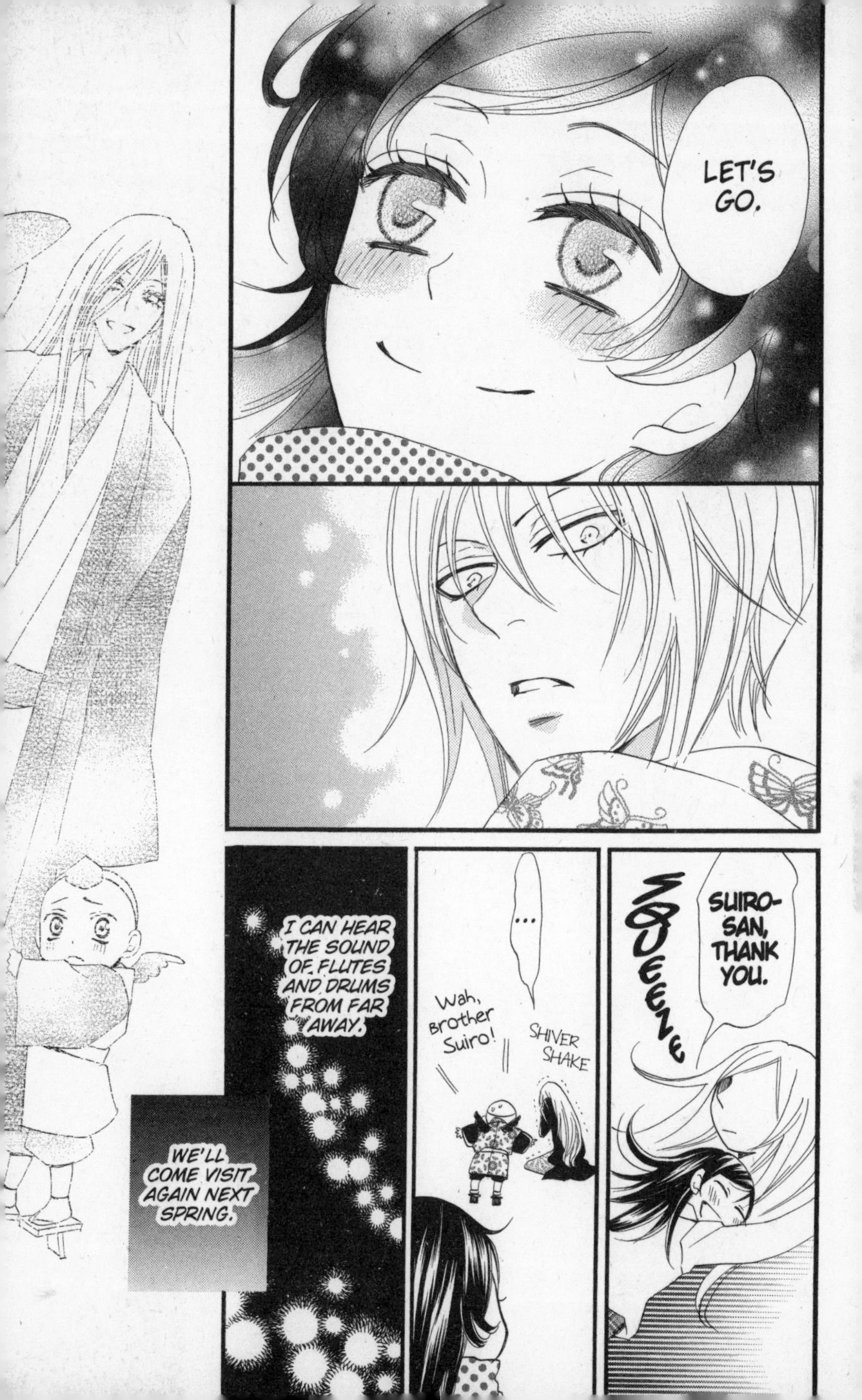
LET'S GO.
SUIRO-SAN, THANK YOU.
SQUEEZE
...
SHIVER SHAKE
Wah, brother Suiro!
I CAN HEAR THE SOUND OF FLUTES AND DRUMS FROM FAR AWAY.
WE'LL COME VISIT AGAIN NEXT SPRING.

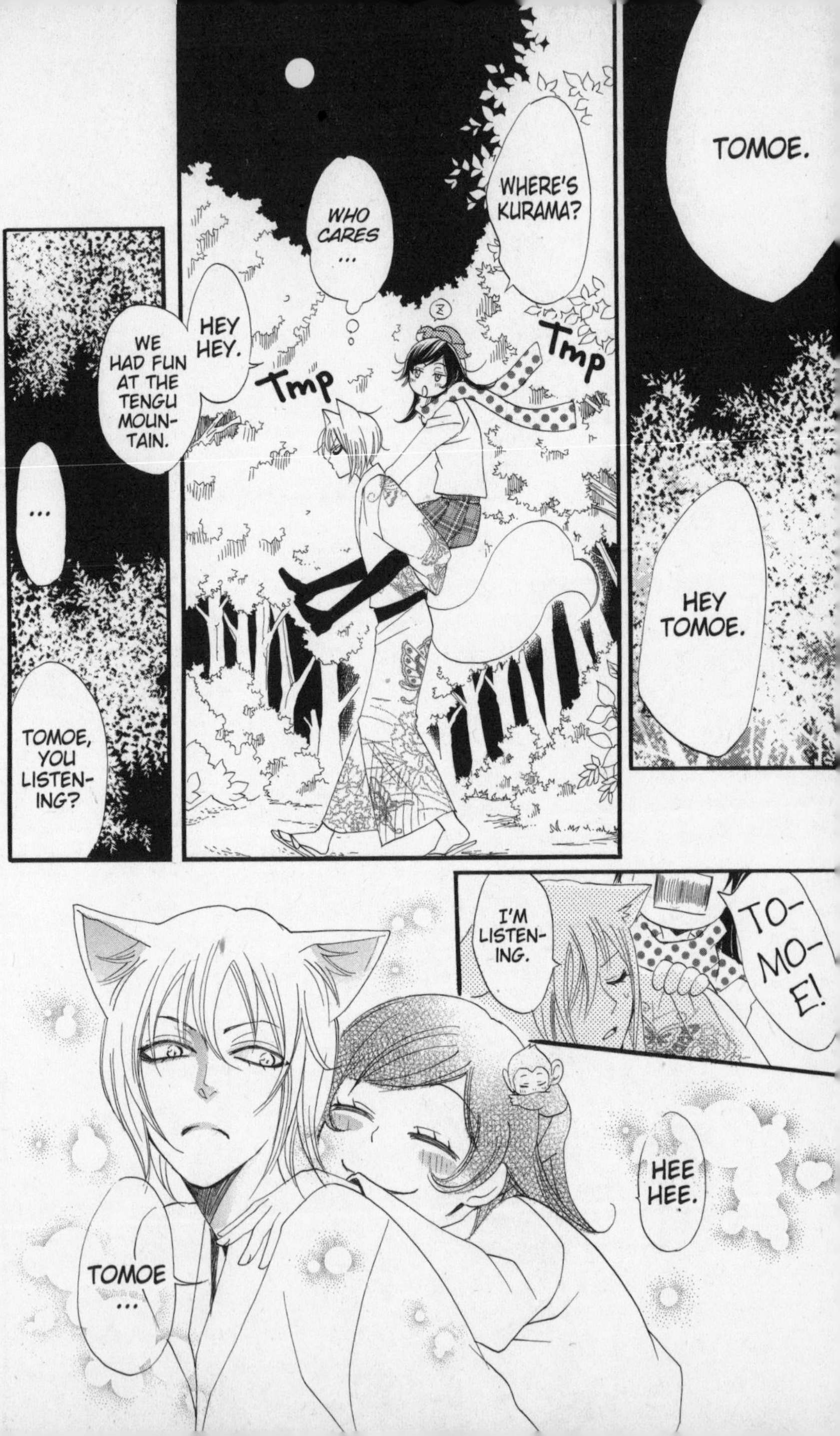
TOMOE.
HEY TOMOE.
WHERE'S KURAMA?
Tmp
WHO CARES ...
HEY HEY.
Tmp
WE HAD FUN AT THE TENGU MOUN-TAIN.
...
TOMOE, YOU LISTEN-ING?
TO-MO-E!
I'M LISTEN-ING.
HEE HEE.
TOMOE ...

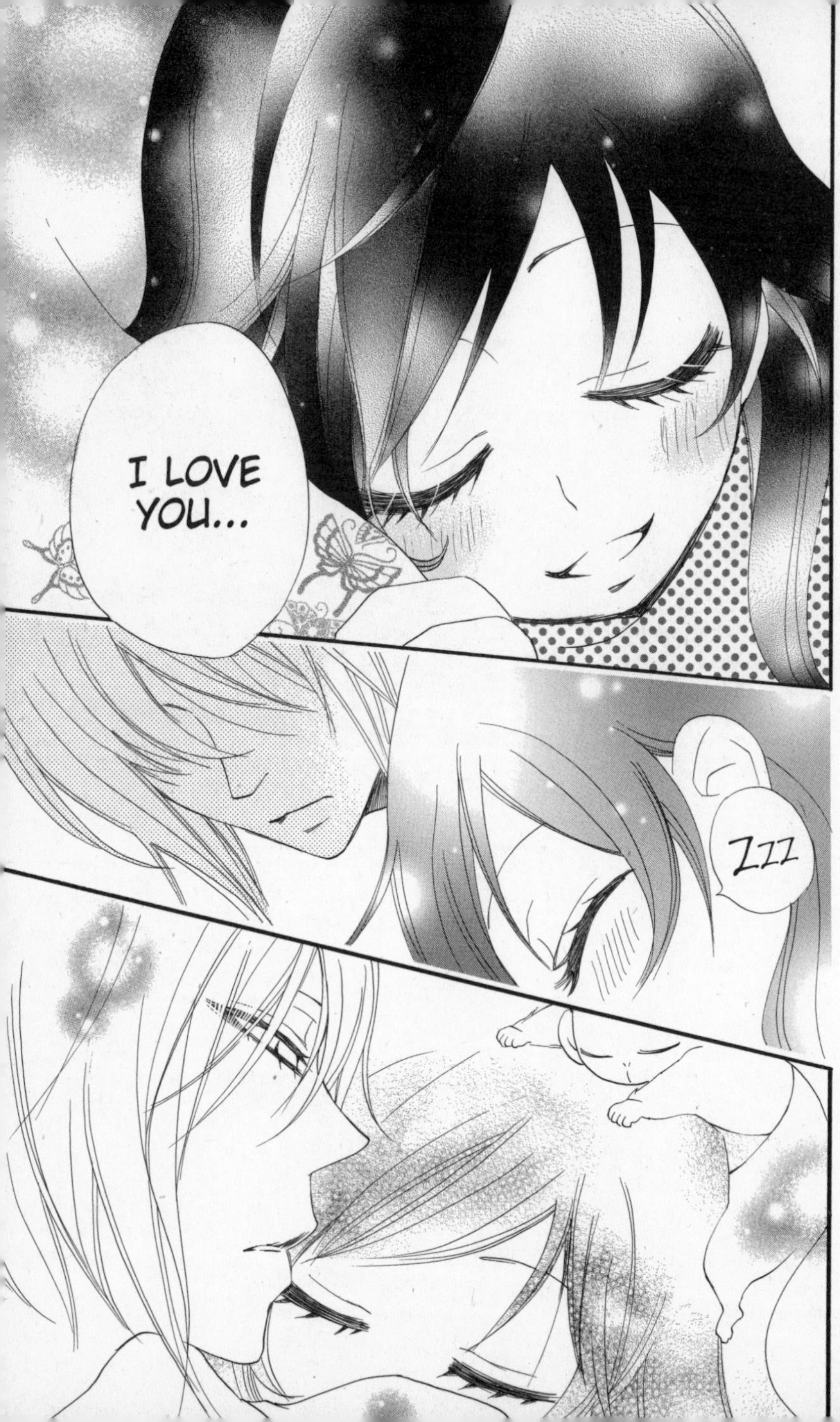
I LOVE YOU...
ZZZ

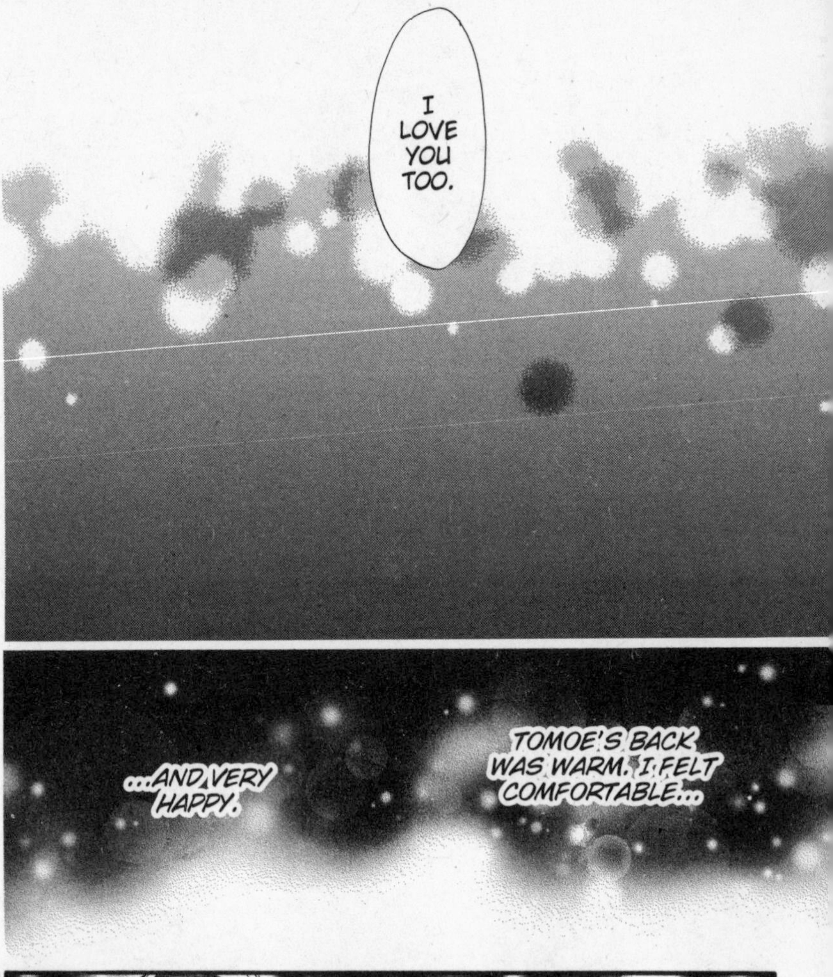
I LOVE YOU TOO.
TOMOE'S BACK WAS WARM. I FELT COMFORTABLE...
...AND VERY HAPPY.
I'M LEAVING TOO!
On this!

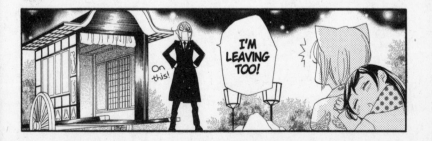

The Otherworld

Ayakashi is an archaic term for yokai.

Kami are Shinto deities or spirits. The word can be used for a range of creatures, from nature spirits to strong and dangerous gods.

Onibi-warashi are like will-o'-the-wisps.

Shikigami are spirits that are summoned and employed by *onmyoji* (Yin-Yang sorcerers).

Shinshi are birds, beasts, insects or fish that have a special relationship with a kami.

Tengu are a type of yokai. They are sometimes associated with excess pride.

Tochigami (or *jinushigami*) are deities of a specific area of land.

Honorifics

-chan is a diminutive most often used with babies, children or teenage girls.

-dono roughly means "my lord," although not in the aristocratic sense.

-san is a standard honorific similar to Mr., Mrs., Miss, or Ms.

-sama is used with people of much higher rank.

Notes

Page 38, panel 1: Ofuda
A strip of paper or a small wooden tablet that acts as a spell.

Page 58, panel 5: Maoh-den
Literally means "demon lord residence."

Page 98, panel 2: Statue of Nanami
This is a spoof on the famous statue of the dog Hachiko at
Shibuya station. Hachiko is renowned for waiting for his master
at the station every day, even after his master passed away.

Julietta Suzuki's debut manga *Hoshi ni Naru Hi* (The Day One Becomes a Star) appeared in the 2004 *Hana to Yume Plus*. Her other books include *Akuma to Dolce* (The Devil and Sweets) and *Karakuri Odette*. Born in December in Fukuoka Prefecture, she enjoys having movies play in the background while she works on her manga.

KAMISAMA KISS
VOL. 10
Shojo Beat Edition

STORY AND ART BY
Julietta Suzuki

English Translation & Adaptation/Tomo Kimura
Touch-up Art & Lettering/Joanna Estep
Design/Yukiko Whitley
Editor/Pancha Diaz

KAMISAMA HAJIMEMASHITA by Julietta Suzuki
© Julietta Suzuki 2011
All rights reserved.
First published in Japan in 2011 by HAKUSENSHA, Inc., Tokyo.
English language translation rights arranged with
HAKUSENSHA, Inc., Tokyo.

Printed in the U.S.A.

Published by VIZ Media, LLC
P.O. Box 77010
San Francisco, CA 94107

10 9 8 7 6 5 4 3
First printing, August 2012
Third printing, April 2015

www.viz.com   www.shojobeat.com

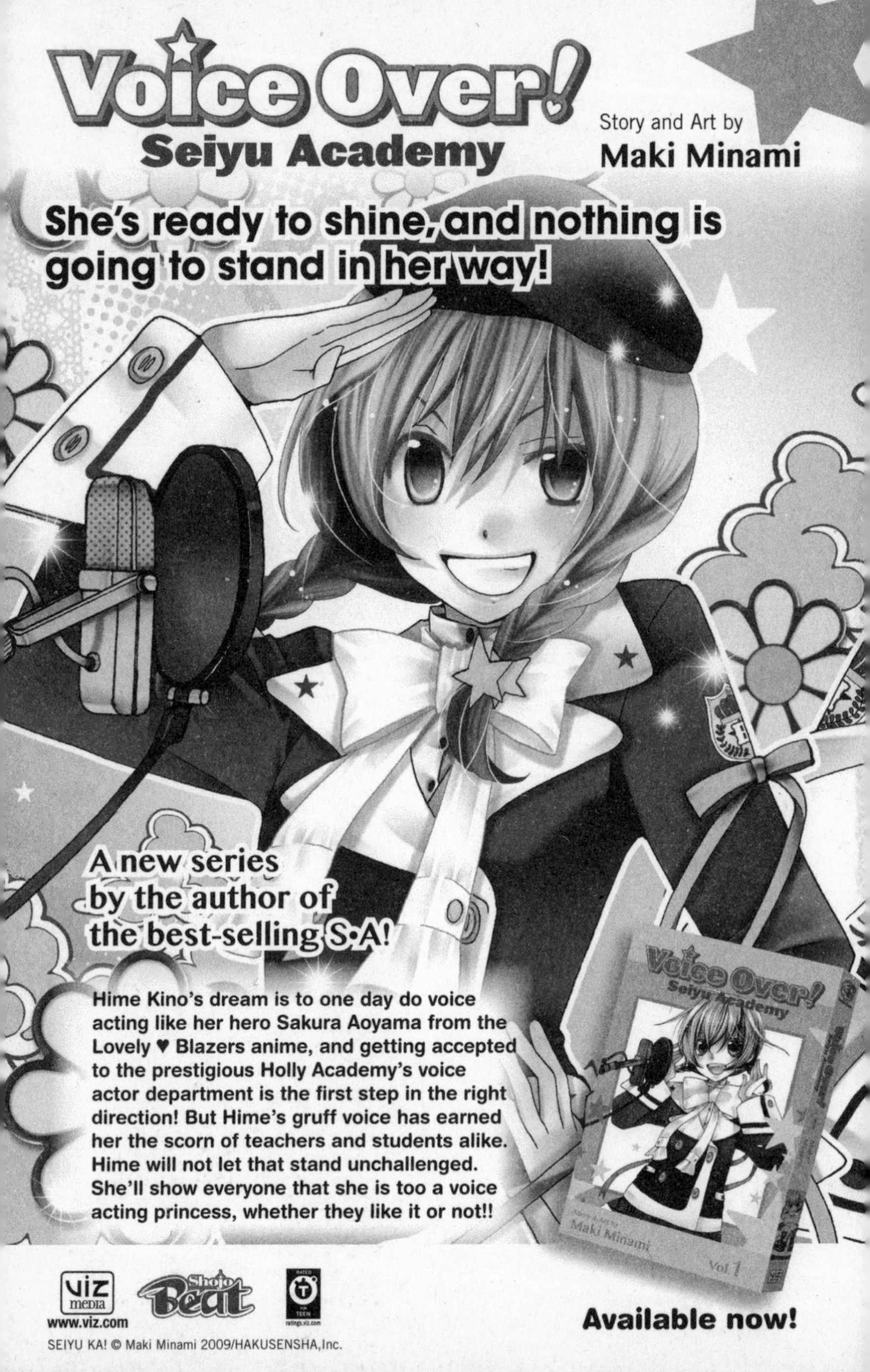
Voice Over!
Seiyu Academy
Story and Art by
Maki Minami
She's ready to shine, and nothing is going to stand in her way!
A new series by the author of the best-selling S•A!
Hime Kino's dream is to one day do voice acting like her hero Sakura Aoyama from the Lovely ♥ Blazers anime, and getting accepted to the prestigious Holly Academy's voice actor department is the first step in the right direction! But Hime's gruff voice has earned her the scorn of teachers and students alike. Hime will not let that stand unchallenged. She'll show everyone that she is too a voice acting princess, whether they like it or not!!
Voice Over! Seiyu Academy
Story & Art by Maki Minami
Vol. 1
viz media
www.viz.com
Shojo Beat
Available now!
SEIYU KA! © Maki Minami 2009/HAKUSENSHA,Inc.

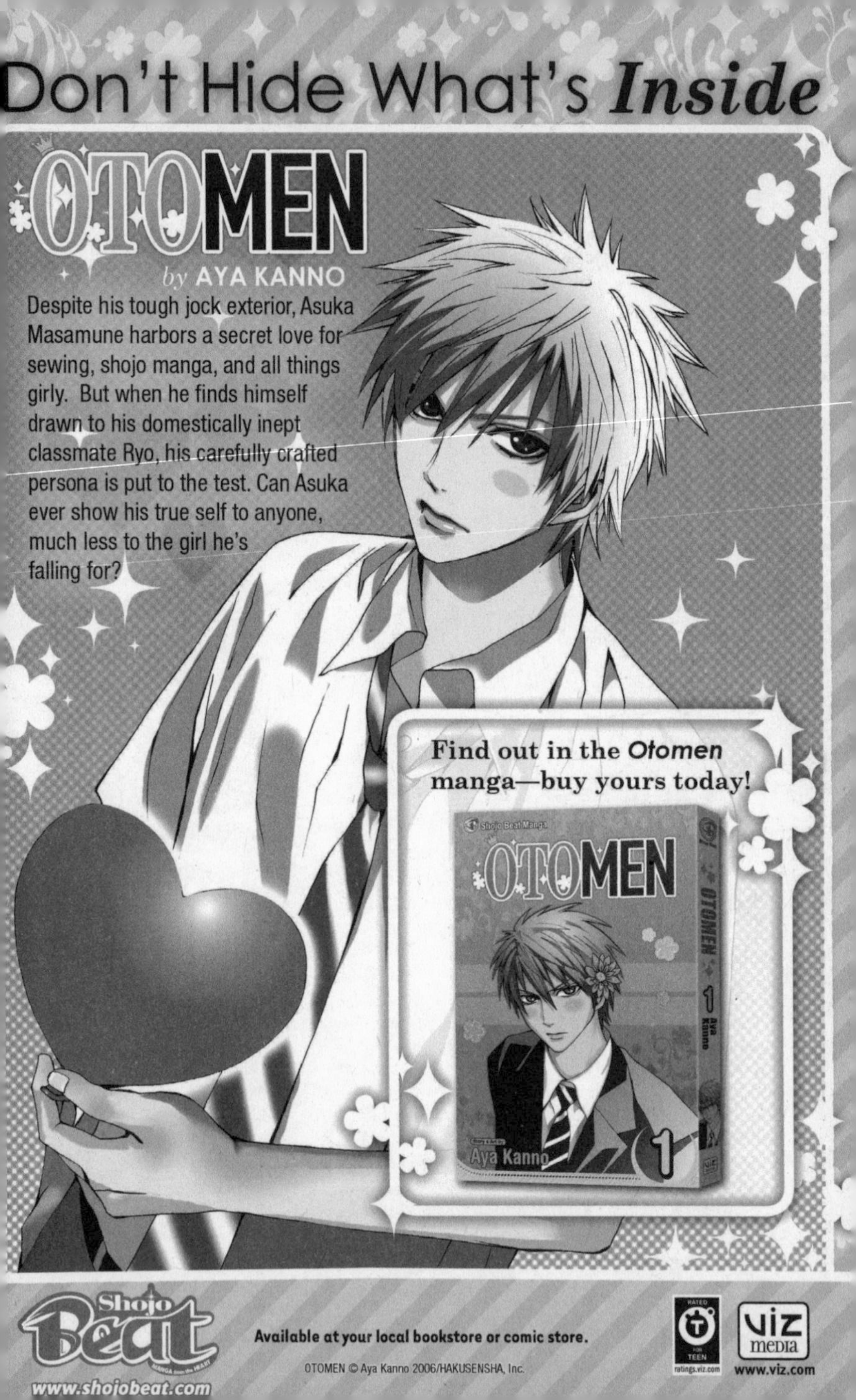
Don't Hide What's *Inside*
OTOMEN
by AYA KANNO
Despite his tough jock exterior, Asuka Masamune harbors a secret love for sewing, shojo manga, and all things girly. But when he finds himself drawn to his domestically inept classmate Ryo, his carefully crafted persona is put to the test. Can Asuka ever show his true self to anyone, much less to the girl he's falling for?
Find out in the *Otomen* manga—buy yours today!
Shojo Beat Manga
OTOMEN
Aya Kanno
1
Shojo Beat
www.shojobeat.com
Available at your local bookstore or comic store.
OTOMEN © Aya Kanno 2006/HAKUSENSHA, Inc.
RATED T FOR TEEN
ratings.viz.com
VIZ media
www.viz.com

This is the last page.

In keeping with the original Japanese comic format, this
book reads from right to left—so action, sound effects, and
word balloons are completely reversed. This preserves the
orientation of the original artwork—plus, it's fun! Check out
the diagram shown here to get the hang of things, and then turn
to the other side of the book to get started!